GREEN HELL

Massacre of the Brazilian Indians

GREEN HELL

Massacre of the Brazilian Indians

by Lucien Bodard

TRANSLATED BY
JENNIFER MONAGHAN

OUTERBRIDGE & DIENSTFREY

NEW YORK

DISTRIBUTED BY E.P. DUTTON & COMPANY

Originally published as *Le Massacre des Indiens*, © Editions Gallimard 1969

Standard Book Number: 0-87690-030-9
Library of Congress Catalogue Number: 72-178895
Translation Copyright © 1971 by Outerbridge & Dienstfrey
First published in the United States of America in 1971. Printed
in the United States of America. All rights reserved including
the right of reproduction in whole or in part in any form.

Design: Anne Hallowell

Outerbridge & Dienstfrey
200 West 72 Street New York 10023

CONTENTS

GLOSSARY

AGUARDENTE   a distilled alcoholic drink, sugar-cane brandy
ALDEIA   a village or settlement
ARUANA   a large river-fish
BANDEIRANTE   a member of an armed band of early adventurers
BARRACÃO   a trading post
BORRACHA   a latex, gum of the rubber tree
CABOCLO   half-breed of white and Indian; a rural peasant
CACAIUM   an alcoholic drink
CACHACA   raw, white rum
CACIQUE   chieftain
CAHUCHU   Indian name for the rubber tree
CANGACEIRO   bandit, outlaw
CAPATAZ   foreman, overseer
CAPITAO   captain, chief; master
CARAIBE   Indian term for white man
CASA DOS MORTOS   house of the dead
CATINGA   any region of stunted vegetation
CEGAMONEN   the renting of women
CHACINADOR   a professional assassin
COMPRADOR   a buyer
CORONEL   political chief in rural areas
CORRERIA   foray, hunt
CRATO   disorder of the skin
CRUZEIRO   Brazilian currency, about four per $1.00
DEFUMADOR   a smoke house for rubber
DESBRAVADOR   one who tames or cultivates
DESBRAVAR   to tame (animals); to cultivate (the wilderness)
DESPACHANTE   broker
DOBRADIMA   double salary
ESCUDO   Portuguese currency
ESTRADA   the part of the forest tracked by a rubber hunter
FAVELA   slum, shantytown
FAZENDA   a plantation, an estate
FAZENDEIRO   planter, large scale rancher

FEIJAO   bean, bean pod; cooked beans (pl: feijões)
GARIMPO   diamond bed; gold field
GARIMPEIRO   prospector for diamonds, gold
GRILEIRO   claim jumper, land grabber
GRINGO   Americans
IGARAPÉ   a narrow waterway
JAVARI   an Indian battle ceremony
(MADEIRA DE) LEI   a rare hardwood
MACULO   a type of dysentery
MALOCA   an Indian camp or village
MANIOC   plant akin to the cassava
MARACA   a gourd rattle
MATE   Paraguaian tea
MATEREIRO   trader
MATEIRO   woodsman
MATO   jungle, thick forest
MOROCOCO   an alcoholic drink
PAJE   witch doctor
PISTOLEIRO   hired assassin, gunman
QUILOMBO   a hiding place for runaway slaves
RAPADURA   hard square of raw brown sugar eaten as food or candy
RODAVIA   highway
SAVANNA   tropical grassland
SECCA   drought
SELVA   jungle, esp. the Amazon rain forest
SERINGAL   a stand of rubber trees
SERINGALISTA   owner of a rubber plantation
SERINGUEIRO   rubber gatherer
SERRA   mountain range
SERTANEJO   inhabitant of the wilderness
SERTAO   wilderness; remote back country
SURICU   anaconda
TRONCO   instrument of torture
URUBU   black vulture
VAQUEIRO   cowboy

I THE MASSACRE
OF THE INDIANS

THIS MORNING I left Rio de Janeiro; I left civilization and the twentieth century behind. In the space of a few hours I was dropping back through eons of history to the Stone Age and burying myself in the past. What a strange country Brazil is! It takes so short a time to go from skyscrapers to the jungle huts of naked men.

I had just flown in a small plane over the scrawny, harsh expanses of Minas Gerais, the treasure land—a land ransacked for centuries by adventurers of all races, who in the brotherhood of adventure and death, had left the coast for the unknown interior in search of gold and precious stones. Minas Gerais is the eldorado of suffering and of greed; its soil is drenched with the blood of all the Indians slain since their epic began. Their survivors have retreated farther and farther into the terrible Amazonian jungle, the most poisonous and pestilential anywhere on the surface of the earth. Once there were Indians on Sugar Loaf Mountain which towers over Rio de Janeiro, the cosmopolitan city of the white man and magical city of the black man; today, an Indian there would be a museum piece.

It was the Indians that I was going to meet—at least, those that are left, in the biggest "Far West" of the modern world, in the heart of darkness and barbarism, where "pioneers" filled with brutality and savages with hatred still war with one another.

Then, flying above this wild country, I caught sight, suddenly, on a sort of plateau, of something incredible. It rose before me like a mirage—the most futuristic city in the world, a city of modern beauty and of human love: Brasilia. A masterpiece, created in a few years in the wilderness by the will of man. Beyond sumptuousness, its simplicity springs from the most costly materials and from forms that are no more than lines. The city might be called a harmony of algebraic signs. It is at once a model of idealism and the symbol of the destruction of the Indians, for idealism, even more than elemental passions, is killing the Indians.

Underneath the facade of its humanitarian pretensions, Brasilia is the march of progress. It is official conquest. By its creation, Brazil mastered the interior of her immense and savage continent. Where there were none but outlaws, authority has been and is being established. A far-reaching decision, because for centuries the real Brazil was the coast.

First, though, Brazil had been the black slaves of the shores of Bahia and Pernambuco—a civilization of sugar and sugar-mills and of Creole overlords, elegant aristocrats in their plantations, masters of ebony-skinned Africans imported to replace slain Indians. Then after the suppression of slavery, the Creole civilization collapsed. And then came the Brazil of the coast, in the South, much whiter and much more powerful, with all the dynamism of money and technical progress, of wild speculation and moneymaking energy. This was the Brazil of São Paulo, the then brand-new Southern metropolis, set in the midst of red earth, tamed jungle, and coffee bushes. A São Paulo of skyscrapers, banks, factories, endless suburbs, in which everything was possible because everything was new. Ugly but utilitarian. Millions of Germans, Italians and Japanese were slowly but surely assimilated with the native Brazilians. It was a happy union: the arrivals gave free rein to their vitality and technical ability, and the Brazilians contrived to share in the profits. German Brazilians and Portugese Brazilians mingled in an aristocracy of profit, the most snobbish to be found anywhere. This was the real Brazil, with Rio de Janeiro as the capital of politics and of pleasure.

It was the real Brazil until the creation of Brasilia. Brasilia was a fantastic idea: thousands of square miles to desbravar—to tame. Millions of square miles of nature at its most terrifying: the mato, the jungle, an infinity of Green Hell; and the infinity of the waters which make Amazonia a forest set in an ocean. Brasilia is the promise of progress in all its forms, good and bad. It is a progess that has always brought death to the Indians.

We had left Brasilia behind and still had more than 625 miles to fly. We were above the sullen tropics, a dark, glaucous mass of water and trees. I found myself over the geographical center of Brazil, where the Mato Grosso, the great jungle, mingles with Amazonia, at the heart of what, only thirty years ago, was unknown territory, wild and unexplored. Everything then barred entry: the tropical fevers, the immense distances, the dense flora and fauna, and above all the savage Indian tribes. This is the region drained by the Xingu, the most mysterious of the Amazon's tributaries, which the white man could not ascend because of its enormous rapids. The Xingu is revered by the Indians as a sacred river; for them, it is the supreme lord of the universe, the master of water and fire. According to Indian myth, it was on the banks of the Xingu that the hero Maivutsini created the heavens, the earth and men; he made them all, good and bad alike. To the Indians, the good men are those they know, the men of their own tribe. The bad are the others, all the others.

Before we reached the Xingu, we flew over other rivers—immense gray serpents which coil their way against a monotonous background of dark vegetation. First was the Rio Araguaia, which constitutes the boundary between civilization and barbarism. On its banks are the last visible huts; beyond that point the struggle between man and the elements is hidden. Indeed, the next loop of water is called the Rio das Mortes—the River of the Dead—so named, it seems, because no river has ever borne so many corpses: the bodies of garimpeiros—diamond hunters; of seringueiros—men who bleed the rubber trees; of fazendeiros—the landowners; and of priests and white soldiers. But even more so, the bodies of the Xavantes, Capajos, and Tapirapes Indians, all once powerful tribes, proud and cruel, who some thirty years ago, were almost totally exterminated.

Nowadays, it is on the western side of the Rio das Mortes that nature is being assaulted and the Indians decimated. A condemnation of the killers has been issued by the Brazilian government itself. Its main accusations: genocide, the liquidation of entire tribes, machine-gunning from the air, epidemics touched off by presents of clothing deliberately infected with germs, gifts of poisoned food, candy containing arsenic given to children. There were more accusations—of bestial tortures, of the survivors being reduced to slavery, of sexual perversions, of prostitution of the women, of theft of Indian territory, of promises extorted by alcohol and by force, of every ingenuity of destruction: practically every crime in the Brazilian penal code was committed. And all this done with the complicity of the S.P.I., the Service for the Protection of the Indians, which had been dubbed "the Service for the Prostitution of the Indians" by the Minister of the Interior himself. One hundred and thirty-four functionaries of the S.P.I. had to be discharged for homicide, and 200 others were dismissed from their duties for being accessories to murder. Two generals, some colonels and other superior officers were implicated, as well as former ministers and former provincial governors. Nonetheless, the annihilation of the Indians had been protected by a secret and powerful politico-economic group. The investigators had thirty-two threats on their lives, threats which had to be taken seriously considering the great number, in Brazil, of pistoleiros and other killers for hire. There had also been attempts to blackmail and bribe the persons who uncovered the horrors of the S.P.I., horrors making up a dossier running to thousands of pages. And these pages cover only the results of recent investigations, for by strange mischance the old archives of the S.P.I. went up in flames in a mysterious fire in Brasilia.

I was on my way to the Indians who had escaped—to those specifically who had been saved by the Vilas Boas brothers on their reservation on the Xingu; the Indians have been pacified by the brothers' kindness and they live in a primitive state that is only very slightly improved over their usual situation. These Indians are people living 3,000 years before Christ, but who are familiar with the bicycle, the nylon fishing line, the saucepan. But not the Bible. Most emphatically, the Vilas Boas brothers will have no bibles about. The brothers are trying to keep the Indians just about as they are, for everything destroys them: not only the bullets of adventurers but also civilization, with its bacteria, its alcohol and even its philanthropy.

In a region as large as Brittany, the Vilas Boas brothers, Orlando and Claudio, are the masters. There they prolong the existence of perhaps twenty tribes, each of them a remnant with its own language, a group of a few dozen persons, living naked in their respective villages. A curious Eden, where twentieth-century man is forbidden to enter, lest he contaminate the Indians. It had taken a special and exceptional permit for me to get in.

Hours passed in my little airplane above the Green Hell. Then there was a steep bank overhanging huge swollen marshes. Then a clearing and we landed.

A 100 yards away stood some dingy huts made of boards and corrugated iron painted blue. They were all dilapidated and dirty, forming a rough square around a patch of matted grass dotted with dung. The principal building was a very unpretentious ranch house. Inside it there were plank partitions, a few benches and chairs, hammocks and primitive beds, mirrors, shelves with some dog-eared books, a table covered with bits of paper, a sink. Dust was everywhere. The heat was stifling—and not so much as a fan. The atmosphere of a far-off outpost, lost and forgotten.

But a deafening voice was speaking by radio with São Paulo, 2,000 miles away. The barks into the radio lasted almost an hour, embellished by the crackles of the transmission. Orders were repeated twice, five, ten times, in the way that business is done in Amazonia: "Cigarettes? We're all out. Have 220 pounds put in the next military airplane that comes here. I must have sugar and vaccines as well. The pay.... it's three months late ... "

The voice was that of Orlando Vilas Boas, the elder brother, the chief, the leader of the domestication of the Indians. A great, massive, naked torso, covered with sweat, with big mammaries above and a big belly below; a bulk in tattered trousers and bare feet; a wide face with the puffy flesh of a man in his forties. Yet all this conveyed an impression of extraordinary power, and dark, searching eyes showed a warmth mixed with hard, secretive glints born of experience. They were full of unspoken wariness. His features were pasted on like those of some conqueror returning from the wars after undergoing too many hardships. On his thinning hair, at the top of his enormous skull, perched a tiny greenish parrot, as motionless as if it were stuffed. I could sense in his whole personality an authoritarianism, a paternalism, and a sort of irritation all kept in check by his smile, his gestures and attitude, by the art of playing a part. But truculence mingled with fatigue, with the hardship of years spent in the jungle for the benefit of the Indians. Why does he live such a life? From ambition? Or conviction? Nobody knows: it is Orlando's mystery.

The second Vilas Boas brother, Claudio, thin and bearded, looks like a tropical intellectual. And he is, indeed, the theoretician, the man of faith and passion. Mostly he remained silent, hunched up and self-absorbed as if wounded; his feverish eyes distant, detached. When reality was too sad, he always lost himself in the same dream, that of the paradise of innocence, of the love of the "noble savage."

A third brother, Leonardo, died of a heart attack long ago. But he was reproduced larger than life in a portrait, in the guise of a warrior. He had given his name to Orlando and Claudio's pacification post.

We had a glass of whiskey—the whiskey I had brought, because the Vilas Boas were out of everything. They enjoy their poverty—and their legend. As we drank, they told me:

"All our lives we have applied the principles of Marshal Rondon, the soldier philosopher and mathematician who practised the positivism of Auguste Comte. He believed above all in man's goodness. He didn't want the unknown lands of the interior to be conquered as the Americans had conquered theirs in the past—by the bloody massacre of the redskins. He was convinced that it was possible to win the hearts of even the most ferocious Indians in Amazonia. He absolutely forbade the use of guns and forbade killing, even at the risk of being killed himself."

Marshall Rondon, the man the brothers were talking about, is a legendary figure, even though it is barely ten years since he died. A living legend, for at Rio, as in the Vilas Boas' huts, pictures of him are everywhere. You see him

as still a young man, a lean face under a colonial helmet, making the gestures
of peace—he is chatting with some naked and unidentified Indians. And you
see him in all his glory, his features regular and clean cut, his eyes strangely
peaceful, his look distant and almost indifferent, cutting a fine figure in his
uniform. He is receiving the title of Marshal from the Brazilian Congress.
From all sides illustrous hands of presidents, senators and politicians, are
pinning military insignia on him. The most astonishing photo is one taken of
him in his old age, when he visited the Indians for the last time. He is seated
opposite an aged and gaunt cacique. And there is an extraordinary
resemblance between Rondon and this Indian chief. Rondon has the other's
engraved features, dark skin, deep-sunken eyes, and the same gaze, piercing
and, as it were, outside time. Almost a mask. It's a strange affinity—the good
genie of the Indians is almost an Indian himself; the only almost pure Indian
to have arrived of his own will in our time and our world. It's a miracle, a
miracle that has made of him a great white man, who has prolonged by some
decades the men of what was almost his own race.

Rondon's history was only possible because there are two—directly
opposed—Brazils. One has issued from the Lusitanian race, the terrible race of
merchants, smugglers and traffickers, the Latin equivalent of the English
merchant adventurers. The second Brazil is the Brazil of "the enlightened," of
fine minds and noble spirits, which were nourished by the encyclopedia, and
the France of Voltaire, Rousseau, and the first humanitarian socialists.
Reflections of the "Rights of Man," of Auguste Comte's temple located in
Rio de Janeiro, they were solemn gentlemen who believed in the Supreme
Being. This was the Brazil of the suppression of slavery, national Independence, and the end of the Empire; and it had, as its instrument, an army
imbued with liberalism and spiritualism, the only army of its kind that has
ever existed in South America. This Brazil has all but disappeared, but it
permitted the adventure of Rondon, the little Indian-saver of the Indians.

Rondon was a half-caste Indian, born in 1865 in the Mato Grosso, which
was at that time almost unexplored, and where most of the cities that had
risen beside the coal mines were dead. At that period there remained only the
fevers, the menace of savage tribes, and the incessant war with Paraguay. The
child had a very bronzed color—his mother had the blood of three western
Indian tribes in her veins. His ancestors had been gold-seekers, who had come
from São Paulo by the long route of outlaws. Instead of killing the Indians,
they had become their neighbors. His father had "married" a girl of the race
of the Guanas Indians, but died before his son, Candido Rondon, was born.

His Indian mother died in her turn, entrusting her two-year-old son to her own parents, almost pure Indians. They had been "assimilated" for a long time, for Rondon's Mato Grosso stretched toward the South, a huge prairie which reaches to Argentina, wild grass cut up by long strips of jungle along its rivers. These rivers flow into the great rivers Paraguai and Paraná, which meet to form the huge estuary of the Rio de la Plata, dominated by the great Spanish city of Buenos Aires.

In the interior, this Mato Grosso of the prairies had been the first Brazilian Far West, where white men had come long since, because nature permitted access. Hard men had come for gold, others for the Indian slave traffic, from the Brazilian shores of the Atlantic, from São Paulo. There had also been men of God, who had ascended the great rivers from Argentina. These huge regions, where murder jostled against the Gospel, were called the Paraguay of the famous Jesuits, the ones who had subjected the Indians to an absolute Christian civilization.

At the end of the eighteenth century, everything collapsed in what was then Paraguay. The mystical experience was condemned by the Pope, and there was no more gold or Indian slave traffic. Paraguay was dismembered, one part of it going to form the South of the Brazilian Mato Grosso. Whole cities were abandoned, the largest of which was Villa Bella, a proud city with even, well-lit streets and splendid buildings, forsaken because of the maculo fever, which appears at the beginning and end of the rainy season. After an incubation of a week to a fortnight, it causes pain, a loss of sensation and lethargy. Occasional survivors suffered from the disease of indolence.

Of the Mato Grosso of the past, there remained only the huge herds watched by the vaqueiros on horseback, and one special race, a mixture of the former Jesuitized Indians and the slave hunters. The Indian half-castes had learned to be horsemen, progress which was due to the whites, for the Indians had no previous knowledge of the equestrian art, horses being an importation into the prairie. Mato Grosso was forgotten, until the lusts of the twentieth century reawakened the region.

Brown and bare, Candido Rondon used to swim in the perilous waters of the Rio Mimoso. At nine years of age, he was a little vaqueiro. He even acquired the rudiments of learning from someone who turned up at the village of Mimoso, in rags and a beard, a former sergeant from the battalion of the "Volunteers for the Fatherland," which had fought against Paraguay.

His grandparents died. Candido went to what was the "city" of Mato Grosso of those days, to Cuiabá, the province's new capital. He had an uncle there who welcomed him, adopted him, and sent him to public school.

Cuiabá, however, was only a village at the end of the world. The age of gold had ended there no less than anywhere else but the survivors of earlier times had moved there because the climate was relatively healthy. New pioneers would come to Cuiabá too, for the village is the point of departure for the mato and the selva.[1] Close by, the dark mountains rear up, the frayed Cordilleras where the great rios are born, which flow not only towards the more civilized South, but also northwards to become the aquatic corridors of the great rain-forest, the tributaries of the Amazon. Cuiabá was the most advanced point of civilization—beyond it, the serras and rios were lost in the unknown, a huge white stain on the map.

Cuiabá was the terminus of the land route from São Paulo. To go farther, as far as the waters of the Amazon, was now the great design. Then Brazil would be one. The most direct route from Cuiabá would be to get through to the Tapajós and the Xingu, but these two great rivers of central Brazil were too tumultuous to be the arteries of life. So the solution was to make a long detour, and reach the falls of the Madeira; after that, the waters had been navigated for centuries. But to penetrate that far, thousands of miles had to be surmounted in a nightmare of man and the elements. But there are always men for the unknown, men who generally do not leave so much as a name behind them. It was left to Rondon to be the great desbravador—the great tamer—of this terrible tropical savagery, and to proclaim that all men there were good.

But before civilizing, he first had to learn civilization. At sixteen, Rondon obtained a teaching diploma. He left Cuiabá for Rio de Janeiro, an unknown who charmed the court of Pedro II. It was a brilliant court, and prone to the "enlightened." It was the century of philosophy for Brazil.

Pedro was the enlightened despot of a country, almost a continent, of whose savagery he was ignorant—Pedro the noble, almost an atheist, permanently under the influence of his old teacher, who was the great master of Brazilian Freemasonry. Rondon was admitted to the palace's military school, which was reserved for the children of noblemen. He studied astronomy, physics and mechanics there, under the auspices of Benjamin Constant—not the original, the Frenchman, but a Brazilian who had chosen his name, a very distinguished man, himself a disciple of the "enlightened." Everything was "enlightened" in the Brazil of those days—to the point that the enlightened sovereign renounced his throne without much difficulty in favor of a much more enlightened republic, the finishing touch being given by an enlightened army in which Rondon was an officer. He was rewarded for

1. See Glossary.

his revolutionary action by receiving bachelor diplomas in mathematics and in the physical and natural sciences. Moreover, he was promoted to military engineer. All he had to do was remain a braided intellectual in a professorial chair or military headquarters for the rest of his life. But this was the moment when the fairy tale turned into the Rondon myth.

It was an unexpected application of the doctrines of Auguste Comte. In the positivist temple at Rio de Janeiro, in the lodges of Freemasonry and the books of free thought, young Rondon had learned that there are no inferior men, no submen close to animality; there are only men and women united in humanity, but who are at different levels of civilization, running the whole gamut from savagery to mastery, thanks to natural factors such as the climate, the soil, the water, geography, geology and flora. There is no God, and no one is to blame: it is because of the elements that, in the tropics, human beings are savages. But they are "noble savages," and neither their body nor their soul should be destroyed. Having first accepted them as they are, and being willing to keep them true to themselves, one must make them mount a few rungs up the huge ladder of progress. That should be the great task of the "gentlemen of reason" inspired by Auguste Comte. They would consecrate themselves to the Indians as "enlightened despots," ruling the jungle in the name of Auguste Comte, who had been forgotten in France and classed as an outmoded bore, but whose thought dominated Brazil. In fact, in that huge country, there was everything necessary for the triumph of positivism, for the believers in positivist humanity to bear this message to the savages: that they too were men and the equal of all men—even if they needed to be schooled somewhat by the bearers of the good news.

For centuries only outlaws and missionaries had plunged into the jungle. There were theosophic discussions at Rio, but no disinterested man to go to the aid of the Indians who were being exterminated faster than ever at the beginning of this century—this time, because of rubber. Not until Rondon, the whitest Indian, said: "I want to bring the civilization which I have acquired to my Mato Grosso and my Amazonia, to the jungle and its tribes." So began the legend which was to make him one of the five great modern explorers of unknown continents. In the New York Geographical Society his name would be inscribed upon a plaque side by side with the names of Amundsen, the explorer of the South Pole; of Peary, the explorer of the North Pole; and of Carcot and Byrd, explorers of the Arctic and Antarctic. He would be looked upon as the man who had penetrated the farthest into the unknown tropics.

The legend began prosaically enough, by planting poles, thousands and thousands of telegraph poles. First in the prairie, as far as Cuiabá, Rondon's town. He was accompanied by an army of officers, engineers, soldiers, guides, interpreters and merchants. They were exposed to their first temptation to kill the Indians. It was the first time that Rondon said, "Don't kill them." And, after long parleys, the Indians nearby refrained from destroying Rondon's "wire," which amused them instead of frightening them.

From Cuiabá on it was the great Mission, the creative exploration towards the Madeira and Amazonia. To put the telegraph in the unknown rain forest was to plant it in the wilderness. Nothing came to the serras and rios apart from a few men in canoes or on foot. Where before there had been nothing of the twentieth century, suddenly there were hundreds and thousands of miles of wire, the voice of modern man across the jungle, which preceded the white man's flesh and blood presence by some twenty or thirty years—a presence that would not be a result of crossing the jungle but of flying over it. The telegraph would give way to the plane only when Rondon was an old man. And the road, which was to change everything, would not be made until Rondon was dead. However, there was an odd exception: before any of this, a railway would operate over 125 miles, right in the Green Hell, all along the Madeira—the path of the borracha and of death.

Titanic difficulties for Rondon's "wire." The jungle in its raw state had to be vanquished. Nothing was known, not even the routes of the rios under the inundation of the green jungle. He had to advance with the workers and the materials, make the men work, carry the tools and the food, and carve a path. It was an achievement just to sink a stake in a bottomless swamp. As always, there were deaths from disease, fever and dysentery. Wooden crosses on some riverbank. Rondon radiated health. He sent off small groups in all directions to find their bearings in the patchwork of swamps, rivers and forests. He was constantly going off to reconnoiter himself, in a gargantuan nature where the stakes that were set up and the wire that was strung on them seemed miniscule. They were not in scale.

There were Indian tribes—the Parecis, the Pacaas Novos, the Parintintins, the Caripunas, the Nambiquaras, the Bocas Negras, and many others. Terrifying and invisible, constantly near at hand. The sound of their war dances could be heard. Sometimes the savages would rush out to demand gifts; they would shout—but in an unknown tongue. Discussions would be held by gestures, mimes and grimaces. There was a great temptation among the men to slaughter them by gunning them down. It was formally forbidden by Rondon: "There is to be no more massacre; not one Indian is to be killed."

He gambled on his art of seducing the Indians: he would soon be called the Indian-charmer. He pronounced the hallowed phrase: "I bring you peace." To overcome the Indians' mistrust, Rondon would resort to the great oath of the jungle, and take part in magic ceremonies—he turned himself back into a red Indian, if necessary. His was exhausting work, for it was not enough for his men not to kill the Indians—it was also necessary for the Indians not to kill his men. All too often, despite everything, one of his comrades was struck by arrows. Another jungle grave. Every time the moral dejection of Rondon was profound. Every time he asked himself if he had the right to demand of his people that they let themselves be killed without even defending themselves.

The whole expedition wanted revenge. Sometimes there was almost a revolt. But Rondon, his face an impassive mask, would order: "Let us weep. Let us weep, for I loved this man who has perished for my sake. But I command you to do as he did. Never shoot."

The Madeira was attained. Amazonia was attained. Eleven hundred miles of wire were placed in the Green Hell. Twenty thousand miles had been crossed by Rondon, in the depths of the jungle. He was never affected by anything, not by fatigue or disease. His feeling for the pacific war was unparalleled, his courage absolute. In a region of cannibalistic tribes, his men begged him to wear a coat of mail. He laughed. His tours became longer and longer, the skin withering on his frame as he looked more and more like an old eagle. He was modesty itself: "What have I done? Nothing by myself. My colleagues did all the work." Yet he had learned ten dialects and discovered fifteen new rivers. From now on he was accompanied by scientists. Science was on his side—more than 30,000 specimens were dispatched to museums. But the consecration was Theodore Roosevelt's participation in one of his more perilous adventures: the descent of a deadly river, one of the least salubrious, and highly populated by Indians painted for war. A friendship developed between the former President of the United States, a huge, jovial, and powerful character, and the silent Rondon. Roosevelt's name was given to this rio, where the telegraph line went next. And still not one Indian had been killed.

Rondon was to survive another fifty years. The good conqueror, the saint, the man who believed in justice as the norm of life. A personality which was both modest and glorious. He had a simple home in Rio, where he lived in a bourgeois style with his wife and seven children. It was to this home that the emissaries of tribes came to see him. Every day he went to his office, where he studied all the dossiers scrupulously. Sometimes he went to some international congress in the United States or in Europe, where he was acclaimed. He had his disciples, and famous men came humbly to see him. Paul Claudel found a sort of divine grace in this atheist. "Rondon," he wrote, "had the impact on me of a figure from the Gospel." The Brazilian Congress revered him as one of the "fathers" of the country. He was a Marshal, but a Marshal of the jungle. When advanced in years, he still visited the distant regions that he had earlier subjugated by his goodness. In 1956, almost a mummy, his cacique's face fleshed out by old age, he went to Rondonia, the territory of the upper Madeira which he had once entered as the pacifier.

He is said to have been almost a myth to the Indians. When, summoning up his last reserves of strength, he went to the Mato Grosso, Rondon, the white cacique, embraced the cacique of the Bororos. It was a sentimental display of emotion. Rondon turned to his escort: "Do you know what the chieftain has just said to me? He invited me to come and die here, because I am very old, and my end is surely near. And only the Bororos know how to bury me worthily." And so Rondon was assimilated by the Indians as one of their own at the great moment when he would confront the spirits.

He died in 1958, and received a state funeral. It was then that he fully became a myth, a myth of goodness—to the Brazilians, to the whites. The Marshal, in his simplicity, had not even realized that times had changed, and Brazil with them. He had created the Service for the Protection of the Indians, and he believed to his last day that the S.P.I. was serving the Indians, whereas it was serving them by killing them. Lost in the night of time, lost in his memories of his epoch, Rondon had remained in the Brazil of positivism and the philosophy of the "enlightened", at a time when Brazil was caught in the coils of technical progress, development, nationalism, power and money In this Brazil, it was absolutely necessary that there be no more Indians Rondon was the camouflage of reality. He died at the moment when a new genocide was just being prepared.

"So you yourselves have never opened fire on a dangerous Indian?"

"Never. That would spoil everything. Better to run the risk of being struck by an arrow, because the Indians are very vengeful. They never forgive a murder. You either have to destroy them all or know how to persuade them all, to make them believe in you. Once you have inspired their confidence they are marvelous. But getting to that point is an art."

"Then why do you have that collection of revolvers and rifles in that rack?"

"We have to have them. Apart from the Indians, there are a great many ferocious men and animals in the vicinity: garimpeiros, seringueiros, and every kind of adventurer. In their search for treasure, they systematically slaughter the Indians: it's safer, more practical, and causes less fuss. We have to defend our charges. And anyway—arms are our hobby."

For at least an hour, the Vilas Boas brothers went into ecstasies over models from an enormous arms catalogue. Their bible. Endless technical discussions. Oddly enough, it is the humanist, the wheezing Claudio, who is the most fanatic. He is an extraordinary shot. These death machines are a great distraction to the lonely dreamer in love with humanity. He has fifteen of them, very rare and expensive, and accurate.

He smiled indulgently as he said: "They keep me happy. Cleaning them is really something."

The brothers lovingly displayed their finest pieces. A Smith & Wesson with a hunt engraved on its breech, and a pistol with a mother-of-pearl butt.

Orlando said suddenly: "Look at this Winchester rifle. Doesn't it look modern? It was made in 1873. It's the model used by Buffalo Bill and the Americans when they were wiping out the Indians. When they no longer needed the guns they sold them in Brazil for the same purpose; after being used for the extermination of the Sioux and the Comanches, the guns are being used for the extermination of our Indians. They arrived in whole cargos in our ports, and were bought cheaply by all the adventurers who wanted to plunge into the interior.

"This rifle has quite a story. Fifty years ago, the most formidable Indians of the Xingu, the Capajos, killed its owner, a good prospector, with a poisoned arrow. They couldn't use it for lack of powder. I became a friend of one of their tribes. Here, this is the boy who gave us the rifle."

Around us, watching us, were Indians. The men wore feathers, and were tatooed and in a variety of hues, while the women had neither feather nor ornament. Most of the Indian women were naked, clad only in their long hair; they had no hair on other parts of their body. All big eyes and innocence. Some, more "civilized," were half dressed, sometimes the upper half, sometimes the lower. Almost all of them were already old, even though they were perhaps only twenty. The men were better-looking, with faces like masks, and hair cut in a bob; their genitals were enhanced by the remains of red paint from their last magic ceremony. In spite of their dignity, the Indians were somewhat beggarly. They pestered for cigarettes, and clearly looked on the Vilas Boas' wretched hut as a palace of marvels.

One of the group was a young Indian with long hair—an Indian in the style of Fenimore Cooper, but modernized by blue jeans and a sweat-shirt. He had a far-away, mysterious look. He looked like a hippie. He was the Indian who had given the Winchester rifle to the brothers.

"His father," Orlando explained, "is an Indian of the plateau. He has an enormous disk of wood distending his lips. His face is marbled all over with bluish scars, made with thorns. His name is Cretire. A true savage. He is the chief of a particularly primitive tribe, nomadic warriors who don't use bows and arrows, but huge clubs hewn from tree trunks. They attack other, more civilized Indians. They even attack the garimpeiros—the diamond hunters. The latter are now too numerous and so the terrible Cretire came to ask my help. We had months and months of negotiations, of those parleys where the Indians never express their thoughts, and you have to guess them. We used to say to Cretire: 'You must no longer kill, you must no longer steal, you must respect other tribes.' At which point he would get wildly angry.

"Everything came to a head when Cretire and his warriors stole a large pig from the station. We went to Cretire to tell him that we would not give him anything anymore. The next day he came to the station with his warriors painted in black, the color of war. That particular day Claudio was alone here. Cretire came up to him shouting: 'Claudio, you are not my father. I'm not afraid of you. I'm going to kill you. My people are stronger. I'm going to destroy you and everything you've built.' This all took place in this very room. Claudio was relaxing peacefully in his hammock. No revolver within reach. Anyway it would have been absurd to use one. The thought never even crossed Claudio's mind, even when Cretire was brandishing his club. Claudio spoke for two hours. Two long hours. Again and again he repeated: 'I don't care if I die, but you need me. You are children, you don't know anything. You are not the most powerful. Without Orlando and me, the garimpeiros will wipe you out.' And finally, Cretire laid his hideous head on Claudio's shoulder: 'It's true. The Capajos don't know anything. From now on, they will be good. From now on, they won't paint themselves black any more.'

"And, as a pledge of peace, Cretire presented me with the Winchester via his son, this boy who's here, who is so handsome, so calm, who seems so modern, without discs or paint or marks."

I asked Claudio, who wore the most child-like smile as if this drama had had nothing to do with him:

"How did you charm this barbarous Indian? With what marvelous words did you touch his heart?"

Claudio, bland as ever, murmured, "What I told him wasn't enough. So for a long time I explained to him the philosophy of Kant."

Orlando's loud voice broke in, "It's true. That was just like Claudio. He can say anything, he always persuades the Indians. But the friendship we've established with the Capajos is a burden, because the garimpeiros fear and hate them in particular. Their aim is to liquidate the Capajos so they feel safe. You have to have a certain respect for the garimpeiros. They are rough people, half-castes of half-castes, the sons of all the rapes of the centuries, a mix of whites, blacks and reds. But even though they have Indian origins, their war with the Indians is inexorable. For every garimpeiro killed, 1,000 Indians would be killed if we weren't here."

Indeed, I learned that the Vilas Boas brothers had just saved another tribe, the Tchicoes, who were also "bad" Indians. At least the brothers had saved the Tchicoes who were left. Fifty-four men, in very poor condition, of the 120 that they used to be. The tribe used to roam the fever-laden banks of the Rio Jatuba, an eldorado which was almost their tomb.

IT WAS humid. The hour of siesta. Orlando was snoring in his hammock stretched across the office. As always, Indians were there to watch him. They were huge, reddish masses of muscles, with buttocks and chests like blockhouses. A suggestion of prize cattle.

But some pitiful human forms were among these somewhat blasé stalwarts. Stunted, grey-skinned, barely alive. They gazed furtively at Orlando in his sleep and then slipped away. I followed them into the courtyard, in the direction of a shed which was used for both the kitchen and the dining room of the Vilas Boas brothers. In the shed I saw an Indian as thin as a rake, like some Asiatic "boy," preparing the unchanging stew of *feijoas* and rice. But the poor wretches passed by and walked toward their own shanty town. This was nothing but rabbit hutches made of planks from a crate. Inside these structures in a circle around a fire that had gone out, sat men whose ribs stuck out, women with pendulous skin, and children with swollen bellies. These living skeletons, herded together in a heap of silence, did nothing. They had nothing to do.

Claudio appeared. "These are the Tchicoes. We've lodged them here while waiting for a proper village to be built. First of all we have to get them on their feet again. Vaccines and rice. They've already put on several pounds. They were at death's door when we took them in."

And from him I heard a drama of the jungle, a primitive and bloody tragicomedy.

The Tchicoes are the terror of the other Indians, the hereditary enemies of peaceful agricultural and fishing tribes. Though always outnumbered, they used to raid the more civilized villages, which had the secrets of pottery and stone axes, and where the women were prettier. They would overwhelm a village, burning and killing, steal the pottery and axes, and carry off the girls. This went on until the warriors of nine villages that were regularly sacked united for a punitive expedition—a strange and complicated coalition of Indians speaking different languages and strangers to one another. A white adventurer was reported to have guided them—an outlaw like so many others in the supposedly impenetrable jungle, capable of anything, even of making some curious pact with the Indians—unless he was an agent of the Vilas Boas. At any rate, under the guidance of this white chief, the "army" fell upon the Tchicoes' lair and massacred them. Only the children, the old men and the women were left alive; they had hidden themselves in the depths of the jungle.

A few weeks later, Claudio and Orlando learned that these wretched survivors were dying. They had nothing to eat in their green desert. They were too weak to burn an acre of mato and plant manioc in the cinders. Without stone axes, they were disarmed. Disease raged among them. They were a woebegone flock, frightened, hiding in the immense vegetation of the Jatuba, a river rotten with malaria. Orlando dispatched emissaries who took two weeks to find them. The Tchicoes refused to listen, and moved camp farther and farther upstream. They were afraid of everything, of other Indians always ready for vengeance and every kind of white man: why should the Vilas Boas brothers be any better than the garimpeiros and the seringueiros?

The garimpeiros were just then arriving from all parts, by the thousand, diving over each other's heads into the Jatuba. Its bed was a mine of diamonds. Before exploiting the treasure, these men obeyed the unwritten law of the jungle: first, liquidate all the Indians. They machine-gunned the unfortunate Tchicoes. Once again the remnant of the tribe cleared out. In their exodus they died one after the other, condemned by the flu virus—most viruses of the civilized are fatal for the Indians.

When they heard of the Tchicoes' distress, the Vilas Boas brothers began to

Lucien Bodard, the author, with Orlando Vilas Boas.

Orlando and Claudio Vilas Boas. The Vilas Boas brothers have given their life to the Indians. Orlando is a giant, bearded and truculent, and the head of the "Reservation." Claudio is an intellectual with a lean look and the eyes of a visionary. The two men live and do their work on a minute grant from the Brazilian government.

search for them with their little airplane. At last, in the middle of the clearing, they caught sight of shriveled bodies. It was a row of corpses: twenty-two in all. A little farther, eight other Tchicoes were dying from a cold in the tropical heat. It is possible that the garimpeiros had contrived to contaminate the tribe with germ-laden clothing. This is an old trick and one of the hundreds of locally known ways of getting rid of the Indians.

Corpses and dying, but no sign of any living Tchicoes. Were there any? Orlando and Claudio flew over the treetops all along the Jatuba, but in vain. They finally abandoned their search.

Meanwhile, the expeditions of garimpeiros were thinning on the river. It was necessary to dive deeper and deeper into the waters, and the diamond hunter had to use professional divers to rake the mud from its bed and bring it to the surface. In a few weeks, the underwater mine was exhausted, and the cabins, the stores, everything that had been built as if by magic, were abandoned. One after the other the men left, returning to the Mato Grosso, to the "frontier," to the first civilized villages. The Rio Jatuba returned to its loneliness.

But four garimpeiros, instead of retracing their path, decided to seek their fortune farther away. So they descended the Jatuba by boat to where it flowed into the Xingu. As they traveled they felt as if they were being watched, spied upon by Indians hidden in the vegetation of the banks. In these parts, a seen Indian is a dead Indian. On the other hand, invisible Indians are a danger. They do not attack armed men as long as the latter are on their guard, but at the slightest slip, the Indians leap to the kill. Generally this is just before dawn, when the man on guard becomes drowsy. At night, the Indians are afraid of spirits and keep away. The hour of peril is when daylight begins to filter through the fronds 100 feet above, daylight which barely arrives.

Each dawn, the garimpeiros hurriedly left the bank, their asylum for the night, a haven lit by a fire. They crowded into their canoe, and plunged into the currents of the Xingu to throw off their unknown pursuers. But at every dusk, and at every halt, they always felt the Indians were near. At last, one night, just as dawn was breaking, the invisible Indians showed themselves. No madmen painted for murder. Almost dead. They were the last of the Tchicoes. What did they want? Did they still want to kill these few garimpeiros, their eternal enemies? No, they wanted help.

Miraculously, the adventurers did not wipe them out. No doubt the garimpeiros knew they were in the fief of the Vilas Boas brothers, who would not forgive such a massacre. In any case, they prudently informed Orlando of what had happened. They hoped, in recompense, he would let them pursue their journey across his territory, towards the mighty Amazon.

The Tchicoes were brought to the station. The Vilas Boas brothers arranged matters well. Orlando mobilized all the "good" Indians from his reservation to form a formidable welcoming committee. For days, they arrived at the camp, tribe after tribe, with wives and children, by river and jungle trails. All naked. All a little nervous. To reach the station, some had paddled or walked for weeks. Those were Orlando's orders. They had to come. They had to take part in the first large peace congress of Indians in upper Xingu. But the anxiety was great: would not the sanguinary instinct of all these Indians who were forever warring on one another reassert itself on this unprecedented occasion when the Indians would all be united? Would it be reciprocal slaughter instead of a permanent reconciliation? Everything depended upon Orlando's strength and upon Claudio's charm. As each detachment arrived, the brothers bade them welcome, cracked jokes, and—most important—gave them magnificent gifts—from guns and bullets for hunting, to fishing lines worthy of Miami millionaires. Magical power of gifts upon the Indians. On all sides, wide smiles, great bursts of laughter. It was a camp without precedent. As much to eat as you wanted. At night, around the fires, feasts, while by day incredible preparations for the guests, the outcasts, the loathed Tchicoes, who were still not there.

In the camp, there were rehearsals. Songs and dances to the sound of enormous flutes. Throbbing rhythms, rather slow, that went on and on. No sorrow in them, but no frantic, sensual gaiety of the Brazilian blacks. A sort of endless rehearsal. Men and women set out like pieces on a chessboard—one man, one woman, one man, one woman, indefinitely—but each separated from the others by a yard or two, each performing in his place. Sometimes they formed into a procession, still alternating one man, one woman. Always the same sounds, the same gestures. They would shake their heads, adorned by the rainbow diadems of parrot feathers. Arms poised, feet tapping the ground, whole bodies in motion. Music and melody like muffled rumbles from the forest. Seriously, noble, almost hypnotic, a communion of man with the world. The women often passed their hands over their bellies, as if in thanks for what they had received, signifying man's seed more than his food. It was clear that this could turn into an orgy, but there was no question of this in the official presence of the Vilas Boas brothers. A more pressing preoccupation though, was that this dance of joy not suddenly turn into a war dance, with the instruments of death suddenly appearing—bows, arrows, clubs, spears . . . .

The wait lasted endlessly. It took the Tchicoes three months of canoeing and walking to reach the Rio Jatuba. They had fled that far from it. At last they appeared. And the Indians of the Vilas Boas brothers saw, instead of the six-foot giants they expected, phantoms, dwarfs four-and-a-half-feet high, dying men who barely had the strength to drag themselves along, and who literally used their last reserve of strength to fling themselves upon the food. This reassured everyone, and the fête started, the fête so carefully prepared to accomplish the solemn rites of friendship with these remaining Tchicoes.

Suddenly, in spite of everything, tragedy—or very nearly. It took all Orlando's authority to avoid it. Among the throng an old Indian woman began to wail. In the ranks of the arriving Tchicoes, she had recognized her daughter, whom the Tchicoes had kidnapped twenty years before. Since then, she had grown almost as withered as her mother. She had had a daughter herself, who had in turn had a daughter. She still carried a child on her deflated breast—her own, her grandson, or her great grandson? No one knew. In any event, her mother began to moan. She implored the daughter to rejoin her true clan. But this Helen of Amazonia (the nickname given her by the Vilas Boas), said firmly that she was now a Tchicoe, and wanted to remain one. Guttural sounds. A total impasse. All around, the thousands of Indians also began to weep and wail like the old woman. The Indians stopped in the middle of their dance and became enraged. Gesticulating furiously, they closed in on the poor grubs of Tchicoes. The chief of the Tchicoes was a gnome with a large nose, wide chest, and miniscule legs. In vain he tried to speak. At any moment this could be the massacre of the last Tchicoes.

Orlando roared. Orlando carved himself a passage with his voice, his eyes, and his all-powerful body. He obtained with difficulty a respite which he used to whisk away the Tchicoes. He shut them up in a shed, under the pretext of giving them more to eat. The old woman began to prowl around the Tchicoes' hut. She recommenced her groans and pleas. The daughter remained indifferent. The old woman's clamor lasted a long time. But the problem no longer interested anyone. The mood of the Indians, as often happened, had changed. Their one idea was to return to their villages with the Vilas Boas brothers' gifts.

As for the Tchicoes, they slowly began to fatten up. Men from a neolithic age. What was to be done with them?

The four garimpeiros of the Rio Jatuba, still at the station during my visit, were absolutely furious with Orlando's order: "I forbid you to descend the

Xingu with your canoe, which I have confiscated. It's your punishment for having dared to penetrate my territory. You will leave by the first plane. Until then, don't bother me, and make your own arrangements for finding food."

In order to eat, the garimpeiros began to kill crocodiles. By day, the Xingu is extraordinarily calm, without a ripple to indicate the presence of the beasts. But the Indians will tell you that they are there by the thousands, hiding in the flooded jungle, "where the river has no banks." And indeed, at night, if you sweep a flashlight over the surface of the Xingu, you could believe you were in a parking lot: everywhere, in pairs, two little red stars on the water. To kill the reptiles, all that is necessary is to dazzle one of them and take aim between the luminescent points of his eyes. The Indians used to attack the crocodiles with javelins. Now they have lost the habit. With their carbines, the garimpeiros made successful hunters, and for almost three weeks their menu was composed of crocodile tails.

I spoke with one of the men. He had a wide-brimmed hat, a cruel face, swarthy, emphasized by a fine moustache, an aristocrat of adventure. Like his companions, he was very reserved and secretive. He refused to speak of his past. I asked him about his projects for the future. He replied: "How do you want me to know? We live from day to day. And it's hard for us to live." Everything is hard in the Amazon.

ORLANDO HAD his usual look. The look of a powerful and dirty condottiere, an intentional dirtiness, which is both virile and philosophical. He covered his chest with a sweater, with such tears that you could see his whole navel. His skin was greasy with sweat, his face overgrown with beard under the shade of a straw hat. He barked out his orders. He was totally concentrated, leaning over his maps, preparing a peace expedition like a military expedition. It was a matter of putting an end, by sheer personality, to a hodge-podge of a war that involved a bit of everything. Some completely savage tribes were tearing each other apart; others, somewhat more civilized, entered the fray by "collaborating" with the whites. The indifferent functionaries of the S.P.I. were receiving the corpses in their stations; half-caste turtle-hunters were distributing poisoned sugar to the Indians; rich American pastors, proselytizing in the heart of the jungle, were getting ready to move out in their small private planes; and stout, bearded Catholic missionaries were also escaping, but on foot.

All this was happening north of the Vilas Boas brothers' reservation. The reservation itself was always calm, because Orlando and Claudio had a thousand eyes. It only took a tiny clue for them to be aware of something and take action. Here, they are at home, and their four stations are theirs alone. But to the north, beyond the rapids of the Xingu, lies the most appalling part of the whole Amazonian jungle, a land of terror between the middle reaches of the turbulent Xingu, and the Tapajós, the river of fevers, another tributary of the Amazon, as large and mysterious as the Xingu and running parallel to it. Even more dangerous are the smaller rivers, the tributaries of tributaries, like the Rio Juruena and the Rio Arinos, which spring up in the serras, those bedlams of rocks, vegetation and humus.

It was on the banks of the Arinos where this particular trouble began and where an American Seventh-Day Adventist, forlorn in that mad world with all his puritanical good will, almost lost his faith in God. From his little lost temple, scrubbed and clean with its electricity and air-conditioning, he sent out his cries of alarm: "The Brazilians are doing today what our ancestors perpetrated a century ago in our own country. It's so terrible that I would rather the Indians remained savage and heathen. To convert them under these conditions makes no sense. It's to betray them. God is far away . . . "

The missionary named an employee of the official society created for the development of the center of Brazil. This gentleman was the boss at Fort Gauchos—a few plank huts on the Rio Arinos, making up a village. He had had almost the entire Beiço de Pau tribe poisoned, and had the survivors finished off by assassins. He had then had 193 square miles of their land made over in his own name, after some transactions with those oily, exigent gentlemen, the politicians and policemen of Brazil. He was grateful for the good offices of the "grileiros"—the real estate go-betweens—whose services are almost indispensible when the laws regarding real estate are as uncertain as those in the Brazilian Far West.

What happened was that all the stragglers in the jungle who were not too dark, neither too black nor too red, wanted their part of the spoils of the tribe. They were all determined to become fazendeiros—proprietors—even if the properties, now that the Indians are dead, are only lost empty hells far, so far, from everything. There is nothing but the desolation of the waters, and the unbridled fury of the cannibal jungle which devours itself. But, for the "purchaser," there is hope, the hope of cutting the jungle, selling the wood, or reselling the soil, to an American, a trust, or a big operator who might turn up. It's a lottery. There might also be hidden treasure, rare trees, precious juices, medicinal plants, saps, a vein of gold, a cache of diamonds. Perhaps a mysterious prospector will appear, some kind of American, with the most up-to-date equipment, and an interest in unknown metals, which will prove unexpectedly valuable for the almost magical super-industries of the great modern nations. Even if the visitor proposes nothing, absolutely nothing, the rumor of his presence alone makes prices rise 100 per cent.

The Rio Arinos. How can the Indians, whose only tool is the stone axe and who still live 4,000 years before Jesus Christ, how can they resist? The fazendeiros want to be rid of them all. Droves of assassins. The hiring of pistoleiros. Sometimes some whitish adventurer or mulatto is killed, his body riddled with long vibrating arrows. Then all the "civilized" men of the region, in a chorus of imprecations and appeals for help, demand that the army undertake a punitive expedition with all the modern resources of planes and machine guns. Sometimes this is done, but often, rather than expend money on an onerous bloodbath, the authorities prefer to appeal to humanistic specialists to calm, tame and pacify the Indians who are left. The Vilas Boas brothers often serve this purpose.

As a matter of fact, Claudio and Orlando are not always very keen on it. Saving the Indians is their profession. They do it with love, they are proud of their technique of approach and contact, they tame by kindness, and their charitable exploits are legendary. But they would like other regions, all the upper and middle Xingu, to be theirs, completely theirs, to be the kings of one large Indian kingdom. And so to intervene and, in effect, serve the interests of the fazendeiros, seringueiros, garimpeiros and the other killers, revolts them. They detest all of them, look upon them as intruders and murderers. Moreover, the brothers distrust the S.P.I. people, who are weak, profiteering, and have no ideals. They detest missionaries of any religion, cassocks and dog-collars alike. "Those people," they never stop repeating, "don't kill the Indians physically, but morally. They're murderers too." The brothers exude an old secular, atheist positivism; and they are incapable of tolerating any rivalry. The Vilas Boas brothers believe in their unique destiny. This often creates difficult situations for them.

The principal enemies of the Vilas Boas are the big fazendeiros, the powerful landowners, the speculators on an international scale. Orlando's and Claudio's dream would have been to carve themselves a fief grandiose enough for them to let all the tribes in central Brazil live in happiness, in nature, according to a natural philosophy. They both believe that there are some tens of thousands of completely wild Indians between the Xingu and the Tapajós, Indians who have been swallowed up by nature. These Indians have their own frontiers, which they signpost by strange marks, knotted grass or bundles of branches. When the adventurers violate these taboos, the Indians sometimes retreat still farther towards greater hunger and degeneration. But sometimes they attack the invaders, whether it's another tribe, or a band of whites. Then there is war in the jungle. The Vilas Boas are convinced that they are the only beings able to approach, pacify and protect all these free, brave Indians, who are now dying out from hunger and disease. To save all of them, the Vilas Boas would have to have an immense territory.

They obtained only 13,500 square miles, a tenth of the area necessary to accomplish their great design. And what difficulties they had to obtain that. Poor Orlando! He had to battle in surroundings more treacherous than the Amazon—the senators, capitalists, generals and the cops, all linked together by immense secret interests. He did everything to further his cause. He dressed up for the occasion as a subtropical gentleman, which made him look rather like a fazendeiro. At one time, everything was let loose against him. A press campaign was instigated, denouncing the Indians as cannibals and belligerent madmen, with the implicit conclusion that they should therefore be destroyed. But Orlando has his wiles. He is very Brazilian despite everything, with an instinct for a possible deal—in a good cause, of course. So, in 1961, he extracted a decree from the president of the Republic, Janios Quadros (a strange individual, whose symbol was a broom—he was due to sweep himself out of office a little later by resigning during a nervous breakdown). This document founded Orlando's reservation, "his" little reservation, with its area comparable to Brittany, with fourteen tribes, 1,200 Indians, one or two planes, a tractor, a pump, three electric generators, and a stock of medicine, ammunition and clothes. Orlando received a salary of 6,000, Claudio of 3,000 cruzeiros.

Hemming them in with what should rightly have been theirs were gigantic territories extorted, thanks to influence and money, by the powerful fazendeiros hand in glove with the politicians of Cuiabá, the Mato Grosso's capital. Cuiabá is comparable to what Chicago was supposed to have been a century ago. It is a city of the past, of the gold rush, on the river of the same name. Children are now forbidden to scavenge for any gold remaining on its banks, to avoid their collapsing. But Cuiabá is also a city of the marvelous future, with skyscrapers among its huts.

Orlando was growing more and more irritable. He was debating whether he should go up the Rio Juruena to the assistance of his enemies, the fazendeiros.

In the dark night of the forest of Juruena, there had been more bloodshed. This time the Indians had been fighting each other. In a clearing of the jungle, hallucinating war-dances, alarming war paint and the sinister chants of war. The ceremony of the Javari. Incantations for the death of the enemy. Solemn oaths to fight fiercely. "Dead or alive, after the war, we shall have peace. If we win, we shall have peace at home. If we lose, we shall find peace beside our ancestors." The naked bodies are a grey-black, with terrible green designs like the coils of two huge snakes climbing up their buttocks and meeting along their spines. Other white and green marks, like scales, are dotted about. A mask around the eyes—not a real one, but a dark varnish ringing the sockets like tortoise shells. It's a sign of abandon, but it reminds one of masks in a masquerade, or of sunglasses on the Riviera. The Javari lasts for days. It's a complicated ritual relating the episodes of a war legend lost in the mists of time. Brandishing their arms, the warriors depart, melting into the vegetation towards the village that is to be destroyed. The women have taken no part in this, but have remained in their huts. If one of them glimpsed something, she would undergo terrible punishments, in conformity with the ancient native law of many centuries. The Indian women wait for the issue of the combat, aware that their existence is at stake, because they constitute the first, and most precious, spoils of war.

The Mencromotires against the Kraiacaras. A long and indecisive war. Even during respites, hostilities still threatened. At least twenty Indians massacred, and a dozen Indian women killed or kidnaped, a considerable loss for an intertribal quarrel, for the tribes are miniscule. The figure of twenty is minimal. It is the figure known to the whites, for the Indians laid the corpses near a station of the S.P.I., who haven't even gathered them up. There are certainly more. One wounded Indian told a priest, "There are more deaths than I know how to explain. I'm going to show you how many with my fingers." The man agitated his fingers for some minutes. This meant "many, many." In most of the tribes, the Indians don't know how to count beyond four or five. They don't have the numbers for more. To express quantity, they use their knuckles, or the expression, "as many as the hair on your head."

The hostilities had a complex plot. It was the Mencromotires who attacked. They are experienced killers, but semicivilized. They have had a relationship with the whites for a long time. The latter have often used them as their eyes in the jungle, as guides and spies, and also to "contact" wild tribes. This time the contact seemed particularly brutal. It is only one step from there to the thought that the fazendeiros or the garimpeiros instigated the quarrel. No doubt they gave the Mencromotires gifts, perhaps even arms.

War among Indians is also a way of getting rid of Indians. Moreover, the white adventurers of the Arinos were particularly anxious not to be further annoyed by the Kraiacaras, who are a very individual people, very distrustful, and very much in the way. They were a special branch of the Capajos; descended from half-castes who had been absorbed by the jungle, forgotten, degenerated, and Indianized; they had become Indians opposing the new half-castes of the present time.

But the Mencromotires were too numerous, and their setbacks only served to increase their rage. They were determined to kill all the Kraiacaras, or to make them move elsewhere, far away. As it happened, the Kraiacaras ended up by leaving. But where had they gone to? Had they escaped to a distant jungle hide-out, or were they going to reappear suddenly and dangerously where they weren't expected? A certain fear hung over the upper Xingu, and as always in Amazonia when one kind of Indian is dreaded, the rumor spread that they—in this case the Kraiacaras—were gigantic specimens, over six feet tall.

The Vilas Boas planned their strategy at their second station, the ranch where I was staying. It's quite possible that they knew where the Kraiacaras were, since the Indians were enemies, like themselves, of the "bad" whites. The brothers had been in touch with the affair for a long time, and there was every indication that they were preparing a denouement in their own style, and a recuperation. But this was the moment when misfortune struck, a real misfortune, which obliged Orlando to mount, before my eyes, an urgent expedition. He had to retrieve an incredible blunder.

The Vilas Boas brothers are on bad terms, in the Xingu, with pretty well the whole of the civilized world, with the exception of the pilots of the Brazilian air force, the F.A.B., who replenish the brothers' supplies by plane. In exchange, Claudio and Orlando have taught the pilots to trade in a small way with the "good" Indians of the Xingu, and to exchange bazaar trifles for the fine feathered ornaments that the pilots sell for exorbitant sums to American tourists in Rio. It would seem that Orlando encourages his "protégées" to make pottery and ornaments from feathers, shell and bone, with an eye to this legitimate trade which benefits everybody—the Vilas Boas, their friends the pilots, and their friends the Indians . . .

The airmen had a large base at Cochimbo, 100 miles or so from the station where I was with Orlando and Claudio. In Cochimbo, there was a cement airstrip set in the middle of swamps, one in the chain of twenty or so strategic airstrips which extended from Rio de Janeiro towards the United States, across the desolate interior of Brazil. They were built during the Second World War, when the United States needed rapid communications across the world, so that her large planes, which flew over menacing continents and dangerous seas, could touch down to refuel before they arrived at the combat zones—once again, the wild rubber of Brazil had become precious. Since then, in peace time, these concrete slabs in the virgin jungle had returned to normal use.

For a long time, a garrison had been stationed at Cochimbo, with its small business and its understanding with the Vilas Boas brothers and their Indians. What had recently happened and was so unexpected was that one day the pilots panicked. Some Indians had appeared one fine morning, but not looking at all like the others. They were brandishing their bows and their primitive weapons, shrieking, painted for war. These warriors burst into the military property apparently with the intent to attack it. The airmen believed it was an attack, and shot at the ground with machine guns. Others succeeded in taking off and skimming over the Indians' heads. The garrison was so panic-stricken that it demanded reinforcements, and a Dakota airplane with twenty-four soldiers was despatched from Rio de Janeiro. The plane never succeeded in finding the airstrip at the end of the world. The gas ran out, and plane and crew were lost.

"It's so stupid," Claudio, the thinker, was telling me while Orlando, the man of action, was on the move. "The Indians who appeared at Cochimbo are the Kraiacaras, whom we've been waiting for for so long, and whom we've persuaded in secret to join us. Of course they'd just come from a desperate fight on the Juruena to defend the land which is their only wealth. They hated the whites who were trying to exterminate them, but they knew that there were some other whites, like ourselves, who were their friends. They were coming to us. Why did they show up at Cochimbo? No doubt because they'd heard that the pilots were our allies, and had concluded that they were also their allies. They'd emerged from the jungle at Cochimbo, not for war, but just the opposite—for the end of the war, for the peace festivities. They had painted themselves for joy, not for bloodshed. No, I can't understand how the garrison could have fired."

Claudio's expression was less friendly than usual, his face even more thin and wan, unshaven, bristling with thin, flaxen hair. When Claudio is thinking, his hands almost unconsciously grope around him in search for his glasses, which he always loses. This time they were on his nose, which gave him a look that was hard to understand, bewildered and myopic, and yet, in an odd way, incisive and resolute.

"What a tragic error. For of course it's an absolute rule that the Indians, when they've been the victims of a betrayal or a trap, become rancor and revenge personified. Sometimes it takes fifty or even a hundred years to calm them. And how can we make the Kraiacaras understand that this time there was a misunderstanding? Misunderstandings are outside their comprehension. Orlando and I are going to have such trouble trying to explain to them and regain their confidence. We're going to attempt it as soon as possible."

The news was not good. As expected, the terrified and angry Indians had taken refuge in a particularly putrid and inextricable swamp. This time they had painted themselves for war. Orlando knew more or less where the Kraiacaras had hidden, and for some days had been studying a route to approach them. A hard task, because the place was really appalling—fevers, wild animals, stagnant waters, vegetation as thick as a wall. No question of landing a small plane in a clearing. Contact could only be achieved after a long expedition of hacking a path with axes or risking an unknown river. In any case, it would take days and days.

And what kind of welcome would they get? These were alarming Indians, with their heads shaved in the front, their hair falling down their backs, their pierced ears, and their lips with discs. However, the brothers did hold a possible trump card. One of the Kraiacaras, a giant who in fact was some six-and-a-half-feet tall, had fallen into their hands. For a fortnight they had treated him with every kindness, and had then released him without any conditions or messages. Their only hope was that he would say to his tribe, "These whites don't want to kill us. They are good."

How many times in the past have the Vilas Boas taken the risk of appearing, unarmed, with gifts, in front of savages bending their bows or brandishing their clubs?

"Each time it's a toss-up," Orlando explained. "We know that somewhere there's a village or a tribe which we can perhaps rally. Where exactly, we don't know. What these people really feel, we don't know. Our own Indians are no use because they're not familiar with unsubjugated Indians and don't even speak their language. What a stroke of luck if, by some extraordinary fluke, we can detain an individual here from the group we wish to pacify. We send him back with his hands full to his own people, to bear witness that we are good. But that's a rare case.

"We depend upon the first contact, the first moments, on the unknown reflexes in the unknown heads, to find out whether their desire for our offerings is greater than their temptation to kill. It's essential to divine the state of mind of the Indians to be recuperated. Indians are so complex in their simplicity. They're masterly at concealing what lies in their hearts.

"There's the enormous weight of the distant and recent—sometimes very recent—past. It's so often believed that an unknown tribe is "virgin," that is, that it's never seen a white face. What a mistake. The wilds of Amazonia are full of ancient history. There's almost no tribe that has not had, one, two or three centuries ago, trouble with those whom we call civilized. The tribe we believe has stepped straight out of pre-history, has had a history. At one time, one doesn't know when, it was certainly part of a powerful race which was splintered and crushed beneath the blows of its white conquerors. This explains that extraordinary mosaic of tribes—the rump of Amazonia—which waste away in some corner until they're rediscovered. We don't know of the dramas of former times. But these tragedies remain in the collective memory of the Indians.

"The past. The frightening responsibility for the past. Now Claudio and I have to proclaim: 'We're not like the other white men.' But as we say this, we don't even know if the tribe that we wish to rally has forgiven ancient crimes. We often don't know whether it's been the victim of a recent atrocity. In such a case, we run the risk of paying for the faults of others with our own lives.

"Paying for others happens to priests, too. You mustn't forget the missionaries. Centuries of missions. All these fathers, churches, naked Indians dancing the baptismal dance and singing Latin hymns and the Ave Maria, kneeling and prostrating themselves. But it's often come to a bad end. I've heard a story about the last century, during the period of official slavery. Some Jesuits had built a fine church on a fine river. They'd told a tribe of Indians living upstream that they'd come to get them the next year, to bring them home to their mission. A swarthy man arrived there by river, with a very large canoe. 'I am coming on behalf of the fathers. They are anxious to have you at home and told me to transport you there at once. They're waiting for you.' He selected the forty finest males, as well as women and children, packed them all into the interior of his craft, and made them voyage for weeks. The Indians had not the slightest suspicion. But instead of disembarking at the church of the fathers, they disembarked at Manaus, where this person auctioned them all off as if they were his own slaves. The remainder of the tribe waited patiently for months in the hope of good news.

None came. None, except, a long while after, the rumor of the infamous sale. The tribe obviously believed that this was a treasonable act by the good fathers, descended upon the mission, and burnt and killed everything in sight. They continued the war against the missions for long, long years. It cost a great many human lives, and made numerous martyrs."

Did this martyrdom of the priests move Orlando? It didn't look like it. In any event, he explained to me his technique for not becoming a victim himself—he was no keener on being sacrificed in the name of Rondon than he was in the name of God.

It takes flair. In fact, Orlando is an ace at Indian strategy. His glory is to "feel out" the Indians. He treated me to a heroicomic exposé of his methods.

"It used to be much more difficult when we were obliged to travel on foot or by canoe. The problem used to begin when we reached the 'frontiers.' There were several successive frontiers, marked each time by the classic signs of grass or branches. We used to put the gifts on the boundary, and, if the taboos were removed the following night along with our presents, we would continue. We made our way as far as the village, which was symbolically defended by sorts of hooks stuck in the ground. We would hang on them some fine merchandise. If it disappeared, it meant that we and our gifts were accepted. We could go on, hoping not to be hit by an arrow.

"It's been a bit easier since we've had a plane. We can search for the village and discover it in its clearing, a dot in the immensity. Instead of bombarding with dynamite, we bombard it with the eternal gifts. We keep watching. If, at the end of two or three days, there are no hostile signs, war dances, men taking potshots at our plane, etcetera, we land on any firm surface that we can find, unarmed, but without cutting off the motor. This is the nasty moment when the Indians appear and look at us without saying a word. Their silence against ours. We wave our offerings. Are there going to be smiles—or snarls, shrieks, savagery let loose, and a swarm of arrows?

"Once a little boy climbed into our plane. That turned out to be a lucky break. We took ourselves off in the middle of an attack and kidnaped him. The child served, later on, to attract the whole tribe.

"In the course of one operation of this kind, to pacify the Jurunas, we really thought we had had it. We had landed calmly and entered the village. Nothing. And then, suddenly, armed men everywhere, raising their spears. I knew the name of the cacique—the chief—a seventy year old grandfather who weighed 200 pounds: it was Takara. As a last resort, I shouted, 'Takara! Takara!' Immediately a man of twenty came out of a hut, beating his breast as if repentant. 'I am Takara,' he said. It was the grandson. All the agitation stopped. The warriors smiled at us.

"Unknown to us, we'd been saved by an extraordinary chance, thanks to Indian 'theology.' In the eyes of these Indians, the paternal grandfather and the grandson were identical, to the extent that, if the child were sick, the old man was nursed, and vice versa. Together they made one person. In our case, it happened that the older Takara was dead, but the young man was also Takara, and he considered it a sacred sign that we knew his name."

"But have you experienced any failures?"

Orlando swaggered.

"Oh yes. Sometimes it took many expeditions, great diplomacy and incredible efforts, sometimes lasting for years, to recuperate a score of Indians, who were the only ones to speak a language which no one else understood. It has happened that we ended up with nothing at all. Once all I brought back from an infernal expedition in an infested spot, was a blond wig—a wig made from palm and cotton fibers with amazing artistry; it even gave the effect of having a wide hairband, cleverly waved, ending in a long tress like a pony tail. It wasn't large, just large enough to cover a mummified head. And yet, in those regions of the Xingu, the Indians didn't know how to shrink heads. The color was sandy, the color of white-skinned women's hair, hair that fascinates the Indians.

"There's been everything in Amazonia! Even the legend of the Amazons, a tribe of proud Indian women who used to give themselves to the males once a year by the edge of a lake called 'Reflection without a Moon.' Apart from that single day, they used to kill all the boys mercilessly. They were tall, pearly-white, lovely, muscular caryatids. Isn't it just a fable? And yet the first Portuguese explorers of the Amazon swore they'd seen them, and even that their boat had been riddled with arrows by these mysterious Amazons. It's probably a fable, but a fable of desire.

"Anyway, what incredible trouble we had getting this wig! It happened miles downstream, where the Xingu becomes very broad, and divides into a network of arms flowing into the estuary of the Amazon; where a mixture of water, plants and land stretches over areas as large as a European country.

"Civilization has been eating away here for centuries. At the time of the Portuguese conquest, there was a slaughter of Indians which ran to hundreds of thousands. Odd towns were built on anything resembling a bank, many of which have died and been reborn in turn, following the varying values of the products of the jungle. In spite of the rubber, and the march towards the West, not all of these cities have been resurrected.

"One of them, Pôrto de Moz, has existed since 1754, on the lower Xingu, almost at its confluence with the Amazon. Along with the white men, there used to be civilized Indians—their slaves. And, as they used to be poor workers, they'd almost all been exterminated. So the few who were still alive fled into the jungle in small groups, and formed a single tribe, which plunged ever deeper into the stifling greenery. Their tactic was never to show themselves. They were nicknamed 'Shaven-Heads.'

"But the Shaven-Heads became more and more menaced. For the jungles and valleys of the lower Xingu, the part of the Xingu without falls, was being peopled with the creatures of progress, from fazendeiros all the way down the social scale to caboclos, the lowest of the halfcastes. There were 10,000 settlers near the modern city of Altamira, on a bend of the river, and whites had already penetrated into the rivers Jaraucu and Penatecaua. When construction was begun on a road between Altamira and the more important town of Santarém, on the Amazon, the Shaven-Heads believed that the trap was closing, for the road finished off a triangle, whose two other sides were the Rios Jaraucu and Penatecaua; a triangle inside which the Shaven-Heads lived.

"So, in their anguish, they attacked a group of ragged workers who were piling up the earth to make the road. One man was killed and the others wounded. Work was abandoned on the highway, the whole region paralyzed, and there were appeals for help to the mayor of Altamira, whose mother was an Indian. Planes and helicopters were unable to pierce the secrets of the jungle where the Shaven-Heads lived, a jungle without clearings. There was no way of bombing or machine-gunning the invisible, nor was there time to mount a real military expedition. Their only chance was to use the 'specialists in Indian pacification,' that is to say, me, Claudio, and our colleague, Morales.

"First we encountered the beauty of the Xingu, and then sweat, hunger and cold. The mattress of vegetation was so dense that the humidity below seemed to freeze us to the marrow of our bones. Flu beneath the tropics. In Amazonia, flu, even when not in its virulent Asiatic form, just the normal kind of flu, is deadlier than cholera. It's the curse of the Indians. One man with a cold can spread the scourge over whole provinces. It kills more surely than gunfire.

"We found the flu when we set out—the Indians of the region had it. We didn't know whether it had been spread on purpose or by accident. But at the last station of the S.P.I. there were twenty-two Indians dead; they hadn't been buried—they were food for the urubus.[1] Eight others were stretched on

1. See glossary.

the ground, waiting for their end. Nobody was taking care of them. Claudio saved their lives by having them carried to Altamira. We wondered if the flu had spread further and had attacked the Shaven-Heads.

"There were fourteen of us. We ascended the Rio Penatecaua aboard two motor boats. The rio is a vegetable jail. We had to leave our boats to cut away the trees that had fallen on its bed.

"We could see nothing. Under the foliage of the banks, it's always night. Yet we strained our eyes to penetrate the impenetrable, the monstrous forest. For we knew that the Shaven-Heads were there. They had already shot at an old fisherman, fishing for giant tortoises, who had fled with his fourteen tortoise-shells, and never returned. They had also shot at an S.P.I. detachment, weighted down with gifts, who had retraced their footsteps. We were in the domain of Indians at war.

"We plunged into the jungle on foot. All of us, Claudio and I, and even an old man named Chico, sixty years old, carried on our backs from fifteen to twenty pounds of presents. They were our only hope.

"After journeying for days, we found a huge abandoned hut. A week later, we found another straw hut, larger than the first. It had been abandoned too, but this time there were recent traces of life: a rat and its young eaten by ants; a monkey's skull, human hair, fruit peel, some mats, and the barrel of an old gun, which must have been stolen from a settler. There were other things, indefinable and frightful, which lay everywhere. Also a mirror, which was almost new. I was sure the occupants had just left. They were certainly the Shaven-Heads. They were outside, we thought, surrounding us silently. It was useless to stay and be caught in a siege. Our only chance was to go to them . . .

"We journeyed on. As night approached, we found another hut, empty of the living, but full of graves, the *casa dos mortos*, the house of the dead. We stayed there, and slept in a heavy, almost deathly sleep. Outside was the normal cacophony of the forest. But one sound, out of all those sounds, awoke me. It was one sound too many; it was the song of the uru bird. Outside it was pitch dark, and I knew that the uru only sings at dawn. It wasn't the bird, and yet the sound was a perfect copy—too perfect. It could only be the Indians. The Shaven-Heads had approached little by little, with, as their agreed signal, as their sign for a rally and perhaps for an assault, the whistle of the uru. This time we were truly surrounded.

"Claudio decided to reconnoiter outside. He took with him an old Indian whom we had brought from the Xingu. We called him Da-à, "the interpreter," and he did indeed speak almost all the languages of the tribes in the center of Brazil. From our hut, we heard his lonely calls breaking off in the silence, a silence suddenly reestablished. 'I am alone with the whites, and they are good. Come to speak with them and they will give you presents." Da-à called no more, and Claudio returned with him into the hut.

"Four o'clock in the morning. The attack we were waiting for never occurred. We continued on our way, leaving a pile of gifts. We journeyed on for days and days. Hunger and thirst was weakening us. We entered the royal way of the jungle, an Indian path leading to a village of five immense huts, camouflaged under gigantic trees. But, on the raised center of the alley, two huge pieces of wood—two sacrificial stakes—were planted. It was there that the Shaven-Heads celebrated the magic ceremony of calling to their slain, and where they tortured their prisoners to death. We could have been tortured there ourselves.

"There was no one there. But we picked up a strange, pale ornament from the ground, jungle fibers intertwined with threads of cotton. It took us some minutes to realize that it was a wig, one of those blond wigs which the Shaven-Heads used, one doesn't know what for. Blond haunts the Indians. There've been many white kings, or rather half-caste kings, in the heart of Amazonia. There've even been white queens—generally white girls who've been kidnaped.

"Beyond the village there was a still better kept way, and a yet larger village, but everywhere lay the taboos and the warning fires. There was habitation quite near, but we were forbidden to go any further, under pain of being pierced by arrows. The warriors were near at hand, surveying our approach, to pass sentence, their bows arched, invisible. I saw on the ground the sign of the final warning. We stopped and deliberated.

"We were all in agreement. Beyond that mark, we had to kill, or be killed. You know that it was our rule not to kill. We had done all that we could, but we had reached an impasse. We decided to return to the Rio Penatecaua, where we would wait for the Shaven-Heads to show themselves at last. They would certainly follow our withdrawal. To defuse their anger, we would leave behind us, all along our retreat, a line of gifts, frying-pans, plates, knives, nylon, swatches of colored fabrics, etc. After many days, we reached the Rio Penatecaua. We crossed it to camp on the opposite bank and stayed for another three days.

"The first was a night of alarm. At least 100 Shaven-Head warriors were marching on the opposite bank. There was total darkness, because the Indians didn't even carry in their hands those lighted brands which they normally use as torches in the night. I don't know how many times in my life I've seen the obscurity studded by hundreds of points of fire, each representing a man with his brand; it's a tribe departing, nocturnally but peacefully. The black-out of the Shaven-Heads had a dangerous implication. The Indians were advancing silently, but all the same we could hear the branches cracking under their feet.

Da-á, the interpreter, called once more: 'I am alone with the whites, and they are good. Come and speak with them.' Then I, Claudio, and the others joined our shouts to Da-á's, each one trying the different dialects that he knew: 'We don't wish you any harm; come speak, come speak.' And then the silence closed back in upon us. Total silence.

"We spent the last hours of the night on the alert. We took shifts as sentinels until dawn. But there was no trace of the Indians. They had come neither for peace, nor for war. Camped on the same spot on the bank, we passed another two days and nights in a useless wait. The Shaven-Heads had brought us to their frontier. Without even attacking us, they had shown us that they wanted no more of us than they did of the other 'civilized,' and that they could not believe that there could be a species of white men which was 'good.' They remained in their splendid isolation. We descended the Rio Penatecaua as far as the lower Xingu, as far as Altamira and civilization. That adventure was over for us. For days and nights we had been continuously surrounded by Shaven-Heads. We hadn't even seen one. But, as a souvenir, we brought back the memorable wig."

Orlando has force in everything, even in his voice. A rumble, reflecting his full, exhausting, bubbling life, swells up from his throat like lava.

"There are still quite a number of 'bravos' Indians on the Xingu and the Juruena. If exterminations depopulate, rapes reproduce. So it is that two, three or four centuries ago, from the Indians they raped, the whites begot men who are lost in the night of time and who've returned to the primitive state. They've formed primitive tribes. You already know of the Kraiacaras, the issue of forgotten half-castes, and of the Shaven-Heads, who descended from escaped Indian slaves, and who have blond wigs. But there is something even more extraordinary: white Indians.

"These are savages with fair skins, sandy hair, and blue eyes. They are a well-proportioned people, of a height normal for Brazilians. If they were in suits, you'd take them for gentlemen from Rio de Janeiro. But naked and painted, they are terrifying. There are 2,000 to 3,000 of them in the jungles of the middle Xingu, the region of waterfalls and fevers. They are called the Acurinis. They attack everything. They kill anybody who comes within range of their arrows and clubs. They are incomparable with the bow, and their valiance is heroic. They have no fear of death for themselves. It is sometimes said that Indians are cowards, because they operate by ruse and surprise, and avoid being caught by whites armed with guns. The Acurinis have none of this prudence. They rush openly into the attack in waves, even if they have to charge against hails of bullets.

"The Acurinis are handsome and they speak softly. Yet they seem to have a general hatred of humanity. Is it because, unconsciously, they have not forgiven the violence from which they issue? They do not know their origin. Nobody knows it. It goes back, no doubt, to the time of the Portuguese bandeirantes who committed so many massacres and tortures. I think to myself sometimes that these white Indians are the descendants of those men of war who shed enough blood to redden the river Amazon itself.

"There are black Indians, too, or at least almost black. They exist, especially in the Mato Grosso. They're the descendants of African slaves who escaped in the eighteenth century from the gold mines of Minas Gerais. The mines were convict prisons, where under the whips of the overseers, the Negroes crushed rocks, bored through mountains, and sieved the rivers to collect the precious powder. Six slaves fled into the jungle among the Indian tribes of the upper Xingu, which was then a white blank on the map. These blacks, instead of being massacred or eaten, were highly esteemed. They even formed a quilombo, a community, where they were the protectors of some fifty Indians. As these Negroes were Christians, they proselytized, and made some conversions among the Indians. The result was not only a mixture of skins, but also a carnival of all the gods of Europe, Africa and America.

"Strange rites were celebrated in the clearings, with crufixes and Latin words, tom-toms and Bantu melodies, totems and Indian dances. But most of the slaves who'd become masters ended up being killed by their Indians, in quarrels over women. Today the Indians hate the blacks who come to them, not as the whites' victims, but as their capataz, their right-hand men, brutalizing the Indians as a favor to the seringalistas, seringueiros and garimpeiros."

He paused.

"Amazonia. The past which returns like a breath—and the future, which

must atone for this past. I'm a weak man to take part in such a task. But now
I am absorbed by the Kraiacaras. We have to correct this at once, if we don't
want any nasty complications. I know these Indians and their grudges. Next, I
think, I shall go on to pacify the white Indians, the Acurinis, from curiosity,
and because they are the scourge of the middle Xingu—which will become
much safer when these mysterious whites of the jungle have become 'whites'
once again."

Such was Orlando's program. Then, abruptly, thanks to a decision of higher
authorities, his expedition "à la Rondon" for the recuperation of the
Kraiacaras was deferred until later. No explanations. Orlando was furious, and
Claudio grieved.

ORLANDO SWIFTLY mastered his anger, for he has to be "proud" all the
time, even in the rags that he arranges to prove his lack of concern. He also
has to be "concerned," that is to say, sustain his work. And he has to control
himself all the time. Were he to permit himself the least weakness, his whole
system would shatter. It would shatter in the civilized capitals, where people
involved with business, politics and money, are forever saying: "What's the
use of this nut who defends the savages? It's his affair, not ours." It would
shatter even more swiftly in the eyes of his own Indians, for whom he must
always be a "man-god," a supernatural being who, by a sort of magical power,
assures their good life on earth. At the smallest failure, he would fall from his
heaven, and in their eyes turn back into a poor type, a charlatan, a white just
like the others. It's all so contradictory. The Indians have enormous difficulty
in believing in an all-powerful Lord, in a God in the religious sense of the
word. How priests have labored throughout the centuries to make them
swallow a little of Christ, and with what adjustments and compromises! No,
what the Indians esteem are the mythical beings, the incarnate forces of
nature, forces which command and constrain nature, and make what civilized
man calls miracles. Legendary beings, of whom it is not known whether they
are alive or dead, whether they are gods or men. Dazzling the primitives by
identifying themselves with these genii has always been a tactic of those
conquerors of the Indians who have used the cross rather than the sword. But
Orlando is first and foremost an atheist, a Freemason, a materialist, a
humanist, a positivist, a philosopher straight out of the old encyclopedia and
its "noble savages." Yet he knows quite well that in practice he must also be

revered as the Lord of the thunderbolt, waters, and fecundity . . . a difficult role to play.

The whole of his Xingu reservation is based on one act of faith: that the Indians are men like other men. But Orlando is Brazilian—he sometimes appears to have some difficulty believing in his credo. Often he behaves toward them as toward wayward children, children who are unpredictable, suspicious, deceptive, demanding, who wish to have everything, but give nothing, and who do not comprehend any effort. Arrogant children, who do not tolerate an order, and who suddenly have mad crises of weeping, stamping, and shrieking, a sort of folly which can lead to bloodshed, to barbarous rites, to murders undertaken as a joke, and committed after long hypocrisies. All this has been proclaimed by the priests for centuries. Obviously Orlando claims the opposite. But, in his heart of hearts, does he really believe he's not superior to them? It is clear that the Indians, with their keen instinct, sense that he considers himself of another race.

Orlando behaves like "a man who knows what's what" with the Indians. Confronted by Indians who never reveal anything, he reveals nothing either. He is as mysterious as they. Then, suddenly, he has the magic word, the magic gesture, which resolves everything. Truth does not exist among the Indians. Irony is a catastrophe. What is necessary is mutual dignity and respect, and also an outburst of good humor, of clowning and fun, which emphasizes the joy of all living together. This is why Orlando abandons his intentional solemnity for a policy of "farces and booby-traps," including the "kick in the ass," not the colonialist kind, but the anticolonialist, which expresses fraternity. When Orlando sees an Indian looking down in the mouth, he whacks his bare toes on the Indian's bare buttocks, jovially, and with resonance. The other Indians turn around—then Orlando claps the person whose behind he has just kicked, on the back, saying, "Kiss me, fat beast."

The Indians also know how to play the clown, but sometimes their clowning is unpleasant or menacing. It can mean that they are burdened by some wrong; it can be the sign of a smouldering fire. Their resentment must be divined and appeased. Orlando knows how to sense which way the wind is blowing with his Indians. It's a task, almost of divination, which needs infinite patience. At other times, the fury of the savages is due to their frantic desire to improve upon their "state of innocence" by the objects of the white man. To yield is to corrupt the Indians and aid their downfall. To resist is to unleash their passions, and the white man's reprisals, in a time-honored and fatal cycle. A strange perspicacity is necessary not to give too much nor too little. It is in this frail equilibrium between two abysses that Orlando's genius lies. While he is around, there is no open drama. But secretly, the contest of wills continues interminably.

The Indian, apparently quite content, is nonetheless trying to wear Orlando down. He doesn't stretch out his hand, but wherever Orlando goes, there's almost always an Indian following him, like a red shadow, his face expressionless. It's the Indian way of asking for something, the polite way, acceptable to Orlando. At length, after some hours, Orlando says suddenly to the man who is dogging his footsteps, "What do you want? Soap? Cigarettes? Cartridges?"

Does Orlando really love the Indians? Nobody knows. He defends his noble work harshly, bitterly, if need be—a harshness which wounds Claudio, who is all love and silence. Except for an occasional flicker made in the name of the friendship which still endures, the two brothers speak little to one another. They are generally silent in each other's presence. This creates a curious situation in the "refectory." At meals, the two or three Indian men and women of the kitchen, indefinable individuals, who "work," mixing smiles with filth, bring in three large dishes on a sort of tripod. Everyone in turn goes to help himself with a ladle from the enormous cauldrons of brownish, glutinous broth, in which float ignoble morsels which were once huge fish, monsters of the Xingu, or emaciated chickens, saved from the boa constrictors who regularly attack the farmyard. There is a hierarchical procession. Orlando returns to "his" table, more enormous still by what he is about to devour, more prestigious still thanks to the joyous belches that he emits between mouthfuls, which are themselves resounding ingurgitations. Beside him sit the most important subalterns, whose skin is not too dark, all very respectful. At another table sit inferior individuals, half-castes of all the colors that still claim to be white, who don't say a word. Finally, at a distance, completely alone, quite apart from Orlando and the entire assembly, Claudio is isolated in front of his plate, his body slack, his thoughts wandering, not even putting himself to the trouble of lifting the food to his mouth. He remains like that, almost motionless, forgetful even of the fork in his hand.

While the elder Vilas Boas taps on his table, like a tipsy adjutant, healthy and paternalistic, Claudio dreams, like a monk whose haggard eyes never focus, a monk whose body is gnawed as is Claudio's by venom, fever, and drink. The venom came from a tiny snake which once bit him. In Amazonia it is the quantity of the poison which is believed to kill, not its toxity, so the most dangerous snake is the one which can infuse the most venom. His fevers have been caught in his solitary wanderings. Then there is all that alcohol drunk alone—the cachaca of the civilized, which drives them mad in the jungle, and which they use to drive the useless Indians mad. For Claudio, cachaca is used only for his own destruction, and his own consolation. To it he adds the ancient, orgiastic drinks of the Indians, like cacaium or morococo. But within him, the orgy is always the same, the orgy of thought.

Claudio, the ferociously anticlerical "monk" who believes in humanity. Ah, but how he believes in it, and how deeply! From time to time, his thoughts escape him. The cry of the believer. Suffering in the face of suffering. Sometimes, emerging from his silence, he shouts, "If anywhere in the world a child dies of hunger, if anywhere in the world a child is killed by the hand grenades of war, who can atone for that cruelty? God? The government? No. I think that such a monstrous crime is the fault of our civilization. Every time a boy or girl dies in this way across the world, the whole of civilization falls back to zero, and everything has to be begun again."

The idealist in the jungle of savagery. More and more turned in upon himself. For most of the time, far from the whites whom he no longer tolerates, far even from Orlando, Claudio shuts himself up in another station of the reservation—one even more removed, more buried in the interior, sitting in a nature that has a more terrifying form, some sixty miles away from his brother. This station is truly Claudio's. It is called Diaurum—a few planks, where he lives surrounded by the jungle and "his" Indians, like a happy hermit.

Claudio the Good. With the whites, he forces himself to be pleasant and natural. But for the Indians he has the spontaneous gestures of a mother. At Diaurum, there is nothing that recalls the almost patriarchal discipline of Orlando. Here the Indians are fully at home. Claudio swings in his hammock, to read or meditate. To read great tomes of philosophy, starting with "Science and Religion" of Bertrand Russell, who sent him a copy dedicated to him. To meditate on the great problems. Usually he doesn't have his electric generator working, because the noise disturbs him: it's too civilized. At the uncertain hours when darkness falls, Claudio continues to read by the feeble light of a little oil lamp. And then, in the darkness, enveloped by the numberless clamors of the jungle, he dreams. He hardly sleeps, just as he hardly eats. His food is similar to that of the Indians who are all about him. But they gorge themselves as if they could never satisfy so ancient and ravenous a hunger, and he watches them gobble.

His face is worn. His clothes are long and tattered, washed by himself, and never ironed. His air of neglect is not calculated like Orlando's. What his smile expresses, and what his eyes betray, is his mistrust of a materialistic world. To him, the universe of truth is that of the Indian playing the flute. Whole tribes arrive at Diaurum at any hour, night or day, without any embarrassment, when they decide to, when they like. Parties of men and women interrupt Claudio in what he is doing and do what they want, and Claudio is enchanted.

A fete. A pagan fete in Diaurum lasts for a long time. Songs and dances by the Indians. Claudio loves their haunting stamping, and their melodies. It is more poetry than barbarism: human sentiments, those of all men, expressed by the savages—savages, according to Claudio, with a tender heart. Of all their songs, he prefers the one dedicated by the young to the old, who can no longer enjoy life to the full. Claudio explains it:

"It is a beautiful and sad song, which you should hear at night or dusk. It recalls the joy of childhood, the enthusiasm of youth, all the pleasures of the hunts and feasts of other times. When they hear it, the old men weep and sometimes I do too."

But from time to time, Claudio drops off to sleep during the fiesta that never ends.

Claudio's asceticism. No women for him. Orlando satisfies himself, from time to time, with white women, whom he has come in from São Paulo. There is no question of that for Claudio, nor of any union with an Indian woman. His brother Leonardo, who is dead, used to have an Indian woman. It caused a lot of trouble.

"Why not sexual abstinence?" cries Claudio. "It's a heavy sacrifice, but I have accepted it for humanity."

Claudio has accepted the sacrifice for the love of the Indians, a total, mystical love. Any intimate relationship with the daughters of the jungle would spoil the fraternity. For it would embroil Claudio in the inextricable and particularly dangerous sexual conflicts of the jungle. The ease of carnal access is nothing but a trap. Thereafter, a man is the prisoner of primitive complexities, the prisoner of a tribe. Renunciation of the flesh is therefore necessary, in order to enjoy more fully and completely the "noble savages" who are so superior to the evil "civilized."

Yet this Claudio, who is petrifying from idealism, this Claudio who is ill, misshapen, and stunted, who looks like an insomniac, who digests books and theories, little Claudio, a fanatical admirer of the Indians, is no ennervated visionary. When he gets up from his hammock, his muscles resemble some medical diagram, his sinews have an incredible power. One can hardly believe it, so little does he look like what he really is: the master of the jungle. No one else, not even Orlando, has so tamed the Amazonian jungle. Nobody is capable of walking into the mato as he does, indefinitely, with slow precise footsteps. He can travel enormous distances, carrying loads of more than sixty pounds on his back. He never quickens his pace, but he never stops. He doesn't even have the sensation that he is walking, so natural is it to him. Nothing is a burden to him, not even the sweat drenching his clothes, nor the humidity falling from the eternal vault of the trees, nor the night of the vegetation, nor the water, nor the myriads of devouring insects, nor the ferocious animals. He walks with his body bent forward to avoid obstacles, his eyes fixed on the ground to pick his way. While he walks, his eyes search the ground. A myopic look, which marvelously notes the invisible clues to the dangers of the jungle. And as he walks, he listens, picking out from all the huge noises of the jungle, the miniscule noise which is a sign of peril. He walks inflexibly, yet his step is marked by an almost permanent hesitation, as if to be better able, at the last moment, to make a snap decision and side-step.

In the heart of the vegetation, he is almost like an Indian. Like an Indian, he can reproduce the sounds of dozens of species of animals, birds and reptiles. He knows a great many recipes: "If you are lost and hungry, only eat the kinds of berries and fruits that the monkeys eat: it's a sign that they're not poisonous." He has more modern tricks as well. For example, in regions infested by jaguars, hold a dog on a leash. The cat will leap upon the dog, not upon the man.

He is almost as knowledgeable as the primitives of the jungle, but he considers himself greatly inferior to them. For the Indians never get lost, even in the most monotonous places in that uniformity of water and trees which is the chief snare in Amazonia. Once an Indian has passed by a place, he can locate it for the rest of his life. There is no need for him to mark the trail by chipping the trees.

"But I," says Claudio, "have often got lost. To walk in circles in the limitless jungle is the worst of tortures. You can go everywhere with salt, bread, and an absolute confidence in the Indians who are with you, who always arrange matters, and always know how to find the right path—on condition that they too are sure of your friendship. In that case, they will do everything for you, and will not abandon you."

Frail Claudio, with his look of a brushwood intellectual, is in fact absolutely indefatigable on his treks. In the course of expeditions which last for weeks and months, each morning, while his companions are still sleeping, their exhausted bodies hunched around the dead fire, Claudio is the first to get up. Fresh and cheerful despite his fatigue, in good health even though his face is cadaverous. It is he who, still a shadow in the lingering darkness, prepares the coffee for his companions, who are starting to open their eyes and begin the new day—one more oppressive day among the endless days of an Amazonian journey. Claudio, at that hour, in the depths of the jungle, hums Viennese waltzes, forty-year-old souvenirs.

And, in the course of his campaigns, Claudio knows how to do everything. He has an extraordinary facility with his hands. In these myriads of creepers and trunks, he knows how to choose a forked branch, and cut it within a centimeter to make the support for the ratatouille. At the halts, while the others rest, consumed by exhaustion or a fever, he is up and about, making a meal for them, somehow preparing dishes for twenty famished people. He is always on the move; a volunteer cook, volunteer hard-duty man—which is a title of glory in the jungle, for it presumes an extraordinary resistance. None of this prevents him from being alert to the smallest danger. He is a vanguard in himself. It is he who, in difficult situations, gives advice to the captain, Orlando. It is he who goes on ahead to make reconnaisances and dangerous contacts. He has no fear. He believes that even the most hostile Indians will not kill him; and yet he knows quite well, inside, on another level of his consciousness, that he is at the mercy of a trifle, of a tribe's deceit, a savage's bad humor, or a malicious arrow.

Claudio the solitary. When he is back at his station, or at his brother's, there often comes to him the yearning to escape to the whites. Then he goes for a walk in the mato close by. In the course of these rambles, he is again gripped by his distraction. He dreams. He carries a gun with him on the pretext of hunting, but despite his extraordinary skill with the gun it is distasteful to him to kill even the animals. Sometimes, all the same, he can't resist the appeal of an acrobatic shot. For example, when it's a matter of pursuing a monkey, of hitting this almost human beast as it runs on all paws through the black and indistinguishable branches some fifty yards above. There's nothing but a tiny point, a spot making its aerial way through the suffocating vegetation as easily as if it were travelling on the subway. Claudio, below, drops to the ground, until he shoots the bullet which causes the animal, the spot, the point, to fall from above. Then he says, "I couldn't resist the finesse of this hunt—the only kind that's really difficult." But he's remorseful later.

Claudio, usually so even-tempered, generally happy even in the midst of his sorrow, sometimes plunges into frightening despair. There are whole days, whole weeks, when he is prey to fearful doubts, as if he had lost his faith. It is then that he drinks massively, that he wants to kill himself, that he treats himself like a hippie.

At first Claudio was taciturn with me, but one heavy leaden afternoon, he began to talk to me, with passion, interminably, like a visionary. A strange confession in which he unburdened himself of his sufferings. More than ever he was the poet of the Green Hell. How he loves the great jungle, his terrible beasts and his "good Indians." In his eyes, the only evil of this terrifying universe is the whites. But, that day, he was gripped by an obsessive idea: that everything he and Orlando had been able to do seemed a mockery. For evil, the evil incarnated by the whites, was going to triumph.

"It seems so long ago since, as a young man, I entered the enchanted world of the past, with my brothers. I was looking for adventure, and I found it. The adventure of the human spirit. At that time, my humanistic upbringing led me to see all beings as men, and all men as brothers. I used to think that goodness would triumph over cruelty. Yes, I used to believe in progress, in the building of a better world, where there would be a place even for the Indians. Yes, all of that appears to me today as naïvete and illusion. I know now that the law of the civilized is the law of the stronger, which gives no quarter.

"I am finished. The Indians are finished. My brother and I are too alone, and the Indians too weak. You will tell me that the Vilas Boas are famous, that they have the distinction of a world press; but isn't this victory an illusion, not to say a swindle? Think of this number: only 1,200 Indians in our reservation. And tell me that this represents Orlando's and my entire lifework! The truth is that extermination is triumphing, directly or indirectly, surreptitiously, or by open massacre.

"What are we to do? We have reached our limit. We would have to have a new Rondon. He, long ago, stopped the perpetual killing of the Indians. With neither tanks nor cannons, he knew how to pacify them. While the Americans had conquered their Far West by living off the redskins' food, Rondon brought to Brazilian civilization the farthest distances of Amazonia, simply by planting telegraph poles in the national wildernesses. A wise man, an engineer, an explorer, an ethnographer, a friend of men, and finally a marshal. He won the Indian war peacefully, at the level of a drum of wire—and it wasn't barbed wire. Most important of all, he was actually able to convince the Brazilians to accept the Indians in a real way. Yes, Rondon's thought was inspiring and spoke to the heart. Yes, he saved the tribes of the jungle. But we, who are his disciples, are discovering that his peace was only an intermission in the long massacre, which has started again, and is now more terrible than ever. For the Indians to survive, we need again another great man, a mighty voice . . .

"I even ask myself if Rondon understood everything. Wasn't he duped too? He ended his long and noble life in 1958, covered in glory, without realizing that all his work on behalf of the Indians had been turned against them. He had given them land: it was the signature on their death sentence. Yes, the whites and all westerners have a passion which is stronger than all else—the passion to create, to exploit, to construct. A passion for wealth. It's a magnificent and terrible instinct. Clearly civilization on the march needed the Indians' lands. So the most obvious solution was to liquidate the primitives whom Rondon had made landowners. An ownership recognized by numerous laws. It used to appear a monument of solidity and morality. But what is the law in the face of the reality, the violent desire of greedy men. The law which was intended to save the Indians has contributed to their extermination.

"Poor proud Rondon. He showed that it was easy for the whites to seduce the Indians with gifts and fair words. He was absolutely sincere, yet here, too, there were appalling consequences. For once the Indians had been tamed by a man of noble spirit, they were then defenseless in the face of the adventurers who arrived hotfoot after him. These hordes did what they wanted with the Indians—which usually meant killing them. Once again history was repeating itself. Throughout the centuries, great hearts have converted the primitives, and every time these same savages have been subsequently killed, a hellish repetition which should have warned Rondon. He and his lieutenants, when they pacified the Indians, assumed terrible responsibilities without knowing it. They were, in fact, delivering their charges to evil.

"Poor Indians beloved by Rondon! Where there wasn't murder, there was debasement and total degradation. The Marshal never answered this question: what to do with the Indians who have not been killed, but are in one's care? He created the S.P.I., which took this principle over from the priests of old: to civilize the savages, there is nothing like work. Obviously, the fathers had spiced this with prayers and ceremonials, which Rondon, the Freemason, spared the Indians. But even secular integration—which is primarily hard work—destroys a tribe just as surely as a band of seringueiros. While they are trying to assimilate into our world, the Indians first have to cross the barrier of epidemics. By the time they are finally immunized, half the population has died. It is to the weakened, disorganized and panicky survivors that we say: "Produce!" Although they have triumphed over bacteria, they are in no condition to face the malice and wickedness of civilization. It only takes a few years for whole tribes to be composed solely of beggars, drunks and prostitutes.

"What to do with the Indians? For years and years Orlando and I have debated this question. It has never ceased to torment me. To understand our agonizing situation, you have to find some way of measuring the intensity of the plight of the Indians who are forced to integrate. It would be the same for us if we were to come face to face with Martians. Oh yes, in the eyes of the whites the Indians' customs are laughable, and their laws of no value. They are called animals. And they are incapable of leaping through the millennia into our civilization. They cannot overcome this obstacle without some exceptional help, such as is generally attributed to apostles.

"Orlando and I don't want to be apostles. We don't want to do charitable works. We look upon ourselves as the Indians' friends, friends seeing to their education. We are betting upon the passage of time—it all depends upon proceeding slowly. Once the Indians have conquered the flu and the measles, and are protected from their killers and enslavers, we are counting upon bringing them into the twentieth century by a very slow rhythm. We reckon that it takes fifty or sixty years to "adapt" a single tribe, which need only comprise some fifty souls. You can see the greatness of the need! Everything is very difficult—even finding nurses. The ones in Rio don't want to come to the Xingu because of the poverty and the loneliness, and also because of our Indians' alarming faces, their long hair and long lips. It's all of a piece.

"So it takes almost a century to save a tribe, and only a few days or a few minutes to destroy one, thanks to the new methods. Annihilation is always way ahead of conservation. Death is proceeding now at top speed. Soon there will be no more Indians, unless a new Rondon appears to awaken the Brazilian conscience. The man whom we so greatly need would have to be much more modern. Can such a man appear, or are the Indians, in fact, already condemned by progress? That's what I'm afraid of, and that's why I feel so despairing."

Claudio was certainly the most fervent and the most disenchanted of Rondon's disciples. He finally said to me:

"What is the use of good works? Fine men and noble minds have taken pity on the Indians. People are always citing Rondon. It's true that he planted thousands of telegraph poles in the most savage part of Amazonia, at the foot of the Andes, between Cuiabá of the Mato Grosso, where men dreamed of gold and then of diamonds, and Manaus on the Amazon, from where the billionaires who lived there used to send their shirts to London to be ironed. It's true that not an Indian was killed throughout Rondon's expedition, even though his soldiers were often pierced by arrows, and it's true that he created the Service for the Protection of the Indians. And now it's in the territory called by his name, Rondonia, that the worst horrors are being committed. Rondon or no Rondon, never have so many Indians been killed as now. Yes, what is the use of good works?"

II CENTURIES OF BLOOD

THE VILAS BOAS' bungalow was a haven amid the raging elements. Outside, since morning, a deluge had been beating down upon the unending tangle of water and greenery that the Xingu had become. It had risen seven feet since the night before.

"It's the very image of the Green Hell," Claudio agreed. "But what difference do the horrors of nature make to the Indians? They adapt to them very well. Left to themselves, they are perfectly happy; all their misfortunes come from the whites, their killers.

"The Indians have always been killed, ever since Pedro Cabral and the sixteenth century. First by the bandeirantes, the bandits, then by the garimpeiros, and the seringueiros—the adventurers in diamond and rubber—who ascended the Amazon and its tributaries, and who set off from São Paulo to penetrate deep into the interior of the Mato Grosso. They had only one slogan: "descer Indios"—"kill the Indians." They didn't kill them in the name of Christ and the cross, as the first Spanish conquistadores had, the Pizarros and Corteses; they killed them for commercial gain. The Indians have always been outside our world and time. It is impossible to make them enter it—as producers, as slaves, or as anything else. They can't understand; they can only understand total liberty. They would rather die than work—so they died, or were put to death. There used to be two, three, four million of them in Brazil. How many are left? Barely 200,000 or 300,000 in the entire country.

"The massacre has gone on for centuries, and is still going on."

Four hundred years of death. In the early days, for one or two centuries, the civilized made fantastic efforts to tame the Indians and get something useful out of them. The settlers wanted to use their bodies for hard labor in their plantations and mines. The men of God, while trying to save their bodies, wished to acquire their souls. First it was the Indians' arrows, and later their resistance (through a passivity equivalent to suicide), that touched off the whites' rage. So the whites killed. No living Indian had brought them any gain, except for the women who brought into the world those dour, tragic and abandoned half-castes who were eventually to become the instruments for liquidating other Indians.

All might have been well, were it not for the inexorable need of the explorers, a sort of interior necessity, to transform the Indians' nature and make them creatures of the West as slaves or Christians. How implacably the whites ravaged the dream of the golden age—of the "noble savage." Yet the first Indians they saw had been quite ready to receive them with a sort of adoration. Weren't these whites divine beings—or at least, half-gods, half-men with their white skin and beards, their strange accoutrements and their magical powers displayed by their curious boats, by the iron machines which split the jungle, and their weapons of fire which blasted the beasts? The Indians asked only for a share in their miraculous power, and offered them their wives and their daughters. There were banquets in the jungle; a belief in friendship. But the whites, far from being content with this primitive hospitality, lost no time in using gunpowder and the sword to exterminate their hosts.

Manhunts in Amazonia. What use were the edicts of kings and Popes in protecting the Indians? There was a fatal correlation: strong arms were needed for the sugar mills of the new white landbarons of the coast, and the Indians came to mind first. Men penetrated ever deeper into the interior, on the Amazon and its tributaries, to capture them. From 1640, the waters of the furthest rivers were defiled by swarms of adventurers attracted by what was called "Indian fishing." Fishing because the savages by the river banks were the first to be captured; the "hunting" would come later.

The heart-felt cry of a Jesuit priest: "If you think of the Amazon as the greatest river in the world, I tell you that the thirst for blood is greater than the river."

Nothing stopped the traffic in flesh—neither disease nor fever, sixty-foot floods, rapids, the unknown, nor the long distances. Although sometimes someone would operate on his own, or by trickery, generally there was a genuine expedition financed by a "capitalist," or ordered by a governor. Whole fleets would depart, crammed with soldiers, and their arms and provisions. The principal backer was the Mayor of Belém—the town at the mouth of the Amazon and the center for slave auctions—a man brutish in his rapacity for Indians. Silent columns penetrated deep into the jungle to take villages by surprise. There were Indian "collaborators" to give information and act as guides. Sometimes the hunters resorted to deception: they arrived with gifts and fine words, and, upon a sign from their captain, attacked. There was a kind of frenzy of lust and slaughter in the jungle—shrieks and the crackle of burning huts, gunshot and slashing sword. Throats were slit, and the human cattle herded in. As the men and women were naked, their market value—their physical strength and their capacity to reproduce—was judged then and there. The captives, still naked other than for their chains, were thrown into boats. Then came the return to Belém. As always in slave-traffic, there were deaths during the voyage, from beatings or exhaustion, which reduced the profits, even though only the pick of the crop was brought back. What could not be sold—babies, the old and the sick—had been slaughtered in the jungle. Sometimes a cacique or warrior was also tortured on the spot, if the hunters hadn't cared for his behavior.

In order to escape, the tribes plunged deeper into the jungle, where pursuit was more dangerous, for now the Indians began to kill—tribes of shrieking, elusive demons, who tore apart and devoured their white prisoners. The ferocity of the hunters was sharpened by their fear. The killing and tortures escalated. There were all the barbarisms at once: those of civilization as well as those of the wild. Amazonia was being depopulated; the wandering remnants of the Indians dispersed into small groups, and warred upon the whites and each other. Up to the Rio Madeira there were still outlaws, whores, and white pistoleiros, lusting and dying in the indifference of Amazonia. On the coast the planters prospered.

Amazonia paled by comparison with the abominations occurring in the Mato Grosso, where the bandeirantes of São Paulo were operating. At this period of the seventeenth and eighteenth centuries, São Pauo was only a village of diamond adventurers and Indian hunters; its total activity consisted of brigandage. There was a perfectly organized hierarchy of "financiers," "captains," of half-castes who were used as "corporals," and a rabble of Indian "soldier-serfs." Throughout these centuries, a gang of sometimes several thousand set off each year towards the heart of the continent for the great pillage, sometimes going as far as Peru and the Pacific. The orderly horde looked like an army. The "general" had his staff, the "Portuguese" were armed with muskets and had padded tunics of cotton to protect them from arrows. Under the shouts of the half-castes, the Indian serfs carried their loads or hacked open paths through the mato with their cutlasses. Important people were on horseback, the rest on foot. They had one aim: to take everything that they could—gold, diamonds and slaves—and to destroy whatever could not be sold.

These columns were an extraordinary scourge; the whole of Latin America feared them. They profaned even the churches of the missionaries, laughing as they stole the host and ran their sabres through the faithful who had taken refuge there. Their path left a trail of fire and corpses. They were experts in torture, and in torture for a joke. They used every device: they passed themselves off as good Christians if necessary, to deceive the priests, and they used kindness to capture the Indians. The gang had a few Indians who would promise paradise to mistrustful tribes to ensnare them. If the bulk of the tribe had disappeared into the jungle, the hunters would seize the chief and some women to oblige the tribe to return. If some babies had been forgotten, they were kept until their mothers reappeared—and then battered against tree trunks.

The place for rounding up Indians was the interior, where the bandits chasing men and gold penetrated farther and farther. This is how Brazil acquired her present enormous size: "Indian hunting" pushed back her frontiers.

After a year or two came the glorious return from the jungle with the booty: holy vessels, gold and precious stones, and the prize troop of Indian captives. The bandeirantes who made it back to São Paulo divided the spoils according to a very precise mathematical formula. And for several weeks they went on a binge, a more civilized one, paying for prostitutes instead of raping Indian girls. And they offered grateful prayers to the Blessed Virgin, for the bandeirantes, when not on campaign, were usually devout.

The market for Indian slaves was the coast, where the first settlers dreamed of a fine Creole civilization in the style of the French of Haiti or the English planters of Virginia. A familiar sort of civilization, with its "chateau," its pleasant life, its elegances: the white wife, perpetually fatigued by her pregnancies, reclining on a divan, the colored mammy looking after the children; the household composed of privileged slaves who devoted themselves to every refinement of service. There was the master, choosing captive beauties for his pleasure and through them producing a slew of half-caste urchins, or shouting orders at the capataz, his overseers, to make the ordinary male and female slaves work harder in the vast sugar-cane fields. In short, a classic civilization, but one that would not work with the Indians. The Indians, by a sort of aristocratic and frightful privilege, have a talent for unleashing the sadism of the whites. What is the mystery of the Indians, which inevitably makes them victims? They have physical beauty and a feeling for the beautiful, even for art, in their primitive life. They live only for a total and unrestricted liberty, created for their convenience. Their misfortune is that this degree of liberty looks like a defiance. It is not; it is the spontaneous, elemental, vital refusal of everything imposed upon them by nature and man. It is this natural, untamable liberty that enrages the whites. The Indians are still Indians in the worst misfortunes; they are still Indians in resignation and in death.

To slap, and slap again, is the reaction of the civilized man in the face of what is not a refusal but an impossibility. And to torture. There were tortures during the raids as well as on the great estates of the planters. Refinements of physical cruelty in an attempt to triumph over a will that could not be vanquished because it was not a will. Weren't the Indians so stupid that they died in droves from diseases and epidemics, jeopardizing the profits of a crop? Wasn't it impossible to get them to work in an orderly and regular manner? So to tame them tortures were used. What imaginative tortures! All too many engravings of the period show the whites—warriors leaning on their swords, or land-barons dressed like Portuguese noblemen—looking proudly down at a mound of massacred Indians, warriors in feathers or skeletal slaves. But killing served no purpose at all. Killing did not correct. The Indians wept: it was the only "human" quality they had, in the western sense of the word. To get something more from them, a comprehensible reaction, to obtain obedience and servility, in short, their adaptation, the whites burnt them, hung them by their feet, cut them in pieces, gutted them, impaled them on stakes, fed them to ants and other creatures, and availed themselves of the tronco—two planks, with three semicircular holes, which were put together in such a way that the Indian's neck, arms and feet were squeezed, and he was suffocated from all sides at once. In Bahia, nobody could imagine how so many Indians could be used up in so short a time.

Only sperm produced. The whites were prey to a kind of genetical exasperation. They were relying upon themselves to produce a qualified working force. But the Indian half-castes were equally useless for everyday work. What resulted then were the caboclos, the poor, solitary devils of the jungle. But there would also, one day, be the hard, sunburnt, mystical half-castes who would be the seringueiros and the garimpeiros; not children like the Indians; but naive, yet sly, extraordinarily tough, without hope, and yet resolute—a people of desperados. There soon would be many of them on the lands of the petrified forest, lands of drought and burnt ground, on Ceará, a sort of thorny desert which rose above the landbaron's plain: a peculiar race, closed, silent, completely unpredicatable and ferociously obstinate, which would later serve to desbravar—to tame—the interior of Brazil in the era of rubber and diamonds.

Then the Indians as a source of manpower were forgotten for a time. In the plantations and the mines, the work was done by the blacks. For the landbarons, the solution was the blacks. There was a massive slave-trade and the same scenes of capture on the coast of Guinea as there had been in Amazonia. But in this case the blacks who survived adapted very well to Creole civilization. Bahia, Natal, and Fortaleza prospered mightily, as did Ouro Prêto in the Minas Gerais. The old dream of the southern civilization was realized: pleasure and wealth, churches glittering with golden tiles, a galaxy of saints, the triumph of rococo, parades of cowled penitents, flagellations and processions; Voodoo, too, and trances, religious chants alternating with African rhythms, the presence of Africa.

Reproduction among the blacks was encouraged by the white landowners: empty Brazil must be populated. It was essential that the prices fall on the markets of men and women. A policy of lust for every man; no need to heed the commandments of God and the Church in this particular. Anyway, in the Brazil of those days, carnal pleasure was scarcely considered a sin. It was said that the priests enjoyed it . . . The result of this policy was every shade of skin, including remnants of Indian blood. And on the coast, it was nothing but a remnant, for it had disappeared under the black avalanche. But in the interior, Indian blood prevailed under men's dark skins.

SO AMAZONIA was forgotten. The true Indians were forgotten. They had been sacrificed in vain. There were, however, those who had kindly feelings towards the Indians who were left: the pious. They knew that the surviving Indians had a soul. To be sure, the Indians were not aware of this themselves, but the Pope had decided it for them, by a papal bull. They were therefore to be offered to Christ. Of course, one needed the grace of God to convert them. By themselves, they were animals, who had only instincts. There were many who liked to eat human flesh; they killed one another to eat one another. They enjoyed the most ignoble vices: every kind of fornication, extraordinary drinking bouts, orgies that lasted for days; almost all the women were available to all the men in one tribe, and there was every manner of making love. A shamelessness in all of this, and in their total nudity. And there were their songs and dances, with their bodies painted and decorated, herbs which gave them hallucinations, along with the witch doctors' strange remedies, tobacco smoke which was breathed onto the sick, and maté, or Paraguay tea, a stimulant which they drank. Fantastic and drunken pagan ceremonies. No sense of the divine or of personal sacrifice; no sense of adoration or of grief Nothing but myths of supermen of the jungle, magician genies.

The devout first tried to save the poor Indians bodily. The missionaries, particularly the Portuguese Jesuits, came to the aid of "these poor creatures trampled underfoot, who are waiting"—presumably for God. Indeed, what would be more exalting than to bring to the Lord complete pagans, creatures of nature, so far removed from all revelation? So priests of the great orders set off across Amazonia to hunt the Indians, in order to catch their souls.

To achieve this, it was essential to have living Indians. This was difficult for many reasons: firstly, when the men of God were approaching a tribe, soldiers or adventurers often secretly followed them, and would either kill the Indians or kidnap them. In this way a captain renowned for his brutality, Tavares, kidnapped entire cargoes of future catechumens, who were made to embark on his own boats, and found themselves on the Belém slave market. As for the good fathers, they were captured by other Indians for the purveyors of human flesh. It was a struggle between the men of God and the soldiers and adventurers, who, in common with others of their ilk, were devout except in business matters.

But what trouble it was to ascend the remote river, a tunnel under the verdure, to reach the Indians. Most of the time, the apostle voyaged for weeks upon a wooden raft attached to Indian canoes carrying other members of his party and paddled by civilized Indians, who, equipped with rosaries and loin-cloths, moved rhythmically, barely touching the water with their oars. The holy man lay upon a few planks with his impedimenta: the portable altar for the mass, the instruments of worship, iron axes to cut the vegetation, and piles of gifts to convert the Indians. Often he wore a holy relic.

The rivers were full of obstacles—trunks and floating islands which were pieces torn from the jungle, still growing in the waves. The rivers narrowed, dashing against rocks, and became furious currents that had to be ascended inch by inch, or which drew the navigators torwards the terrifying noise of the approaching cataract. The rafts traveled as swiftly as an arrow, and the missionaries, giddy with fear, stretched their hands automatically towards branches on the bank; prayers were intoned in chorus, chanted by the Indian oarsmen, who remained impassive, marvelously skillful in this crisis. Sometimes they passed the falls by zig-zagging through the foaming waters, whirlpools and sharp rocks. Sometimes they had to by-pass the rapids by disembarking, setting foot in the indescribable mud, and to advance by carrying their burdens.

But to triumph over a cataract was to plunge infinitely further into the unknown. Each cataract represented centuries in reverse. The missionaries could hear not only the noise of the water, but also the sound of the maraca, the sacred instrument of Indian tribes made from gourds, beaten to inspire terror in the enemy. It meant that the travelers were forbidden to go further. There were other strange sounds, duller, coming from hollowed trunks that the Indians drummed. There were also all kinds of taboos, little odd things found in the jungle, whose meanings were unknown, but which perhaps meant that arrows would soon be whistling around their heads.

The rio was now only an igarapé, a trickle, which could become an enormous swamp deep enough to drown in or dry up in the dense vegetation. Then the missionaries had to walk, with the good Indians hacking a path with their axes. They had no idea where they were going. With the priest could be some fifteen or twenty men carrying God's baggage. Little civilized Indians, or even small Portuguese children who had been brought over from Lisbon, marched behind the adults. The Portuguese children had their hair cut Indian-style, and their skin was as tanned as the Indians'. These "Infants of Jesus" continually sang canticles in which adoration of the Lord mingled with Indian words and cadences. It was the rule to use music, because it had been observed that the pagans were very susceptible to it, particularly when the musicians were children, for children are kings in the eyes of the Indians. The bearded priest advanced in the middle of the procession, his face bristling with hair, his skin torn, his eyes feverish, his body emaciated and devoured by vermin; he himself was often barely sane from his own doubts, from his insomnia, or from his mystical exaltations. He brandished a great wooden cross, carefully sculpted and painted. Each day he donned his chasuble over his wretched rags and celebrated mass, raising the consecrated host towards the dark, stifling vault of vegetation which served as the sky.

Every time that the missionary felt that he was getting near to a tribe, he prepared for combat for the Lord—a pacific combat, even if one or two Indians did have their guns cocked and ready. The stage was set to impress the savage imagination, to make them believe that the expedition was bringing not only a flesh and blood magician, but one who had at his disposal a God who was more powerful than all the other Gods. The ragged troop transformed itself into a magnificent procession. The priest marched in his sacerdotal robes, supporting himself on the enormous cross. All about him the good Indians carried the banners of the Blessed Virgin and all the saints. The children in their surplices shouted, "Hosanna!" The magnificence of the hymns and adornments was paralleled by the magnificence of the presents, ordinary merchandise for the Indians such as salt, knives, pans, mirrors and cloth. The host and the monstrances made a powerful impact—as did the axes, so coveted by the Indians, representing, as they did, the miracle of iron.

The next seconds that passed were seconds of glory or martyrdom, or, even more often, seconds that were useless or ridiculous. What would happen could never be predicted. Often the procession of God entered a village whose huts were empty: the occupants had just fled in dread of epidemics and massacres—all that they knew of the whites. Sometimes the emaciated priest, walking in a throng of naked Indian women and scarred and painted men, was brought up to the chieftain, who looked more like a mask than a man, with slivers of wood, claws or disks inserted in his nose, lips and ears. The stench was overwhelming, the colors a pagan orgy. The priest, his eyes shining, announced that he brought the true God, the Lord of the Indians. "Do you want to believe in God?" he asked the chieftain. No matter that the language was incomprehensible, even with the vain translations of the good Indians— for the upper Amazon is a Babel of 150 different tongues. One of these priests recounted: "In spite of what we say and what we see, we are all deaf and blind. But words count for little. The essential is that the Indians feel that God is there, and that they accept Him."

But often the missionary had no idea whether the Indians accepted Him or not. He offered God, while savages flexed their bows against him. Sometimes everything turned out so well that he was offered their wives, which was embarrassing. On other occasions, great groans responded to the discourse of the convertor—but this was only a rite of hospitality. Yet again, the smiling chieftain and his Indians could be transformed in a few seconds into ferocious savages, who would throw themselves, shrieking, onto the priest, strip him naked, and put him to death, while they danced around in his sacerdotal trappings, mimicking his preaching and the mass. It sometimes happened that the entire tribe emerged from huts and the surrounding jungle, to fall on their knees and put themselves under the protection of the priest. "We are going to die; we believe in your God, who will save us." These were generally people who had suffered so much from being slaughtered or defiled by soldiers and adventurers that they turned to other whites as to a last hope.

But even if a tribe surrendered to Christ, the apostolate had only begun. The goal of the priest was to convert their souls, furnishing them with the true treasure of faith. For as long as the Indians lived in the jungle or the mato, they remained far from the divine light, and were prey to their paganism and their bestial nature. They had to be uprooted from the jungle. It was a long and difficult task to say to the Indians: "Abandon your jungle and your villages. Come with the priest, and he will give you food for the body and the soul. With him, you need no longer fear the adventurers or white soldiers, nor famine and the calamities of nature. You will be happy on this earth, and in the next you will go to Paradise." Once the migration was proposed, it took years for it to be accepted. The priest generally left some good Indians on the spot as overseers of the Truth. He himself revisited them often. Everything was easy when he cured someone who was dying, or when he revealed his miraculous powers by prayers which controlled the elements, by making it rain or not rain. There was a kaleidoscope of holy pictures, of visions or archangels, of apparitions of the conquering Virgin, shining haloes of saints, the thunder of the celestial trumpet, and the revelation of the joys of the Trinity. The ceremony of baptism was a great day in the jungle. There was not too much insistence upon Hell and its torments, or the fate of the damned—the Indians didn't like the pain. One Jesuit played the violin—a sensational success. In all, there was a fantastic gallery where the parables of the Bible were muddled up with Indian myths, in which the priests sought out Indian characters corresponding to God or the Devil, in order to render the new religion more easily assimilable.

Eventually the tribe would move. To receive it, the missionary founded an aldeia, a civilized village, built in a favorable place, a high river bank, for example. In the center were the church and its records. From now on, life was an eternal renewal of the liturgical year. There were all the holy days, perpetual Adoration, choirs, the credo and the Hail Mary. The intoning of the ten commandments, an ever increasing number of hymns, communions and banners. But there also had to be the revealed Truth, confession, catechism and prayer. The true God must be made to enter deep into the Indians' hearts in the place of the rather too easy-going God of the first period of their conversion. Endless explication of dogma, with its practical applications, along with the sort of existence dominated by what would later correspond to Marxist self-criticism. One had to achieve a transformation in the Indians, a change in their all too human nature, so that they arrived at the concept of God—a fantastic task which required the constant vigilance of the priest. He paid particular attention to the children, who were less tarnished with superstition, purer receptables.

It was essential to make the Indians work—to make them build a house for each Indian family, not the huge orgiastic family, but the little Christian family; to make fields, and work the fields for the food of the shepherd and his flock. One had to impose a disciplined life: always the same hours, always the same tasks, working together in a sort of primitive communism. And there was always a constant struggle against adultery, murder, theft and lies. This was difficult, because adultery, theft and lies were concepts unknown to the Indians in the sense that they practiced them naturally. Some idea of sin had to be drummed into their heads; they had to be taught both what it was, and that it was wrong. They accepted more readily that they should not kill, at least when it was not a matter of people from another tribe. The priest waged war against lust, against evil thoughts, and against spontaneous actions. To combat all the sins, he tried to manufacture an automatism of good. However, he had to make several accommodations, but for which the Indians would simply have left.

This explains why the Fathers gave their permission for a little alcohol to be drunk: "Total abstinence from spirits would be pharisaical, and impossible to practice under this appallingly humid climate. Each person may take a drop now and then." Permission was also granted for secular festivities to be held until eleven o'clock at night, including dancing and singing. Of course the women were clothed, the men had trousers, and even the girls wore veils for their first communion. But in the course of a pagan night, even though one invoked from time to time the memory of a dear departed, everyone began to strip. The priests were obliged to turn a blind eye to it—even if the fete turned into an orgy, and the drop of drink became a wild drinking bout. Of course there were penitences the morning after, but they were not too harsh . . .

Still, the results were most uncertain. Everything had always to be done over. The splendors of the liturgy were not enough: the savages remained savages in their souls. They used to spy, with a mistrust harkening back to the Stone Age. They were never content; always on the point of revolt. If a Jesuit told an Indian to build himself a cabin, or clear a field, or admonished him upon a point of doctrine, or used texts which the Indian didn't understand, the Indian wanted to be off. A primitive strike. There always had to be gifts to restrain him, and the gifts weren't adequate. The disgusted Indians would complain to the Fathers, "You promised me food, and I am hungry. You promised that your God would make the crops grow, and you tell me to go and work. I don't want to. I'm lazy." Everything was dangerous for the Father; it was a risk even to tend the most suppurating wounds. When the priest gave medicine to a man who died shortly after, he was immediately accused of murder: "You killed him; you invoked your God, who is bad." To remove a corpse to the cemetery blessed by the Father was to gather the genies of death among the living—to menace the Indians and provoke an epidemic, that evil introduced by the whites.

Some chieftains agreed not to have more than one wife, but some were arrogance and blasphemy itself. These Indians had the gift of sarcasm: "I want to have all my wives, and live as I used to. Why shouldn't we eat you, as you eat your God?" Then there were the paje, witch doctors who cured the sick by sucking a man's mouth, making a black stone come from his lips, which was the evil that had got into him. The priest couldn't extract stones from bodies. Even so, they were afraid of the priest's magical power, so certain Indian men-gods built temples in the jungle where smoked human flesh was preserved. The temples, made of leaves, bamboo or reeds, were built in imitation of churches. They even had altars equipped with ornaments which had been stolen from Christian communities, and a ciborium filled with the flesh of young boys, particularly the children of the choir, who had been kidnaped and killed, and who were eaten in place of the host, while the faithful were told to go kill the white priest.

The Indians suffered from depression and nervous debility, fretting for their jungle. But this melancholy could rapidly change into an excitement marked by sweating, panting and stamping, and become a murderous frenzy. Sometimes the priest found the cross burnt and the aldeia, his "civilized" village, deserted, with only a few "tarts of the fount" left—for there were such women. Sometimes the priest was killed by the Indians, who screamed, "You are not the strongest—we are, because we are killing you."

If not death, arguments. The Indians have a curious dialectical capacity as long as they haven't been brought to total submission. But sometimes, after dozens of years of successful functioning, the faithful from a Christian commune disappeared into the jungle after eating everything eatable and stealing everything that could be stolen. European objects have been rediscovered a century or two later in the hands of naked Indians. Why did they flee? First, because they wanted to turn back into men and women of nature who made love and war, and secondly, because they never quite overcame the suspicion that the priests were really the accomplices of the other whites, who brought death and disease.

Even when an aldeia became prosperous, with praying Indians and growing crops, it was at the mercy of every calamity. Savage Indians attacked the civilized ones, kidnaping the women for their pleasure and the men and children for future feasts. The attacks of the white adventurers or soldiers were worse yet; after a frenzy of rape, murder and robbery, they departed with the chalices in their knapsacks. Then there were floods and the black fever, all the poxes which flattened the Indians like flies, and the syphilis implanted by rape. The cancers of civilization were added to the horrors of tropical diseases.

If the priest's vigor or health failed, the aldeia became gradually more and more Indian, with mangy dogs barking among the straw huts. Endless rains washed down upon the plumage of huge Indian parrots, rainbow-hued over the filth. The Indians shuffled through dirt that was a mixture of manure and a layer of insects, clouds of mosquitoes and columns of ants. By night, the fires threw into relief the shadows of drunken men and naked women embracing. The father tolled the church bell against these evil spirits. He himself, worn by hard work and sickness, crawling with worms and lice, lived under constant nervous tension, under the constant pressure of finding the soothing word or gesture to prove his power. Negligence was not forgiven, and every mistake was exploited immediately, often with terrible consequences.

Nonetheless, there did exist, in the heart of Amazonia, fine, prosperous, and content aldeias. Sometimes they were moved to a more easily defensible site to escape the bandeirantes. In 1784, however, the Indians of Madeira revolted. A text of the period declares: "This (the revolt) has caused so many deaths among the priests and the faithful that we have never seen so many." Where there had been churches and processions, there was only scorched earth. In a few weeks, the vegetation regained its hold. On orders from Rome, the Portuguese Jesuits were obliged to abandon their missions. The order of Saint Ignatius was dissolved, and the last faithful Indians returned to the jungle. God had not been able to subdue their souls for worship any more successfully than the planters had subdued their bodies for work.

Unfortunate Jesuits: the colonial administration of the King of Portugal, the governors, and the capitaos denounced them. They were accused of "enslavery," the "humanist" accusation of hounding the "noble savages" to despair and death. One of the representatives of the crown wrote to a superior of the Brazilian Jesuits, before their expulsion: "You have used cruel and inhuman methods against these unfortunate people. You have made them work for you without pay. You have made captives of their goods and of their souls. By putting them under your yoke you have criminally attacked their liberty as well as the country's economy. To satisfy your voracious appetites, you have gotten control of poor wretches and installed them where it suited you. But as these people had no love for the houses that you made them build, and detested the agricultural labor you imposed on them, they neglected the land that they were supposed to be cultivating, which impoverished the countryside. You have been absolute tyrants over indigenous peoples, no matter what their age and sex. Instead of instructing them in Christianity, you let them revert to barbarism. How can we fail to be sorry for the wretched fate of these unfortunate people, who now have no faith, and no masters."

In the abandoned jungles, a few priests remained. But these were renegade priests, adventurers of the cassock, who were usually to some extent in league with the other adventurers. They reigned as absolute sovereigns over a few last faithful and degraded Indians. One of these behaved like an ecclesiastical lord at the time of the Renaissance, enjoying every temporal power. Another received this epistle from his distant superior: "Your Excellence has the fire of Purgatory in his throat, and a land of Libya in his stomach, a land capable of absorbing in one day a Jordan of cachaca. It is so ugly a vice that it renders you unworthy of the presence of God or man." Another renegade jungle priest was characterized as a "wolf who attacks his sheep, and who rides on the rump of the prostitute with whom he lives."

Apart from these few shepherds and their flocks there were a few large and still savage tribes, who plunged deeper into the jungle to escape "civilization." The remnants of tribes that had once been catechized had forgotten almost everything from their period of "collaboration." But although they had almost completely reverted to Indians of nature, they no longer had the qualities of "noble savages." They wandered about in the regions abandoned by the priests, maintaining intermittent contact with the "poor whites" of the jungle, the caboclos and the adventurers—a strange relationship which led either Indian or white to mutual murder or to a derisory trade. They were similar in their ferocity, and equal in their misery. These wretched and degraded Indians, rotten in body and in soul, deformed by dropsy and scurvy and by terrible eruptions of the skin called "crato," coveted the shoddy wares offered them by the commercial travelers of the jungle, half-castes almost as wretched as they. For a bauble, the Indians were ready to prostitute their wives, and themselves—they were prepared to do literally anything. In their abjectness, they retained a few vague memories of Portuguese words, and some uncertain recollections of prayers. Poor Indians, abandoned and covetous . . .

Darkness closed back in on Amazonia for nearly 100 years. Not until the middle of the nineteenth century did another wave of missionaries break upon its shores. Once again apostles took up the task of earlier days. From all that effort, that sacrifice and dedication, they found only a few, almost imperceptible, and sacrilegious signs, as if the jungle had wished to take its revenge on God, who had wished to tame it.

One of these new priests told the following story:

"After ascending the river for weeks, I saw about ten savages on the bank. They gestured to me to approach them. What a state they were in. They were all ill, coughing, on the point of collapse. Between sneezes, one of them spoke a few words in Portuguese. I didn't understand much of their gibberish, but I finally made out that all that this human offal wanted was to "exchange gifts" with me. Wild with desire, they asked for the "hardstuffs" of the jungle—axes, knives and pans. What disappointment when they saw for themselves that I didn't have anything! They asked me when I would return with the goods. I said, not before eighteen moons (about eighteen months). The number eighteen surpassed their mental grasp. It was too large. I explained it with my fingers and my toes. Silence.

"I attempted to pursue the conversation: 'Are we friends?' 'Yes, we're friends.' 'Are there many tribes round here?' 'There are.' As if to encourage me to give them a small gift anyway, some of them made the sign of the cross, fumbling awkwardly, not knowing what it meant. I explained to them: "It's the sign of Christians. Do you want to be Christians?" They didn't answer—they didn't want to answer. They were very close to me, in a sinister circle, their faces devoid of expression. I didn't insist, but lighted a cigarette, and again their faces shone with desire. This had a meaning for them, a beneficent one—much more than the sign of the cross. Again they became importunate, begging, almost menacingly, for the luxury articles of the jungle-salt and cachaca. These tastes that they hadn't been able to satisfy for so long put them in a state of frenzied desire. Their hands reached out to me, in supplication and in menace. I gave them two quarts of cachaca and a pound of salt. They presented me with a few feather necklaces, with great solemnity, as if they were responding to my generosity with equal generosity, instead of cheating me outrageously. I couldn't extricate myself in any other way. They were perfectly happy, and didn't need me any more, letting me leave while they fought among themselves for the bottles.

"The Indians will do anything for gifts—and yet they are very jittery about them, because they know all too well that for centuries people have enticed them through gifts, to capture or kill them. What tricks they think up to collect gifts without being caught themselves!

"I had once been riding on horseback for days and days with an escort of three men. I could no longer bear the sensation of being weighted down by the vegetation and the humidity. That oppression of Amazonia! Imagine what it's like not to glimpse the sky the whole day long, to be in darkness at midday, to be cold in the heat. Every morning we left early in the hope of finding a clearing before dusk. What a sense of liberation to see one, with the marvelous light pouring down in a great jet! We used to pitch our tents before darkness and its infernal orchestra, the choir of birds singing mournful songs.

"Our horses would start in the moonlight at the approach of some animal. I noticed that for several evenings in particular they had been very agitated, snorting and whinnying. So I wasn't surprised the next day when Indians leapt from the jungle, cutting off our path. They emerged from the thickest part of the jungle, which seemed absolutely impenetrable to me, as if they were immaterial beings. But they used to go through it as a sport, coming out where they wanted and when they wanted. Such appearances were very dangerous. On this occasion, my heart skipped a beat as I faced these men, who were painted and strung about with their bows. But their chieftain said to me: 'We have been following you for some days. You've come from the church which has been built on the big river. You are a priest.' 'I am, and I come in the name of God, with three of the faithful.' 'Very well, but never come back here with a Negro.' I did indeed have with me a mulatto, who began to pray, believing that his last hour had come. 'Let the Negro remain here,' went on the Indian. 'He has nothing to fear this time. We are going to bring you and your two other companions to our village. Be sure to bring your baggage with you.'

"Where were we going? It would soon be dusk—which we knew thanks to our watches. In the jungle, there was scarcely any difference between day and night. All of a sudden—the sky, an immense slab of daylight: real daylight, the glorious golden light of the last rays of the setting sun, the brilliance of the dying day pouring down upon a clearing beside a stream. An Indian clearing. Here was a village such as I had never seen, better concealed and larger than I had ever imagined, dozens of huts which were revealed at the last moment, all at once. A few minutes later, darkness fell. I was thrown into a cabin with my two remaining companions. There was nobody near us. Silence. But a dog began to bark. I drew the revolver that I kept under my cassock. Suddenly the night was illuminated by stars: Indians were all around us lighting their way with torches. The chieftain said:

" 'Give me some more gifts.'

" 'I don't have any more.'

"He said nothing. The darkness was peopled by purple flames, great fires which had their own language. What they meant, why, and how, nobody knew—except the real savages, the Indians who had remained primitives. These pyres could mean that we would be killed at dawn. I kept awake until four in the morning, the dangerous hour. Nothing. The chieftain said to me:

" 'You can go. But when you come back, bring more presents.'

"I departed with my companions with nothing to my name but my cassock. Our Negro was found for us. But hardly had we plunged two or three yards into the jungle when I asked myself if I hadn't been dreaming: there was no village and no Indians. Everything had disappeared as if by magic. Once again there was nothing but jungle, trees, creepers and leaves mingled into a solid mass, where it was difficult to distinguish one trunk from another, where everything was intertwined in this cathedral of vegetation. I was sure that the Indians were following us, spying upon us to assure themselves that we were departing in earnest, without second thoughts. They wanted no more of us.

"It was the first time that I had been near a large tribe practicing a policy of 'wildness,' making itself invisible in such a way that it could see the whites, but never be seen by them. But all these precautions would be in vain when the armies of seringueiros arrived, the hordes in search of rubber."

Who could have suspected, around 1850, the next carnage, the next stampede of men who would plunge into the forest to die and kill? There was still tranquility in the jungle, an uneasy peace stemming from the earlier failure of the white man.

1850: at the mouth of the great Amazon—where the dirty sea tangles with the land and where the colossal waters of the inner sea flow incoherently into the true sea, the Atlantic Ocean—a town slumbered. It was Belém, the old Indian slave-market, the sleepy town which was adequate for all the traffic of the interior; Belém, the old colonial city, scented with spices, girdled with the endless monotony of water and foliage. For centuries ocean breezes had rocked the palm trees enclosing the town. It was restful in the shade of the churches, restful in its mixture of races—and there were no more auctions of men. Almost no swollen sails, or boats came from the jungle rivers or the Atlantic Ocean, just the tolling of the bells to the glory of God.

Belém of the quiet tropics—a harmonious civilization of the forgotten past. Old commercial buildings patinated by time alongside the docks. One modern invention—a trolleycar line whose carriages were drawn by mules. The conductor signaled a car's departure by blowing a little tin trumpet, and the trolley rolled off at a walking pace along the deserted quays.

There was still the quarter of the poor people left to its own plagues, with black bands of crows ever circling above it. The hospital was filled with the sick, their skin ashen with malaria. Most of these were adventurers who had escaped the lonely death of the Green Hell, and who were dying here with the blessing of a priest, and with nuns to close their eyes. There was still the quarter of the rich, with fine buildings and large avenues. Flowers, old porches, thick walls, inner courtyards with water fountains and stone urns. An aristocracy comfortably established in tropical luxury and piety. Every day, from four o'clock in the afternoon until the small hours, the distinguished enjoyed a sort of perpetual springtime of life. During the siesta, while their masters slept, the servant class was up and about; half-wild Indians, taciturn blacks and half-castes of every kind. Down the paths ran laughing, naked children, little half-castes of half-castes.

Impossible to believe that hundreds of thousands of Indians were once sold in this torpid town. In Belém, there were so few Indians that the King of Portugal decided upon a policy of Indian repopulation, or rather half-caste Indian repopulation, by the sacrament of marriage. Belém was short of women. It had been the practice of the authorities to procure girls of ill repute from Lisbon to be regenerated by penitence and then given in marriage to the pioneers. Suddenly the representatives of the crown announced their wish to assist the whites who united themselves to Indians in the holy bonds of matrimony. Every white man who made an honest woman of an Indian girl received the following presents from the state: an axe, a sickle, a pickaxe, a saw, a hammer, a gun, two pairs of scissors, some cloth, clothes, two cows and two bushels of seed. This allowed him to start off as a planter. The priests, for their part, made great efforts to increase the number of marriages of the civilized to the daughters of the jungle.

This is what Belém had become before the new boom, the boom of the weeping wood, of borracha, which was to be called "black gold." After the Belém of pitiless enslavery, and the Belém of drowsy piety, Belém was to become the gateway to a Green Hell that would be quoted on all the stock exchanges of the world. It would be the gateway through which the damned would pass in search of the great, smooth, round trunks and whitish bark of the rubber trees, which spurt upwards in a great jet, like pillars, to bury their silvery leaves in the ceiling of intertwined vegetation. Through Belém would enter the outcasts on their way to exterminating each other and the Indians. But from Belém would leave the balls of rubber neatly stacked in the holds of cargo steamers, one on top of the other like so many Dutch cheeses.

Among the tattoos, scars and marks on some of the most savage Indians, there were sometimes unusual ornaments inserted into their ears or lips—tubes or disks made of a hard, evil-smelling substance, which added to the horror of their faces. It came from the "wood which wept," cahuchu. An Indian name. An Indian product. Whoever could have imagined that this disgusting gum was to be the cause of the second great liquidation of the Indians at the beginning of this century?

It is a remarkable fact that it was the "almost Indians" who were to become the seringueiros—the "blood-letters" of the rubber trees—and who were to shed so much Indian blood. The seringueiros were themselves the half-castes of half-castes, the results of love affairs of long ago with whites, Indians and blacks. But these were not the ones who had been manufactured in Amazonia itself, or in Belém by the policy of repopulation. There weren't enough of those—what was needed was quantities of complete brutes; and there were plenty of these in the country of the drought, in the sertao. The men from this burnt, parched sertao—a nightmare of rocks and thorns—were to become executioners in the Amazonia of waters, rivers and mists, nature's most luxuriant vegetation.

The sertao is twice as large as France, a desert with twenty-five million men. Far too many. It is a high plateau stretching between the old coast of the sugar civilization and the huge trough in the interior of the continent, made by the Amazon and its tributaries. Its scorched earth has traces of water courses and occasionally a glittering reflection of a rivulet which turns out to be only the outline of an empty riverbed at the bottom of a dark gorge. Nature gone to rack and ruin, chaotic nudity, decomposing granite, the stains of reddish clay or slabs of blue shale, erosion, strange deposits, cliffs gnawed by deep grooves or riddled with caves.

Upon this grim and stony ground stands the catinga, the petrified forest, extending dustily over the ground like a huge hair shirt. There are so many spines that men and animals alike have to be covered with leather carapaces—living oxen protected by the hides of dead ones. The stunted vegetation boasts only thorns and a few thick, almost varnished, leaves. But the true forest is subterranean. What you see are shrubs and tufts. If you want to uproot them, you can't. They are the tips of branches which are buried in the ground and which get larger, become enormous and belong to a trunk which is itself buried. Ten or twenty-yard stems are drawn down by their roots into the depths of the earth in search of moisture: a troglodyte network.

Sometimes a shower of rain brings forth nature's exuberance. But then the leaves and flowers fall, leaving only dead boughs against a rocky landscape. The desert sags beneath the devouring sun. The light is implacable. Squalls of wind from the northeast bring the drought, the secca.

In every normal year almost a half of the children died of famine. An egg was a treasure. Families rested motionless in their clay hovels, to conserve their strength. The old and the weak perished. But some years it was worse—there was total drought. Day after day the men of the sertao, the sertanejos, recited propitiatory litanies, and joined in processions behind an enormous cross, demented processions where they beat or flagellated themselves, or were crushed under the flagstones that they carried on their shoulders. The exhausted cattle scratched at the ground with their hooves in the hope of water. Bats fought over the oxen, their deadly teeth concealed under hundreds of wings. Streams of rattlesnakes, in a living pathway of death, attacked villages by the thousands. Men struggled at knifepoint with the jaguars that prowled around the huts in the hope of carrying off children. Huge ditches had to be dug for the dessicated carrion of the oxen. Men and women grew more and more skeletal. All the horrors of hungry flesh: swelling, dropsy, and edemas. If the sun shone fiercely, and the secca continued, if everything vibrated, the people had to flee, sometimes without even having the courage to inter their most recent dead. A wretched exodus of people in search of life, destroying everything in their path in an hallucination of violence. Still hungry, they went farther and farther, sometimes walking thousands of miles and then disappearing. But at other times, after their journey, they retraced their path, and if the secca was over, they survived in their sertao.

Throughout Brazil, the seed of the white conquerors had been diluted by a wide range of cross breeding. But here in the sertao, it had created a separate and very homogeneous race, thanks to peculiar circumstances.

You have to imagine, four or five centuries back, bandeirantes storming the catinga in quest of mountains of emeralds or silver. Instead of treasure, they found Indian girls. The savages and the civilized, and even priests who had surmounted the thorny paths, shared in this debauchery of peacetime, as they did in the debauchery of war. The whites killed and procreated.

This was a commonplace in the Brazil of those days. But in the sertao, solitude closed back in on the survivors and preserved them. The adventurers departed after their orgy (except for a few who became feudal barons over oxen and men, and used their own offspring to tend their herds), and religion put the finishing touch to the isolation.

The sertao was considered a land of faith whose inhabitants had been converted and were pious and who musn't be corrupted. The priests procured royal letters which forbade access to the region by white men from elsewhere. Even commercial dealings with the coast or with the Minas Gerais were forbidden. Within the sertao, the flocks of the faithful preserved in this way were domineered by crazy priests, who threatened the flames of hell and extorted the most degrading submission.

The sertao had always been a poor land, a land of hatred, of mystical delusions, and of worship of the dead. The earth was an insupportable exile, and death constituted a deliverance. A child's death was an occasion for a holiday. His parents rejoiced through their tears that heaven was opening its gates to him. The sertanejos were also subject to extraordinary collective neuroses. Often the people of the sertao entered a state of hysteria because some visionary had just perpetrated a bloody sacrifice. Always the same kind of hallucination—of the coming of the enchanted kingdom on this earth. In the state of Pernambuco, a huge solitary cliff towers over a sheer cliff gorge: Pedra Bonita. A prophet once preached to the surrounding population that they should shatter the rock, not with clubs but with the heads of their children. He foretold that after the holocaust the great king would come in gleaming majesty to punish human vice and heap wealth upon those who had proved their faith in him. Mothers as they listened to him lifted their babies in their arms and fought among each other to be the first to make the sacrifice. Blood was soon flowing on the rock, tumbling down the walls of the gulf to make a sea of blood below. The Indian ancestors of the sertanejos had lived in the "land without evil," where magic assured their happiness. But their half-caste descendants were overwhelmed by the miseries brought by the whites. For them the only deliverance lay in heaven, and their lives were passed in an expectation consecrated to an obsession with death and the somber joys of bloody ecstasies.

For 300 years the sertao was a closed vessel, where half-breeds reproduced

half-breeds like themselves, according to a single mould. There was a
uniformity about these taciturn creatures with their ochre-colored skin, their
smooth, hard hair, and their ungainly distorted bodies which seemed made of
steel. Sometimes the sertanejos revealed, in a ferocious uprising, everything in
them that had been repressed—from their barbarous rites of fetishism to the
fantastic superstitions of a Catholicism gone mad.

At the end of the nineteenth century the purest part of the sertao gave
itself over, body and soul, to the "Counselor," Antonio Conselheiro, the
madman, the paranoiac, visionary, saint, prophet and demon. With his
emaciated body and hollow cheeks, his long hair tumbling over his shoulders,
he was the anchorite of lunacy. He walked for days without eating, supported
by his pilgrim's staff, his spare frame concealed by a poor cotton tunic. He
never smiled or spoke, except to make his terrifying predictions. He foretold
the end of the world, the apocalypse—when water would turn into blood, the
stars would be quenched and a sinister planet would be seen in the east. He
told all the oppressed of the sertao to come with him to the abandoned town
of Canudos, amidst the serras and the desert, for it would be the last holy
land.

So crowds converged on Canudos, piling into its ruins and bringing the
stones which would be used for building the "final church"—a church-
fortress. They were people without a penny to their name, because each
person had been obliged to give ninety-nine per cent of his worldly goods to
the Counselor, as a proof of his faith. Canudos was a town where all that
mattered was adoration for the Counselor, where the only hope of salvation
lay in prayer, and where vices were of no importance. What did all the
degradations and defilements matter if one could only shed a loving tear at
the sight of the ravaged face of Anthony the Counselor, who had taken upon
himself all the sins of the world, like Christ.

The fantastic adventure had begun. Canudos was not only a camp of
hysterial destitutes, it was also the armed camp of these destitutes. For
denying the laws of the world, and for killing, stealing, and praying to glorify
the Counselor, their only master, they had been declared rebels by the
authorities. So the men of the sertao prepared methodically for combat—with
a few old guns. Anthony the Counselor remained supremely cool, promising
his faithful supporters that they would make mountains from the bodies of
their enemies. When Brazilian armies marched against the land of Canudos,
Anthony's and his ragged crew's incredible assurance was justified—for the
soldiers of the government fell in the hundreds. Whole battalions exhausted

their strength in the dust of the catinga. The Counselor's fanatics were everywhere, in great numbers, precise, methodical, and relaxed, finding their mark every time they sprung an ambush, fought hand to hand, or slit a throat. Already the drama of modern troops against guerrillas. The government forces marched again on Canudos, and again their soldiers were battered by the Counselor's fanatics. The sacred village of Canudos was thronged with sertanejos flocking into it. Almost the whole population of the sertao was there, swarming around the church.

There was a new military expedition, and Canudos was besieged, a siege which ended in disaster for the authorities. The "Brazilian" prisoners were tortured, and the survivors, most of whom were mutilated, put to grotesque flight. Victorious sertanejos staged a macabre scene. They amused themselves by assembling all the corpses of their enemies that were lying on the thorns of the catinga, withering beneath the heat and being devoured by ants. Their heads were placed in a straight line on each side of the main highway which led to Canudos. Great care was taken to get them opposite each other so that they still looked at one another—the pathway of derision. Above these naked skulls, the sertanejos hung on spiky bushes all the bric-a-brac of military pomp, so vain amid the sand and cactus. The skulls were adorned with abandoned equipment—trousers, caps, jackets, capes, waterbottles, epaulettes, braid and sword belts. This extravagant decoration was presided over by the leader of the regiment, or what remained of him; his corpse was propped up at the end of the mortuary path, impaled on a sharp branch of a spiny plant. As the days passed, the cadaver, waving in the wind, became more and more obscene.

This mocking specter greeted the combatants of the fourth expedition, the "great expedition." It would take an expeditionary force and a colonial war to dispose of Anthony the Counselor and his land of Canudos—the land which had been unknown to the civilized world and which was yet a mystical challenge to the whole of civilization. The vengeance of the conquerors was as terrible as that of their opponents. Anthony was exterminated along with his dream, and everything that was found alive in his holy city or in the huts, alleys or the gigantic church, was put to the sword; Canudos returned to ruins.

There were no more "lands of Canudos" or "heavenly kingdoms" in the catinga. This mystical episode only made the sertanejos revert to a yet deeper misery. It was at this time when, to escape their lot, they turned to the Green Hell of the accursed rubber.

At every great drought, there was an exodus towards the watery world of Amazonia. After five appalling seccas in one century, when the plants of the catinga that were built to resist died of thirst under the relentless sun, the people fled. The survivors marched towards the coast and to the cities nearest the coast, particularly Fortaleza. But they had walked among so many corpses that they carried with them, in their rags, appalling epidemics—smallpox, the plague, cholera and yellow fever. In the towns that filled up with these human waifs and strays from the lifeless desert, almost half of the population perished, as happened in Fortaleza in 1877. Death struck equally the good citizens who caught the contagion, and the wretches from the sertao who had brought it. But the youngest of the sertanejos, those with slender hips and long muscles, escaped: natural selection.

The recruiters, the seringalistas, who were sent by the rubber barons, had their work made easy for them. All they had to do was appeal to the men who had survived—they didn't even have to choose. They told them that they could stay in Amazonia for a short time, to the profit of their patrons. They convinced them with the marvelous words: "Go and collect borracha in the jungle. You will be paid for it as for gold. You don't need any money to begin with. We'll pay for everything. In a few years, you will have paid us back, and will return rich and powerful to the sertao, where you can buy yourself a fazenda and cattle." It was important that the proposition be accepted quickly before the secca ended, before a rain restored the sertao. For if the sertanejo were to hear of it, he would never leave for the Green Hell of Amazonia—he would return home.

Amazonia was empty. Slaves had to be brought there for the rubber trees. Ancient skiffs disembarked their human cargoes at Belém—the same Belém that had consumed so many Indians of the jungle in the olden days, Belém which was to consume so many shepherds, herdsmen and gauchos of the sertao, for the jungle. The sertanejos abandoned the proud leather armor they had worn in the thorny desert in favor of the shirts and trousers of ordinary men, already ragged and drenched with sweat.

The whole of Belém was organized to cheat them. It was the usual game. The blasé population scarcely spared a glance for these men who believed they were escaping slavery—and who were going to be propelled into an absolute slavery, by an implacable system which permitted everything to be extorted from a man until his last breath. It started sweetly enough, by hypocrisies which ended in misery and violence.

Belém of the borracha, the gum. It lay about everywhere, heaped up on the quays, in the hangers, in the warehouses and the huge sheds. Dry, hardened borracha or soft, shapeless borracha. Its odor hung over the whole city. Gum fever. It was the "backside" of the Far West—it was the entry gate, the outlet and the headquarters of the gum. "Nice" people administered the business, that is to say, those who concealed the terrible reality of organized exploitation. There were several categories among these honorable persons. At the top of the ladder were bankers and exporters, unctuous bourgeois gentlemen in collar and tie. These were the chief beneficiaries of crime. Below them came the politicians, rather more vulgar, with more of the fast talk. They legalized the crimes. At the bottom there were veritable gangsters, sharp-eyed, sometimes scarred, or an eye short, with diamonds on their fingers. These were the seringalistas, the contractors for the gum, the killers and gentlemen in one.

The sertanejos, when they disembarked, were no match for this array, particularly for the seringalistas. There were seringalistas everywhere in the jungle, each in his own compound, to make his seringueiros work. The average was two deaths for every ton of borracha. This was really not important, because the seringalistas had on their side the law, the cops, their private assassins, and their capataz, their overseers. And they had the account book and the scales as well. Enslavery through grocery was infallible. Once he was caught up in the circuit, the seringueiro had no way of extricating himself. The seringueiro was a man who handed himself over to the seringalista without knowing what was in store for him.

So it all began again at Belém. The sertanejo, with the knife of his forefathers stuck in his belt and his old hammock rolled around his neck—his only worldly goods apart from a blessed medal—had no idea that he was selling himself, body and soul. He was even given ready money, lots of it, for his pleasures in Belém—it appeared that the next boat for the interior didn't leave for two weeks! No receipt was requested, one was among gentlemen. Two weeks of alcohol and girls, Belém girls whom the sertanejo would never see again, because the promissory notes that he gave them would make him a serf for life.

The wide longboat toiled up the great river. It was an open boat covered by dry palms, with an upper deck for a few well-dressed people. Below, packed-in humanity. Chickens and gasoline, hammocks slung from every side, hands and feet muddled up at night in one gigantic puzzle. The noise of the engine was added to the cries of children, the groans of the sick and the shouts of a brawl. Here below there was absolute equality, as if at this level there was no longer any difference between men and brutes. The proletariat of the jungle. People were so crammed in that everybody had to cooperate for one of them to shift his position.

Days on the water without sight of land. Sometimes there was a storm—the wind got up and the waves rose higher, with a muffled rumble. The boat no longer steered well. It was like a shell tossed about by the boiling, foaming waves which dashed madly past. At any moment it could capsize or be smashed against a rock. Terrible zig-zags. It was at this point that the old pilot, so tanned and withered that he seemed to be made from bark, said in a calm voice: "The danger is considerable." Then he added, with the same serenity, "God help us." During these crucial moments, as he clung to his tiller, his eyes riveted on the foam to find the best course, this ancient mariner managed to roll a cigarette meticulously with his fingers, lift it to his lips, lick it, stick it up and smoke it in short puffs. He would be clenched tight with the tension yet completely unafraid.

The humanity packed into the craft didn't flinch—not a cry, even from a child. Most people remained in their hammocks, swinging chaotically. Only the merchandise banged about. Was it heroism or passivity? It was a kind of indifference bestowed by their inurement to the great jungle.

Calm returned, and the banks, though they can scarcely be called that, began to be sketched in. There were even people living there, a great many caboclos—the castaways of the jungle—each in his own hut with his own canoe. There was a lot of movement, which remained miniscule—so lost in the amplitude of nature that it was hardly noticeable.

Now and again on a pile of earth, a town would appear, in the air, supported on its stilts, with whitewashed walls and even patches of corrugated iron among the huts. Often there would be a seringal there. This was the seringalista's castle. It was there that he had his "store." Around the seringalista, his face purple with authority, stood his capataz and his clerks, pale, jaundiced creatures, but dangerous. Nothing but men, and armed men at that.

On the counter were displayed all the products which are such treasures in the jungle: rapadura, dried meat, and dried fish, piles of beans, mounds of flour, knives, guns, and fish hooks. Marvels. The sertanejo, the man who was to become a seringueiro, a bleeder of the rubber trees, was told to make his choice. While he picked out what he wanted, a clerk wrote numbers down in an enormous account book. The sertanejo stood by. "Here's your account.

A Seringueiro village and one inhabitant. The seringueiros are virutal slaves, the descendants of all the marginal races that teem in Brazil. They live out their miserable lives in incredibly isolated sites, extracting latex from the rubber trees and producing "borracha." They are subject to attacks by the Indians, who are no less poor and ragged than they.

Check it and sign it." The sweat and alcohol, the nervous intensity, the solemn menace of the occasion made for an atmosphere which discouraged the verification the sertanejo had been going to make. It would be insulting to the seringalista's honor; it would even be dishonorable to himself to betray any niggling doubts. The question was better disposed of since he didn't know how to read, write, add or even how to sign his name. He was made to put a cross at the bottom of columns—he had hardly any idea of their amount. This cross he would carry about with him until his death—a death without a cross, without prayers, miles and miles from the nearest man.

The account book and the scales. This was an enormous instrument for weighing the balls of borracha which the seringueiros produced after months and years of work. These balls should in the long run have assured the liberty of the rubber workers, but in fact they never did. There were never enough of the balls for that. And then the scales, like everything else, were fixed . . . this was enslavery by grocery.

In honor of the brand new seringueiro, there was a party that lasted the night—a wild fiesta of brutes drunk on cachaca, chanting and dancing obscenely—obsessed by women who weren't there. There were so few women in this Amazonia . . . but in spite of the alcohol, nobody used their knives in this heady junketing—this was not in the interest of the seringalista, who was watching over everyone's deportment.

The morning after, and the days after that, there was the voyage in canoe on a river, a tributary of the great river. The seringalista was the owner of this little rio. He controlled access to it and exit from it by means of his capataz. Towards the interior, the waters narrowed, and became increasingly darker and enclosed by vegetation, and finally mere streams. A world of terrifying isolation. But even here, on these wild banks, the jungle was a gigantic allotment. Each allotment belonged to a seringalista and was worked by a seringueiro.

The beginning for the seringueiro was on the edge of a creek, with a cabin erected on a tree stump—a stump high enough to be above the level of forty feet high floods. It was nothing. A hole. A palm roof full of snakes. There was humidity, the man, and the stocks of food for which he had paid so dear. The seringueiros were alone in their wretched huts in the bosom of the forest. Not even the illusion of a challenge, as there was for the garimpeiros, the diamond seekers. It was an existence more rigorously regulated than in a factory, but worse, without a moment of respite. And the seringueiro had to force himself to follow the same appalling routine, day after day, year after year, even when he was feverish, had every kind of wound, and his body was rotting. Each man in his own little corner of the Green Hell which had been assigned to him, made his same round, took the same path among his well-numbered, clearly marked trees. For hours and hours he followed paths that had been traced between tree trunks that were often miles from each other.

His knife was in his hand to make headway down the trails eaten up by vegetation, and to hack down the poisonous, thorny stems. Sometimes he grabbed for his gun because of a suspicious noise among all the other noises, a sound indicating that a wild beast was watching for him or that Indians were at hand. He had to grope his way to cross streams full of all the dangers of the Amazonian water. Death menaced him from every quarter, from crocodiles, stings, arrows or poisonous fumes, but he could not slacken his pace. It was as though time, which has so little meaning in the jungle, were measured by chronometer. It all took place in a double night: night which was night and a night that was the night of the jungle, where a daylight worthy of the name does not dawn.

In this darkness, the same operation was repeated upon 100, 200 trees, the same gesture to wound the rubber tree, to gash it as high up as possible and fix beneath the wound a pottery saucer, into which the tree could weep its tears. And when the blood-letting was completed and the man had barely returned to his hut, it was time to set off again into the glaucous green veil of the noonday jungle. The same paths, the same round, trudging along again to confront the same trees, the 100 or 200 scattered about the vegetable ocean, each one of which he knew by heart much better than he knew any human being. The seringueiro was condemned to exist only through his flock of trees, which were as fragile as human beings, and which suffered from one fragility that was the worst of all—how often did the weeping tree weep no longer . . .

His second round. Only his gesture was different. He poured the contents of each bowl hung on the tortured bark into a sort of milk bottle. Often the tree, covered with wounds and scars, looked like an old and hideous corpse. It had been bled too often, it had run dry, without sap, without gum, without latex, and without hope. So many seringueiros had passed over it before, most of whom were dead themselves like their trees. What despair the present seringueiro felt when he could collect almost no sap on this old battlefield of rubber. He had been given a bad section, he had been cheated. He was filled with a vain rage and hatred against the trees who had deceived him—who had not let him pay back his debt and who would never give him back his freedom.

Once more he was in his wretched hut. It was dusk, and he had to stir the pot. When the jungle was once more rent with sounds, the seringueiro was seated in his cabin in front of a fire which was warming a copper full of the gum he had harvested. As the man crouched there, his skin red from the flames, iridescent with white fumes and beaded with blood, filth, and residue from the rubber, he stirred what was inside his pot. The cooking lasted for hours. The kitchen of the Green Hell. Every evening, the seringueiro poured his new latex into the mixture at the bottom of the cauldron, made of half-cooked gum from the preceding days. He started to stir this half-solid, half-liquid mixture with a huge wooden spoon, always stirring in the same direction. Half-burnt and half-asphyxiated, he had to continue this exhausting, stinking rotation until he dropped asleep for a few hours, before setting off on his rounds.

So he would walk in the oppressive jungle, and then with his last reserves of strength he would stir what he had brought back, which had become a nameless material in the pan. He would stir until it started to skin over, and the skin hardened and thickened and eventually became a ball weighing forty pounds. But it took weeks and months to make these cakes of borracha, on which the seringueiro stamped his mark with a hot iron—a mocking mark of a liberty that was never to be his.

When the seringueiro had twenty or thirty of these balls, he packed them into his canoe and went off to deliver them to his "patron," his boss in the seringal. The latter gave him credit for the balls in his great book. But on the opposite page was marked what the seringueiro owed, what he had purchased in alcohol, bullets and red beans in order to return to the jungle. A few hundred cruzeiros for his balls, a few thousand for his shopping. He was already a man exhausted and facing death. The capataz surrounded him, ready to beat him if he protested. He said nothing. It was the seringalista who said harshly: "Try to do better. You owe me a lot of money." That night at the seringal, there was more cachaca, feasting and dancing. The dancing was macabre, for the man who was to depart to his rubber trees knew his fate.

The destiny of the sons of the dry sertao was to perish, each in his own corner of the jungle, from making his rounds between his rubber trees; to go on until the last seringueiro perished from fever, exhaustion, scurvy, loneliness, madness, the diseases of the jungle, the bites of wild beasts or from Indian arrows. Many of them sank into the swamps and were swallowed up.

But most of the time the seringueiro saw himself die. He lay stretched on his hammock. Often he was nothing but an open wound, corroded by insects, millions of germs and frightful kinds of worms: there were some which entered by the soles of the feet and insinuated themselves further and further into the flesh, until they came out at the belly or the navel. He had fever, diarrhea; he vomited black substances. Sometimes he found it impossible to stand up. The hammock swung until his last sigh.

The most common death was that brought on by beri-beri, which devours the nerves and causes the dissolution of the skin and muscles. The vastness of the useless vegetation mocked him—a salad could have saved him and there was not one to be found among the unfurling trees, creepers and flowers. The food that the seringueiro was eating was what he had bought at the price of gold in the seringalista's "store." But every vital element had vanished from this food on its journey to the galley slave of rubber in his estrada—as the portion of jungle was called where the seringueiro made his round, stirred his mixture and swallowed a few mouthfuls. Dead mouthfuls—a few morsels of rotten meat or biscuits that were both dried and sticky, because they had decomposed at the bottom of holds, or on the counters, or in the sacks of food brought by canoe. A useless pile of provisions in one corner of the hut that had already been gorged by Amazonia, by the humidity, by the length of time, and by larvae before being eaten by the man. Nourishment which did not nourish. When the seringueiro felt flaccidity spreading over his body, he could have saved himself by cultivating a patch of garden or by picking wild fruits and berries. He did nothing of the kind. He hadn't the strength. He didn't even want to. He was limp in his hammock.

In this way, within some ten years or so, 500,000 to 1,000,000 men of the sertao perished.

After some time spent in the jungle, these people knew very well that they had been atrociously deceived; after their exhausting work, they felt the approach of death. Why then did these proud creatures of the sertao, these mad mystics, these brutes of honor, why did they not revolt in the jungle as they already had in the land of Canudos? An extraordinary impotence. Even when everything was almost used up, it was rare that a seringueiro tried to escape. Certainly flight was very difficult to achieve because the only way out for the fugitive was the river. This was a dead end, because where the river flowed into a larger river, it was overlooked by the boss's seringal. It was a system from the Middle Ages, with an observation post as the castle-keep and capataz as sentinels. Even if, by a stroke of luck, the seringueiro slipped past, he was easily caught lower down, so visible was a solitary paddler on the surface of the water.

After his failure came his punishment. The seringalista's face was purple with fury as he bawled: "You wanted to cheat me. You . . . " Around him he saw the servile, insolent faces of his killers waiting for their orders. The seringalista had the power of life or death over him. Usually he snarled: "Only 50, 100 strokes of the whip, if you're sorry." This meant that he believed that the man could still be of some service after his punishment. The condemned man was tortured. Emaciated in his nudity. The sallow body became bloody, the skin split. But if the culprit submitted to this very humbly, begged for forgiveness, recognized all his debts, and swore to return to his rubber trees, and not to be an ungrateful swindler, but to work like a madman and to pray to the Lord for the good seringalista, then he was not beaten to death. But if a man were too reticent, or an example were needed, he was beaten until there was no breath left in his carcass. He was thrown into the river for the piranhas. For the obstinate, the people of really very bad character, there were executions that were much crueler, the whole gamut of torture. That's what it meant, the rights of ownership in the jungle . . .

Escape was difficult, reprisals were atrocious. But this would not have been enough to tame, humiliate, and exploit to death the men of the sertao—if they had remained themselves. If they had remained those half-castes of Indian blood, who, wildly ferocious and implacable though they were, still had in the darkness of their souls true passions, as it were, and a sense of their own worth, something that was like a search for God, and a despair of injustice, a dark, bloody and moving despair. This is what the sertanejos had been on their desert plateaux, in their dusty catinga under the purity of the sun. But in the dank heat, the ennervating steam bath of Amazonia, their souls had surrendered with their bodies. A kind of blight had been produced in the organism. The intelligence that these men used to have, the tone of their brains and muscles, their grasp of certain values like honor, pride and vengeance—all this had disappeared. In its place, nothing but night; this time a starless darkness, without hope and without refusal, in which those who were physically weakest sank into disability, and became the amorphous men of the jungle, complete slaves marked by the automatism of their submission.

It was their indifference that saved them—for a time. Without this, how could they live without any human experience, without feeling, without any living presence, with no organized family and generally no women? These degenerates reached the point where they didn't even help one another, where they had lost all solidarity, even against nature or their masters. Victims of force, they were also its instruments. They killed if they were told to, they tortured if so ordered—it was all the same to them: to massacre, torture, live, or die. They no longer felt anything; they were far beyond resignation. All that remained to them was the kind of unthinking sadism that was scarcely enjoyable, that was the law of the jungle. They still had a few instincts, a taste for alcohol or a prostitute, or a raped Indian girl. There was plenty of cachaca, but a female was rarer, unless a wily trader organized the barbarous traffic of the cegamonen, the renting out of women transported by canoes to the end of the Green Hell. The girls were exchanged for borracha. But if the seringalista was not involved in the bargain, it often ended badly. In any case, the best solution, as far as the seringalista was concerned, and the least burdensome, was to have Indian women kidnaped by his henchmen, and then offered to his seringueiros.

The weakest cracked quickly. The master always kept his eyes open to find out strong natures among the people of the latex, those who had been "acclimatized," who had adapted to a world of violence, that violence which is the only law of Amazonia. In the sertao, even the creature most stained with blood, the pistoleiro, had something of a soul. In Amazonia, no one could succeed except by becoming an animal.

This happened to certain seringueiros; while their conscience atrophied, their body hardened. They became like stainless steel—even in this watery world where everything rusted. Their reflexes functioned. If their guile, cruelty and energy were equally developed, and if the transformation into a complete brute was achieved, their chances of survival increased. Instead of cracking up themselves, they cracked up others. These were the people whom the seringalistas made their capataz—their overseers, spies, killers, henchmen, their slaves who ruled over slaves. It was very important for the boss to have good capataz, who knew how to get the work out of men, and how to extract the maximum profit from the weak, the listless and the submissive—from the doomed. Everybody was doomed in the long run. So were the capataz, at the smallest error; they had to be more ferocious than all the ferocities of Amazonia that they had to repress or exploit.

The seringalista was the only person in the jungles of the rubber trees who had all the chances of surviving. He began to prosper so remarkably that a few years later he had acquired the manners of a gentleman. And if he didn't, at least his son would.

The Indians, in the jungle of the rubber trees, were superfluous. Of course, they did defend their territories against their invaders. The whites' invasion was constantly increasing. They were always penetrating farther in, where there were the most rubber trees and also the most Indians, towards the upper part of Amazonia, the great cascades and rapids where the land is drier. Their dreams of wealth were encouraged by the mateiro, that mysterious person, a half-breed of almost completely Indian origin, who could scarcely count but who could slip through the most impenetrable jungle, returning from month-long sojourns in the Green Hell to say: "All about the banks of a great distant river are the trees that weep, thousands of them, waiting to be bled."

So the Indians were bled before one began to bleed the trees—so that one could work in peace, without annoyance. Genocide was practiced on the tribes who had been discovered because of the rubber trees, who were, as it were, intertwined with the rubber trees, but who attached no importance to them: to such tribes, the trees were a very ordinary plant from which dripped an ordinary juice. The value of latex was an incomprehensible mystery to them: how astonishing to die for that!

The whites had to kill the Indians so as not to be killed by them. It was necessary, and it was also absurd. For the Indians had no idea that the borracha was liquid gold. They had no notion of what gold was, or what it represented. They had no idea of what a piece of money was, or a bank note, much less currency or dividends. They were supreme innocents, impervious to the mental fever of the civilized, that crazy cupidity which drove the whites, the less white, and the half-breeds of all colors, into the fabulous and fatal adventure of the jungle. The latter died of the empty hopes that had brought them to brave hell. But the Indians died in complete ignorance.

The Indians had to be killed, because, although they were indifferent to the borracha, they were certainly not indifferent to what it entailed—the white invasion. They defended their territories bitterly, with their arrows, their war-chants and their war paint. They were one with the unfathomable vegetation, invisible, spying savages, darting out to garnish the bodies of the whites with arrows like hedgehogs.

The Indians didn't manage to kill many, but they themselves were killed in abundance, because they were confronted by a formidable and systematically organized apparatus. The jungle was partitioned up like a chess board—on each square was a pawn—the seringueiro walking among his rubber trees. Backing him up were the seringalistas, with their seringals and their stores. The unknown river had been domesticated, cluttered with shanty towns, landing stages, boats and canoes bringing ever more men and "grocery items," and carrying off ever more borracha. Much further away, in the metropolis of profit, sat the politicians, the bankers and their associates. From its offices, civilization, which seemed quite close, authorized the horrors that yielded the white blood of the rubber tree, the slow death of the seringueiro, and the massacre of the Indian.

Genocide—a necessity, and a pleasure. The seringueiros delighted in killing. What happiness to be rid of the shadows that darted arrows at them. At first the isolated seringueiro lived in an agony of fear, easy prey in his hut or on his trail, anywhere and everywhere. Then his fear turned into hatred, which turned into vengeance, which turned into a murderous sensuality. There was more than fear. When these sertanejos found themselves face to face with painted and bestial Indian tribes, they killed. They liquidated the primitives as if to prove to themselves that they were "civilized." They refused to see their own image in these naked and barbarous creatures of the jungle. So they exterminated, while being themselves condemned to a slow death.

The news spread from estrada to estrada—"So and so has been struck by arrows. His corpse has been carved up into tasty morsels. The Indians are here." Then all the slaves of the rubber tree, the whites, the half-breeds, and mulattos, started to hunt the savages. They banded together for the great chase. Treks of death which sometimes lasted for wearying, joyous weeks. As before, and as always, they used old "civilized" savages as collaborators, guides and beaters. The seringalistas and their staff of capataz took command. The crack of rifles, hails of bullets in the jungle. Shadows materialized, becoming Indian bodies, but riddled bodies in their death throes. It had all begun again: just as in earlier times, the "hunters" caught the fever that Amazonia gives to the whites, the fever of cruelty and sadism. The Indians who were caught alive were slaughtered, often after being mangled first, in accordance with the ancient tradition of torture handed down by the bandeirantes. If a few were left alive, it was to be used as beasts of burden. They did not last long. And naturally, too, the lonely seringueiros lusted after the naked Indian girls. The captains used to distribute them, long ago, to their soldiers, and now the seringalistas offered them to their seringueiros for their collective gratification. Then, after these commonplaces, the men of the rubber relapsed into their solitude and isolation.

Sometimes a tribe was powerful, resolute and formidable. The seringueiros on the job were pierced one after the other. If they abandoned their toiling after borracha for the toil of extermination, they achieved little or no results, except that other whites were killed. The Indians had learnt to triumph over guns with their bows. They were literally nothingness, completely invisible; and yet they were there, close at hand in the bosom of the vegetation, discharging clouds of arrows upon the band of seringueiros who were inching their way across the Green Hell, one behind another in Indian file upon the path that they were hacking out slowly and painfully with their axes. Often they were laden with their wounded or with their sick, and their provisions had run out. They were lost. They had to retrace their steps if they could. It happened that whole troops of killers were killed. But these seringueiros were not really professional assassins. For that the seringalistas had only to address themselves to the craftsmen, the gentlemen whose profession it was to wipe out the Indians. It was very expensive—so much per head—but the seringalistas made the necessary financial sacrifices: the rubber was worth it.

These were the infernal columns in the Green Hell. They were composed of specialists who knew all the tricks of the trade. Nothing stopped them. They let those who had been hurt perish on the spot. There would be fewer to share the spoils. Sometimes they killed each other off on their return from a victorious campaign, so that there would be fewer for the pay-off. In any event, the work was well done; there were no more Indians in the jungle they had traversed.

But there was a genocide worse than massacre. This was the enslavery of Indian tribes by means of the rubber tree, an enslavery which was much more economical than importing the "blood-letters" from the sertao. It could only be practiced in the most far-flung corners of Amazonia, thousands of miles from anywhere, in virgin jungles that were almost unexplored, yet accessible by barely navigable waters. It happened in the fabulous jungle where the upper Amazon takes on the name Solimoes, where Columbia, Peru, and Brazil tangle in the wilderness. It is so far removed from civilization that the official boundaries between the countries that shared this fragment of the Green Hell barely existed at the time. Here the seringalistas were able to improve upon their normal methods. Instead of butchering the Indians en masse, without extracting any profit, they annihilated them a little more slowly by using them as seringueiros.

Two conditions were necessary for the success of the operation: First,

Indians who were so behind in time and space that they had never heard of the whites and their horrors and who still did not possess that atavistic, congenital mistrust of the "civilized." The first task was to lure the Indians, to reel them in like fish while they were still strong and free and could flee forever into the jungle. Two or three gentlemen, perspiring in tropical dress, introduced themselves amiably into the village of the tribe to be captured. They arrived with pale skin, flashing eyes, fair words and plenty of gifts. They had one sole aim: to entice the Indians into the trap which they had prepared—an age-old trap, for nothing is ever completely new in the jungle. Every kind of trickery and deceit had already been tried out long ago. They said: "Come with your families and your children to our camp beside the river, where our chieftain will be happy to greet you and offer you in person marvelous gifts, whose beauty and splendor you cannot even imagine." If the tribe followed its temptors, it was lost. What it found at the camp was training by atrocity.

The second condition for success was sadism—not only for the pleasure of it, but as a technique, a necessity for the revenue, a solution to a psychological problem. To dismantle the Indians, to turn them into vagabonds, beggars and prostitutes, served no purpose. The rubber barons wanted much more—to make them work for them in a disciplined manner. To accomplish this, they were obliged to create a fantastic terror, sufficient to surmount the fantastic inertia which was the Indians' power of resistance.

But the Indians' death through slavery for the borracha, was not the achievement of the small Brazilian seringalistas alone, but of great international finance as well. The principal responsibility rested on the shoulders of the City of London, which at that time was the greatest stock exchange of the imperialist world. English decency. "Colonial" companies presided over by lords. The operation was underwritten by gentlemen attracted by the twin prospects of gain and evangelism. It was done in the name of the Lord. One company distributed prospectuses boasting of its forty-five centers of latex in the Amazonian forest: the product and the producers were being improved. "Purified" gum was obtained to be sold at a very high price. The indigenous collectors were being civilized by work, ethics and religious proselytism. Chapels had even been built for 40,000 or 50,000 Indians who were being retrieved from savagery by employment. That, at least, was how it was described.

The truth lay in the extermination, for the sake of "business," of the Huitotas Indians, the Cocomas, the Andoques and the Boras Indians, unknown Indians of the unknown Rio Putomayo, a name that was to become infamous. This mysterious river is born on the peaks of the Andes, and is already huge when it flows into the Amazon a great distance from the Ocean. Near it were discovered hundreds of thousands of rubber trees, and also several Indian tribes buried in their barbarous customs. These discoveries allowed a transition from the era of prehistory to the industrial age, in the heart of the unexplored jungle. Thousands of dollars were poured out to produce tens of thousands of dollars. This could only earn profits by a rational "improvement," or butchery. Only if the Indians shed their own blood, as they shed the juice of the rubber tree, could gigantic dividends be made in this remote part of Amazonia that was too distant for conventional returns. For dividends, a systematic slaughter was necessary.

It had to be kept a secret at all costs. Hands were greased—straw men, every kind of accomplice, and of course policemen and politicians were paid off in every city in Amazonia, from Iquitos in Peru to Manaus in Brazil. Governments were bought to maintain the wall of silence. The indiscreet were punished—eyes were pierced, eyelids stitched up, hot oil poured in their ears. Those who "talked" were tortured and abandoned in the depths of the jungle as food for the beasts.

All the same, it was a hard secret to keep as the "good years" rolled around. Of course the agents of the English Company of Putomayo were on the watch to keep the secret from getting out. But there were rumors. This was put right fast enough when the source proved to be small-timers, half-breeds, small whites, drunk seringueiros or even jealous seringalistas. In reality, everyone was in the know to some extent in Manaus. It didn't shock a soul. The most respected citizens kept quiet. Paying them off—that was the golden rule for the society's representatives (who all rejoiced in Lusitanian or Hispanic names because the English lords didn't dirty their hands).

All would have been well, had there not been foreigners, real foreigners, meddling in what was no business of theirs. Two American engineers, Walter Hardenburg and Perkins, eventually learnt a good deal, and wanted to reveal the truth about the "reeducation" of the Indians. They even wanted to produce a report! Orders were given to reduce them to silence; there was no way of liquidating these Yankees—it would only increase the scandal—but everything was done to try to muzzle them. They didn't want money, so stronger measures were taken: even if they couldn't be killed, at least they could be made to believe that they would be. The English Company had the two Americans thrown into an appalling jail by real policemen, with real warrants. They were visited by sinister gentlemen, sanctimonious yet menacing, self-styled lawyers, who told them to "sign" papers, which were, of course, confessions. Executioners appeared, and made preparations for their execution. But if everything is possible in Amazonia, there is still one impossibility—killing two citizens of the United States. And in this case the State Department had been informed. But for that . . . Even so, it took the whole might of American diplomacy, almost ultimatums in the face of blackmail and deferred payments, to restore Hardenburg and Perkins to liberty.

From this point on, the horrors were exposed. There was too much bloodshed for Her Majesty's Government to defend the Putomayo company—particularly as the rubber seeds which had been stolen earlier from Brazil had by now grown, in Asia, into marvelous great plantations of well-behaved, peaceful trees. Instead of protecting the dividends that had been obtained by corpses, she condemned them herself. A name made Amazonia tremble—Sir Roger Casement's, the man who earlier had been sent to the Congo by the British Government to open an enquiry into the atrocities committed there. He had dared to publish a terrible condemnation of certain English companies in Africa. And it was this same Casement, the implacable lover of justice, who had been assigned to shed light on the atrocities of Putomayo.

England: after the puritanism of immorality, she was indulging in the puritanism of morality. She could afford to, because, in 1876, she had pulled off, in Brazil, the most extraordinary coup of commercial gangsterism of all time, which had nothing in common with the tortures of Putomayo, and the other macabre trivia: this was a stroke of genius—the idea of obtaining, by fraud, the seed of the Brazilian rubber trees, those wild and inconvenient jungle growths which didn't conform to the laws of good economic production. From these filched seeds, the idea was to produce a new breed of nice, tame, civilized trees, whose yield would be huge, and treatment practical, which would grow in artificial forests under the British flag, at the other end of the world, in the exotic land of Malaya. Just as wild animals could be broken in, so would wild plants.

It took meticulous planning. First, the seeds had to be filched. The great obsession, the haunting fear in Amazonia, was that seeds might leave the country. Brazilians felt a terrible mistrust, those who died from the borracha as well as those who lived off it. There was a coalition between seringueiros, seringalistas and the simple caboclos, between outlaws and policemen, custom officers, politicians and the government—a ferocious unanimity between men who, under other circumstances, killed one another: the stream of latex must remain Brazilian. To this end, every precaution was taken. Brazilians who were suspected of having been bought off by spies to hand over seeds were executed. Foreigners who were suspected of being in the country to commit the irremediable theft were followed in the cities, in offices or bordellos, upon the rivers or forest-trails. But noble England was to triumph over this formidable defensive network.

Hand-picked Englishmen were working separately, yet together, as special agents in the conspiracy. For it was a conspiracy, relating to a few, large, ordinary-looking seeds, of which there were so many among the infernal, miraculous flora of Brazil. The conspiracy's headquarters were located in the Botanical Gardens of Kew, near London. In Amazonia itself, as its executors, were so-called explorers, real and phony scientists, old sea dogs, respectable businessmen affiliated with Her Majesty's Secret Services, and some very official consuls. Agent number one was Henry A. Wickham, who for many years had been exploring the innermost secrets of the jungle, supposedly as an orchid hunter, those marvelous yet terrible flowers which look like open sores or emerald smears upon the giddy summits. Wickham emerged as the compleat adventurer, the gentleman of fortune. In reality he was absorbed by one task—to find a way to carry off the seeds.

But while he played his part of the big spender, high liver, gambler, the superb rake who would risk anything, and the crazy man of the jungle, the Brazilians suspected his real role. Around him at all times were men on the alert. He had no way of getting hold of the seeds while this dangerous web was woven around him: if he betrayed himself by the smallest error, it would mean death, or perhaps the derision of a prison sentence—an irreparable setback. He found it impossible to act—until he had a stroke of genius: in the rainy season, when fifty-foot high floods submerged vast areas, the Brazilians relaxed their vigilance: it was agreed that the spreading sheet of water would put a stop to the most evil of designs. But they reckoned without Wickham's Englishness, his British obstinacy and guile, his British perfidy.

Wickham had discovered a distant plateau, far from any watchful eye, which stayed above the waves every year, even at the highest flood, an island in the giant sea that Amazonia had become. A jungle island with rubber trees full of seeds amid the interlacing vegetation. When the rivers began to invade nature, Wickham was there, with a few trustworthy men. All he had to do was select, pick, collect and camouflage the seeds, and to recount later, "I was taken by surprise on the plain by the rapidity of the flood. To save my life, I walked and swam desperately towards high land that I saw on the horizon, and took refuge there in this providential haven."

As if by chance, an ancient English trawler with a cargo of scrap-iron, a vagabond of the sea, was crawling along Amazonia from one landing stage to the next, as if in search of a cargo. Wickham brought it his—2,400 seeds at the bottom of boxes. Clandestine cargo. The old boat descended the Amazon with its camouflaged treasure at a crazy speed, born by the smooth currents. There was considerable anxiety on board during this mad course. All was not yet won. There was a standing order for all foreign ships emerging from the depths of Amazonia to present their credentials to the authorities at Belém before taking off for the open sea—for search and inspection. A general precaution against the theft of rubber seeds. But did the Brazilians entertain any particular suspicions in the case? Anguish. The ship was moored along the quay side for a long wait. The lengthy negotiations lasted for days and days . . . Was it for the usual greasing of hands, or was it something more? It was at this moment that Consul Green intervened. There was no need of conversation for the two men to understand each other. Very calmly, in the most natural way, Green brought Wickham to the house of his Most High Excellency. Double or nothing. Wickham had left orders with the crew to maintain the boat's steam pressure, so as not to lose a second in making a bolt for it, if it were to be nothing.

The visit passed with the full protocol of diplomatic courtesies. Anglo-Saxon breeding and Latin blandness. Marvelous compliments from both sides, spare from the lips of the consul, warm and flowery from the Brazilian dignitary. "My friend Wickham," said the diplomat, "is being delayed in an inopportune manner . . ." Simple words, but enough to denounce some blackmail, to imply that the port officials were demanding hush money. His Excellency was startled: "It's only a matter of routine. Stupid red tape. Of course the regulations don't apply to an acquaintance of yours. I'm going to give some instructions . . ." A few hours later, the steamship was in the open sea, and the rubber revolution was under way. But it would take thirty years of devoted work before Malaya's first regiments of rubber trees would stand by for inspection in their camps, trunk by trunk, column after column, where the jungle had been eradicated to make room for them. Perfect soldiers for the blood-letting.

Thirty-six years later, just on cue, came the verdict of Sir Roger Casement and his commission on the Putomayo. A verdict like the blow of an axe. The guillotine of justice. It revealed atrocities more horrifying than the most perverted imagination could have invented, sadism's dreams. Yet it was the truth. At least 40,000 Indians liquidated, one after another. Crime as an economic stimulant. A crescendo in assassination to achieve a parallel increase in yield: a merciless progression in horror and profit.

Such a simple procedure! To begin with, the joyous fiesta. The "noble savages" as the hosts of the "good" whites. The Indians in their gala get-ups, painted and plumed, handsome despite the bones, claws, and shells piercing their faces and the scars that remained as proof of submission to fire and thorns, to show their mastery of pain, their virility. Laughing naked women, quantities of children, babies and dogs. The old solemn chieftain cracking jokes. The savages' primitive alcohol, and the marvelous taste of the civilized's cachaça. Mirrors to look in, to recognize oneself and say, "That's me." Dancing, singing nights of orgy. A feast, where the meat of wild animals was mixed with the strangers' meat that came out of closed boxes. In the largest hut, the Indians' "great house," a ceremony of friendship in which the Indians and their visitors dipped their fingers into a gourd full of magical substances to bring one to a still better world.

Then the party at the home of the civilized; here is their camp—what a difference from Indian huts emerging from the jungle clearing! It is on the bank of a great river, and the jungle has disappeared. On the bare earth rise great buildings made of logs and corrugated iron. Another world. The miracle of light: pitiless brilliance of lamps, which are only ordinary oil lamps. Stars soaring towards the heavens, the fake stars of fireworks, a salvo of welcoming gunshot aimed at the nearest treetrops—exalting, flaming thunder. A deluge of cachaca in things called bottles, given to everyone, everyone drinking from them at one gulp, until the bottles are empty, and then starting over. Women, girls and children drinking too. Cadavers of bottles—the first cadavers.

Two or three hundred of the civilized merry-making with the Indians. They drink too. They have skins of every shade. The great chief is thin and very white, ashen white, with features as sharp as a knife. Seated around him are his assistant chiefs, somewhat less pale, some of them obese and smiling, while others are skin and bones, and have glittering eyes. Then, in a descending hierarchy, are all kinds of people, whose skin gets darker as their clothes get fewer. First the Indian half-castes, who had so completely forgotten their Indian origins that they named themselves the "rationals," as opposed to the Indians, "who are animals." Then the blacks, ebony and colossal, the executives for any job; lastly, Indians from a distant tribe, who had been captured when they were young and trained up as hounds for the Indian hunt. These were the civilized who presided over the frenzied fête.

The drunk Indians collapse, some on the ground, some in their hammocks which they'd managed to hang up. The white chieftain shouts, "Wake up—I'm opening up the palace of marvels for you. It's all for you." He takes handfuls of tawdry baubles, such as have been used to snare the Indians for centuries, and, laughing, flings them before him on the turf. All the Indians grovel to pick them up, their crouching, frantic bodies struggling and jostling.

Savages gorged with cachaca and gifts. Savages who are becoming uneasy because the whites who are deployed around their pell-mell bodies have an alert, tense look. These whites have pointed their rifles at them. Their chieftain, the great chieftain with the ashen face, says: "You have accepted my presents. They are worth more than you or your lives are, so from now on, you have to do what I want: you are mine. To satisfy me, you must bring me borracha. You know the trees it comes from. You will be shown how to make it. Look at this." The white chief flings open the door of another shed filled with thick, heavy balls and the reek of rubber. There are thousands of them. The chieftain says: "You will learn how to make me ones just as nice and just as heavy. You will have a few hours for sleep. The rest of your time, night as well as day, will be mine. Each man has to bring me five heavy balls every moon. Then you will get other gifts."

After this speech, a kind of discontent rustles through the Indians. Their ill-temper is not defined, because so many are unmanned by drink and gifts. There is fear, too, which will paralyze them much more after the first blows. For the whites, the moment has come to kill.

The occasion for the necessary murders is offered by a few Indians, who, despite everything, are courageous enough to shout: "We're giving you back your presents. We want to be free." The blacks immediately grab them, fling them onto the ground and beat them with whips or tapir hide, until the blood flows, the flesh splits and the bones are left bare. Some Indians try to escape into the jungle. They are joyously felled with gunshot. From that point on, the remainder of the tribe submits.

The martyrdom of a tribe. They are sent back to their village, but surrounded by the "rationals" and blacks, whips and guns in hand, who strike and kill the second anyone says "no."

But the men of the village no longer say "no." The agony is too great. It's startling—the Indians no longer hunt, or cultivate manoic. They are hungry, very hungry. Always on the run, their ribs showing, they bleed the trees and fashion the balls. Not a minute of respite. And the men who used to have no notion of time, who used to live without working, now work like convicts. When the appointed time has come, they return to the whites' camp in a long procession, stumbling under the weight of their load. At the camp comes the hour when the Indians know the torture of the scales, of the needle that doesn't rise high enough when the borracha is weighed. The white chief, purple in the face, orders them to be whipped. Dozens of them, hundreds of them are whipped, and left to die untended, their backs no longer backs, with worms crawling over what is left of their bodies, and the scavenging urubus wheeling overhead. The bodies are thrown into the river, but even so, around the camp there are human bones.

Alcohol and gifts for the Indians when their borracha weighs enough. But they learn how to cheat: they put pebbles in the center of the balls, and secretly cut down the accursed trees. The civilized are aware of all these tricks. So they cut off their arms, and throw them to the dogs—arms cut off as the rubber trees were cut down. Tortures: bodies dismembered, burnt, the tribe's chieftain hung by the feet and his head used as a target. An unspeakable stench. Alcoholism, sadism and insanity attacks the whites too, the executioners, who occasionally slaughter each other. The chief restores order among his troops with the tronco's vise.

A sensual frenzy. The tribe is made to bring its girls. The chief has first go at the prettiest—he always has at least a dozen around him. He has dresses given them. Along with syphilis, of course. Within the camp, the Indian girls descend the hierarchical way with white men, off-white, chestnut, brown, black and even red men passing over their bodies. At the moment of ecstasy, some of these kill. At the end of the course is the little house with hammocks. Girls who have been used up are suspended there, and men climb upon them and cling to them until they are torn and broken. The river is their tomb. Bleeding girlish bodies, with the flowers of the fiesta still in their hair.

No more than a few Indians left alive in the tribe. In their despair, they find the courage to flee. Shadows, cadaverous shadows in the bosom of the night. Then it's the correira, the foot-hunt. The "rationals" and the Negroes don't find the fugitives, but the Indians do—those from another tribe, who have been trained and fattened up as bloodhounds. Capture. The useless, the children and the aged are beheaded on the spot, on the jungle trail, with a blow from an ax. Red balls upon the dark green. The men of any vigor are brought back to the camp. The chief chooses their punishment: "For every five escapees, one will die. The others will return to work with more enthusiasm." A huge tronco is made for the many culprits: ten, twenty Indians are laid side by side, each in his groove, their bodies crushed by the wooden frames tightened upon them. The lower parts of their bodies die, then they die altogether. The living and the dead, the one next to the other, are flattened alike by the machine, and attacked by insects, by swarms of ants. Every morning, the whites come to see the results. The Indians who aren't quite dead are left there. The corpses that really are corpses are removed and hurled into the infamous river. In their stead, others are put to dry out and rot at the same time, until they slip out of life, unobserved by any, even by the other sufferers, remaining until the morning visit, when they are found completely, and for the better, dead.

At last Sir Roger Casement's verdict came, in July, 1912, and spelled the end of the Putomayo slaughterhouse, and the other Indian slaughterhouses of upper Amazonia. And to other things as well. For there were other insanities that arose from the borracha and were affected by Casement's verdict—insanities of the imagination rather than of physical cruelty, fantasies which led up to an incredible reality: after a century of onslaught against nature, the jungle, savages, and death, finally, on April 30, 1912, the first train of the Green Hell blew its whistle at Pôrto Velho, on the Madeira, great tributary of the Amazon.

THE TRAIN had a heroicomic look. It was the sort of train you see in old American Westerns. It looked like the trains that once brought the Yankee pioneers across the great plains and the Rocky Mountains on the Pacific Railway of olden days—indeed, it was bought from old stock in America. Outmoded grandeur. There it all was, the engine with its wooden furnace belching black smoke through a wide conical chimney, and a bell clanging to warn goodness-knows-what creatures. On its front hung the big lantern to explore the way. It was a train in a world where nightmares were simple daily realities which could break the little train like a toy. And there, in front of the wheels, was the iron cow-catcher, the metal broom which, instead of being used against the buffaloes, swept away pythons and alligators. It swept a way which went on, mile after mile, a tunnel under layers of vegetation. But the real danger came from nature itself, rather than from its guests, with the exception of the Indians and their arrows. Knowing the hours when the train passed, they discharged salvoes of arrows against the chugging little train loaded with borracha and humanity. The engineers were protected by iron plates installed on the sides of their cabin, and returned the shots from a machine gun installed on the roof. Too bad if one or two passengers, in the crush of hammocks slung up in the wagons, got hit by mistake.

At the origin of this crazy railway, lay, as always, a dream. Even in the countries of nightmare, there were mysterious people. How they had gotten there, or why, nobody knew. For them, the word adventure was inadequate. They were obsessed by a fabulous idea. They were of all races—but American, English and German in particular—of every age and every past. Their living dream was to find a way to reach a treasure trove. They believed they had found it when they explored the Madeira beyond São Antonio.

Up to São Antonio the great tributary of the Amazon is peaceful, but further on, towards Bolivia and the Andes, the Madeira is a liquid riot. Cataracts and currents grip like lassoes, whirling upon rocks as pointed as teeth. Nineteen consecutive waterfalls in all. But beyond them lay the eldorado of the Brazilian nineteenth century: the largest forest of rubber trees in the South American continent, at the foot of the last slopes of the Andes, where the water from the mountains accumulates before flowing down. Worse than anywhere else, even though in Amazonia, one always believes of any nook or cranny that it is worse than anywhere else.

Whose was this eldorado? What country did it belong to? No one knew; it didn't belong to anybody. It belonged to the Indians. Those who were there were terrible: cannibals, corpse-eaters, not at all peaceable or trainable like the tribes of Putomayo. These Indians of the Madeira scoffed at the rubber trees and killed all the whites who meddled with them. This eldorado was ownerless in another way: even if one could extract the gum, there was no way of disposing of it. Nature's blockade. On one side the Andes, on the other the rapids of the Madeira and Mamoré rivers. And then the idea occurred to the vagabonds of the jungle; the idea of the railway—to build, in the depths of the Green Hell, the iron way to by-pass the liquid demons of the Madeira, and carry the borracha as far as São Antonio, as far as Manaus, as far as civilization.

The idea went back to 1851. It was the brain child of a lieutenant of the American Navy. Others were inspired to take on the idea. Such was its power that international capitals were obsessed by it as well. There were crazy investments. Work was started off in the unknown; there were disasters, malaria, typhus. Merely identifying a lay-out was frightful. Rivers, streams, feverish swamps, hills of porphyry harder than steel. Nothing on the spot—no men, no food, and no materials. Everything had to be brought up by way of the Amazon and the lower Madeira. It was a slaughterhouse, where men fell like flies. In 1873, the English company which had been the first to undertake it abandoned the project: too many deaths. Scarcely had the first rail been laid when it was known as the "Railway of Death," "The Devil's Railway." One human life per tie.

Ten years later the Americans had a try—P. and T. Collins, the stalwarts of Philadelphia, of the species "empire-builder," who believed in muscle power. They knew nothing, nothing whatever; they didn't have much capital, and had no medical knowledge. It took years to start the line off. In the jungle, the ties, ballast and rails were washed away by the rain. The machinery that had been brought up by special boats and unloaded with such care, rusted. Not only did the savages kill, but every night they stole, even the rails that had been laid during the day. Nature drowned groups of lost, dying men, who kept on working all the same. It was too terrible. It was too distant. There were no results. If one piece were botched, everything came to a standstill. It took months and months to replace. If one cargo of food missed a boat, there was nothing left to eat for a long time.

On the banks of the Madeira was a patch of trampled earth: the landing stage. Further on, emptiness. Condemned men and criminals were taken from the prisons of Brazil and sent to work with their jailers. They all escaped. Brazil was scoured for recruits, but even the outlaws were afraid to come. Men were pressed into service across the world, across the ports of Europe and America. Fabulous pay was promised to poor immigrants. Italians were hired, who were believed able to put up with anything. But even for the Italians, it was too much. They used to attempt to escape from the work sites, which had become convict camps where capataz armed with guns and whips supervised the workers. As the Italians were unable to make off by way of the Madeira, because of all these jailers, they chose to plunge into the jungle in the direction of the Andes, rather than remain. Not a sign of them. No doubt they were eaten by cannibals, transformed into the strips of smoked flesh that the Indians keep for years, for galas. A few haggard, gaunt men did appear at Manaus and Belém, fugitives terrified of being recaptured.

Rows of crosses. Lonely crosses for men who died alone, by an arrow, a fever, or an animal. Mass graves and cemeteries for the workers who perished in groups from an epidemic or particularly pernicious fever. Suicides and alcohol. Desperadoes, trying to buy the Indians' wives, and hunting them down for this purpose. There were said to be as many as 300 deaths per day. The expenditures were staggering. Not a rail that wasn't worth the price of a bar of gold. Eventually thirty-two tons of gold were expended for 128 rails, laid parallel to each other, which represented a half mile of railway. Eventually four miles of rails were laid. A third of the qualified laboring force were in their graves, not to speak of the caboclos dead and the Indians assassinated. In the end, the rough and ready Americans of Philadelphia, who had wanted to force destiny's hand no matter what the cost, gave up, because of the bodies and the expense.

But the idea of the railway for the borracha still held its fascination. Much later, in 1907, other Americans entered the stakes. These were Yankees from Maine, realists with a lot of money. The weight of their wealth and technology had to overcome Nature, or so they believed. It was impossible to triumph by courage, dedication or folly—this had been proved all too often before. But couldn't the dream be realized by money and men, materials and medicine? Giant construction camps, quantities of machinery, masses of workers, came from thousands of miles away, pouring onto the Madeira's banks.

Once again they recruited throughout the world. They hired men with experience, the former excavators of the French Panama canal. Some of those were such veterans that they had already survived the previous hecatombs of the Railway of Death. These hardened men withstood the hardships, but not the others, full of illusions, who had come from poor old Europe, particularly from Germany, naive, fresh young men. Some were scientists, lured by the prestige of science, which recognized no obstacles, and which rewarded effort with huge profits. They died anyway. Half of these specialists, overseers and engineers became spectres, withering and dying at the end of two or three months. How many died? About 10,000. Nobody kept count.

There were supposed to be over 20,000 men on the construction, but the actual number never exceeded 3,000, for the others lay in hospitals, nursing homes or huts, attacked by all the diseases of Amazonia: malaria, yellow fever, dysentery, and so on. (One always has the impression in Amazonia that death must have an accelerated rhythm, in a frenetic dance; but it's not like that. There, more than anywhere else in the world, each man dies alone in indifference. All the corpses and despairs and bloody orgies disappear into the immensity of nature, in the endless continuity of the crushing tropics. You need a fierce resignation to endure that.) The workers on the railway who had been imported from Europe, deserted, like their predecessors, into the fathomless jungle. And, as in the previous attempts, there were crosses. But this time the railway was extended a bit.

Cemeteries were banked up alongside the Madeira, whose waters foamed like steel soapsuds. Almost every mile of the line was marked by a cemetery. On the tombs were sometimes inscribed the words: Mortos pelos Indios. More often the tombs had no words, no name, no explanation of any kind. Of the 600 Germans who had been engaged as shock troops, there were eventually no more than sixty, who fled in their turn into the jungle. Was technology, contrary to belief, going to be vanquished by nature?

The solution was war: war against the mosquitoes, against the larvae of the deadly malaria which produced a glacial fever, which stretched men out, their whole body shuddering to their very bones until they shuddered their last. There was one particular species, unique in the world, where the liver became the size of a watermelon, while a deadly anemia gnawed the body, not producing much fever but paralyzing the motor nerves and dislocating the joints. The man was like a stem which became stiffer and stiffer. The whole countryside was a hotbed of fever. Malaria, in one form or another, attacked ninety per cent of the line's working force, and caused the majority of the deaths. War was also declared upon the stegomyias of yellow fever, which caused men to vomit black blood while the skin acquired the color of a lemon; in this case the liver didn't become too big—it was devoured.

So war was declared against the thousands upon thousands of mosquitoes in the jungle. The only method: to sanitize the swamps in Amazonia, which is all swamp. Great expanses of land were dug, trenched, dried, and drained by canals, artificial ditches which had to be cleaned almost daily—so that one day a train would at last run over the 227 miles of the dream railway. To kill the mosquitoes so that some workers might survive to finish the line. To make the jungle habitable. This is what the United States had done to bore their Panama canal after the distressing failure of the French. It had been the first clean up of the tropical jungle. And it was begun again on the Madeira, by the Americans of Maine: it had to be the end of the mosquitoes or the end of the line.

But the line had to be finished, no matter what the cost, no matter how, because of the fabulous profits still to be made. For it turned out that there were new tons and tons of borracha to be transported, for another war had been won. This incredible war had occurred farther up the Amazon than the Madeira, farther than the Mamoré, in a great pocket of jungle that stretched somewhat more to the north, between the spurs of the Andes. This was the "territory of Acre," the no-man's-land between Bolivia and Brazil, inhabited only by some terrifying Indian tribes. The deeper one penetrated, the more rubber trees there were. Here several thousand seringueiros had been locked in combat. The first to establish themselves in the area were men of Hispanic race, mostly Bolivian, who had come down from the Andes. The latex that they gathered was transported by caravans over the mountains, massifs of ice and snow, along dizzying tracks towards the Pacific Ocean. But then bands of seringueiros from Amazonia had appeared, after ascending the rivers, surmounting the rapids, and marching for months in the jungle. There were many more of them, so they attacked, and in an atrocious war the Brazilian adventurers put everything to the fire and the sword except the jungle, which was virtually indestructible. There were no prisoners taken, and no quarter was given. The Bolivians, when caught, were assassinated, their depots burnt and all their borracha stolen. In response, one Nicolas Suarez, a Bolivian colonel, organized guerilla warfare against the "invaders." Hostilities between Bolivia and Brazil were officially declared. This was the first conflict in the world over a mere vegetable juice. Then Brazilian regiments came to the rescue of the Brazilian seringueiros, most of whom had by then been captured or killed. In the end, the territory of Acre was assigned to Brazil; blood no longer flowed, but the latex still did. So the railway was essential, absolutely essential, to bring the borracha of the victory towards Brazil, Manaus, Belém and the factories of the world.

During all these years, during the wars of the railway, the mosquitoes, the Indians, the rubber trees, the seringueiros and the Bolivians, the upper Madeira was teeming—with misery, vice and the thirst for gold. Its capital was a notorious and unruly town by the name of Santo Antonio. A town of filth—no water-mains, no sewers, and no system of lighting. The garbage was hurled into the alleyways, piling up in mounds against the walls of the buildings. Excrement. In the center of the city, huge holes filled up with rain and flood water, and were transformed into quagmires, from which swarms of anophele mosquitoes spread death among the population. There was no slaughterhouse: cattle were shot on the open road. The pieces that no one wanted—the heads, horns, entrails, viscera, and hides—were left there to putrefy in a pool of blood. An indescribable stench arose, a smell of carrion that invaded the whole city.

Into this cloacus gathered people from all over the world. Brazilians from every corner of their immense country, Englishmen, Italians, Spaniards,

Germans, Greeks, Arabs, Levantines, Chinese, Peruvians, and Bolivians. Into the cabins packed a changing, varied unpredictable population: pure adventurers, riffraff from labor camps—and the rich, people whose lives had already been shattered. Daytime saw the rhythm of work—the work of secret conversations, plots, speculations, wild projects, and scheming calculations. But at night it was the rhythm of the fiestas, music, discussions in every tongue in the dark taverns, the rigged gambling houses or the innumerable brothels. Elbow to elbow with the prostitutes were the homosexuals. For drink, there was champagne, beer and aguardente.[1] The poor ate the fish of the Madeira, and the rich tasted the finest preserves imported from the best houses in Paris and London. You could even find pâté de foie gras.

In the cool period of the year, when the waters were low, from June to August, the cold, or what could be called the cold, took its toll. It killed all the adventurers who had been weakened by alcohol or exhausted by the trafficking which they had hoped would make their fortune. Exposed to the winds in the rabbit hutches in which they had taken refuge, death chilled them definitively.

1912: the railway's victory. The bizarre, astonishing whistle of the train in the jungle. So man's will had proved the stronger. The Madeira-Mamoré Railway Company—the dream, from this moment on, was a reality. Festivities—rockets, firecrackers and fireworks. A low bow to the directors of the railway company, who were now the kings of the country. The emaciated survivors of the construction watched the first train departing. Every hope was permissible; prosperity dispensed with the law, for now, more than ever, fortunes were available to the strongest.

Santo Antonio was too wretched for this grandeur and these riches. Three miles from the unworthy town a new little city with 800 inhabitants was born, named Pôrto Velho. From now on, Pôrto Velho was the key to the future. It was more the Far West than ever, more violent, crazy and rotten than Santo Antonio, but a lot better-looking. More external conveniences. One stage more advanced in the evolution of exploitation.

It was the railway's Far West now, with a conglomeration of buildings looking vaguely like mills or factories grouped about the railway station. The center was the station, with piles of borracha emerging from wagons and being humped on the backs of slaves as far as the boats. Surrounding the station, there were almost houses: buildings with real cement columns and French tiles. The simpler dwellings were in wood—planks, but roofed with

1. See glossary.

genuine zinc. A hotel opened up, the Grand Hotel for all the gentlemen who arrived: the civil servants from Manaus and Belém, doctors of all kinds, traders, financial promotors, magistrates, employees and overseers. Of course the adventurers came as well, but very respectably clothed and portfolioe English gentlemen in white tropical outfits, drinking whisky; oeaming German Herren, who drained tankard upon tankard of beer; pot-bellied seringalistas, swarthy seringueiros, persons who claimed they were political refugees; the occasional banker . . . a throng in search of pleasure.

The most select spot was the "International Club," with its big ballroom. Gentlemen by the bushel. A triumph for the little French girls from Marseille who, with unflagging professional dedication, ogled the wealthy, the provisional winners in the adventure. Actually everything was provisional, and everything was pretentious. In this forlorn spot, women in evening dress danced the fox-trot to the sound of jazz, while their cavaliers sported fob watches in their waistcoat pockets. Everything was possible, and everything was illegal. It was the law of the strongest, and the conquered, like the fox, went to earth in straw huts to commit crimes.

There was no doubt about it—the police were the most dangerous. A dozen cops had arrived from Manaus, ruffians who blackmailed the most respected people—with the exception of the worthies of the Madeira-Mamoré Company, who were too powerful. The police were quick to pull their guns and quick to shoot, for their arsenal of weapons was protected by the classical legal arsenal of the Far West. But even they sometimes got it in the neck. And even the secretary of the superintendance was arrested one day for embezzlement, extortion and impropriety. No doubt he had tried to put the screws on someone too highly placed. Thus was the equilibrium established, one way or another, within the societies of adventure.

Madness of Pôrto Velho, inhabited only by outlaws, whores, bankers, crooked magistrates and swindlers. From time to time yellow fever—in addition to malaria—took its toll. No children. No school. What was the use? People were there to profit from the borracha, whose price on the stock exchange in 1912 was still rising.

The most daring of the adventurers simply took the train at Pôrto Velho. They went to the terminus of the line, the line which would have dissolved into the jungle in a few weeks if it were not maintained daily. It was the toughest who went to the end, to Guajará-Mirim, a dreary little harbor on the Mamoré, beyond the falls. Bolivia faced the travelers; there were soldiers and barracks on both sides—but what is a frontier for traffic?

Yes, in this tiny civilized point in the middle of the wilderness, the possibilities for wealth were even greater than at Pôrto Velho. All about lay denser jungle, less explored, and richer in latex and everything else. Borracha and contraband. From the heart of the jungles skeletal white seringueiros and garimpeiros arrived at the station of Guajará-Mirim. They came by boat or on foot, accompanied by Indian slaves to carry the loads—not only rubber, but cocaine from the Andes as well. For the latter product there was a huge network, that much better organized because it was largely controlled by the police and the authorities. Mounds of borracha and sachets of cocaine left on the train.

In this world of gangsterism, the nouveaux riches lit up their cigarettes with bank notes of 10,000 reis. They were brought white bread sometimes from as far as Paris. Now and again these gentlemen heard that an Indian tribe was ready to attack the city, that it had burnt a seringal or a settlement. There were still too many Indians. Expeditions were organized to kill them. All was going well.

Far away from all this, in the heart of Amazonia, the madness was multiplied a thousand fold. Manaus, the metropolis, was the Babylon, the Sodom, and the Paris of the borracha, all in one. It rose from the water and the mud, from the jungle and because of the jungle, close to the confluence of those two enormities, the Solimoes and the Rio Negro—the river of the troubled waters and the river of the clear waters which mingled under the name of Amazon. All about lay Amazonia, a world of its own, a world of non-existence, so isolated, so disparate from Brazil itself, that you were nearer to Paris, London, or New York than to Rio de Janeiro. Amazonia looked straight towards Europe—Manaus was almost a European city. A throbbing, distracted city, of inequable wealth, of extraordinary luxury in the splendors of its vulgarity. Manaus flung its rubber out onto the world and received in return countless billions and all the treasures of bad taste. Steamships from Anvers, from London, and Le Havre made fast mid-river in the Rio Negro to floating docks, which replaced banks that did not exist because the waters could rise or fall fifty feet. Manaus—an outpost of the Europe of the Belle Epoque. Manaus, worthy of La Vie Parisienne of Offenbach in which the Brazilian sings: "I come so that everybody can steal from me what I stole over there." Manaus, debauched blossom of civilization. And all around it lay the jungle of horror.

Manaus was the supreme society of injustice, the city of high life where billionaires behaved in a way that they would never have dared to anywhere else, even in those days. A society of criminals in uniforms and frockcoats, with their women collected from every continent and dressed by the great couturiers of the Place Vendôme. Diamonds twinkling on every finger, each one corresponding to a certain number of corpses. Brothels everywhere. Mean brothels, splendid brothels, the most beautiful brothels in the world, with the girls from the Rue Saint-Denis at a premium.

It was symbolic; the jungle was not far away, but what people saw was a temple of glazed tile, bushes pruned like wedding cakes in the flower beds, and the monstrous thing that rejoiced in a Renaissance portico, a Hellenistic pediment, a French colonnade, and a Byzantine cupola. All the rococos. Amazonia so far away and yet so near, because sometimes somebody slipped this remark into the conversation: "The yellow fever's just broken out in a suburb. My uncle, the seringalista, has caught it. What a catastrophe if the German singer has been contaminated. I'm off for Paris by the next boat."

The "Tout-Manaus," after the elegant observations and the flowery compliments, went home to its palaces. There were almost as many palaces as brothels: brand new palaces in all the ancient styles—Gothic, à la Versailles, Venetian, Buckingham Palace, and à la Florentine. Candelabras, gigantic crystals, but not yet abstract painting—this would be Rio de Janeiro's luxury fifty years later. There was a whole population of flunkies and ladies' maids brought in from Paris who knew how to flatter their mistresses, most of whom were former shrill-voiced whores. Men sent their shirts to London to be ironed. Sons of scarred Manaus billionaires were despatched to the best European colleges to learn the grand ways of the son of the family. Daughters were brought up by nuns in the convents of Paris or London, to be initiated into prayer, good taste and the refinements of snobbery.

One could indulge in anything while the price of borracha soared upwards on the stock exchange. One competed to see who could have the most beautiful palace and the most imagination in stuffing it with horrible marbles. Nothing was too expensive in Manaus. Yet the jungle was always near. So was the population of prostitutes, sailors, and brothel keepers, of cops with their bribes, politicians, eminences grises and ministers. Millions were spent on greasing hands. Fortunes were made and unmade. Important people were mysteriously assassinated. Under the vests, a loaded revolver. But the world still asked for more borracha. Increasing numbers of ships tied up to the docks of Manaus. It would never end.

Madness, but also a desire for dignity, and a desire to endure. Manaus, baroque pearl of the jungle, wanted to become the capital of Brazil, of Latin

America, a unique city. So she claimed the whole apparatus of civilization—in marble. She acquired all the marbles of Italy—only white marble for the four balconies of the famous theater, the monument which meant that one had bought art. Manaus paid not only for the prostitutes, but for the greatest actresses, singers and dancers, for the sirens of the world. Pavlova, Sarah Bernhardt. The peak of refinement, when these celebrities, these legendary princesses, played upon the stage of the great theater of Manaus. The finest materials were brought in for the service of God, law and justice, in the form of a cathedral, numerous churches and a law court. Manaus, hysterical in its self-confidence, wanted to possess the complete panoply of progress: to be the metropolis with bridges, canals, sewers, electricity, and tramways. No, it would never end. Manaus was the miracle of pride long before Brasilia.

Manaus on its sea of latex. Amazonia dripping with latex in 1912. Its prosperity thanks to the weeping wood.

1913: the blood of the Indians, the blood of the seringueiros, and the blood of the rubber trees came back to haunt the billionaires. For Sir Roger Casement's report condemned not only Putomayo, but the whole of Amazonia. We have seen how opportune a condemnation it was as far as England was concerned. It was the year 1913, as if the time for justice had been meticulously chosen, that the armies of the rubber trees in Asia began to produce. A deluge. An organized deluge, prepared and planned methodically, peacefully, a vast, boundless deluge which would swell and swell, which would attain hundreds of thousands of tons, millions of tons if need be. The 2,800 seeds filched by Wickham had become tame forests, forests subject to the will of man; not the adventurer any longer, but the engineer, the botanist and the financier. Rubber at one's disposal, which could be improved like a breed of poodles, and which was bled by teams of coolies supervised by a few white men. Colonization had killed barbarism. It was Singapore's turn to be the city of billionaires—much better policed ones, white and yellow alike, than those of Manaus! It was a time for trusts and dividends. This was something of quite different dimensions, and the "boom" that people had longed for would last at least until the appearance of synthetic rubber. But now, in 1913, as far as Amazonia was concerned, the adventure was over.

Amazonia. Manaus. Faith in the miraculous latex. Suddenly from this summit a collapse whose like had never been seen. The collapse of the stock and the collapse of everything. Dizzy from the inexorable, pitiless, total plunge. It was like the brutal death of an empire after a plague, one of those empires of which hardly any trace is found thousands of years afterwards in some desert. But we know how Manaus died. It was not an army, a disease, or a cataclysm of nature, but the stock exchange of London. The perfect murder.

A few years later Manaus was gobbled up by the jungle, and became a city of ruins where a few inhabitants wandered. The population had long since fled. The theater with its white and rose marble remained an inexplicable monument to a mysterious and all-to-brief splendor. No more Pavlova or Sarah Bernhardt, no more ladies and gentlemen in evening dress—nothing that even resembled them. Emptiness and dust in the nave and a few reunions of charitable societies. Houses in the colonial style, once rich and beautiful with their colonnades and wrought iron balustrades, were being dismantled by the jungle. Gardens returned to the wilderness. Roads became sewers—no more electricity, just mosquitos and fevers. A few ancient steamships in the port loading or discharging the occasional ball of borracha. Just a little bit of borracha. The death of a city.

Pôrto Velho was abandoned too, with its adventurers gone and their stucco board and zinc buildings collapsing, turning into piles of mud and iron junk. The whistle of the trains in the virgin jungle could still be heard. Useless trains—the marshaling yard was empty, as were the wagons. So much work for nothing. A train crossing the unbridled jungle which had become the jungle of destitution. On the railway line were a few ragged workers who were barely paid for their trouble; it was very hard to struggle against a vegetation which was gaining the upper hand. Nobody had any money, not even the last seringalistas who had sought refuge in the town, or what could be called the town. But there were still some old seringueiros in the jungle, lost in time, who had no more idea of anything, who were isolated in a hut at the end of the watery labyrinth. They were still the prisoners of their capataz, still unable to escape. Where would they go? The whole of Amazonia seemed to have died. The fevers had gone but the days trailed on endlessly. And those trains . . .

In a final uprising, the seringueiros attacked the railway lines, tried to demolish them and destroy everything. In their simplicity they believed that the borracha was no longer being sold because of the astronomical prices of freight in the wagons. They would rather have carried the balls on their own backs or the backs of their slaves, or loaded up the canoes and faced the terrible rapids. The railway of death. For when one of these seringueiros was dying, his boss, to avoid the expense, had him carried out close to the railway line and left to his fate. Often poor travelers, caboclos or people of very few means, made a collection among themselves to pay for a ticket for a dying man to go as far as Pôrto Velho, where there was a hospital.

From the stupendous rubber rush, there remained only a few madmen, a few "rubber barons," the son succeeding his father in his seringal. Some of them turned up in Europe, as particularly likeable and jovial Brazilians. But the whole thing was a facade. The reality was gilded misery. Those who remained did so hoping for a new eldorado based on something which they couldn't even guess at. Something the whole world would need. So a few gentlemen were still masters of great chunks of jungle, where there was nothing to glean except for a few gums and nuts. But they would be well placed for the future miracle. When would it come about?

Amazonia was deflating, emptying out. Apart from these few colonial gentlemen, there was only a wretched rearguard—those who didn't even have the strength to leave.

The jungle triumphed once again and with it the Indians, even though the habit of killing them persisted, and whenever people met them, they let loose their usual violence. But massacres were rare and of small dimensions because the civilized no longer had any reason to penetrate deep into a jungle that had lost its wealth . . .

IN AMAZONIA, epochs of blood have always followed on the heels of epochs of forgetfulness. A tragic alternation. So it has been in the past, and so it will be in the future, to the end of the last Indians. The logic of death. After the slave hunts of the sixteenth and seventeenth centuries, the diminished Indians had had a time of grace. But the civilized had returned more powerfully than ever, with the rubber rush. They had killed whatever they could, men and trees, in their rage to be satiated. They had ravaged the wild rubber trees without even imagining that it was possible to civilize them, improve them and make plantations of them. So you can imagine what, in this state of insanity, they were able to do to the Indians, who were much more difficult to domesticate. There was a time for massacre; there was also a geography of massacre. Previously the bandeirantes of the Renaissance had liquidated all the tribes of the great rivers, the ones by the mouths of the Amazon and the rivers which flowed as broadly as seas. More than two centuries later, the searchers for borracha had plunged deeper into the jungle and ascended rivers where there began to be banks. This entailed the liquidation of all the Indians living on any space where any kind of land could be distinguished. Anything that had been left alive, trees as well as savages, was beyond that, beyond the great falls.

Cataracts, cascades, rapids. On every river—absolutely every one if you went far enough—you would arrive at stretches where nature was not just the crushing uniformity of the jungle. She took on a solidity, a shape, she became hills and plateaux as she approached the Mato Grosso or the Andes. At this point there was always a cataclysm of terrifying water. The jungle was still the Green Hell, but it was more: the fury of mighty waterways crashing down in gigantic falls or currents. There was one moment when you could go no further, and it was here that the last tribes subsisted.

So it came about that the last great Indian tribes were no longer in the heart of Amazonia but on its periphery, where the falls were; where the rivers that were born in the mato, in the vegetation of the plateaux, thundered down upon the soft jungle. All the killers coming from the direction of Amazonia, all the garimpeiros from the virgin jungle, were halted by the obstacle of the falls before ever emerging into the savanna. In the opposite direction the garimpeiros searching for diamonds and gold who had sieved the rivers of the Mato Grosso were unable to descend any lower into the jungle. Two invasions were blockaded in opposite directions. Here were the greatest and finest tribes. They were on the Araguaia, the Rio das Mortes, the upper Xingu, the upper Tapajós and its terrible tributaries. They were also on the wild and dangerous rivers which flowed into the upper Madeira, like the Rio Aripuaña, the Rio Roosevelt and many others. It was feverish, unknown country, on the boundary between the jungle and the mato. The last Indian races were established in rings around the cascades, from the Xavantes of the Rio das Mortes to the Pacaas Novos, who were established on a massif that towered over Guajará-Mirim and its railway. These were the ultimate Indian territories of Amazonia, Central Brazil, the Mato Grosso and Rondonia, where the mato—the forest that is smaller than the jungle but just as terrible—was more prevalent than the jungle. There were more malaria and more cataracts to impede civilization and help the Indians survive. They remained almost free, almost their own masters, until about 1940. Then the last genocide began, the genocide which has continued to this day.

What caused this massacre? Not an eldorado, not solely the notion of wealth and greed, but the modern world; quite simply, progress. All those complex, contradictory, and compelling forces which constituted the march towards the West, the occupation of Brazil by Brazil. And eventually by other countries, beginning with the United States, in the shape of money and bibles. Not one Indian may escape from it, not one of those Indians whose virtues Claudio Vilas Boas continued to praise in the hut on the upper Xingu, where I still was.

III IN THE JUNGLE

THE LIFE-GIVING sun over the Xingu. For four months the skies had emptied themselves upon the earth, raining heavily and steadily, night and day. The river had risen thirty feet and had since remained stagnant, a gigantic pulp of rotting trees, plants and grass. This is the time when the Indians have difficulty surviving; their food shortage is extreme. Their only advantage is that they are no longer killed by the whites: throughout this whole period they are rid of the adventurers, particularly the garimpeiros. For months there has been nobody at the diamond holes of the Rio Jatuba, which has become an unnavigable cataract.

We were at the end of the deluge, which had begun in August. The beginning is terrifying. Nature is placid, with fine calm days; then the hot humid squalls blow for many days. Stagnation and a terrified expectation. Not a movement in the trees of the jungle; even the birds are motionless. Heavy cumulus, a sky filling up like a witch's cauldron, a copper, stifling, oppressive sky. Then the cataclysm. Flashing lightning, air transformed into water, land transformed into water, rivers on the attack, making one smooth sheet out of what had been their beds, of everything that happened to be between their beds, of the indeterminate world of pools, ponds, swamps and streams. A white, heavy, dismal rain drenches everything. Everything disappears under the waves, as in the Bible. The complicated land becomes a smooth sea, and is painted with fantastic landscapes when the sun, as often happens at dusk, emerges from the night of the clouds before being blotted out in the real night. For a few moments, its rays are reflected upon the waters, and the entire jungle is mirrored there, or rather what remains of the jungle—vast expanses of unsubmerged greenery rising above drowned trunks.

Every year the water begins to rise on exactly the same day: the day of the weather's change. Just before the storm clouds burst, huge female tortoises climb out of the riverbeds; they run towards the beaches before they can be engulfed, easing their ponderous bellies over the ground. Each of them, with every step, lays an egg, in a sort of necklace of 120 to 180 eggs. Animals and men alike jump at this manna, cracking the eggs to make huge omelettes. The Indians gather as many as they can, and carry them off to their huts, for they face the bad months of imminent starvation.

Then there is nothing left but great watery solitudes without people. When the waters are at their highest, in the course of a few clear days, icy tempests arise from the south, from distant Antarctica. The thermometer plunges. Fish die in the water, birds fall, feathery corpses, from the treetops. Even the wild animals cower in their lairs. The traders, the adventurers, and the civilized shiver around fires. The Indians are hunched up in their nudity, their bellies are empty. The more courageous of them climb into their boats and set off to stab with their arrows the fishes nibbling the fruits of submerged trees. But soon there will be nothing else to fish for but the piranhas, nothing to hunt for but the monkeys. In their cabins, the reserves of manioc and maize give out. Many Indians die.

The months pass. It is the wait, the great wait for the ebbing of the waters which, when it happens, means that they will survive. And it is on St. Joseph's Day, March 19, that the waters go down every year; with the same regularity as they came, they depart. Then life returns in every form. The birds are there, parakeets and parrots which attack trees in large flocks, surrounding the trees in obedience to mysterious commands. In the water, fish, and on the earth, animals reappear, and the flora, greener and more vigorous than ever, leaves its bath, bejewelled by monstrous orchids. The air is rinsed blue.

On the Xingu, the sun had been shining for some hours, and the ebb's pump primed. It is a fantastic drainage, as the waters fall almost visibly five or six feet a day. The watery world gives way to an almost solid one, where men can live and kill. New worries for Orlando Vilas Boas; the garimpeiros were about to reappear on the Rio Jatuba. How many of them would there be? A few hundred, or a few thousand?

Orlando's preoccupations left the Indians unconcerned. They knew that they were protected by an iron hand, and also by the quantities of rifles and Colts which could blow off a head 100 yards away. With Orlando as their commander-in-chief, the tribes had nothing to fear, and could be abandoned in their enjoyment of the fiestas in all the villages, at this time of the resurrection of nature. Fiestas where Claudio was intoxicated too—but with the joy of his beloved Indians. He took me along to one of them.

A clearing. A rainbow fell over our jeep: it was in fact a huge bird gliding just above our vehicle, a menacing shadow which seemed to attack like a dive bomber. The bird alarmed me—at least until a great burst of laughter exploded from Claudio and his companions. It was a parrot, with a tail-span of over a yard, of every color of fire, water and forest, and it flashed dazzlingly in front of us as a guard of honor. It was the "papagayo" which the village had dispatched to greet us—the village towards which we were heading, whose festivities were in full swing.

Colors. A world of hues. In the "big house," a hut soaring up like the nave of a church, I could have been in the wings of the Folies-Bergère, with a company of fake Redskins in the middle of making up. But the Indians I saw were real, still primitive, and even virily naked, painting themselves for a magic ceremony. Yet they proceeded with theatrical artistry, very calmly and gaily, very sure of themselves, and taking their time about it. Huge but avuncular fellows. They were supposed to be alarming, but they weren't at all, even when they transformed themselves into "man-beasts." Each of them was painting himself on his front, drawing bands around his legs, and even on his chest making red spots on a black background. A neighbor worked on the back. There was a whole range of tints to use, quantities of phials and bowls which contained as many colors of the jungle as would paint bottles from a supermarket. With their genitalia imbued with vermilion, they put on necklaces, feathered headdresses and cords, bejewelling themselves like prima donnas. As soon as they had caught up their hair in a sticky mass, they made up their eyes in black. For this last delicate touch, they looked at themselves in mirrors, which they held at arms' length. All of this took a great deal of time, but these gentlemen weren't in any hurry. They were still enjoying themselves as they finally adjusted a trumpet on their faces. You'd think they were going to a carnival, whereas they were preparing for a rite of ancient witchcraft to chase away the spirits that haunted the huts.

Two of the Indians tapped their feet, swaying on the threshhold of the huge "big house," looking out. They blew into a kind of portable organ, which was made of very long wooden pipes, fastened together and producing animal grunts. Still thumping their feet, still swaying, still trumpeting, they came out into the great bare courtyard of the village which served as both patio and cemetery. This courtyard was hemmed in on all sides by Indian huts of plaited reeds, huge ones, sort of motionless ships made from slabs of grass stitched together with vegetable fiber. The braves entered each of these dwellings in turn. Each time, they started their exercises and their music again. From the outside, we could only see the instruments making their heavy noises, only these extensions, six-foot-long tubes whose ends were invisibly fastened to lips. The pipes jigged about strangely, seeming to be animals themselves, snakes which advanced or recoiled. In each hut this took a very long time. It was a painstaking task to expel the ill-disposed spirits.

But nobody gave a damn, least of all the women. They sat in the courtyard, crushed together, a gaggle of gossip and chatter, just like any other women in the world. The strange part was that this distinguished assembly was quite naked, and there was the primitive aspect of jostling flesh, a hodge-podge of breasts, limbs and babies.

In the hut where I was staying with Claudio and the "pilot," the Brazilian airman who had brought me to the Xingu through the storms, the latter was discussing business matters with the chief, who was dressed banally in his skin, not having got himself up for the ceremony. Business came first.

The "pilot" was a strapping fellow, quite young, clean-shaven and well-groomed; beneath his linen outfit, he was almost as broad as he was long, and had hands like scrubbing boards. All the same, he was well-mannered. In coloring, he was more of a ginger than a brunette, and his hair was discolored where the skin showed at the nape of his neck and upon his arms. His face was equally massive, and his eyes light. He had all the heartiness of the cunning rascal, and was wearing an enormous smile that was both paternal and commercial. It was quite clear that he could fend for himself.

He had been there a short ten minutes when he opened up a duffel bag full of old clothes. The chief and those Indians who were not doing their duty by the magic quivered with desire. The women came up surreptitiously behind the men. Some of them crouched around the fires where a whitish mixture bubbled eternally in pots—manioc flour. Others lounged in the hammocks that were everywhere, stretched between pillars made from enormous trunks, roughly squared off, which supported the frail, lofty roof. On the floor of beaten earth sat children, monkeys and dogs, and up above, in the half-light, lit up obscurely by the flames, fluttered or perched all kinds of parrots. Laughter. The sacred music that came from outside was barely audible. Yet the primitivism had been modified: among the utensils, an open umbrella rested on its spokes beside the bows and arrows; there were pans, sieves, a cane and a gun. Good nature reigned. The Indian men, in their most natural dress, were both dignified, a little formal and marvelously engaging. Still more people came in. There was just one corner of silence, a separate place that was closed off by partitions. It was here that there were isolated the girls who were to become women, and the boys who were to become men.

The pilot, like a door-to-door salesman, drew out from his duffel bag the most unmentionable old clothes that he'd picked up at Rio de Janeiro for a few cruzeiros and laboriously brought here in his plane. He unpacked article after article, and every time he'd exhibited a piece of second-hand clothing as if it were a remarkable buy, he'd toss it in the most gallant way—and with a sure instinct for social proprieties—to the savage whom he had chosen for it. "This magnificent dress is for you, Grandma," he began. "Claudio will like you in it . . . " And he threw it to an old woman of a little over thirty, whose great eyes remained young, although she was so shrunken and her skin so pleated that I could no longer see her body. She was the chieftain's mother—it was very proper that she should be the first to be honored. Then there were shorts for the cacique, slips for the young women, pants for the children.

Once the duffel bag was empty, the Indians looked like bums, and the pilot was a sort of empurpled Nero. For every time an Indian received a piece of clothing, he covered the airman with feathers—feathers in tiaras, in crowns, in pendants, in bouquets, feathers of every color: somber colors, greys and blues, reds, scarlets, a fantastic ballet of feathers. With every item, there had been a quick glance from the Indian, who judged the value of the gift received and who calculated in a second what he should offer in return. The Brazilian, who by now looked like a parrot, was beside himself with delight. Everything he sported he was going to sell for a high price at Rio de Janeiro. He could fend for himself. So could the Indians. For their trinkets, bagatelles and feather ornaments didn't cost them a thing, not even trouble. All they had to do was regularly clip their tame birds that fluttered around the village.

The pilot, delighted with the way his business had gone, was strutting about like a peacock. Was his intention to show me how foolish his customers were? At any rate, he put philosophical kinds of questions to a little old man:

"Do you know who I am?"

"A man who flies in the air with the help of a plane."

"What is a plane?"

"A bird which carries men."

"Do you know what Brazil is?"

"No."

"Do you know where we are now?"

"Where the plane appeared from, there is a river. And where the sun sets, there is a river. This is where we live, between these rivers."

"Do you know what's at the other side of the river where the plane rises up from?"

"It's the land of the white men, the land of the Caraibes. It's where Claudio came from. Now he belongs here. Sometimes he goes off there to look for remedies and bullets."

"Who is Claudio?"

"A different Caraibe."

The whole tribe had gathered around us. A shrunken old man asked me for a cigarette—cigarettes seem to symbolize the superiority of the whites. Puff, puff, and inhale voluptuously—it's the supreme joy of the Indians. That was the only solicitation.

I was offered a little cluster of feathers. I recognized the man who gave me the present—he had come to the Vilas Boas brothers' station and had planted himself in front of the door of the cabin where I slept, and stayed there for hours, with a faraway look, to watch and wait. I hadn't understood. I was supposed to give him something, which would have allowed exchanges to be begun. The man, disappointed, had left, but this time he had me. I had to repay him for this bouquet of feathers by another present, otherwise I should disgrace myself. I had nothing but money, a worthless offering, so I took off my sweater and offered it. But, as it was most unlikely that I should undress myself further, the Indian realized that the commerce was going to come to an abrupt stop, and departed again sulkily.

Claudio said to me:

"You know, with the Indians it's not only a matter of self-interest. Everything amuses him as well. When a civilized arrives, the great joke is to dump feathers on his head and look at him. The Indian is even happier, of course, if he receives objects that the whites have taken the trouble to manufacture for him. He distrusts the whites, because they work. He is free, he never works, or, at the most, pursues certain noble activities like fishing, hunting, and a small amount of farming—the smallest possible amount of farming, which consists of burning a patch of the forest and throwing some seeds in it."

"Was today's magic festival just a farce?" I asked. "The chief's just told me that he'll have them do it over tomorrow, if he's brought some more gifts."

"It's not really a swindle. But this year the Indians are happy. They have enough to eat, they make love, they're living well. Nobody kills them here, and nobody reduces them to slavery through gifts. I have forbidden anyone to give them alcohol and salt, because salt, to a primitive, creates extraordinary and fantastic need. What they do need, I provide myself. I set limits on trade. Of course, this makes the Indians grumble a bit, but they know I'm right. So, altogether, they are as satisfied as they can be. So why bother chasing evil spirits, when they're obviously so inactive? Not to do anything unnecessary is their first rule.

"There are no more war dances either, thanks to Orlando's and my guns. What matters is that the jungle be full of game, the rivers full of fish, and the earth fertile. The great festival which they still celebrate is the festival of fecundity. In every village there's a separate and sacred hut which the women cannot approach. This is the hut where the rites of abundance are celebrated. The men dance naked for the ceremony of the Aruana. The Aruana is a marvelous and mythical fish without bones. The witch doctor hands a mysterious sign to the boy as he says to him, "You are the Lord of the Aruana." It is a festival for fertile males. Any female who approaches exposes herself to great danger. If she's a little girl, she becomes a woman; if she's a woman, she dies.

"The Indians celebrate fecundity, the fecundity of the Green Hell, where they are happy despite the horrors. What is more outrageous than the dragon of the waters, the anaconda? The Xingu is full of these enormous snakes. Sometimes, close to a canoe, you can see its head rising from the water, with its huge teeth and a mouth like a pair of bellows. Some are from forty to fifty feet long. They coil and then uncoil to snap up a man and drag him to the bottom of the river, where they swallow him. The Indians are not in the least afraid of these monsters. In the Suija tribe, the warriors, the women and even the children jump on them, tear them apart with their hands and spears and reduce them to impotence by breaking their point of support—the extremity of their tails. To the Indians, this fantastic beast symbolizes the world—horror overcome."

We returned to the Vilas Boas brothers' camp, and along the way Claudio continued to enumerate for me all the abominations of the rivers and the jungles. In the waters, there are sly alligators, gobbling piranhas, the condirus—a little fish which insinuates itself into the openings of the body and leaves its stings to swell there—sting-rays, with stings as big as fingers, numb-fish which emit a deadly electrical discharge, and parahilas weighing from 60 to 80 pounds, whose tactics are to drag their human prey to the depths, like the anaconda.

And what quantities of reptiles there are. The jungle is teeming with them, from the boa constrictors which let themselves hang down from the trees to drink the water from the rivers, to the terrible rattlesnakes. The other kinds of snakes blend into the leaves and flowers where they are invisible—except to the eyes of the Indians, who know how to spot the almost indiscernible nuances of their skins against the dark green vegetation. It's an almost miraculous power, because everything is the same color in the virgin jungle, except for the orchids. It's very rare that an Indian gets bitten. As for the famous snakes that come to suckle women's milk, this is a myth, a symbol. Is it the sign of the reconciliation of the Indian with the frightfulness of nature?

There are still more hideous creatures—enormous black spiders, brutes which spit jets of poison, bats that bite, and even vampires which suck the blood of men asleep in their hammocks. There are the "monkeys of the night," which strangle the peaceful sleepers with their hands. These monkeys are the Indians' only real fear.

What they call "ounces" are all the members of the cat family: there are a great many of them, and they are to be found everywhere—in the mato, the jungle, and the savanna, some of them weighing as much as 330 pounds. They lurk in the Green Hell, completely concealed, a bundle of muscles ready to pounce, of fangs and claws ready to tear apart. Often they scratch the trees, and when you see these scratches on the bark, you are afraid, for you know that they are lying in wait for you.

And then what can you do against the hundreds upon thousands of germs, microbes and insects, which transform men into rotting, gaping wounds, into men dying distended or emaciated, into men who go mad. Immense pitiless world of insects. In addition to clouds of malarial mosquitoes and plague flies, there is everything that pesters, lays eggs, or secretes, that eats the flesh, in the form of eggs, larvae or worms which sting, infiltrate under the skin, or penetrate into the intestines and the entire body. There are also scorpions, leeches, ticks, and every kind of vermin known to man. What can you do against a kind of ant, an inch long, which stings like a centipede? Or against the trails of ordinary ants, whose columns stretch for miles, and which eat everything on their path—plants, animals, even entire huts? There's nothing else to do but flee, if you can.

Everything is poisonous; venemous thorns, dappled glades imbued with fevers, and water reeking with noisome fumes. You reach the point where you can no longer distinguish between the vegetable world, the animal world, the world of larvae and the world of imagination. Among these fantastic shapes there are things which could be flowers or butterflies, or nothing at all, just reflections, unless they be some hybrid product that partakes of everything, fibers and seeds and flesh.

He went on:

"How is it that the Indians have been able to remain real men in the Green Hell? Civilized man turns into a bloodthirsty brute. It's fantastic, these ' noble savages ' in this jungle with its prodigious strength, where all things multiply fantastically, with the sole aim of devouring each other. The jungle is the cruelty of the elemental world. From every quarter and in every way, the jungle confronts you with its fullness, its immensity, its emptiness, its mysteries, its secrets and its noises. It crushes you beneath its vaults, assails you with its burning bushes and watches you with 1,000 eyes. Everything is alike, eternally alike, in a uniformity which is the worst of snares, with suddenly something different that is usually monstrous. Everything is possible, from trees which move to fish that walk. There are no limits set on anything, no reality to anything—everything is immensity, cannibalism and decomposition. The ground is water, all this accumulated humus, these putrifying layers of foliage, of leaves and vegetable and animal corpses. It's the world of the unnamable, and yet a world of splendor. Over and above the stench, you get marvelous wafts of perfume. In the vegetable anonymity, a sudden vision of flowers towering like branches. Amidst noises expressive of death, sometimes the honeyed sound of sweet music like a latent silence—rare moments of consolation before the relapse into the barbarous grandeur of the eternal night, the unspeakable humidity, the constant gestation and the constant death.

"Everything devours itself: you no longer know which eats and which is eaten. The jungle is the final mistress over everything. But from what is she herself made? One half of the jungle supports the life of the other. There is no parasite that is not itself parasitized. Not a branch that does not nourish with its own blood some succubus, which does not have creepers or flowers which are not its own, and which live off it. Everything is embroiled in one immense fertilization, in one immense digestion, in one immense excretion. There is life in all of this, but it is a global life, a total life, a life that is almost undifferentiated. In the jungle you no longer exist as an individual, you have lost your personality, you have become the slave of the vegetation, a vegetation which makes you long for death. In order to survive, you need an unexampled cruelty, and if I love the Indians so much, it's because they survive without this unexampled cruelty, and it's because they, in this demented world, are healthy and are free."

Once again we were in the camp. We found Orlando joking with his girlfriend—a slender sparkling beauty, white-skinned (a rather dark white), in nurse's uniform, who had come from Rio. Civilized games. Claudio said nothing. In the courtyard, in front of the veranda, two Indian kids were playing. One of them was absorbed by a bow and arrows and the other was running with a little plywood model plane in his outstretched hand, to make the air turn the propellor. Two children at each extremity of time . . .

But Claudio's thirst to talk, his fever of the moment, persisted:

"You must realize that the Indian of Brazil is a man of nature, but a nature which would be naturally good. He's a man without complexes. He's attained complete psychological equilibrium; he has reached the point where the frightening universe which surrounds him is not, in his eyes, a world of terror. He worships no cruel gods, nor even any good ones. He worships no kind of god at all. He doesn't know what prayer is, or any kind of worship.

"Of course he has to have emotional control over himself. How could his imagination not be imbued with obscure forces? So he lives according to somewhat surrealistic myths. He is haunted by fabulous creatures, sirens, ogres, fiery serpents, gnomes and Amazons—the jungle of dreams amid the nightmare of the Green Hell. The fantasia of the jungle becomes an unclear zone between the real and the unreal, with plants that sing, birds that announce evil, vaginas implanted with teeth, and liquids that are sperm and blood. Yes, but the Indian is capable of handling all of this by a magic which is primarily a practical science. He chases out his fantasies by dances, songs, secrets and recipes known to the witch doctors. His fears, in fact, are the spirits, the multitude of evil spirits, but he reduces them to impotence in the same way. Dances, dances, and at the end of the dances he has attained fulfillment, he is planted in the visible world much more than in the invisible one. The hereafter is simply a world somewhat like this one, which prolongs this one. In the final summing up, the Indian doesn't even believe in death.

"His characteristic attitude is joy, the most simple joy of all, that of being alive. He is content with being, and that's all. It is a state of happy indifference augmented by pleasure, every possible pleasure. His ideal is to sleep for twelve hours at night, to eat as much as possible, to make love and to be handsome and strong. These "noble savages" are just the opposite of savage; they avoid passion and everything that resembles it. They do not like to be upset, and nothing is more of a nuisance than outbursts of anger, greed or desire. They have no concept of money, self-interest, or egotism. They have to have freedom without any limitations, to the point that good and evil, sin, remorse and fear—at least the fear that fills the soul—do not exist for them. In fact, they do not really claim a soul for themselves, but only a second state, vague substitutes for their being. Concepts like intelligence or reason elude them. What we call ideas or abstractions elude them. Each of them has his body, nature and the world. It's not what I call savagery—as I see it, it is, in a certain way, a natural civilization and a natural morality that is superior to our own.

"You know, the Indians generally live with thirty or forty couples in a large—very large—hut, with all their children and animals. But each of these communities is a republic. Nobody decides what an Indian has to do except himself. There are plenty of chieftains—caciques—who are more or less hereditary, but each of them has to make himself acceptable by virtue of his "value." Indeed, even the greatest of the caciques has no physical authority; he's a "counselor." He doesn't have the right to judge or inflict punishments. His role is to be the master of ceremonies; to suggest commercial exchange with other tribes, to propose fishing or hunting expeditions, or to give his advice upon moving the village—they change sites because the ground is exhausted or because the game has disappeared, or upon the smallest fantasy. The chief only speaks at dawn, at the door of the "great house," holding in his hand a bow and a quiver of arrows. It's an impressive spectacle, but it's really mostly a stage effect. Because it isn't even the community, it's each man and each woman who makes the decisions.

"A tribe is a harmonious society. People behave well towards each other; they laugh all the time—it's their natural state. They have the art of not being embarrassed, and also of not embarrassing others. If someone has had the misfortune to cause an embarrassment to another person, he makes up for the awkwardness by a gift. When one woman's child forgets its manners upon another woman, the mother has to offer a small object as a token of apology. There is a whole code of courtesies, consisting in never showing one's temper, never behaving badly, and avoiding coarse words, vulgar brawls or losing one's temper. This doesn't mean that everything is perfect. You can't say that an Indian doesn't experience any feelings of discontent. He can find certain things disagreeable. If he is genuinely furious, he goes off for a few hours, a few days, or forever. He departs to build a hut somewhere else. I know an old man who moved off in this way—he was in the middle of building a "house" on the other side of the river when his daughter and son-in-law turned up. He was exasperated, but didn't show it. All he did was destroy his hut, his arms, and everything that belonged to him, and then go further away where his solitude would be respected. This explains why it is sometimes said that the Indians are hypocrites: it's because they do not reveal their thoughts, but still pursue them, and can reach the most unexpected results, an explosion replacing their excess of resignation. But all this happens with a self-control that is secret, obstinate, variable, harsh and good-natured, all at once, profound instincts which result in what civilized man calls treachery, and I call good breeding.

"The only restraints the Indians feel are those of tradition, usage, custom and superstition, which can be very rigid, but generally aren't at all. This is how it is with marriage, even though it's a sacred institution. Every union is negotiated by the parents, who often betroth their two-year-old girl to an 'old man' of fifteen years or fifty. In spite of all the ceremonies for nubility and the wedding, love is pretty well free. A crime of passion is inconceivable. The wife preserves a great sexual independence. If she goes too far, her husband wallops her behind and denounces her in public. Generally everything sorts itself out. If they really no longer get on, they try someone else, officially. In any case, this never prevents a lot of horseplay. Smutty stories are very much enjoyed. They play a kind of truth game at the festival of the Javari: the men, when it's their turn to throw the javelin at a dummy, tell each other what they've done: 'I slept with your wife.'

"There are no really rich and no really poor. A certain collectivism for the cultivation of the fields, and for hunting and fishing. They don't yearn for difficulties, so the recommended method for catching fish is to poison the pools with a venom extracted from a creeper. All sorts of aquatic monsters float on the surface, half-dead; they are finished off by a hail of arrows. In some instances, the Indians admire heroism. But it's the ease, the power of doing things comfortably, that's the great gift.

"They live from day to day, doing the bare necessities—which means hunger and want at the most minor catastrophe. But what beauty, what supreme luxury not to pluck so much as a fruit that you don't want, even at the risk of dropping dead from starvation next month when the water's covered everything.

"Odious work is reduced to a strict minimum, but all the same, there is a division of labor. The women are involved in anything to do with water. This is why they cook the fish in large vessels filled with water they've gone to fetch from the stream. But if it's a matter of smoking the fish, it's the man's job, because it's his duty to go into the jungle to collect the wood. The jungle, hunting and animals for the men, the water for the women, who share in the fishing, by helping to haul in the catch. Women of the waves: the legend of the Amazons. Indian women in giggling groups are always bathing while the men watch and make appreciative comments. The river is the love court.

"Idleness but beauty, a sense for ornament, a sense of gesture, a feeling even for the words they speak, pride and arrogance, decorum and fun. These are the reasons why I love the Indians, because, as well as all of this, they possess true generosity of spirit.

"Nothing is more touching than the Indians' relationship with their children. The women have the right to abort themselves if they want to: all kinds of potions extracted from plants and creepers exist for this purpose. But the little ones who do come into the world are cherished, whoever their father is. The actual father hardly counts. The kids grow up in a very natural way, as their own masters, absorbing almost unconsciously the life of the tribe and surrounded by tenderness from every side. Parents never punish their offspring; but the children must not get them mad; a gentleman's agreement. And oddly enough, most of the time, everything goes fine. If a kid takes off, there are cries and groans, but afterwards not even a reprimand. The young fugitive almost always returns of his own accord. His father says, 'Why be hard on him? He's a child, and a child can do what he wants.' No, they never resort to punishment, not even when a little Indian sets fire to the big hut. They just say, 'It's a kid . . . '

"To the Indians, life is good, extraordinarily precious. Isn't it marvelous to reject death as they do? If someone falls sick, or dies, it's not normal or natural. Suffering and death are outrages not contained within the law of nature—and don't forget that this nature is the Green Hell. So they have to be the effects of evil spells. They ask the dying man, 'Who delivered you up to deadly spirits? Who disturbed the functioning of your eternal body?' If the man, before his last gasp, pronounces a name, the family avenges him by killing the person he's designated. This is the only occasion when there are executions within a tribe. But generally they find the person responsible outside it . . .

"If a man dies without naming anyone, the family members devote themselves to a positive medico-magico-police investigation. They appeal to the paje, the 'good witch doctor,' to hunt down the agents of evil, sinister shadows, immaterial and dreadful creatures which have been despatched at the instigation of the 'criminal.' Dreams, narcotic trances and hypnosis; the paje journeys into the realms of the uncertain in his quest. Sometimes while the man is dying, the witch doctor exorcises the spirits—if one can say so—and the prostrate man returns to the excellent existence of this world.

But if the man passes on, the Indians pursue their investigations harder than ever, because there is always, inevitably, somebody guilty, somebody who willed the 'murder.' Usually he has paid a 'bad witch doctor,' who has sent the deadly spirits to assassinate the victim. If this witch doctor is unmasked, he is killed, and so is his 'client.' And as the latter nearly always belongs to another tribe, there is then war in the jungle.

"But peace is restored. War between the tribes is rarely very serious, it's more like a game. And when the party's over, each tribe enjoys its life in its own territory with its well-defined boundaries. How a tribe loves its patch of virgin jungle! How sensually a tribe is attached to it! This is why the tribe defends it against invaders. And when the invaders are the whites, the tribe struggles desperately, vainly—just enough to be a nuisance, enough for all the Indians who make up the tribe, men, women and children, to be killed. Little genocides and multiple ones, because there are many tribes which are already very diminished. The last great races like the Chavantes disappeared some fifteen or twenty years ago. It's a terrible price exacted from innocence."

It was then that I made Claudio really angry:

"Innocence. But aren't the Indians also innocent in what we call evil? It was your brother Orlando who told me about some very cruel customs—killing the children of a woman who has just died; strangling new-born twins; burying their parents alive when they're too old. And aren't all these tribal wars much more than a mere diversion, aren't they also the Indians' reason for living? What about the war dances and chants, war paint and shouts, the mutilations which they inflict upon themselves to inspire fear? There are endless struggles in the jungle involving trickery and torture. Orlando told me all of this. He also alluded to the eating of prisoners to get control of their powers. I've been told that there are nearly always grim masks and human bones to be found in the villages of wild Indians. Isn't it true that side by side with the Indian Eden there is also a sort of Indian Hell: a sullen terrifying atmosphere, full of taboos, mysteries and burnt offerings . . . Side by side with the legend of the "noble savage," there is also the legend of the Indians as pure schizophrenics, as lazy, vicious, beggarly, inquisitive, very mercenary, quarrelsome, unstable, swindlers, and horribly arrogant. In short, bad people."

Claudio responded heatedly:

"It's not true. It's only slightly true. Yes, Indians remain Indians. There lies their nobility. If they do evil, it's because they have no sense of evil. Anyway, they only do very little of it, much less than the whites, even the whites who call themselves good. Yes, the Indians have this marvelous quality of loving life, true life, the life of nature. And within this appalling form of nature, they prosper . . . They protect themselves from monsters and insects—the viruses of the jungle don't affect them. They escape from all those fevers which devour civilized man. It's true that we others, the whites, give them in exchange our refined viruses of the twentieth century. In all of these exchanges it's the Indians who lose. Not only are they killed, but they are called evil."

Claudio relapsed into silence. How could he completely deny the innocence which the Indians exhibit in evil as well? Cannibalism as a means of disarmament, for example. In many tribes, choice morsels are removed from the corpse of the slain enemy and then eaten. A magical operation which seems barbarous. They take from each body the eyes, lips and tongue, and the muscles of the legs and the right arm—and they gorge themselves. This is to render the uneaten survivors of the hostile tribe incapable of taking revenge upon the consumers, because they will no longer be able to see, hunt, or draw the bow; they won't even be able to speak or make plans. In short, feasting upon the killed paralyzes the nonkilled.

Dried human meat is preserved for those cases of necessity when there is a new danger of war. It also makes a very precious gift. One desbravador was presented with a piece of an Indian's tongue. The civilized man had at first believed he was being offered any old bit of meat. His host expatiated at length upon the "value" of the meat, which was full of the power of the Mura warrior who had been killed, cut up and smoked ten years before—a power which the Indians were turning back, through absorption and digestion, against the still hostile race of the Muras. There was no question of the white guest's not swallowing with gusto this marvelous remnant—his fellow diners would have been annoyed. His only solution was to pretend. He said that he had lost it. The company began to search for it on the dirty ground, crouching on their haunches, overlooked from above by the head of someone recently slain which had been hung on the wall; a well-polished head, withering nicely, which was being preserved with pride, while the usable meat had already been prepared and stored for the years to come.

There was another method of preserving the sacred meat—by keeping the captive alive, healthy and well-fed, and provided with everything, even a woman. At the wished-for moment, he was slaughtered. Blood and entrails everywhere; children paddling in the carnage, with the approval of their mothers (it would give them strength). The warriors of the tribe—for this was generally the moment when they were mobilizing to depart for the war—swallowed their portion of flesh solemnly, as if it were a regenerative sacrament, a kind of fortifying communion. At the same time, someone from their tribe was probably being similarly savored by the people of the tribe that had furnished the devoured prisoner. The rivalry in appetites thus preceded the combat, and in a way influenced the outcome in advance.

But is this tasting only ritual? Isn't it gastronomic as well? Some Indians from one tribe asked the whites who had just massacred the Indians of another tribe, enemies of the first: "Our neighbors have disappeared. Did you eat them?" Astonishment. "You didn't? We would have had a feast." A sense of waste. They were furious with the whites at their negligence, to the point of wanting to eat them in compensation.

Innocence in evil. If the Indians kill the children of a woman who has just died, it's because everything in the world ought to have a living mother. Not only men, but trees, water, rocks and the sky. There is a mother for the yam and a mother of the storm. There is a mother for the smallest particle of the smallest thing. So it's sacrilegious for children to be able to live without her who created them. Sacrilegious not in the religious sense, but as a breach of the taboos, which is unpardonable; it would entail frightful misfortune. So the little innocents are killed by the big innocents. But is it innocent, a consequence of ritual, to bury the old alive?

There is not much cruelty within a tribe. It is the other tribes that are the enemy, and the whites even more so. But how can one deny the hospitality that the Indians offer the whites? Is it from fear of a magic more powerful than their own, or from the desire for magical gifts? Gifts which end in death. In Amazonia, the civilized see no prospect but death. What greater evil is there than that of not recognizing evil? That is the curse of the Indians. They have to be killed. Garimpeiros, fazendeiros and seringueiros still pursue this task with the same zeal. But the "new men," who bring the modern world into the jungle, are more murderous than they, and more terrible, for they destroy as if automatically, by force of circumstances, sometimes without wanting to, sometimes without knowing it.

IT LOOKED as if the garimpeiros were already on the move towards the diamond beds of the Rio Jatuba, whose waters had barely begun to fall. This took up more and more of Orlando's attention, an Orlando who was still huge and stalwart, a kind of bare-chested king, but an Orlando who is growing old in spite of his Herculean strength; there are too many killers for his Indians.

He growled:

"You never know how many of the garimpeiros will turn up. If they think that the Jatuba's vein is exhausted, and their luck lies somewhere else, there won't be very many of them, and I shan't have any problems. But if they still believe in the Jatuba, 10,000 of them will come, 20,000, 30,000, I don't know how many, in big groups and small, in a migration that will never end. And they'll set to work like madmen, from dawn to dusk. It's the gambling fever. I've seen it often enough these last twenty years by the Xingu. And every time, the first concern is to massacre the Indians in the surrounding countryside. It's an enormous problem to stop them—enormous because although these people are wretched, there's a great deal at stake, and with all these outlaws I'm up against a society that has its own laws, the laws of the diamond.

"Sometimes they stumble across a real treasure. Then, even in the most forbidding swamps, they create practically in the riverbed they're sieving a temporary town, a shanty town, but with its own logic. There are stores, cabarets, brothels and inns; every kind of woman and every sort of trade. Not just cheap hardware items, but luxury articles to gratify the big winner, the finder of the big diamond. Expensive guns and clothes, brand names of alcohol, and even dresses for the ladies. All this reaches the town on foot, with people travelling for months carrying the stuff on their backs. But it also comes by air, by taxi airplanes, at $100 an hour. The jungle is burnt to make a rotten little muddy runway, crawling with people night and day, who clutter it up with junk. Sometimes you see a ragged man departing for his moment of ecstasy—a winner, who'll come back in the same pitiful state. But it's usually the men who buy and sell, the moneylenders, the police and the landowners who get on or off.

"This group has a very precise code. Most of the garimpeiros are controlled by 'patrons,' respectable, important men who might live in Bahia or Rio. Each patron finances a team of garimpeiros, and provides his men with work clothes, dried meat, rice and beans, shovels, pickaxes, and sieves. If the garimpeiro finds a diamond, he has the right to make a deal with anyone—he always sells it there and then. But he's obliged to give half the sum he receives to his patron. No use a garimpeiro trying to conceal his discovery of a stone and flog it for his own profit thousands of miles away. No need to search the man. For wherever he tries to sell it, the purchaser looks at him oddly and says, "This comes from such and such a place. Is your patron aware of this?" A few days later the 'swindler' is riddled with bullets.

"It's all very well organized. In addition to the patrons, there are the gentlemen buyers called 'compradores' or 'carpengueiros.' They come from the city, armed with scales and a magnifying glass screwed into their eye. A down-and-out will halt in front of one of them, and take a stone from a bamboo tube. 'I've found a diamond,' he says. The comprador takes the stone in his white hands, holds it up in the air to look at it, fingers and examines it for a few seconds in an offhand way, and then proposes, with distaste, his generous offer: '50,000 cruzeiros.' '80,000.' 'No, there's a shadow. Look at it yourself with the glass.' The unfortunate garimpeiro has to accept because he's controlled by a formidable system. Over the comprador, who's only a poor kind of guy in spite of his city suit, there's a bulk buyer, then a bigger bulk buyer, two or three other buyers who are even more important, then the company at Rio, and then the international company. Each one bawls out his subordinates in exactly the same words, descending from the summit of the hierarchy to its base: 'Too dear, much too dear, you're paying crazy prices.'

"A good diamond hole is worth millions, and represents formidable interests. The police don't risk going there for the first few days. Then the cops arrive, increasingly higher ranked. I'd rather not tell you what they do. Next a gentleman in a tropical suit introduces himself, panama hat on his head and buckskin shoes on his feet, and exhibits a document smothered in stamps. 'I am the fazendeiro, the landowner of this place. Take a look at the paper—it's official. Anyone can enter my territory, and anyone can leave it, but I require ten per cent of the price of whatever is found here.' The senhor is surrounded by some self-confident, cheerful types in linen suits, who bulge with revolvers and cartridges: his pistoleiros, his collecting agents. And far away in the first available city with a skyscraper, Cuiabá, Goiânia or Brasilia, sits the politician who provided the paper, the seals and the signatures, who gets a certain per cent of the ten per cents.

"Naturally, everybody is in agreement over suppressing the nuisance—the Indians, if there are any. And of course there is no lack of ways and means. The big people, those involved with finance, the 'patrons,' the fazendeiros, the various kinds of cops, all the buyers and sellers, the whole indeterminate marginal range of intermediaries and straw men, all shell out for that. The S.P.I. people—you know, the Service for the Protection of the Indians—close their eyes, or even assist in the massacres. What can the S.P.I. representative in his station do? He's generally sodden with booze, and he's faced by people in high places and a crowd of desperadoes with their crazy hopes. If necessary, they use planes which bomb and machine-gun, but naturally they prefer simpler and less obvious procedures like the common cold or the poisoned candy, or the neat little commando raid. If the big men fork out, the garimpeiros then form a squadron to clear out the Indians.

"Look here, if you want to see a nest of garimpeiros, take your plane and touch down at Aragarças, 300 miles from here; it's just an hour's flight. It's not really a garimpo, but it's the last little town of civilization which many diamond hunters make their winter quarters. There are even some old holes there where the most persistent of these men still sift the earth in the hope of getting their hands on some little stones which have escaped the armies of their predecessors."

That same afternoon my small plane flew over the Rio das Mortes and the Rio Araguaia. Below me, the jungle and its twisted flowers. Then, after crossing the Serra do Roncador—jungle spurs where the Chavantes, once the most famous and feared tribe in all Brazil, used to battle—we came down on the edge of the Rio Araguaia. None of the seething of an ant heap of garimpeiros. Aragarças is just an ordinary little colonial town from which military expeditions had once departed to "pacify" Central Brazil. Orderly. Its mine was something of a veterans' hospital for saving garimpeiros.

It is a marvelous and hellish existence. Some garimpeiros give up the profession, but go back to it after a few months. That's always the way. It's a folly of the imagination, for no garimpeiro has ever made his fortune, and none ever can. The garimpeiro's money is cursed. The garimpeiros know this so well that when they finally find their hands full of wads of notes, they go on a binge to beat all binges. Drinks all round.

Everything is anticipated for the high life, even in the most distant of jungles. There is everything you need in the way of girls, mostly French, but others of every race, even Chinese girls. How do they get there? No one knows. Some are lovely, others hideous, old women who make love in hammocks stretched between trees, attracting their customers by making strange movements with their tongues. The garimpeiros' erotic fantasies usually are enacted in the bordello, a zinc-roofed shed. The garimpeiro takes his revenge on his destiny by making the girls crawl about in search of the money that he's hidden in the corners; he shouts to them, "You're garimpeiros too."

You can obtain anything, even a mink coat to offer to a whore to please her, or for a joke. All you have to do is apply to a Syrian, one of those Levantines who are the business men of the Green Hell. He says: "You give me the stone, and the fur will be here in three days, by the first plane." Its cost is fantastic, five or six times more expensive than at Rio or New York. Everything is fantastically expensive, even an ordinary bottle of beer, even the dirty beans which are the basis of meals on ordinary days.

The binge never lasts very long, because of the prices. But it does last until the garimpeiro has nothing left. Nothing is too exotic. One garimpeiro had a Cadillac brought over in pieces into the heart of the virgin forest, which he put together again and used over the 100 yards of pavement in the place, until it rusted away.

Life is to enjoy yourself like an animal, when you can, and then relapse back into misery. This life is so accepted by the garimpeiros that some of them, after they've gotten their hands on the big money and togged themselves up like gentlemen, get return plane tickets from a travel agency. There's always one, even if it is in a hut. The fantastic run around to Rio or São Paulo and then the reappearance, when there's not a penny left. Once again the rage, the sieve, the hope that leads nowhere. Garimpos only last for a few months or a few years. A tremendous crowd, and then nobody. Nothing but the debris left by things and men who succumbed. Not even the traces of a vanished town, because there never was a town. It was only a shanty town of the eldorado, like hundreds of others in Brazil. Each time with few winners and many losers. Each time it's all forgotten; each time the jungle has reclaimed everything.

On the cement runway of the aerodrome, pilots of a row of taxi planes waited for customers like cab drivers. Surprised looks from these gentlemen— they didn't recognize my plane, and wondered who I was. My pilot, the one who had been so plumaged by the Indians in exchange for his "gifts," was explaining us to some other people who had appeared suddenly. There were three or four of them, in linen suits, with those razor-edged faces and gimlet eyes which indicated policemen. Public or private cops? I don't know, and am not likely to find out. It's public knowledge that in the interior of Brazil "meddlers" are not well-loved—those "revolutionaries" who talk up syndicalism or make the prices go up, "capitalists" who aren't part of the local set-up, or fugitives who are believed to have accounts to settle with some powerful fazendeiro. The account given by my pilot was satisfactory. Smiles. What I wanted, to see the garimpeiros, was judged a foreigner's odd and innocent whim. Everything was organized for me. I was just asked to wait a few minutes in a handy bar, presided over by an enormous matron with breasts like fountains of beer. All very impersonal. It was hot. A jeep was soon there.

We set off. As escorts I had one fellow with the head of an insect, another with the shoulders of a bull. Immaculately turned out and very obliging. We left Aragarças behind, slumbering in its tropical banality, and followed a sort of little laterite road stretching straight across a bleak landscape of thorny savanna. The light was intense. There was a gateway in this nothingness, a show of barbed wire in this void. And suddenly, in front of me, a dizzying cliff, a red gulf with a few ragged men at the bottom, in honeycomb cells, grinding earth and gravel. Some huts around it, so wretched that they were barely distinguishable from the vegetation. The very image of a convict camp.

A sheep track was the only way of getting down into the hole, which was so huge that I thought at first of a valley or canyon, a split in the ground due to some geological cataclysm. But it was man-made. It was what generation after generation of men had dug out. Walls the color of blood, smooth but with jagged wrinkles, the walls of a gigantic prison. The individuals who did their time at the bottom of the abyss were volunteers. They were more than that, they were men possessed, who could only be torn from there to go into some other pit that was fuller of illusions. Each of them, within this jail-like eldorado, was further enclosed inside a little hole at the bottom of the big hole, a regularly shaped, almost rectangular cavity, which he had made himself, and in which he was burying himself still deeper. The condemned man, who had sentenced himself to the madness of carats, flung up around his excavation stones which piled higher and higher: the useless gravel.

A titanic labor for these people, to keep on bending, to keep on collecting the earth, then carry it to a stream and pick it over. Water, on the edge of the watery Amazonia, was rare. It had had to come there through wooden ducts, and it flowed meagerly in miserly dribbles to become a ditch, where the men sifted the earth that they had torn out of their holes. Nothing but the desolation of the raped earth. And the miracle of the water, which could produce the miraculous gleam at the bottom of a pan which meant a fortune, however provisional and however it would be eroded.

The garimpeiros were coolly friendly. They all had rotting felt hats, indescribably tattered clothes, more rips than cloth, and bare feet. They were in such shreds that their principal clothing was the beard and wild hair on their leathery faces. They were all disfigured, without teeth, or with a dud eye, a finger missing or one leg shorter than the other. Bums, and yet not

bums because of their tanned skin—the kippering peculiar to adventure—
because of their taut muscles and the controlled tenseness of men of prey.
Their set faces threw me a friendly but distant glance. They all had the
swarthy complexions of half-castes. The range of skin color is extraordinary,
in a so-called diamond mine in Brazil—from amber to soot. One of them, so
wrinkled that I could scarcely see his color, although he was still young, had
blue eyes—his Teutonic side, no doubt.

After a minute's pause to watch me, the men started to pick again. Still like
galley slaves, but each one alone in his excavation of fifteen or twenty feet. A
chessboard of excavations, with these solitary individuals in a frenzy of
silence and concentration on their work. All separated from each other by
flimsy sides; what hadn't been dug became the walls. They had only the most
primitive instruments, the hand, a shovel and a pick. From close by, I saw
nothing but bent backs. Each garimpeiro made a pile inside his own hole of
the earth which he had grubbed up, the "good" earth. When he had enough,
he carried it to the ditch. Some of the diggers had children, their own sons or
small urchins whom they'd recruited, to serve as beasts of burden. I saw one
kid carrying a basket with a load larger than himself towards a garimpeiro
bent over the stream, in the process of picking over his earth.

He had put several sieves in the water, one on top of the other, which he
was letting soak to get rid of the silt. He lifted up one of these sieves, with all
that it held of the unknown, of mystery; automatically, he gave it four
violent shakes, two this way, two that. Then without even glancing at it, he
threw the worked-over matter onto the edge of the stream. He did this to all
the sieves. Next, he took a twig and meticulously scratched in the middle of
the deposit of mud that he had so painstakingly shaken. Then, and how
intensely, did he look at it! He moved his twig with slow consecrated
movements towards the center of the dripping pile. It is just as intense as the
passion of the millionaires of the gaming table. The same passion lit up this
unfortunate. Was he going to glimpse the stone he sought? If there was one, it
would be there, in the middle. Thirty or forty seconds to analyze the silt and
the little stones with the stick. A grain gleamed, but it wasn't a diamond. No
hint of disappointment on the thin face, just a kind of indifference. The mask
of the gambler who knows how to conceal his passion—his total passion; not
in the least discouraged, the man began to refill his sieves with earth, place
them in the water, and shake them in turn without looking at them. He

The Garimpeiros' treasure. Gaunt, their muscles deformed by constant digging, the garimpeiros tirelessly work the soil under a pitiless sun. Fear is present everywhere: fear of the others, of the landowners, of the Indians. Endless steps are cut into hillsides, trenches are dug into hilltops, but all this prodigious and fruitless activity leads but to the enrichment of a few *senhores* and the gentlemen of Rio, São Paulo, Brazilia, and sometimes the United States.

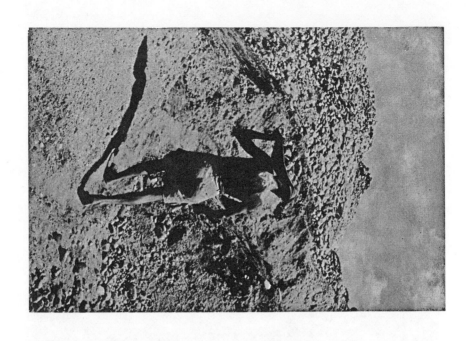

would look at them shortly, in about a quarter of an hour, with his stick. And in all probability, he would find nothing.

He obviously didn't want to talk to me, simply because he didn't have the time. I slipped him a bank note.

"How long is it since you found a stone?"

"Four months. But it was a very small one."

"Have you ever found any big diamonds?"

"Oh yes, many three or four carat ones. One of them as big as a nut. I got several thousand cruzeiros for it [about $200]. I know that it's worth millions in Paris or New York in a jeweller's showcase."

"You were cheated . . . "

"Perhaps, but I can't read. I can't count. That's the way it is. And even so I had a splendid party."

"Have you always been a garimpeiro?"

"Ever since I was a kid. I am old now. Not quite forty. I'm worn out, so I stay in this mine, which is as old and poor as me. But when I was young I went everywhere in Brazil, into the wildest parts of the Mato Grosso and Amazonia, wherever I used to hear that 1,000, 2,000 miles away, there would be diamonds. What I've gone through!"

And the garimpeiro described his trials. He had seen many men die, tough as they were, from exhaustion, the Indians, fevers, from waterfalls or the river currents. The work in the rivers is dangerous. They had to dive, and look with the naked eye at the troubled bottom of the riverbed, while their posteriors and legs waggled absurdly outside, at least when it wasn't too deep. All you saw was this crowd of bottoms. Sometimes they had to dive several yards deep, while their lungs seemed about to burst. Some patrons bought old diving suits for their men, which were worked by air pumps placed on the bank. All of this to wrest out a little earth, bring it up to the surface and then pick it over as they did here. Of course, there were piranhas. It didn't do to get wounded, because they were at once attacked by these carnivorous fish. The mosquitoes were the worst, the malaria. It came when the waters rose, brought by the floods. Half the population of a garimpo could succumb.

"Yes, I've had so many of my companions carried off by malaria! If the boss was decent, he had the dying man put in a plane to be taken to hospital. But almost always the boss found that this was too expensive. Then you dropped dead on the spot. Sometimes you had a priest. I once received the extreme unction. I'm sure it was that that saved me. If the boss is bad, God is good. The Lord will forgive me if I have forgotten my wife and children in I don't even remember which town in Brazil."

I asked: "Is it true that garimpeiros don't steal from each other and don't kill each other?"

"It's quite true. Things are hard enough as it is. Murders in a garimpo almost always happen in the "high-ups," among the gentlemen. The police are particularly dangerous. They come to put things back in order, so they say, but they are there for their own affairs. Funny sort of affairs. They don't take any notice of us; they can't get anything out of us. But it's often happened to me to have my 'patron' in prison or even completely disappear—he has been liquidated for 'lack of understanding.' I can be sure that a few hours later another guy will come up to me and say: 'You don't have anybody any longer . . . ' 'No, I don't . . . ' 'Well, I'll take you on. You will be well protected—I've got friends where I need them.' And everything starts over."

"Have you killed Indians in your time?"

"They don't count. They're animals. Not men. So you have to treat them like animals."

I left him by the ditch and turned back to where the digging was, to the checkerboard of bare holes.

All over Brazil men grub in the ground, collecting not only precious stones, but commoner ones as well, modern eldorados. Nickel. Cassiterite. Black powders. Veined stones. Men didn't know what they would be used for, but an eldorado could happen anywhere, not just in the wilderness but right by the capital. As at Cristalina, the city of colored cristals. Cristalina: the huge illusion seventy-five miles from Brasilia. Beside the road that runs from São Paulo to Brasilia—a magic ribbon of brand new highway leading into the lands of the interior—is, or rather was, the nightmare. For Cristalina no longer exists.

Crowds of men converged on Cristalina, not just garimpeiros, but lawyers, doctors and diplomats, naive men and covetous ones, leaving slums or middle-class apartments, but all alike in having wiped out their property and their families. Cristalina only two years ago. Chaotic. A tragic human landscape of a joyless eldorado. A lunar, bombarded landscape, hacked about by men, in their ant-heap holes. A thankless terrain, without vegetation, whose martyred ground was cut up into thick wedges, into slices riddled by every kind of barb, stain and wound. A terrain like a skin disease. Fifty thousand men, most of them invisible, because the population was subterranean, at the bottom of deep, narrow, dark, stifling wells, "cisterns" thirty-two inches in diameter. Inside it, the man was alone in the entrails of the earth, wedged into the end of a minute fissure which he made himself, prey to cave-ins, asphyxia, and suffocaton. Six feet down there was always a pool of water which had to be dried up. Lower, ever lower, the garimpeiro lived in a sluice, a tunnel of night and swamp. In his well he tore up the earth with his hands; he had to raise it by a hand-winch to make room for himself, to be able to bury himself still deeper. Like a solitary mole, he dug on, in the hope of seeing a light, the glitter of an enormous topaz, the star of the soil.

In twenty days, 20,000 of these perforations! Deaths from breathing in mouthfuls of earth or water. To try to protect themselves, these lonely men were linked to each other by pipes in a huge subterranean labyrinth. At the very mouths of the "cisterns" were all the intermediaries, ears cocked in the hope of hearing the shriek of joy which meant that a man had lit upon a crystal. When he appeared with his great stone, he was sold anything from a transistor to a mechanical piano. Sometimes he was sold the title to a far-off property, which was nothing but emptiness and snakes, but which allowed him to call himself a fazendeiro. For every twenty men curled up in these infernal wells like foetuses in the womb of the earth, there was, on average, but one winner.

Each day at the edge of Cristalina two processions met each other, the losers' and the arrivals', the new players. The desolate expressions and emaciated physique of the men crushed by failure made no impression on the eldorado hunters, many of whom came without experience or money. Some of them didn't even have the tools for digging. Others naively put their cruzeiros into buying a secondhand well. There were so many wells that they were too close to each other, risking everything caving in at the same time. It didn't matter. The men dug on anyway. Some were mere employees, others worked for a patron, and others for themselves. But always, under sunshine or rain, they were confronted with the red earth. A few bored wells that were twenty yards deep, single-handed. No baths, no showers, no time to lose. The ignoble smell of men. Disease. But to a vague project of vaccination that the police talked about, a suspicious, "How much will it cost?"

After the last hope had vanished, the defeated man left without a penny, with the rags on his back as his sole worldly goods. He sat motionless on the side of the road, waiting for the bus to take him away, nicknamed the "bus of despair." Many had come with their own cars, which remained there, because their owners didn't have enough money for the gas. Those who could afford the bus ticket were lucky. Some didn't even have that much, and stayed in the garimpo as beggars, selling cigarette ends they'd picked up off the ground or minute stones that they'd found by scraping the soil with their fingers. And even so, some men apparently died of hunger.

This huge exploitation of human beings had begun in 1964, when two garimpeiros had dug a hole in a sort of a desert, and seen the blue glitter of a crystal. It happened on an abandoned fazenda, called "the partridge farm," whose owners led a comfortable existence in Brasilia. The moment Senhor Odilon de Oliveira learned of the existence of a mine on his property, he made it a gold mine for himself. He left the stones to the men, but devoured the men. He put out a proclamation, a mobilization order, to all the adventurers: "Come one and all to my eldorado. The soil is a treasure trove whose riches I yield you. You have only to help yourselves. Not a penny to pay to start with. One condition only: I shall ask for ten per cent from those whom the Lord smiles upon."

Great promiscuity. Bible preachers clambering onto boxes, ticket sellers for the National Lottery, government functionaries . . . And the prostitutes. Prostitutes in miniskirts, prostitutes in pants and sweaters, all the girls from the brothels of Brasilia. Payment in gold or in stones; not in notes, which devalued too fast because of the inflation. Advertising everywhere. Bars, restaurants, groceries, drugstores, nightclubs, all in shanties, without sewers, stinking, with mounds of empty bottles and cans, mountains of garbage, along with a master of ceremonies and hostesses in evening dress. Profusion. The shopping center, with its refrigerators, shirts, and fruit, had been installed by the fazendeiro upon the debris of his old fazenda.

Le Senhor Oliveira was indeed a very clever fellow. He was a multimillionaire. He was not satisfied with netting his ten per cent through his eighteen fiscal agents; he was the king over the business, over all the businesses, from love all the way to crystals. He bought or controlled the purchase of topazes and other treasures. In the small dark rooms of his heavily guarded fazenda he had fabulous fortunes in the shape of thirty-pound sacks of crystals. Everywhere was felt the hidden law of the powerful. The carousel lasted two years, three years, without anybody protesting or intervening, despite the supermodern Parliament of Brasilia on the horizon, the work of Niemeyer, architect and archangel, who believed he was consecrating Brasilia to humanity's happiness.

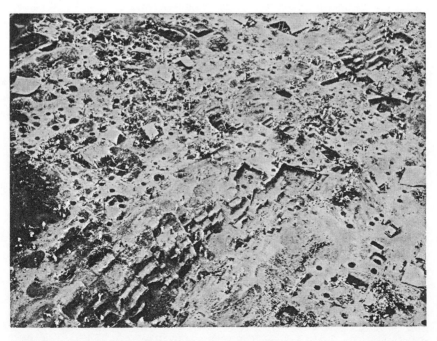

Cristalina, the Garimpeiros' hell. A rush followed when a rock crystal weighing almost forty pounds was reported found in this corner of Brazil. Tens of thousands of garimpeiros transformed the forest into a lunar landscape. The garimpeiros work, eat, and often sleep in these holes, which are sometimes dug to a depth of forty feet.

Golddiggers and prostitutes. Prostitutes are close upon the heels of the garimpeiros. They are rarely beautiful, often sick, and their earnings are for the better part "recuperated" by clever pimps who themselves are often in the pay of businessmen who finance the whole adventure.

Civilization takes over. As soon as a lode has been discovered, and the garimpeiros have begun to arrive, a host of traders moves in to get from them whatever the landlords and their agents may have overlooked. Prices are sky-high. But isn't money to be had for the digging?

Cristalina. Diamantina. Nickelandia. Names of phantom towns, haunted by the thing which gavè them their names, by something which has disappeared. Towns deserted by the garimpeiros who have departed elsewhere to bring other towns to birth, and which are now nothing.

When I returned to the Xingu that same evening, I found Orlando and Claudio in great form. They had learnt that there wouldn't be many people making for the Rio Jatuba, because its gold deposits really seemed depleted. This would simplify life, if only for a time. For peace, in Amazonia, is never more than a truce.

PEACE AT the Vilas Boas'. But a peace which was the more fragile because their fief was situated on the boundaries of two wildernesses: the mato, with its tangled forest and putrefying swamps, and the selva, that immense vegetable fantasy, a bloated botanical nightmare. But at least the selva has its arteries: the Amazon and its tributaries, which men can ascend in boats, as far as the falls—which, for some years past, have also been surmounted by the seringueiros.

In the great Amazonian jungle, the adventure of the borracha continues. There was an abrupt flare-up of wild rubber during the Second World War, after the Asian plantations fell into the hands of the Japanese. Armadas of American seaplanes had landed on rivers. An extraordinary exploit, landing planes where the jungle almost throttles the water. In two hours, each plane brought back to Manaus the gum that would be used for the allied victory, collected by several thousand seringueiros from beyond the cataracts. And then the war had ended. There was no more large need of Brazilian rubber. It was almost worthless, yet the seringueiros went on collecting it. They became forgotten men. They reached the limits of slavery. They killed the Indians, and the Indians killed them . . .

The situation doesn't even have the frightful grandeur of the time of the "folly" of borracha half a century ago, when the whole of Amazonia was one great greed that caused the death of perhaps 1,000,000 men. There's been nothing like that since. All is calm, just the abandonment of everything and everybody, life going on in an incredible misery and solitude which are the norms of existence of the seringueiros.

Seringueiros beyond the cataracts of the Xingu, the Juruena, the Aripuaña and the Rio Roosevelt. Seringueiros beyond the world of men. The largest of these rivers if the Aripuaña. When you ascend it, you meet one last pinpoint of life: Mineraçon, where manganese is extracted. Boats tied up to buoys. Hundreds of men dump loads of mineral into the holds. Here there is still activity, possibilities and money. After Mineraçon, there is no longer the concept of money. After Mineraçon, there is no more need of watches, because time belongs to everyone, because time belongs to no one, because time no longer exists. After Mineraçon, sentences and words lose all meaning—there is nothing to say to oneself.

In the dry season, when the rivers are low, balls of borracha are put onto rafts made of thirty ox skins sewn together. These are released into the current. At each rapid men cling to rocks with harpoons in their hands, throwing them to retrieve the rafts when they are on the point of being impaled or of leaking. Sometimes a man has to go down into the water, in the middle of terrible eddies, with his weapon. If necessary, he jumps into a boat to get up to the grounded borracha, which he aims back into the current.

Apart from this, work is apparently as before. The seringueiro's time is still two o'clock in the morning. Then he gets up, drinks a hasty cup of coffee, puts on cotton pants and a shirt, and fastens to his head a little kerosene lamp to illuminate the night and off he goes to make the rounds of his scattered trees. At the end of the day, the man has collected between eight and thirty gallons of gum. Then he busies himself with the defumador. Once the product is finished, the seringueiro transports it on a donkey or in a canoe along the streams to his patron's barracão. Then comes the weigh-in and the bartering; as in the old days, the good faith of the illiterate seringueiro is abused, and he takes his revenge by mixing stones and bones into the gum.

An accepted existence. No more adventure, but an enslavery which functions of itself, calmly, without treachery, without brutality. There's no more need for it . . .

There are even seringals beyond the waterfalls. On one portion of the bank there's a clearing containing the homes of the patron, his manager and the pilot—there's always a plane and its pilot in any big exploitation. A few huts, a few fields, pastures for domestic animals. Banality even in the heart of the virgin forest, a banality over which the seringalista is the recognized king. Not many killers or hangmen faces around him; now it's paternalism. It's up to the patron to think of everything on behalf of his hundreds of seringueiros and their families. He has to provide their food, clothing, medicine and transport. He has to serve as judge and doctor. He has to open up runways.

A peaceful despotism. The seringueiro learns to live by and for the seringalista. The seringalista is king, but he is often a sorry fellow who doesn't even manage to get rich himself from exploiting men and nature. He climbs into his own plane to go begging in the cities from the big operators— politicians who give him the State's money after a deduction for themselves, or bankers who consent to provide advances at extortionate interest rates. The borracha crop is always sold in advance. In his seringal, the seringalista is constantly haunted by the necessity of achieving the amount of gum that he has already pocketed the money for. A subtle equilibrium: the moneylenders know that the seringueiros will take off if the seringalista doesn't pay them at all, but they also know that the seringalista has the seringueiros in his clutches. His problem is to give the seringueiros the absolute minimum, below which they would die of hunger or sneak off.

Hunger. There is always hunger in the seringueiro's cabin. Not the kind that kills, but the kind that keeps men on the edge of dying. These days the "tree-bleeder," at least while he's still young, is no longer a solitary savage. These days he has a whole family, all wretched. Instead of meeting a swift death, the seringueiro can grow old, very old, treading the same ground. Nothing ever happens to his routine, except misfortunes like falling sick or getting hit with an arrow. Eating inadequately becomes a habit. Burying his wife and kids, another habit. There are some old men who have survived for fifty or sixty years, to find themselves alone, quite alone, in their cabins. Some are pious men who say their prayers and smile as they complain gently: "I have been too poor. It's not fair to have been so poor. I've put up with it all, my body is withered and I use a stick for support and when I die, it'll be as if an ant had disappeared, nothing more."

Hidden hunger, hunger endemic in a multitude of men who die little by little, from not eating every day. Such is the Amazonia of beyond the cataracts as described to me by a little man who was obviously one of Orlando's spies.

"I'd come to the edge of a stream which flowed into a tributary of the Aripuaña. On the bank stood a house, and a woman who didn't dare to look at me. She murmured: 'What is it? Who's that?' It was the cabin of a family of seringueiros, who, on being reassured, offered me hospitality. What hospitality! A sort of slow death. Inside were the father, mother and seven children. The day before the day of my arrival, they had eaten a little maize in the morning, and then nothing else for the rest of the day. Yesterday they'd had a small fish with what was left of the manioc. The day I came there was no more of anything, except for a fish head and a quart of semolina which had been given them by another traveller for a night's lodging. The semolina was their last reserve, which mustn't be touched. I sent a note to the seringalista, their boss, to ask him for a little wheat for them. As we waited for his reply, it was very distressing to hear the children as they drew near the stove: 'Nothing to eat, Momma?' 'No, there's nothing to eat.' The kids didn't cry. To them, it was normal for things to be like this. This sweet temper on the part of kids whose bellies were empty was particularly painful.

"At last the seringalista got two pounds of flour through to me—he couldn't do any more because he had only four pounds left for himself and his family. But what's two pounds of flour for nine stomachs? The seringueiro did nothing. He was living in a continual daze, unable to take any initiative. It didn't even occur to him to look for food in the vegetation, for roots or fruits in the jungle. I sent the kids out to pick guavas. I told the master of the house to take his machete and go cut a palm tree heart, for dinner. But tomorrow, when I'm gone, there'll be nothing left. It will be the same mortal inertia, a kind of resignation in which the unfortunate say to themselves: 'God will provide.' But where is God in the selva?"

A humanity that is bestial in its passivity. People who talk always in low voices. Complete illiteracy, with a vague yearning to learn to read, so as to be able, at long last, to look at the boss' accounts. They speak an incredible jargon, giving names to different parts of the jungle like: "Silk cord," "Little Pillow," "Turn of the Moon," "Hair of the Bun." The kids whose father is unknown have surnames that are equally picturesque. The girls know only that they were born "at the end of the line," "in the month we had flour," or "when there was the storm." The minors are left to the immorality of the bosses or of anyone else.

A blunderbuss and a fishhook can represent the entire wealth of a family. But the men don't have the strength to use them. They prefer to kill one another for a few grains of food or some shoddy item. Everything is precious, everything rare. Sometimes they're without sugar for weeks, and the kids eat licorice roots. A pinch of salt can touch off a knife fight.

The seringueiros don't even have any clothes—the tears in their rags make them so indecent that they can't leave their stream. What civilization means to them is: not to be naked, not to be mistaken for the Indians. So they stay where they are. Sometimes they manage to sew up their clothes, but because there's no soap and they do not wash, they stink, and no one dares to descend the cataracts and go where he will be made fun of.

There are generally no medications, no sanitary aids, no doctor, and no nurse. For an area larger than the whole of France, there is one trunk of remedies in a station of the S.P.I. Instead of distributing them, the official sells them for the price of gold to the fazendeiros and the rich. A poor man who falls sick is doomed. Nobody helps, particularly not his boss. If a seringueiro has had an accident, he's useless for future work and the seringalista abandons him to his fate. It's a favor to amputate a man's arm with a knife. Then the amputee makes out by himself. There are no laws . . .

It can happen that a traveller requests hospitality. So the head of the family, the seringueiro, stays up to talk with him until the small hours; he has a fierce need to express himself, yet he no longer has any language, any conversation, any ideas. Everything that he relates has to do with the different events of fishing, hunting or the borracha, or what happened yesterday, what happened today, if a boat met with disaster, or if there's anything to eat. Sentences that sum up a lifetime . . . They are always linked to practical remarks, like saying to a priest that the pages of his breviary would make good paper for rolling cigarettes.

An obsession for tobacco. Smoking is a vital necessity. A poor defense against the swarms of midges which explode around the men as they talk. Cordo tobacco and molho tobacco, tobacco from scraps and from grass. Visiting one of these men, you wrap yourself up in tobacco smoke, but there is never enough of it. So you wrap yourself up in his rags as if it were mosquito netting, and dress to the neck in cast-off clothing. To hold a conversation under these conditions, breathing in the useless smoke and listening to such monotonous words, is a torture.

Seringueiro. Poverty without succor, hunger without cure, and vice without punishment, unless it's the eternal punishment of complete debasement. For the enslavery by way of grocery still goes on; it actually gets worse beyond the cataracts. After every waterfall the price of everything the seringalista sells rises in his account book.

All the seringalista's groceries that come from Manaus have already undergone an increase of 223 per cent over the original cost before they reach the rapids. They break down like this:

	PER CENT
Original cost	100
Minor damages	8
Losses	10

Risks	10
Costs of transportation	60
Storage	5
Profits	30
Total	223

But at every cataract, these sums double or triple. In the end, you don't even know by how much, and it's really not very important. The seringueiro's debt is so huge that he would need several lifetimes to pay it off. So it's quite understood that it's to the boss' self-interest not to give him things at fabulous prices, but to give him nothing, or almost nothing. It's misery without even the idea of a fiesta or an orgy. They cost too much. It's enough that the seringueiros, among themselves, gratify the vices and crimes of the poor, that cost nothing.

Violence and fear. The seringueiros are haunted by terror. You can never quite kill all the wild Indians. There are still whole tribes beyond the falls. From the fathomless depths of the jungle, hordes of naked men emerge and act with rapidity and precision—attacking all the white men, rich seringalistas and poor seringueiros alike. They massacre everything that breathes.

In 1956, on the Juruena, six seringueiros, young strong men, disappeared. All that was found of them were some remnants of human carcasses beside the carcasses of their huts. The bones of their forearms were suspended from their own cabins. Close by, near the ashes of a fire, some grisly remains of carbonized tibias and cooked flesh. These men had been eaten.

In 1957, on the little Rio Branco, a tributary of the Guaporé, a family was exterminated. The Indians set fire to everything, even the borracha that was ready to be embarked. The bodies had been put into the defumador, and were so crammed in that it took hours to extricate them. No one succeeded in pulling the arrows out of their riddled bodies.

There are countless stories of the cruelty and treachery of the Indians. One seringueiro lived at the north end of a lake. Opposite, some Indians began to build a craft. The white lent them an axe for their work. When the canoe was finished, the Indians climbed in, crossed the water very calmly, and killed the man and his wife, and tore off the hands of their two children, who were sleeping in hammocks.

Another time, four seringueiros met some very friendly Indians who asked, as a peace sign, for two guns and two knives. As soon as the precious gift was received, the Indian chief tapped on the ground with his foot. It was the sign

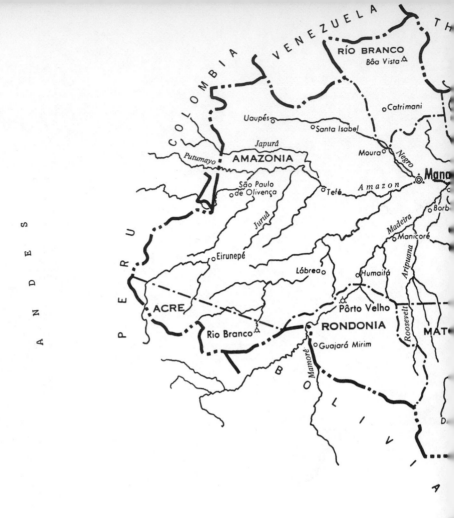

ANDES

COLOMBIA
VENEZUELA
TH

RÍO BRANCO
Bôa Vista

oCatrimani

Uaupés
oSanta Isabel

Japurá
Putumayo
AMAZONIA
Moura
Negro
Mana

São Paulo
de Olivença
Teté
Amazon
Barb

PERU
Juruá
Madeira
oManicoré
Aripuana

oEirunepé
Lóbrea
oHumaitá

ACRE
Pôrto Velho
RONDONIA
MAT

Rio Branco
Guajará Mirim

B
Mamoré
Roosevelt

O
L
I
V
I
A
D

A

P

BRAZIL

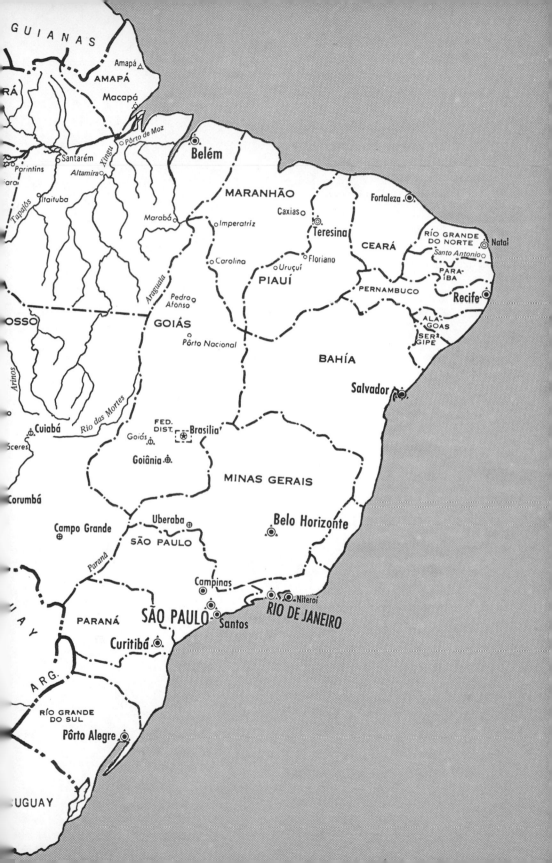

for the Indians to stab the seringueiros with the weapons they had just received.

Terror. The upper Aripuaña and its tributaries are very rich in rubber. The seringueiros go there when the waters are high, and life is, as it were, stopped. They go from tree to tree in a canoe, gashing the semisubmerged trunks. No Indians at that time along the swollen rivers—they have taken refuge in distant hills. But then the ebb begins. The seringueiros are obsessed with the thought of the Indians. Among themselves they talk of nothing but the Indians. From March on, they keep a watchful look-out. Eventually the word runs round: "There are traces of Indians having passed, on the other side of the river." Then it's a stampede. The men of the borracha leave the region to the savages.

The seringueiros' anguish when confronted by the Indians . . . But how much greater is the Indians' anguish in the face of the whites. For one dead "civilized," an entire village is attacked, a tribe wiped out. Endless reprisals from each side.

Still, in all of this, the role of the wretched seringueiros now is secondary, for the collection of borracha is no longer the most important occupation. The seringalista, the feudal chieftain of the jungle, has discovered that there are many other kinds of profits to be extracted from Amazonia. The new wave of adventurers who are arriving, and who include men of every kind, even the incomprehensible American pastors, have given him ideas. He becomes a fazendeiro, owner of the jungle and all it contains. According to his requirements, he kills, subdues or spares the Indians. To help him, he has the S.P.I., the Service for the Protection of the Indians, founded by Rondon, whose employees are prepared to hand over the Indians at the lightest whim of a "big man."

A CERTAIN Father Pucci accomplished an extraordinary odyssey on behalf of the propagation of the true faith, from the Xingu all the way to the Rio Roosevelt, across more than five hundred and fifty miles of hell. His witness reveals the degree of insane anguish which overwhelms Indians confronted by what is called progress.

The last civilized outpost on the upper Juruena. A shack, and, as its boss, an S.P.I. employee, less of a brute than most. Father Pucci arrived there right in the middle of a "nasty incident." A tribal chieftain had been locked up and was in the middle of pleading his cause in the few words of Portuguese he knew, with the gutteral sounds of his own dialect and much gesticulation, to the senhor of the Service for the Protection of the Indians. The latter was bawling him out and threatening him with the tronco. Out of the goodness of his heart, he had gone into the chieftain's village to look after a sick Indian, who died of the fever minutes later. The Indians had then decided: "It's the whites' fault; they will all have to be killed, and we'll begin with this one." Some seringueiros had materialized with their rifles and rescued the S.P.I. gentleman, who had fled to the log walls of his station. Fifty-seven out of a hundred Indians had disappeared into the jungle. Only the old chieftain, who knew from experience that flight was no guarantee of safety, remained behind. He had come to the S.P.I. station with his Indian faithful, some forty men and women, to beg for pardon. But in spite of his explanations, he now was being threatened with every kind of punishment.

It was at this point that the priest arrived. "Leave them to me," he instructed. And he preached to the Indians for nine days, distributing holy pictures and useful presents. Conversion was easy, but the priest was still dissatisfied. "I have to have the others, the fifty-seven who ran away." "It's impossible to get near them," cried the S.P.I. man, "they are very ill-disposed, and nothing is more dangerous than discontented Indians." But the chieftain quavered: "I will send people to look for them, and they will come."

He sent some messengers to the abandonned maloca and to distant and mysterious hideouts. There was a long, long wait. Then, one night, the tribe's witch doctor and the chieftain's own son, the leaders of the "rebellion," approached the station. Instead of coming in, they prowled around it, with their bows arched. Behind them were shadows brandishing clubs—the other deserters. After furtively tramping around for hours in the darkness, they decamped once again.

The priest said suddenly: "I myself shall bring God to these unfortunates. I shall walk through the jungle until I find them. The chieftain will accompany me on this holy expedition, as shall his followers. He and his people have just been baptized; they will guide me until I can confer the sacrament upon their separated brethren." In vain did the S.P.I. gentleman protest.

A short while later, the priest entered the jungle with his converts. They were engulfed in the titanic world of greenery and water. Three hundred yards of swamps, of waist-high watery putrefaction. Then a much vaster inundation, a rio stagnating sullenly upon the plain it had invaded. It took two and a half days to cross this expanse, all the more difficult because it was bristling with a forest of bamboos rising from the mud like stakes. A breach had to be made through the dense mass. At an order snarled by the chieftain, two sturdy Indians took up a position at the head of the column, hacking a path with axes. A third completed the opening with the help of a knife.

During the journey, an aged Christian, an Indian from the priest's distant parish, carried some preserves on his back. The priest had a can opened for every meal, and shared it with the chieftain. One day the latter said, "I want all of it—all the preserves." And by himself he ate it all. The priest was reduced to the Indians' food, a sort of paste which they kneaded at every halt. By using all his authority, he induced them to cut their nails with a pair of nail clippers which he produced from his cassock. It caused general merriment. The holy man soon realized that he had to renounce any hope of cleanliness for the Indians.

A cabin belonging to seringueiros. The Indians refused to go near it and remained hidden. The priest, emerging alone from the jungle, was a miraculous apparition. The seringueiros made him drink some alcohol and asked him to celebrate mass. He explained the kind of natives he was with. They replied that this was a bad tribe which would kill him at the first opportunity, and said, in a burst of pity, "Father, if you would like to be saved from them, our seringalista has just provided us with guns and bullets . . . "

Predictably, when they arrived at the tribe's maloca, it was empty. The huts were intact, but there was no one, not even a dog or a parrot. The chieftain explained to the priest:

"The fifty-seven of my tribe who have disappeared are far away. They are afraid of the seringueiros, but they are even more afraid of a powerful Indian tribe of some hundreds of warriors, who want to kill us all and pursue us relentlessly. So the people of my tribe have taken refuge in a secret place known to us alone. We will make our way to them, but the going will be very dangerous."

Some gashes on the trees. Suddenly, in a kind of clearing, traces of the enemy Indians. "It's the Nambiquaras, who have declared war on us. They passed this way." The only sign of the Nambiquaras was some huge arrows planted in the bark of the trees, pointing in the direction of the hideout of the chieftain's men. At once, a magical ceremony was performed by the chieftain and the new Catholics.

The trip continued. The good priest noticed that the column was missing two men. The cacique told him, "I have sent them off to see whether the Nambiquaras are ambushing our route." Should he believe the old man, this solemn, yet seedy, Mathuselah of the jungle, who resembled an enigmatic bat? But where was the enigma? Was the peril the one which was taking place inside the head of this person, or the one being played out in the jungle? The priest wondered more and more often whether his real assassin might not be the chieftain, with his disconcerting appearance, so noble sometimes, so revolting a few moments later. Could the chief have "invented" the Nambiquaras simply in order to deceive him better?

A few days later, the column came upon the two men who had disappeared. They were taking a peaceful nap beneath the massive shelter of some trees that they had felled. The sleepers, when shaken awake, reported, "There is no immediate danger. The Nambiquaras are not in this area." Then the whole group set fire to three or four great trunks that had been painstakingly cut and stacked up. It made a titanic bonfire which would last for a week. Everyone went to sleep beneath the protection of its flames.

Then, in the darkness outside the fire, was heard the cry of the mucucaure—the wild cock. The startled priest recognized it. But then the chieftain, pursing his old lips, reproduced the sound—it was a pre-arranged signal. Not for the murder of the priest, but for the rediscovery of the tribe. A powerful, muscled body dashed up, making a dancing shadow against the incandescent hearth. It was the chieftain's son. Other bodies arrived, in a flow of bows and muscles. Among them, a stunted figure, the witch doctor, and just a few women, the women's corps of the tribe. In all, the group was the famous fifty-seven who had refused to surrender to the whites and who, since then, had been constantly tracked by the Nambiquaras. They formed the tribe's army, its stormtroopers. Those who had remained with the chieftain were the aged, the weak, the ordinary women and the children.

It had all been calculated, as the cacique revealed to the priest: "The witch doctor had drunk the juice of the plants which gave insight. He had told me to go to the station, and he had told the stronger men to disappear into the jungle. After smoking the grasses which give sight, he had foretold that I would escape from the whites and my warriors would escape from the Nambiquaras. He knew that we would all find each other again safe and sound, but that to do this, we had to go a great distance."

The marvel of fire—for the hunted warriors had extinguished the portable brands which are the electric lights of the jungle and had lived without any light for weeks. Now they plunged their hands into the huge brazier to snatch out burning embers, illuminating the night like so many stars held in the fingertips.

The joy of the tribe . . . but anguish for the priest. Wouldn't this be the moment for the chieftain's people, so overjoyed at their own escape, to sacrifice him? Wasn't he the enemy in their power, the representative of that "white evil" which they detested as much as the "Indian evil" of the Nambiquaras? The priest was afraid of being the choice dessert at the feast which was being prepared.

The children disappeared to look for honey in the jungle. The men departed to hunt. The women cut up balls of manioc—which had been previously smoked and hardened in the three-tiered ovens of the maloca, after being boiled continuously for two or three days. These enormous things, which looked like round cheeses or heads of the dead, were the Indians' preserves, and were edible for several years. The tribe used to bring them with it when it decamped. Now the cooks were soaking several of them in water carried from the river. The manioc reverted into a soft, sticky paste, which the women cooked in a boat-shaped well, between the cinders and the flaming trunks of the bonfire. The result was a kind of Breton crêpe.

The men returned with the corpse of a jacaré—a crocodile. It was skinned and cut up, and pieces of the flesh were stuck onto poles, which were used as spits. Its head, abandoned, lay to one side foolishly. An Indian removed the eyes and fried them. Sputtering. A liquid ran out like egg white. The Indians had a remarkable capacity for gorging themselves.

The best pieces were served to the priest. Despite the general appetite, there was clearly no question of eating him. On the contrary, they made him eat, with the most respectful concern.

They slept like animals. The next day, at dawn, there emerged from the vegetation a kind of monster, a walking bowl. But it was a man, and even an Indian. He was swollen all over. He was suffering from dropsy, his whole flesh loaded with water. And he came to beg for water! He was given some, and by way of thanking for it, he disclosed:

"I live all alone. Nobody wants anything to do with me. But I know everything. The Nambiquaras are advancing towards you. They are two days march away."

The porous bowl disappeared. The captain turned humbly to the priest:

"We want to go with the Father. Where he goes, we shall follow him; for we are too persecuted by other tribes and by other whites. But the priest, he is good. He will protect us."

An igarapé. The priest used its muddy, brackish waters to baptize the recovered fifty-seven pagans. After the ceremony, after a blessing and prayers to the Virgin, they started again on their long march. Weeks and weeks of sinking in swamps. Water everywhere, to such an extent that it was impossible for the column to halt until they located, for the approaching night, a few square yards of firmer ground, a little island where they could stretch themselves out. Without this precaution, they would have been absorbed by this shapeless world, where they sank, where they were, as it were, sucked in, inhaled, where they had to struggle to wrench their bodies from the nameless, vast fetidity, where to survive they had to half-float, half-swim. They advanced, not like real men on their legs, but like hybrid, indeterminate creatures, whose bodies, limbs and heads could no longer be distinguished, so intertwined were they, so encrusted with slime.

Rainy days they crawled ahead, rainy nights they slept like logs, a leaden sleep in spite of the nightmares, the fears that came from the unknown, from an abnormal noise piercing the doors of sleep to reawaken awareness, the yearning to die breeding like a cancer. Danger was like a bell, ready to clang in their heads amid the orchestra of snores. And the priest alone, more lost than a man can be, in the depths of the abomination of nature, the priest alone with his flock of Indians tracked by other Indians, the priest who did not always succeed in having faith in his own flock.

Water, water everywhere. It fell from above as well—from the sky or from the vegetable vaults of the jungle overhead, which, like a waterproof cloth that slowly but surely became saturated and leaked, let the rainstorm drip through, drop by drop. It was cold, too. The chieftain was starting to cough. As he listened to the sneezes, the priest became even more anxious. If a flu epidemic were starting, the Indians would say, "It's the white man, the priest, who's to blame. His magic must be bad. To wipe out the plague, we must kill him." But the next day, they came upon a clearing where the sun shone—the marvelous, redemptive sun. All was yet well . . .

All the same, they were hungry. The balls of manioc had been finished. But a young boy, whose Christian name was Alfonsino, took aim with his arrow at a bird perched in the black roof of the jungle. The tiny point took shape, as the bird plummeted and became flesh to kill, to eat alive. Several other birds fell from the clouds in the same way. The bellies of the priest and the Indians filled up somewhat.

The empire of water. But water that was deeper and more uniform, spreading out like a sheet. It was the great river: the most desolate, fever-laden, and dangerous in Brazil—the river which the young Rondon had explored at the side of the former president of the United States, Theodore Roosevelt. The name of the famous American had remained; so did the telegraph line. A tunnel through the jungle, with its cable, and, beneath, a service path roughly cleared of brushwood.

They walked on. They had to cross the river. The current was raging and a waterfall thundered nearby. The priest's Indians built him a raft. They put it into the water, swimming around it, pushing and pulling it with their hands. It tossed on the waves, on the point of capsizing. One slip on the part of the men—fish, and the priest on his planks would have been sucked down by the whirlpool.

The bank—the liquid which was a little less liquid—was reached.Theywalked on again. Behind them, the thunder of the falls disappeared. A house. Almost a real house. Some telegraph workers with the look of normal men, tanned and withered though they were, snatched up their rifles at the sight of the incredible human troop. Before the gunshot could burst out, the priest came forward from the crowd and made the sign of the cross. He said, "I come from the Xingu with my converts." Incredulity. Long explanations. When they were finally convinced, the white men fell on their knees before the man of God to receive his blessing. But they had barely got up when they asked him, "What are you going to do with these savages? There are too many of them in these parts. We don't need them . . . "

Poor Indians! They were redundant. They were a vast distance from their own maloca, and they could not even return there, walking for weeks or for months, making the fantastic trek again in the opposite direction—because the Nambiquaras, because the whites in that region would kill them. But, by the Rio Roosevelt, would their fate be any better? The chieftain came to beg the priest:

"I and my men have followed you; I have always been faithful to you, I have saved your life many times. So stay here with us. Otherwise we shall die, I know. We shall die, and it will be because of you."

The priest replied:

"I have to return to the city of civilized men. But before I leave you, I will have another and more beautiful maloca built for you. And I will have a church built. The Lord will watch over you and yours. And within a year I shall return to give you communion."

The priest, more of a skeleton than a flesh-and-blood disciple, took the canoe which would bring him to the world of true Christians and the truly civilized. Ceremonies and prayers before he embarked. The whole tribe watched him sorrowfully—a tribe in trousers because a seringalista had offered some old clothes to the priest for his flock, so that they should be decent. The holy man, crouching in his craft, kept his eyes focused on his converts disappearing over the edge of the vanishing horizon. Yet still they stood there, in the same place, silent and motionless. And the priest asked himself, "Will they stay where I have located them? How can one foresee what they will do? They are so suspicious and fickle, so changeable . . . "

IV THE MYSTERIES
OF RONDONIA

"I'M THE loser—but Rondon has lost much more. It's in his Rondonia that the worst horrors are being committed. Most of the whites in the Amazonian jungle are over there, beyond the Rio Roosevelt, and so that's where there is the most greed, and the most massacres."

Orlando Vilas Boas was speaking sulkily. His pout reached from his face to his belly. His features had that thick, tense stupidity which is so dangerous on the face of real killers. But Orlando's heavy mask was only a way of showing that he wasn't pleased. He was a weighty block of dissatisfaction, waiting to be assuaged by a good bawling out. Meanwhile he muttered away, his eyes riveted on goodness knows what.

Claudio didn't seem to exist any longer. It wasn't that he was afraid of his brother, who, in his eyes, was even more of an enfant terrible than a leader. But he was sad, too. Orlando's annoyance weighed a ton; Claudio's was weightless. While Orlando filled the whole room, Claudio was just a human sliver, a bearded leanness lost in a corner. This is how he is when he is depressed.

Claudio can remain in his moods for weeks. Not Orlando. He has to explode. He denounced the Brazilian world and the Brazilian milieu; he was particuarly hard on the higher-ups, the upper crust, in other words the people in the Senates and the billionaires, all manufactured in the same mould, all made with the same fierce, enterprising greed that exists only in new worlds.

It is all due to money that so much that is shameful is perpetrated in the jungle as it continues to reveal new money-making products. But always, always, one has to begin by killing off the Indians. This is so obvious that sometimes an ordinary individual gives the command for a massacre. At Rio de Janeiro, at São Paulo, Cuiabá, Goiana, Belém or Manaus, a peace-loving and respectable businessman can just as easily sign a bill as order the extermination of a tribe which is inconveniencing the profits of a mine or a tree-felling concern. Often a bank is involved in the enterprise, and takes a share in financing it—although the price is not high. The local authorities, and sometimes the federal ones, know what is going on, and of course, you have to have a senator or a governor up your sleeve. Easy enough. Almost always the Service for the Protection of the Indians is at your beck and call. Its agent in the area is positively enthusiastic; he gives instructions for the expedition and assures a moralistic and judicial "cover" for the murder of the Indians. He is prepared to swear that the savages are a bad lot, in open revolt, assassins themselves, and cannibals. Genocide becomes a work of civilization. But this argument is kept in reserve for any snags, when there have been some indiscretions. Which is rare, as everyone has agreed on silence. A fat stack of bank notes for the V.I.P.s of the Senate of the state concerned, and a very small packet for the shabby, diligent official of the Service for the Protection of the Indians.

This is the new face of capitalism in the eternal virgin forest. This is the face so odious to the Vilas Boas. Claudio shrinks from it in horror and takes refuge in his flute. But Orlando is obliged to come to terms with it—with the evil in Cuiabá and Rio de Janeiro.

He had been fighting for days to save at least his Xingu and its Indians. But this time it proved too much, even for him. He had hoped, but he had been overwhelmed. This explained his convict looks, his evil stubborn expression, his glare of defiance and refusal. A refusal which he knew to be futile . . . Poor Orlando! In the end, he didn't explode; he even became quite cheery. He no longer held himself in check, but what he unleashed on me was not his anger, but his truth:

"Eulogies of the Vilas Boas brothers—Brazil is full of them, in the press, on the lips of ministers. We're suffocated, Claudio and I, by these tons of panegyrics. Why all these compliments? Because they need us as camouflage. To hide all the rest. To conceal all the crimes. Because there are always further atrocities in Amazonia, which is reawakening once again to the lure of profit. It's a new epidemic of desire, as so often in the past. These flowers that people shower upon us—they'd like them to be on our corpses! We're a nuisance, and they would like us dead. And, while we wait for that, we are paid only in words. I've just been refused the supplementary credits that I've requested. I've just been definitely forbidden certain projects. This means that I'm completely paralyzed. Thousands of Indians are going to be sacrificed quite close to me, without my being able to do a thing."

I already knew some of this. But for him to pour out on me his bile so completely, Orlando, since hearing of the first refusals, must have completely lost his cause in the big ministries of the big cities. Because, usually, he still had some prudence. But this time he stopped at nothing:

"I never met Rondon, with his eagle's head, his tanned skin and his smile of enigmatic goodness. And yet he's been my patron. He made me decide to dedicate myself to the Indians. It happened twenty-five or thirty years ago. Central Brazil was virgin territory in those days, unknown land defended by thousands of ferocious natives. I wanted to go into it. Perhaps I, too, would have yielded to the yearning to kill. One day, on the barbarous and hostile banks of the Rio das Mortes, I was handed a bit of paper. It was a telegram. I was astonished that a telegram could reach me in such a desolate spot, but even more amazed when I read Rondon's signature: 'I've heard about you. I am trusting you to pacify the Xingu without bloodshed, just as I myself pacified the Mato Grosso and the upper Madeira.' How did he know of my existence? I was a nobody then, just a young nut who wanted to plunge into the mysterious land of Amazonia. So many others had tried in vain, had killed and been killed! And he, the great desbravador, was designating me his disciple! He was then at the peak of his glory, an international figure, a marshal, the Indians' friend and well-loved civilizer, the hero with unstained hands who'd opened up the jungle from the slopes of the Andes and Cuiabá all the way to Pôrto Velho and Manaus. You know all that, of course, but you don't know that I swore an oath to be worthy of Rondon, to make all the vast expanse of Central Brazil into an 'Indian kingdom,' a land where the Indians would be happy.

"A laughable oath, for the whole of the center of Brazil, as impenetrable as it is, has been ransacked by the whites. Their avidity is a terrible thing. You already know about the misery of the seringueiros and the slaughter of the Indians . . . All this carnage for relatively paltry results, for a few thousand tons of poor quality rubber, a few handfuls of diamonds, a few pinches of gold. Yes, I've been beaten by the lust for wealth. I've been crushed by a bloody and empty dream.

"But Rondon, as I've said, is the real loser. The worst horrors of all are committed against the tribes that he protected and loved, on the lands he discovered. In Rondonia we've reached rock bottom. Large-scale murders for the sake of cassiterite, minerals, precious woods, rare gums and veins of gold. It's a jungle of marvels exaggerated by the imagination. There's uranium, petroleum, everything, or so they say. It's madness. But it's a madness based on one solid piece of evidence—the presence of Americans, some of them genuine, most of them men of straw. We are assured that their pilots have photographed the entire jungle, and their geologists have prospected all the soil. Oh yes, there are too many Americans: real pastors and fake ones, agents of trusts in disguise, purchasers, intermediaries of Wall Street, agents of the

C.I.A., military advisers, counselors of all sorts, down-at-heel vagrants, bespectacled university types. You hear every kind of tale—that American companies are operating under names borrowed from good Brazilian families and have bought up half the land, almost all the spongy floor of the jungle, where the ground is barely formed, rotten and decomposed ground whose guts are supposed to be made entirely of metal. Some stories are even more explicit: the governor of Rondonia has been bought by these companies as a tool, with the title of 'technical advisor.' Whether the gossip is true or false, it's deadly. In at the kill are the whole world's adventurers, just as they were fifty years ago.

"The traders of Cuiabá, Pôrto Velho and Guajará-Mirim—the materiros—are actually much more than merchants; they call the game. These are moneyed men, respectable and discreet, with a fat bank balance and those solid 'connections' which you can't do without in Brazil. These are the elderly gentlemen who've seen it all, and 'understood' it all. They probably arrived as young treasure-hunters, but they've grown to understand that, to succeed, you have to be inside the system that really makes money—the grocery business. To hit the jackpot, a man sells no matter what for thirty or forty times its price to people—whom he then controls, and forces to do what he wants.

"The first sign of prosperity is the town store and the seringal in the jungle—with sixty or a hundred miles' range along a river and no limits into the interior. But the seringal is often nothing but a front for other activities: contraband in cocaine and arms, for example. If he's been able to gain people's respect, if he's been able to win the esteem of the police and the authorities, then he becomes a real matereiro—a gentleman seated behind his counter, who is perfectly at home in the corridors of the Senate, yet who goes in person into the most dangerous parts of the jungle. Many of these people were originally Levantines, Greeks, Armenians, men without a country. To succeed, they must fear nothing, neither killing nor being killed. They must have a keen and merciless intelligence.

"The big matereiro is involved in every coup. And God knows opportunities exist in Rondonia, with its rumors, speculations and mining schemes! He's equipped with a plane, a boat, a broadcasting station; he may even have his own aerial armada, his own fleet, and his own telecommunications network. He also has ears everywhere. This allows him to buy, sell and resell all the fictitious or genuine eldorados. He is the real estate agent who deals in mystery, often making money out of nothing, from lakes and jungles which contain nothing whatever of the promised treasure. But sometimes it's the 'real thing.' This always happens very far away, where there are still some Indians surviving. And for every new eldorado of Rondonia, the slaughter of the Indians in that remote spot begins anew, with the efficiency born of habit, the composure that comes from experience, and an extraordinary cruelty, the legacy of centuries of fear and hate . . .

"That's how the Cintas Largas tribe, the 'Wide Belts,' was suppressed. Not a horror was left out, from the poisoned candy, the machine-gunning and dynamiting from the air, to the finishing-off of the survivors by columns of killers. All of this, thanks to an abundance of lei on the 'territory' of the indigenous Indians—it's a wood of considerable market value which a senhor of Cuiabá wanted to exploit."

Orlando fell silent. But I knew about that bit of butchery. It had happened in the valley of the Rio Aripuaña. For a very long time the Cintas Largas had been corpse-eating and cannibalistic warriors, the terror of the jungle until they were put down by military and civil authorities. The army waged 'colonial' campaigns against them and was followed by civil servants who made the peace. A peace which left only a handful of Cintas Largas alive. These few survivors at least used to enjoy some sort of happiness in their last villages. They were so poor, reduced to so little, and, more important, were so remote from anything on the banks of their swampy river Aripuaña, that it seemed that nothing could happen to them. Alas, in the jungle, greed is always on the prowl. A Cuiaban notable by the name of Junqueira learnt that lei—a rare and precious wood used in cabinet-making, and worth a fortune—grew in abundance in the Cintas Largas' jungle. What a waste to leave it to nature! But to exploit it, he had to kill. A very simple equation based not on hatred but upon profit. A matter of business.

It began with a black pinpoint in the sky. A small single-motor plane, a Cessna, was scanning the monotonous black carpet of the jungle. A sudden rent in the vegetation—the hole made by the clearing, the Cintas Largas village. One could see the huts on their stilts, and Indians leisurely going about their small affairs that dated from prehistory. How could they suspect that the thing approaching them in the air was modern death? Like a bird of prey, the plane circled above its objective, the village built just as it had been built millenia ago. Then came the bombing. A perfectly ordinary, run-of-the-mill bombing, rather paltry really. The familiar noise and images of dynamite, explosions and smoke. But to the Cintas Largas, it must have seemed like the Apocalypse.

The detonations shattered the huts, the straw roofs, the beam trunks, the jars of manioc, the human bodies. Flames and ashes. Fire licked up onto the homes: a few moments of red bouquets of flame, and then just rubbish. Men and women toppled to the ground, ravaged corpses. Others fled wildly towards the eternal, immobile, protective jungle, which nothing can tame. But some of these, in their stampede across the chaos, were caught by bursts of steel, and fell. Few reached the wall of vegetation.

The plane disappeared to come dive-bombing down again, almost to the level of carnage. It strafed. Where the cockpit panels had been removed, the gunners shuddered on their machine guns. They couldn't hear much because of the thunder of the motor, but they could see. They aimed their hail of bullets at anything that wasn't completely wiped out or dead in the village—on stumps of wall that hadn't altogether collapsed, on bodies that were still twitching. Finally they 'sprinkled' the first few yards of the jungle . . .

The orders had been for total extermination. But the final liquidation of those Indians who had escaped the dynamite was achieved by the hand, the knife, or the bullet. Some 100 miles or so away was a seringal. Two or three groups of men set off from it armed with Tommy guns and machetes. The expedition was commanded by a Chico Luis. So much per Indian head, he'd been promised. Along with him he took professional assassins only, dipped in the steel of Amazonia.

After sixty terrible days, they flushed the Indians out of the brushwood. A group of some twenty Cintas Largas were encircled in the thick of the jungle. Each 'civilized' man machine-gunned every living thing ahead of him. The Indians were so exhausted from being hunted down, and from fear and hunger, that they hardly defended themselves. Their white assailants were not much better off physically, but they possessed the strength that the fever of murder bestows. Not one Indian escaped. One old woman implored them, but without conviction, as if it were a ritual of good manners; then she was silent, her eyes open: one of them leveled his gun at her stomach and pulled the trigger as he said, "Let's get rid of Grandma right now." Two or three Indian girls were young and pretty. They had to provide amusement for the killers, before they were killed. An ancient law of the jungle. Another ancient law: stabbing the children. The pretext was that if they were left alone in the jungle, they would die a yet crueler death.

One afternoon, a second group of Cintas Largas was cleaned up near a river. After the work was done, the chacinadores—the killers—heard the sound of a child's sobs coming from the scene of the slaughter. "We didn't do such a great job," they said. Under the piles of bodies riddled with bullets, they discovered a young mother and her little girl, still alive. A great diversion. Fun for all. Reward for their hard work. The savage, still sprawling in the blood of the massacre, tried to protect the child by lying on her, shielding her with her body. Coarse laughter. Huge hands of men about to enjoy themselves. The hands seized the woman, turned her over, spread-eagled her for the rape. Other hands fumbled for the child's neck, to squeeze and strangle. But the two Indians fought so savagely that the male group faltered. The child sunk her teeth into a killer's leg and took a piece of flesh out, trying to save her mother. The frightful, taunting pleasure of the chacinadores changed to rage. The Indian woman, seized by panic for her daughter, stopped defending herself, and yielded to the men who came down on her in turn. Her resignation was quite useless, her hope of any pity was vain. An orgy of lust and death. In the intervals between one chacinador getting off her and another crushing her, she looked—and what she saw was that the killer who'd been bitten by her little daughter had started strangling her again, methodically, with the obstinacy of his wounded vanity and his desire for revenge. The child's legs jerked. A 'good' killer took the initiative; he put an end to her agony by a bullet through her head. Her skull exploded in the hands of the strangler, still at his work. The chacinadores began yelling at each other. Chico Luis decided to put an end to all this, grandiosely, by chopping into pieces, with knives, the Indian woman who was still alive . . .

A few more weeks passed in pursuing a few more Cintas Largas. The assassins hardly knew if the Cintas Largas were real or imaginary—they just suspected that there were still some left. And not one could remain alive, because no one must be left to talk. So they continued their exhausting hunt across the jungle and rivers. At last, one day, a victim. One lone wandering Indian woman, perhaps a Cintas Largas, perhaps not. Such was Chico Luis' fury at this disappointing hunt that he forbade the customary embellishments, the usual pleasures. He wanted the woman's blood at once, a river of it. He had her hung up by her feet, and, with a blow of an axe at the level of her stomach, sliced the suspended, inverted body in two. The head and the whole upper part of her trunk fell on the ground. The rest stayed hooked up, a dripping, obscene thing.

It was to Cuiabá, to the Senhor Junqueira, that Chico Luis came to demand his due, for himself and his men: the price of genocide. But it appears that the financier refused to pay him the agreed price, saying, "You've made a mess of the job. Not all the Cintas Largas are dead. Some of them took refuge

with missionaries, and told them everything. There's an even greater
negligence. You let one of your chacinadores take a photo when you were
cutting an Indian woman in two. And the picture's been published in the
newspapers! Thanks to you, I could have problems."

This did not happen. A personality like the senhor is sheltered from any
turmoil, despite the articles and all the evidence. This comes from the fact
that in Brazil there is an established order of things in which nobody bothers
a gentleman who is really rich, especially not one who 'knows how to make'
money. So true is this that Senhor Junqueira continued to display himself
modestly around Cuiabá. Not at all the gallows gangster but the courteous,
urbane, civilized gentleman. He clearly did not change his way of life at
all—that of a fine, respectable citizen; he still had his apertif at the usual time
every day, his whiskey at the bar of Cuiabá's palace. Anybody could
approach him, even people with bad intentions like the journalists of Rio de
Janeiro or special foreign correspondents. He didn't even take the trouble to
defend himself, to wax indignant, or protest. Do believe him, the whole thing
was patently absurd. Questions about the genocide were swept aside by his
moist hands, by his malicious lips. Libels, just libels. If they were true,
wouldn't he have been arrested long ago, instead of letting the pleasant days
slip by? It was a crushing argument. In fact, it was the kind of proof—of
reasoning, rather—that allowed all the senhores to remain untouchable, even
if they had had 200 Indians killed with the whole world knowing it.

As a matter of fact, the kind of violence ordered by Senhor Junqueira—the
aerial bombardment and the manhunt—are frowned upon by the connois-
seurs. According to them, one receives better value by proceeding, these days,
with the gentle approach, by strychnine or smallpox. It is more efficient, yet
less obvious. In Rondonia, how many little Indians died without any fuss,
after sucking candy! Brutal killers, the Chico Luises and their ilk, pursue an
outmoded profession. So much better to have an intelligent, good-hearted
white to go to the tribes in the very heart of the jungle! He must first win the
confidence of the Indians. A long and delicate task. He avoids arousing their
suspicion by an excess of gifts, proposing trade instead. He says to the
Indians: "Kill the animals for me and give me their furs; collect gold from the
river, and in exchange, I'll bring you sacks of salt and sugar." The deal is
made: for several hundred skins and several pounds of precious metal, the
Indians get tons and tons of salt and sugar—impregnated with arsenic. The
white removes himself before the Indians begin to eat and die. It is to his
interest to leave fast.

Is this an increase in sensitivity or is it a refinement of hypocrisy in the executors? In the case of the financiers, it is a perfected insensitivity, an objective insensitivity, an insensitivity that has gone beyond heart, instincts, the emotions or imagination, remorse, or sin. Nothing of the Christian soul, nothing of the conscience of civilized man is at stake. It is as if the Indians were things, just things on the same order as stones, jaguars, or cattle—uniquely destined to serve the superior world of men, in any fashion, by death just as by life. All is permissible because Indians do not exist morally, religiously or metaphysically—except in the eyes of a few priests and ethnologists.

Massacres. Always massacres—but always, or nearly always, in small quantities. Genocides of ten, twenty or a hundred Indians—and who is to hear of them when they occur in the depths of the jungle, when they are, as it were, blotted out by the immensity of nature? It has been done in fits and starts, by continual destruction, by poison or induced alcoholism, for centuries. And yet, if you were to add up the total of the slain, if you could, the figures would be minimal compared with the great hecatombs of Europe, Asia and even Africa. They would be almost nothing alongside the gigantic butcheries of war or revolution that the world has suffered. Despite the hundreds of millions of dead, races repopulate themselves, and even become over-populated. Brazil itself is experiencing a demographic explosion with its whites, blacks, and mixed-bloods. What is peculiar, special and appalling in the case of the Indians is not the number of the victims. It is that they are denied the right to exist; that they are systematically hounded down until there are none at all.

How many tribes have been completely wiped out in what is now the territory of Rondonia! Erased from the world, without even a few survivors. The list of tribes which no longer exist is striking: The Amniapés who used to live on the Rio Mequena; The Apiacas of the middle Madeira; The Aruas of the Rio Branco, a tributary of the Rio Guaporé; The Guarategajas of the Rio Guaporé; The Huaris of the Rio Corumbaria. The Ipotewats of the Rio Cacoal. The Iabutifeds of the Rio Rosinho. The Iabutis, also of the Rio Rosinho. The Caritianas, whose fief was close to the sources of the Rio Candeias. The Caxarabis of the Rio Abuna. The Querquiriwats who once lived along the banks of the Rio Pimenta Bueno. The Macuraps, who used to haunt the rapids of the Rio Branco. The Mialats, formerly settled on the Rio Leitão. The Mondés, who roamed the upper part of the Rio Pimenta Bueno. The Palmeras, men of the interior of the jungle. The Rama-Ramas, who rode along the Rios Anaris and Machadinho. The Sanamaicas, who used to dominate the streams which flowed into the Rio Pimenta Bueno. The Taquateps of the Rio Tamuripa. The Toras, the big tribe of the Rio Madeira. The Urumis of the murky Rio Roosevelt. The Wayoros, who lived by the Rio Colorado.

All these tribes have been exterminated, annihilated, and have vanished. Numerous others have been decimated and almost entirely liquidated, like the Araras of the Rio Gi-Parana, of whom only a few remain, the last specimens, fewer than the fingers on one hand. Elsewhere, where there were once thousands of men and women, a mere ten or so survive, a few dozen, or a hundred human beings, as is the case with the Aricapus or the Maxubis. Sometimes these remnants are "integrated" into civilization at the hands of priests or seringalistas. This is what happened to the last Muras, the last Parecis, the last Bodas Negras, and the last Parintintins. Most of the time the survivors are the slaves of the S.P.I. people who are masters of life and death in their camps.

Yet there still exist a few groups of Indians who are somewhat less subjugated, still somewhat wild. This is an important distinction. There are some who are in permanent contact with the whites, like the Tucumanfeds, the Tuparis, the Urupas and the Wirafeds—in other words, Indians who are controlled, dominated, and in reality serfs. But there are others who have only intermittent contact. These, when they are too ill-treated or too discontented, still have the option of decamping, and of taking refuge in the depths of the jungle and swamps. Sometimes they vanish without a trace, constrained by a fear which counsels them to do nothing, not to fight, but just to hide, to be as if they no longer existed. At other times they make a stand, with their war cries, their war paint, and their poisoned arrows. They are usually won back either willingly or by force—by machine-gunning or persuasion, by bullets or gifts. There are fantastic odysseys of the tribe that is lost and then found—generally minus a few of its members who have been killed in the course of the recuperation. This is what happened to a branch of the Pacaas Novos, a group which still ranges along the Rio Aripuaña. It is the same for the Purubora of the Rio São Miguel.

All this happened in Rondonia—but it is much the same, indeed it has probably been worse, in neighboring Mato Grosso. But in spite of everything, there are still wild Indians, ferociously maintaining their barbarism, such as the Gavios, who number about 1,000. Terrifying. Not only cannibalism, but head-shrinking as well. Numberless men have been eaten—except for their heads, which have been boned and boiled, varnished, macerated and imbued with goodness knows how many juices, and reduced to the size of a monstruous fist which, hairy and simian, is still somehow like the head of the person who owned it in its natural size. A gnomish, bestial yet magical caricature . . .

From the innermost depths of the Green Hell, from the unfathomable Green Hell, painted hordes continue to emerge. Most of the time, they appear only to disappear again—no one knows where. But often that is all it takes. From that point on, these are marked tribes. At Pôrto Velho, the good citizens say: "They must be killed." The priests proclaim, "They must be baptized." The authorities decree "They must be civilized." And sooner or later—depending upon whether the unknown territory of these unknown Indians is of economic interest or not—the process of pacification is set in motion. In other words, the process of the suppression of the Indians, thanks to which the great Indian 'nations' of the centipede river Madeira (each foot being a river or its tributary) have been shattered. There used to be powerful nations from the Madeira's confluence with the Amazon all the way upstream to the rapids, to the serras of the Mato Grosso, and to Cuiabá. One after the other, they were reduced to fragments. All that remains of this mosaic of tribes is a handful of 'integrated' Indians—slaves, servants, collaborators and Catechumens—and a few clans of either semiwild or completely wild Indians. All those corpses, and then nothing but these tiny groups of survivors. The result of the endless punitive or "protective" military expeditions, public or private genocide, evangelism and eldorados—with the coup de grâce given by the Service for the Protection of the Indians. Poor Rondon! Nowhere better than in Rondonia can you see a more precise, a more mathematical application of the system of dismantlement and death.

THROUGH THAT vast stretch of Amazonia, the first battlefield, flows the Madeira itself. It is the axis to be disengaged, the mighty path for penetration; a magnificent river which brings a man to the limits of the jungle, to the Andes of Peru and of Bolivia.

In 1716, the first nation was liquidated, the Toras, who 'held' the banks of the lower Madeira. They were an indigenous tribe who were not too ferocious, and none too 'moral' either. They traded, exchanging their wives and daughters for axes. One lone expedition, commanded by Juan de Barros, was enough to bring them to an end, despite an epidemic which decimated as many Portuguese soldiers as it did Indians. And in spite of a jungle giant—a kind of cedar, with a great sword of a trunk, girdled with huge pendulant branches and garnished with a titanic plumage of leaves. This colossus crashed down onto the leading ship, on the Madeira, crushing Juan de Barros, the greenery forming a sort of leafy shroud over the sunken hull. But the Toras were completely overwhelmed; they were settled in villages, and brought up right; after some years of this solicitude, there was not one of them left alive.

The war against the Muras of the middle Madeira was much bloodier and more bitter. It lasted almost 200 years. The Muras were water gypsies par excellence, pirates of the rios and the igarapés, always on the move, without home or hearth, living on board their slender canoes. Camouflaged, hundreds of miniscule Viking craft used to flash out to attack and grapple. The men used gigantic bows, at least twelve hands high, which were too heavy to be raised in their arms. So they supported them on the planks of their craft, holding one end with their toes. In this way their hands were left free to discharge their equally formidable arrows, which hurtled like swarms of mosquitoes upon their enemies. During the battle, their witch doctors made huge maracas echo in sinister diapasons: sacred music supposed to inspire terror in the victim. After the Muras had finished off their wounded victims, the maracas were replaced, with religious and ceremonial care, upon the portable altars—where they were silent until the next attack.

The whites were waging war against phantoms: the Muras could not be caught. But they were the scourge of the 'colonizers,' returning to the offensive after punitive expeditions had been dispatched against them in vain. They killed the civilized treacherously, robbing and sacking their settlements, their farms, their churches, and even burning their largest ships. They sowed terror with a sort of genius for guile and perfidy, using the art of what would be known, much later, as guerilla warfare.

Towards the end of the eighteenth century, the redoubtable Muras seemed to be tamed. Villages had been built for them, they had been forcibly penned within them, made to till the fields, and converted to Christianity. But many of them escaped from their asylums and used their rediscovered freedom to haunt the whole length of the Madeira once again. Many of the fugitives were captured and executed by the army. Then came the great vengeance of the Muras. In an uprising in their estradas, crazed with blood and blasphemy, they killed, burnt and ransacked everything that lay in their path, rampaging over the country in maddened hordes. The whites' work along the Madeira was completely wiped out.

The nineteenth century. Once again the Muras were cloistered in prison villages. Even their caciques and witch doctors had been corrupted by the concession of privileges, had been won over by the abundance of gifts. They had become the overseers of their own people, on behalf of the white priests who dared not live for long in the place. But the common people protected themselves against the Gospel by sin. They led a life of Sodom and Gomorrah.

The story goes that one day, a "collaborator," no doubt inspired by a wily missionary, said to the crowd: "Your shamelessness is making the protective spirits weep with grief. Do you hear, in the middle of the night, the cocks crowing? It's a celestial warning. If you continue your infamies, one day the earth will shake, the waters will surge, and you will plunge into a bottomless pit." And the story has it that a few years later, the village of the Muras disappeared in a cataclysm.

An edifying legend, no doubt. It appears much more likely that, as the result of a flood, the Muras established their village on a higher bank, and actually grew there in numbers and in demands, until they became a nuisance to the adventurers who were increasingly harrowing the Madeira in search of eldorados. We shall never know exactly what happened, but probably the whites conceived the plan of exterminating the Indians by means of other Indians, and persuaded the Mundurucos, a powerful tribe which had remained in the jungle in its wild state, to attack the Muras, who had been transformed, despite themselves, into 'citizens,' and degenerated by civilization.

There was a second wave of vengeance against the whites, a century after the first. For the Mundurucos had not been able to kill all the Muras. And all the survivors were obsessed by this idea: "The Mundurucos were not the real assassins, but the civilized, who sent them against us. So before we die, we'll at least give ourselves the pleasure of killing as many of them as possible." So the Muras rose one last time, in desperation, against the whites. In their rage, they began by slitting the throats of their own chieftains, whom they looked on as traitors. Once again, they sacked the work of the civilized; they wanted to liquidate civilization. There followed years of lying in wait, of treacherous attacks and bloody treks aboard their warships. But this time the whites were too many and the Muras no longer enough. Whole fleets tracked them on the Madeira, and then up the rivers and the streams. The vise tightened, for no matter which direction the Muras turned, there were tribes ready and able to kill them in flight—as they would kill anyone who crossed their frontiers. A river carousel. The Muras dispersed, hiding by twos and threes. Almost all of them were caught. Of the Muras, there now remain only a tiny number of persons, the ones called 'integrated,' or 'civilized,' who are needed as guides, as beaters in the hunt and as spies in successive expeditions to destroy the other Indian nations. For this is a necessity of the jungle: there is no way of exterminating a group of wild Indians without the collaboration of some subdued ones, who are indispensible as hunting dogs, for picking their way through the indivisible labyrinth of the jungle, and for finding the tribe to be killed.

Now the Madeira was wide open as far as São Antonio and Pôrto Velho. And it was the rubber-crazy Madeira, the evangelical Madeira of the priests, and the Madeira of the Service for the Protection of the Indians. Yet it was all these Madeiras put together that was to result in an infinitely swifter and more forceful technique for exterminating the great tribes of Rondonia. The movement in which everything harmonized to produce the genocide of the most powerful Indian nations. It happened some fifty years ago, well before the little private or semiprivate genocides of these days, which are just the tail end of the whole process.

One of these nations was that of the Parintintins. What an extermination it suffered! These were Indians who were not wholly naked, but whose 'dress' added to their indecency. The men had their penises in very long round tubes—which made them into a kind of elephant trunk. Around their loins, below their buttocks and this monstruous phallus, was a sort of scarf, which emphasized the lines of their bodies. They were very handsome, with smooth, clean, pure features. Around the heads of these Apollos of the jungle was a coronet, with some small feathers in front, and behind, a trail of gigantic, flamboyant feathers, a multicolored river which flowed to their waists. Apart from that, they were without adornment. But, as if in union with the slenderness of their muscles, almost like supplementary muscles, they had marvelously light, powerful bows and arrows. They were great warriors, very numerous and much feared. They were also furiously cannibalistic, and were always battling to procure human flesh. For their expeditions, they had the vast expanse of the jungle between the Aripuaña and the Madeira. Their mortal enemies were the Apiacas and the Mundurucos. They ate a great many of them, and were eaten in their turn, as these tribes were equally cannibalistic. The Parintintins were finally pushed back towards the Rio Roosevelt and the Madeira by a coalition of other Indians. But they remained very voracious.

They displayed a particular rancor towards the whites, who were in the middle of their desbravar of the Rio Roosevelt. Yet these were good whites, for it was Rondon and his men, engaged in planting their telegraph poles. In vain did they offer gifts and propose peace. The Parintintins went on attacking the engineers, the builders and the soldiers who were obliged not to fire, even under a rain of arrows. Rondon himself admitted it: the Parintintins had to be 'civilized.' In 1913, he drafted a plan for their pacification—with, of course, the orders not to kill. He wanted to vanquish the Parintintins by love. He was in the prime of life; he incarnated the State; he was Brazil. It was his greatest moment, and his saddest—for he failed. As soon as Rondon went elsewhere, a collection of sordid interests entered the game, and the upshot was massacre and slavery. The irony lay in the fact that the apparatus set up by Rondon for the safety of the Parintintins was the principal instrument of their destruction.

I am referring to the S.P.I., in its first form. Men were supposed to go and build stations—stations for peace—in the areas through which the Rio Roosevelt and other infernal rivers flowed. They had to remain there, in fortified barracks, constantly besieged by the Parintintins and other savages Constant dread; shrieks from the jungle; the menacing sounds of the maracas. A nightmare of fear. Disease. What a list of fevers—yellow, scarlet and black; what quantities of plagues—abscesses that devoured the blood, the muscles, the very soul of a man. There were no effective drugs in those days against tropical diseases—and even if there had been, who was around to hand them out? The loneliness was absolute. There were no planes. It took weeks and months of hideous treks, by canoe or on foot, to get there, and to get back out. All around lay barbarism; madness watched and waited; one took to drink. Brutality, and the unleashing of primal passions. So how, when the Parintintins launched into a screaming, grimacing, attack, how could the S.P.I. officials not shoot? And so, by pulling the trigger in defiance of Rondon's law, they began the vicious circle of the Service for the Protection of the Indians.

In order not to shoot down the hordes of Parintintins, the S.P.I. men would have had to be saints, like Rondon. They were nothing of the sort—and for many reasons but primarily because of Rio de Janeiro's sabotage. The priests didn't care at all for Rondon, the atheist, the Freemason and the positivist. There were intrigues in the capital. Rondon had managed to get Congress to pass the law which set up the Service for the Protection of the Indians—but he hadn't found a ministry to attach it to. Nobody wanted it, because of the bishops and priests fulminating against it. Eventually an obscure Minister of Agriculture, a somewhat less devout chap than his colleagues, said he would take in the S.P.I. But it was a small, unimportant, ministry, ill-funded—agriculture managed itself in the Brazil of those days—and as a result, the men sent into the jungle to 'protect' the Indians were paid very little. It was as if they had disappeared, ignored and forgotten, absorbed by the vastness of the country. They were left to make out as best they could. Nobody wanted to know about them. And anyway, how could anyone know, when all this happened such a great distance away?

Nonetheless, it permitted the politicians to find a niche for their protegees, who came from the lowest class. They got rid of all the failures, the freebooters, the loonies and the undesirables at one blow. The dregs of society entered the S.P.I., with the title of "officials," entrusted with representing the State where it had never been represented before. A large number of adventurers, with all their wits about them, also 'enlisted.' To make money. To gratify their sadism. What a splendid range of possibilities for daredevils, particularly as they would be covered by an honorable function! They would be sovereigns over the Amazonian dementia. Obviously, these types didn't cherish any illusions about the wages, which were miserly, and in any case, never paid. But if you were bright . . .

So it was that the agents of the S.P.I. very quickly passed from the protection of the Indians to their murder. First, from a vital necessity. They had to kill the Indians, or better still, have them killed, in order not to be killed themselves. The old law of the jungle, forever reappearing . . .

An S.P.I. man was doomed to stay shut up in his post, behind a few poor planks, at the mercy of a powerful Indian tribe. The 'protector' could slaughter a few, some ten or twenty Indians, on his own. But it was not enough. Just the opposite—it was extremely dangerous, for it aroused the wrath of the savages. The one remaining solution for the S.P.I. official was to try to organize a genocide within the rules. To achieve this, he formed alliances with the civilized barons, big or small, of the jungle: all the men in rubber, minerals and contraband. And with the senators, the men of affairs, and the strawmen from the distant States and cities of the Brazilian Far West. Not to mention the police and the military. Every one of them lusting for treasure, territory and trafficking . . .

The S.P.I. man was just a minus alongside these other characters. They owned stacks of money, bands of henchmen, troops of white or Indian slaves, and powerful accomplices. It was up to him to sell himself, to make contacts, to make himself useful—this way he had some extra cash, from services rendered, which stopped him from cracking up from misery and abandonment; this way he could eat. In exchange for this, he was at their disposal. If the head of the station were versatile, he constituted a network of information in the very heart of the jungle; he became a second bureau, operating for the benefit of the senhores whose valet he was. He managed to give them 'leads' thanks to his contacts with the stragglers of the jungle—the caboclos, the seringueiros, and a few enslaved Indians. There was a whole underworld in the world of nothingness. He also played quite a game with the priests or catechumens, who told of this and that despite their suspicions. How could the men of God not speak, even to the 'disciples' of Rondon, when they met up in the middle of the jungle? A word, a gesture of one white towards another, in the midst of these terrors, was a solace.

The S.P.I. man registered all the horrors of the jungle with his ears, and denounced them with his lips. These were by no means news to the senhores, but the value of the poor S.P.I. wretch was that he was an official. As such, he was beyond suspicion, he was telling the truth, and was well placed to activate the administration, the army and the police. Never did he utter sentences such as: "The Indians must be exterminated." But in a sort of ecstasy of honesty, he despatched terrified reports to Pôrto Velho and Cuiabá: "It's a catastrophic situation. The Parintintins are in open revolt. There will be a massacre of whites. You must send volunteers, the militia, the national guard, battalions . . . " The result was indeed a massacre—that of the Parintintins. It was a procedure of extermination which was multiplied mathematically. For the Parintintins, while being slaughtered en masse, managed to kill one, two, three whites from time to time. And as every white corpse was immediately 'paid for' by several hundred Parintintins, the genocide went on in full swing, amid a clear general conscience.

The biggest beneficiaries of the destruction of the great tribes were the S.P.I. people. For from now on they could live off the remnants—as their masters.

There is now an unbelievable number of these "officials." The single primitive shed has been enlarged, and become a squalid labyrinth of cabins, lean-tos, and garbage dumps, a shanty town of chickens and children, and of poor Indians on whom are imposed the rags of minimal decency. Some are barely nourished, others are skeletal. It depends upon which the boss is: good or bad. These days he has an office and an infirmary—and has left them empty rooms: for one thing, he often does not know how to read or write, which means he can avoid the paperwork, and for another, he does not have any drugs, and even if he does get sent some, by a fluke, he usually resells them to neighboring senhores. He has become a rich gentleman, thanks to his store of canned food, his sacks of grain and a muddle of odds and ends, mostly bottles and flasks of rot-gut. And to a few bank notes in whatever he uses as a briefcase.

The ease of the S.P.I. way of life is a product of the work imposed upon the decimated and domesticated Indian tribes. You subject them to the holy law of labor to make them "civilized"—so goes the theory. In practice, the S.P.I. station is a hard-labor camp. The savages are told, "You will cultivate the fields. In the dry season, you will burn patches of the jungle, and plant cereals and vegetables. You will bring us the harvest." The crops form the food of the S.P.I. people, who take everything and leave nothing. If they don't manage to guzzle it all, they sell the surplus to merchants and white traffickers. Total exploitation. What isn't done to the Indians! They are told to chase otters and bring back the skins. To sift the rivers for gold and return with the metal. To gash rubber trees and carry back the borracha. To make trinkets of feathers, bones and clay. These Indians of Amazonia are made to breed animals, when they have never set eyes on cattle, sheep or horses; they are treated less well than the animals they serve. Sometimes their masters in the S.P.I. entrust them with missions of whose oddness they are unaware, like carrying packs of contraband, or spying on and killing someone their masters dislike.

Exploitation. Starvation. Murder. The trilogy of the S.P.I. The Indians are forbidden to waste a second, to sing or to dance. They have to produce, even though they have no concept of "production." The surviving Indians scarcely know that they are Indians.

Some of the S.P.I. people are, apparently, not such swine—but many more span the whole range of executioners and torturers. Extraordinary mistreatment occurs in stations which bear names like "Fraternidad indigena." What punishments! The punishment of "greater starvation"—which must be distinguished from that of "lesser starvation," which is the normal hunger the Indians suffer from every day of their lives, barely eating one meal a day, a few mouthfuls of manioc pancake or fish. For the "greater starvation," the culprit is thrown into "prison," a cell four feet by three. The man has to stay there crouching over the pile of his own excrement, as long as he can produce any. For as he is given nothing to speak of to eat and drink, his entrails wither and his whole body dries up. The Indian's long black hair is like a mad mop over his staring eyes and shriveled carcass, where his ribs seem attached by threads and his limbs are like matchsticks. Sometimes he is left to dwindle away to nothing; usually he is thrown a morsel of bad meat at the last moment—one that the S.P.I. man is trained to recognize.

Punishments of every kind. The whip. The Indian is tied up to a piece of wood, in front of the station. And when the thongs of tapir skin have slit the flesh to the bone, he is left bound to his stake, alone in the sun, with salt in his wounds. And then there is always the tronco. There is the ancient tronco—with holes in a plank, where the limbs are compressed until they become insensible to pain, become paralyzed and atrophy. But there is a more modern one—two wedges which bite deep into the heel, tightened by ropes. These and plenty of other tortures are inflicted to the degree that pleases the official; the degree is sometimes death. It all depends on the official's temper, his pleasure, his fever, his drunkenness or his delirium. The cruelty, the authority over life and death gives him his sense of importance. As he puts it, "There's no other way to civilize these savages."

The S.P.I. is both the instrument of murder and a machine for exploitation. But in spite of this, in the world of horrors which is Amazonia, the S.P.I. is slightly less horrible than the rest. It does "save" a few Indians. That is to say, without it there would be no savages left. For in the last twenty years the senhores and the "civilized," left to themselves, would soon have wiped every Indian out, with their money, machine guns, planes, candy and bacteria. But they had to put the S.P.I. in the picture, for the S.P.I. is, after all, everywhere. Of course, the S.P.I. still helps out in a great many massacres. And it still renders many services. But it also complicates matters, slows things up, stops them from being resolved with a beautiful, definitive simplicity, and even prevents a final solution. For what would become of the S.P.I. officials in their turn if they had no more Indians at all to "protect"? They would be out of a job. So they try to keep enough Indians alive to preserve their bread and butter, while letting enough be killed to satisfy the whites when they are attacked by one of their psychoses of blood. As happened in 1950, in Rondonia, with the Bocas Negras. The S.P.I. played a part in this mighty genocide.

Seen alive, the Bocas Negras are particularly dismaying. They have faces like daubed funnels. Their mouths are painted black, and three black semicircular lines seem to extend their coal-black lips to their ears. This makes a sort of dark hole in the middle of the faces, an oven full of gloom, a yawning cavity to engulf a man. Every face is like the incarnation of cannibalistic cuisine. And indeed the Bocas Negras did eat human flesh, in a stew.

Numerous hordes of these Indians existed where the jungle turned into mato, and the rivers tumbled down from the virtually impregnable serras. In 1942, a reconnaissance was sent out to their territory on the Rio Machadinho. The apparition of some ten armed whites was enough to spread complete panic among thousands of naked Indians—they fled by way of the river on huge boats, they were swallowed up by the jungle, running like madmen. Not an arrow. No one remained in the villages, not even a woman or child. The Bocas Negras abandoned their plantations of manioc, cereals, sweet potatoes and corn. Apparently they did not feast on man alone—they devoted themselves to agriculture. They had fine houses—a genuine primitive civilization. They deserted all of this without the smallest hostile act. How did such a thing happen?

It happened because the Bocas Negras had understood. They knew that if they let themselves be drawn into the most minor combat, if they committed the smallest imprudence, it would be the beginning of the process of extermination, of a death which they tried to escape by cowardice.

Their cowardice was in vain; death would come to them anyway. The civilized had made up their minds. They had only to wait for the right moment to act. They had agents who infiltrated into the tribe's lands, raiding and offering threats and provocations. As their chief spies, they asked one of the most famous and powerful of the seringalistas, Manuel Lobo, who had aided in the destruction of the Parintintins by enslaving those that he could, for two brothers of the Parintintin tribe—such degraded remnants of a glorious race that they would help to destroy another great Indian race.

In 1948, Lieutenant Fernando, an officer of the Brazilian army, disappeared in the jungle, close to the Bocas Negras's territory. The speculations ran riot, and all the whites clamoured for death. The officer's parents proclaimed their son a hero. "A military expedition must be sent to save him if he's been captured; to avenge him if he's been slain." There was a certain amount of foot-shuffling at the S.P.I., where somebody said that some Indians from the mato had reported that they had killed a civilized who had just set fire to one of their villages. But the seringalistas really distinguished themselves. One of them captured forty Bocas Negras, and brought them himself to Pôrto Velho. There was an atmosphere of lynching in the city. Finally, not knowing what to do with them, the authorities had the Indians shut up in the hospital, crowded into a room where they were beaten and given virtually nothing to eat. Their health failed, they caught the flu and began to die. Those who survived were interrogated: they knew nothing about the officer who had disappeared.

The punitive expedition left Pôrto Velho amid an unhealthy excitement. The crowd was hysterical. Women and children stamped and screamed: "Death to the Indians!"

They set off on 16 July, 1948, a strange, motley group of people, with ultramodern equipment. Besides the soldiers in uniform, there were seringalistas, seringueiros, caboclos and garimpeiros—not many of the latter, but the real jungle adventurers, who knew where you could find eldorados in blood. Each was carrying what he could. As their guides, they had the two Parintintins and the survivors of the forty Bocas Negras with head colds, who were made to carry all the heavy equipment on their emaciated shoulders: motors, radio equipment weighing more than 200 pounds, machine guns and Tommy guns, and cases of ammunition. Although they also carried boxes of Vitamin C and all kinds of drugs, they were to serve, without knowing it, as the fatal weapon against the rest of the Bocas Negras, because of their colds. It was their microbes that would settle the matter.

You can see that waging modern warfare in the jungle is a complicated affair, even against Indians. Where is the legerdemain of the bandeirantes of old, where is their audacity and flair? Everything in today's columns is too heavy, too systematic. A slow advance of an interminable file of men subjected to the demands of equipment and technique. It was impossible to discern the Bocas Negras' huts in the monotonous, stony, arid landscape of the mato. The men advanced despite this. There was no water: they had to dig in the ground. At night they stretched themselves out around huge fires. And for all their armament, they were afraid of these invisible Indians.

The next morning a small plane flew over the expedition—a spy plane. Its crew informed the hunters, by radio, that it had at last spotted the Bocas Negras' villages. After parachuting them gifts, the crew had asked the Indians to light three fires on the open space of the "capital," as a sign of peace. This the Indians had done. Conclusion: the column should get there at top speed, to "pacify" these pacific Indians.

Before disappearing, the plane dropped a sketch. The column's first objective was about fifteen miles away. They marched with the aid of a compass in the emptiness of nature. They were soon completely off course, and turned round in a circle. A caboclo appeared, with a message from the airmen in his hand: the spy-plane's radio transmission had broken down. The pilot informed them that he had flown back over the Bocas Negras, and that they were still in their villages. With them was a tall blond man, who, in the middle of a clearing, signalled with his arms to the plane.

A serra: caved-in rocks and a stunted forest, so thick that it was impenetrable. The group made some progress along a barely traced path. The caboclo had told them that it would take four hours to reach the Rio Machadinho. After six hours there was still no river and still no water. At last, at dusk, they encountered, in that landscape of nothingness, a gentleman on horseback, prosperous looking and very much at his ease, in the dress of a gentleman farmer. He was a seringalista. He was interested in the expedition because he wanted to "settle" the Bocas Negras and make them work for him.

"Their first village is quite close now," he said. "Don't kill the natives—there are so few of them left now anyway. Most of them are dying from a mysterious epidemic."

What a spectacle the first village presented! At first it appeared deserted. But there was a stench. Some soldiers, with their fingers on the triggers of their Tommy guns, stooped to enter a large hut through the tiny hole that served as its door. Inside, it was filled with Indians. But—and this explained everything—they were on the ground, covering it with their bodies, a layer of prone figures. The spectacle of the naked and the dead. Some of them were stiffened in motionless hammocks. In the half-light, it was hard to distinguish those who were already dead from those who were dying, and those who were only ill. It was malaria and flu. So the civilizers' task had already been done. Instead of shooting, they had only to order the least afflicted Indians to bury their dead. They sorted them out. Some Indians managed to stand up and keep standing. They dragged the corpses outside, and buried them as one does the garbage, helter-skelter, in such shallow earth that their rigid legs stuck out of the graves. The "grave-diggers" were given something to eat. They didn't have the strength to—except for one couple who were still in very good health. The husband swallowed everything, not leaving a crumb for his spouse. A priest who was accompanying the expedition said that it was a characteristic of the savages not to care about anyone, even their own. Nonetheless, he did his job, baptizing on his own authority sixty Bocas Negras, in articulo mortis, many of whom were children.

In the next village, the troop arrived at the same time as the plague, in fact before it. So the Indians had all the vigor necessary to show their delight and give the expedition a marvelous welcome. They danced all night brandishing bows and arrows, but in a very nice way—it was a ceremony of homage, the ritual of submission. They had accepted civilization. The priest consecrated the maloca to the sacred Heart of Jesus: he cut down trees from the jungle to set up a crucifix, put up an altar with the branches, and celebrated mass.

It was then that a Boca Negra woman died: one of the women who had been to Pôrto Velho, and whom the column had brought back with the remaining of her forty fellows. She expired in a fit of coughing. The population of the village dug her a sepulchre in the side of a hill. Her funeral ceremony took place amid the sobs of the whole gathering. But there was also a deeper sadness, and an overriding suspicion. Had the whites brought the Bocas Negras who had been contaminated at Pôrto Velho back with them to contaminate and destroy all the rest of the tribe, thousands upon thousands of men and women?

The next day there was a raging epidemic; thirty-seven Indians had boiling fevers. Two flickered out at dusk. They, too, were given the customary burial, in deep caverns at the edge of the mato. This time the groans were heartbreaking; the Indians were lamenting for themselves, for they knew that they were doomed. As soon as they returned to the maloca they shut themselves up in their huts to die. On the square of beaten earth outside, there remained only whites—whites who were white enough to resist the virus. In the case of the common cold it is not recommended that killers have too much Indian blood in their veins: it can boomerang.

A hecatomb. Every house was a morgue. It was the men from the expeditionary force who lifted out the bodies—there were no longer enough Indians capable of doing it. Soon there were only a few pitiful survivors in each hut, who were just taking a little longer to die. Here was a youth of eighteen, wandering about alone. Over there were two little old women trying to resuscitate a child already dead. They were pouring water from a pitcher over his body to combat the "spirits of fever." There lay a grandmother in her death throes, with three urchins, one of them still a baby, clinging to her. The children's huge eyes. And when a white approached them, one of them said "good morning." Elsewhere there was nothing but desolation and death.

The next village was deserted. The entire population had decamped before the whites and the evil they were bringing with them. Fresh graves showed that there had already been many victims. The survivors had fled but had first, following ancestral custom, killed the orphans, all the children whose parents had just died. The horror of the savage was added to the horror of the civilized. These children had been buried alive, and the earth trampled down over them by the feet of the Bocas Negras, executing a kind of dance. Other children were found tied up to trees, half-eaten. They had been put there as food for the jaguars, who had indeed deigned to eat parts of them.

The 1,000 or 2,000 Bocas Negras who had not succumbed to the flu were in the wilds. The expedition hunted them in vain. The seringalista on horseback made a reappearance. He, too, had set out to search for them, but for his own benefit. He told how he had been as far as the Blue Mountain, a peak towering over the rocks, but had seen nothing. He confirmed that the Bocas Negras were commanded by a mysterious white man, a madman, a very dangerous individual. "Look out," warned the seringalista. "It's a hazardous situation. According to my information, the Indians have become furious. They are capable of firing volleys of poisoned arrows at you."

The path taken by the Bocas Negras was eventually discovered, thanks to the bodies of Indians who had caught the flu and fallen in the course of the tribe's panic-stricken flight. Curious guide-posts leading to the fugitives, who were too weak to walk fast. They arched their bows against the soldiers' guns. One Parintintin, the "bloodhound" leading the column, collapsed beneath an arrow. The troops for "pacification" machine-gunned . . .

There were still a few handfuls of fugitives, but the seringalista managed to make contact with them before they could be killed. Always the same words: "I'll give you medicine, I'll save you from the soldiers if you put yourself at my disposal." A very old chieftain replied: "We have endured too much suffering. We surrender to you; do with us what you please." So the seringalista brought his naked Indians, his new slaves, to his seringal. There he dressed them and lodged them in two sheds commanded by capataz— overseers—who were Parintintins. The latter started off by beating the Bocas Negras ferociously, to avenge the Parintintin whom they had killed.

So that was the end of the Bocas Negras as well. All in all, there remains the laughable number of twenty-five. Twenty-five men and women. For there were some children, too, whom the seringalista installed in a little hut, right beside his own house. Among them were some little girls . . .

But the end of the Bocas Negras still involved the ancient "romanticism" of the cruelty and sadism of Amazonia. The destruction of the Pacaas Novos is another story. They declined, between 1950 and 1968, from 30,000 persons to 300 or 400. It was a disappearance without convulsions. They died from the building of the rodavia—the new roads. The Pacaas Novos were numerous and powerful—a very great tribe, which had to be exterminated to open up the construction sites on a line between Cuiabá and Pôrto Velho, and the extraordinary highway, as its completion progressed, allowed the completion of the genocide, or at least the bulk of it. It was no longer a question of humanity or inhumanity, just a pulverization by machines and workers.

This had all been willed, round about 1960, by a little man who believed only in the fulfilment of dreams, not in financing them: President Kubitschek, who had had himself proclaimed as "the adventurer of idealism." Kubitschek had said: "I can't conceive of the world without creation," and, single-handed, had assumed the creation of the new Brazil of the interior. Socialism, capitalism, money from anywhere, anyhow—anything was acceptable to implement his plans. If there were not enough cruzeiros, then all one had to do was multiply the bank notes to multiply the futuristic buildings of Brasilia and the hundreds of miles of crude highways. What mattered the impure means one used to transform the universe, or the foul consequences once one had transformed the universe! It was all cleansed by work, an absolutely staggering kind of work.

Desolate stillness of the mato, so dense that a man cannot enter it. The most terrible of all is that this wall of greenery rests on nothing but swamps and lakes. You have both to batter down the Green Hell and pave it. The work sites are battlefields against nature: dynamiting, explosions like bombs, swathes of the mown jungle collapsing with the groans of a cataclysm. On the field of combat, trees undefiled for centuries lie tangled like corpses. Then comes the job of "cleaning up," with the rasping sounds of machines sorting and cutting up the trunks, dragging the vanquished logs to huge trucks. Sometimes the uproar stills, and in the silence you hear a tiny hammering—a bird's call, mingling with the warbles of flutes and the rumbling of organs from birds still perched in the depths of the great jungle nearby—the jungle that has not fallen, the jungle that will not fall.

For the highway is only a slice, a furrow across the Green Hell. Some days the Green Hell burns like hell itself: the soil is lit to get rid of the last animal and vegetable debris. Sometimes combustion is difficult, because there is no land, just watery wastes; the cut branches are left to rot. And as firm ground is needed to go further, it is manufactured. Beneath the uniformity of the covering, concealing and camouflaging jungle hills are sighted, whose invisible flanks are a reddish color. They are cut into pieces, sliced up, and obliterated. It may be 100 miles to get to them. The razed hillock becomes a trail of ochre soil which still stretches out: the highway anchored in the middle of the waters.

And so the road goes forward, letting nothing stop it, raping the secrets of nature. In the swamps and serras so recently haunted by ferocious tribes of Indians, you can chance upon an unknown village—a hamlet of "civilized" men, who have been completely forgotten, descendants of gold-searchers who had come one or two centuries earlier. The garimpeiros had died long since, and the vegetation had closed in over their graves; but they had had mulatto sons by young Negresses whom they had brought with them (bringing as well male black slaves who had also proliferated). The offspring had formed a little population which continued to sieve the rivers without any one being aware of their existence. And yet they did have contacts with the outside world—with Belém, on the mouth of the Amazon, thousands of miles away. They would make their way there by canoe, launching out on a miniscule river, almost at its source, and descending from tributary to tributary on ever widening waters all the way to the distant city of the mammoth estuary. They used to sell their gold there, and buy gunpowder and arms. Each round trip, there and back, lasted two or three years. They hunted to feed themselves. This was less hard than walking to the much nearer Cuiabá or São Paulo, where all memory of them had disappeared, until the highway . . .

On the desolate fringes of the road, the vacant lot where the jungle was no more, a new civilization installed itself, men who materialized from nowhere, caboclos mostly, and with their arrival, the mysterious mato became a "zone." There is always the same grim, painful procedure of setting up a household in the wilderness. First the person stretches his hammock between two half-burnt stumps, whose charcoal is smeared with the reddish dust of the laterite brought there earlier to be used in the road. The brushwood that has sprouted up nearby is painted in the same way. The man sleeps in this desolation, where the squalor of mutilated nature is mingled with the squalor of sordid progress. When he awakes the next morning, he builds a hut of logs and palms, where he sells spirits to poor adventurers like himself, who will one day, like he, be the bartenders of the soiled Green Hell. Then he cleans up his spot with his machete, gun in hand. He battles against the suffocating vegetation, kills the snakes and undesirable creatures that keep on reappearing, but resigns himself to the myriads of insects.

For the time being, the authorities are generous. They've told the simpleton: "Take a portion of territory along the pavement—but not more than 6,000 acres. It's free, and it's yours on condition that you enrich the soil given you, by your own labor." In his allotment, he makes patches of bare earth for planting manioc and banana trees, by burning the eternally luxuriant greenery—for his food, and as a precaution, so that he can say: "Look—I've cleared the ground and improved it as instructed. Now it's mine, and no one can take it away." (Empty words if a big operator, a trust or a bank wants to get hold of the whole region for a major agricultural exploitation, or just to get their hands on some discovered eldorado.) If things are going well, the man's family arrives next, and packs into colorful shanties—colorful because of the range of skins and the gaudiness of tne bright clothes of the chattering women; the men stay in drab workclothes and a dignified silence. A teeming of life which thumbs its nose at all the discomforts. The thatch-roof huts are used for everything; for churches, brothels, and the myriad little commerces ranging from boa constrictors sold alive at the butcher's by the yard, to Branches of Cuiaban banks. To vanquish nature in such a form, to vanquish Amazonia, men have to be, in some way, quite mad. But without this extraordinary capacity for energy, would there be a Brazil, would there be this frenzy of expansion?

It is only a fringe of population that is installed on the edge of the highway, where the area is not too remote or too wild. Most of the time, the highway is just a thread along the immense desolation of the mato; just a thick rut, an unending pothole. There are hardly any embankments or artifacts. Sometimes hundreds and hundreds of miles through absolute nothingness. It is the trail of the terrifying empty spaces: the wagons of Buffalo Bill have been replaced by the heavy trucks of adventure. But the spirit is the same . . .

Men alone at the wheel of their mammoth trucks. Desperadoes, hunted down—by their debts, first of all: they are enslaved to the senhor who has advanced the money to buy their new American trucks, the only ones capable of staying on the road. Trucks as lovingly groomed as horses by their gauchos; tenderly, childishly decorated with statues of the Virgin for luck, little pious lights and curtains with pompoms. But trucks which have to be paid for—and the interest is from seven per cent a month. So the drivers have to go without stopping, until they get out from under or drop dead from their debts. One of them has said: "I'm obliged to travel faster than devaluation."

It is a bleak countryside to drive through, menacing and oversimplified, repeating the same jungles, the same swamps, the same canyons, the same serras and the same rivers. Its uniformity conceals the dangers. Such as rough little slatted wooden bridges, which collapse into the streams. Or the pavement saturated with water, where the rain pours down in torrents. Or the trees which fall like clubs, or the storms sweeping over the steep gradients. The forces of nature can lift up the most mammoth truck like a straw, or crush it with the violence of a sledge hammer.

The drivers have another enemy: the vast distance. Once a driver has committed himself to the interminable miles, he is outside the world, a prisoner in his cabin. He is outside time as well—and yet all he thinks of is lopping off the hours and days in his endless shuttling between Cuiabá and

Pôrto Velho, a round journey of a fortnight, if all goes well. His load can be anything. Sometimes it's simply beer. But at other times . . . One of the freighters may say to him, "Here's the password if you meet any fiscal agents or custom officers." Cocaine or something else? The golden rule is to know as little as possible.

A good truck driver is made of steel. He drives for days and nights without sleep along the ribbon of laterite, in a blinding yellowish cloud. He knows every yard, over thousands of miles, of the dreary, unchanging landscape. The man enclosed in his cage can hear the distant songs of birds and cries of animals, who, unlike himself, are free. Sometimes, by a village, he gets a charming glimpse of women washing clothes, naked, in a stream. Sometimes, on the outskirts of a hamlet, there's a family squatting: it has sat for days on the shoulder waiting to be picked up by a truck.

The "truck-stop" is the only convenient way of traveling in the Mato Grosso, at least where there are no rivers to navigate. So a "truck truce" has been established: a pledge of nonviolence on the part of the passenger, and of nondenunciation on the part of the driver, even when he accepts passengers who have a price on their heads. There is some haggling over the price, for this is a paying proposition, like anything else. Peace of mind is assured in this kind of transaction. If the truck driver catches sight of a man right in the desolate open country, he puts his foot down hard on the pedal—for there are no guarantees here.

The Indians. They are the truck drivers' obsession. The truck drivers' nightmare is to see three or four men, their nakedness adorned with feathers, bounding out of the mato. In a few moments, the Indians are on the edges of the highway, as if to spring an ambush. They can do absurdly little with their bows and arrows to the trucks bowling downhill at top speed. But they have a genius for appearing at a bad moment, when the truck is laboring, or when the driver has stopped for his own needs or his engine's. A hail of arrows and clubs, and it is all over in a few seconds; the stricken whites just have enough time to have a picture of their feathered killers flashed onto their retina. Even these days this still sometimes happens, and explains why every driver, when he slows down, anxiously scrutinizes the shoulders of the road. If he glimpses crouching human forms, he often sends off, without any questions, a salvo of gunshot, following the old principle that one should be the first to kill, in order not to be killed oneself.

You never know the Indians' intentions. There are so many stories. Once, two truck drivers were pumping gas into their truck's tank—there was no service station on that particular highway. A pair of frenetic Indians tore up to them. One of the whites made a movement to draw his gun, but the other said, "No." The more agile Indian seized the gas pump in his hands, plunged the end into his mouth and drank greedily. The second couldn't bear to wait, wrenched the pipe from him, put it to his own lips and gulped. The drivers found this very funny. The first Indian was still spitting, nauseated and not understanding what had happened to him, when his companion began to spew in his turn. They thought they had found an interesting drink, and there they were, sheepish and sick. They suddenly glared at the drivers, who were still laughing, and without a word departed in one bound.

Sometimes the primitives come to the highway like sightseers to a zoo. One day two bearded priests were peacefully waiting for a truck at the outskirts of a village of caboclos. Out of the nearby jungle emerged some colossal Indians, bristling with war equipment, and swooped at the priests, who thought their last hour had come. But the savages stopped short in front of them and began to look at them intensely, at their pale faces, their blue eyes, and the long sandy hair hanging from their chins. An old man gave explanations to the young, like the head of the family to his children. Then, for further information, they began to probe the good Fathers with their thick fingers, feeling their faces, necks, shoulders and ribs. This might be an examination made by cannibalistic gourmets with a view to a banquet. But the priests need not have feared: the savages were only there to see and to analyze. They made particularly lengthy commentaries on the cassocks, fabrics, and shoes, which the Indians fingered over and over. In the end, they simply went off again, very nicely, and perfectly content.

But besides the Indians who appear by the highway, there are others prowling around in the mato. So the drivers, before undertaking the more dangerous and lonely portions of their journey, get information on the situation from villages and small towns, wherever there are senhores, policemen, or the military, and go to interrogate the S.P.I. people. They get a fantastic chronicle of the varied events of the jungle. They hear this sort of report:

"In a village of caboclos, some Indians have just kidnaped a child, to eat him. They wished to get their revenge on the inhabitants, who'd killed one of their people loitering in the neighborhood. An army detachment is pursuing these Indians.

"But it's chiefly on the Pimenta Bueno side that there's a lot of tension. There've been clashes between savages and civilized. A detachment of the civil guard has been despatched to reestablish order. Among the natives in revolt, the most aroused are the Karipuenas. They've attacked Senhor Valmor Meira's seringal. This seringalista had had a little Indian girl captured, twelve or thirteen years old, and was keeping her for the entertainment of his seringueiros. The Indians attacked to get a little white girl of the same age. They slipped into the seringal at dawn, and caught the kid, who screamed. But as they were retreating with their victim, some seringueiros barred their way, and the Indians had to abandon the child to escape.

"Be particularly careful when you approach the Madeira and the Guaporé. There's a war over cassiterite down there. Unskilled workers are collecting mineral in the mountains behind Guajará-Mirim and Pôrto Velho. Some of them are very well-equipped, and are treasure-hunting in motor launches, small planes or even helicopters. Some senhores from the town, with large teams of their own, have organized a system for collection—every week, their garimpeiros deposit their haul in an agreed place, where all the senhores have to do is pick it up. But the men who have less wealthy bosses, or who're working for themselves, bring their booty to the edge of the countryside; it's a dark brown material, put in little bottles. They look like walking wine cellars. But all of this is stirring things up, and several tribes are uprising. Thank goodness there are no more Pacaas Novos . . . "

Clearing the terrain for the highway meant first killing the Pacaas Novos. This was achieved by machine-gunning, poisoned candy and even, or so it is said, by napalm. By 1959, the bulk of the work was done, with greater efficiency thanks to an admixture of measles.

In 1960, official initiative followed on the heels of private initiative, but not in the form of a military punitive expedition. The State entrusted a professional "pacificator," an old hand named Mireiles, with the responsibility of civilizing the remaining Pacaas Novos. He had been a companion of Rondon. He took along with him an aged Indian called Alcé, who had been accepted by the Marshal as his mascot, and brought up by whites. These two had succeeded in numerous pacifications; but they found the Pacaas Novos difficult. To be sure, the Indians made absolutely no attempt to fight. There were only a few small and weak groups left. It wasn't their misbehavior that Mireiles complained of, it was their mistrust. These survivors refused to let anyone approach them. Mireiles deplored the poor spirit of the Indians "who are not genuinely pacific, and who are very resentful over the poisoned sugar." A resentment expressed by a fierce determination to range farther and farther away, to escape the civilized. They chose famine and a free death.

An S.P.I. post. The Indian Protection Agency is a branch of the Ministry of Agriculture. It was set up officially to protect the life and welfare of the Indians, but its agents soon went from protecting to murdering their wards.

An adventurer killed by the Indians. The Indians will pay dearly for tne death of this "civilized man" riddled with arrows. They may even be gunned down. Usually; the means are more subtle: starvation, influenza. No one is to blame: in one case, it is legitimate defense, in the other, fate.

There are still some tattered groups of Pacaas Novos in hiding on the banks of the wildest tributaries of the wild Rio Guaporé.

THESE DAYS the Indians are an excellent business for the S.P.I., thanks to American missionaries. The latter have multiplied ever since China was closed to their evangelization. They are just as they should be: austere, good-willed, serious and materially rich. But they do not know how to spread among the savages the Bible, the dollar, and the American way of life. On their own, they have virtually no contact with the Indians. Primitivism is beyond them. So they have realized that, as their human raw material, they have all the S.P.I.'s Indians ready on a plate, as it were, for their proselytism and their pocketbooks. The more so—and this must not be forgotten—because the S.P.I. has that musty odor of anticatholicism, dating from Rondon, so delectable to puritanical nostrils.

Many missionaries, therefore, congregate in the wretched stations of the S.P.I. They do not live inside them; these shanty towns of stupid Indian serfs and tyrannical bourgeois bureaucrats are intolerable to the worthy citizens of God and the United States. They do not want to see too much, either. The pastor is usually quite near, on the side of the station, in his bungalow, which is a chapel, dispensary, pharmacy, office workshop and depot all in one. The H.Q. of the Lord. No Indians trailing around. The place is very neat: sacred quotations painted on the walls, account ledgers, files full of carbon copies of letters and reports to the sect's superiors and benefactors somewhere in the U.S.A., and even the occasional statistical curve. A generator for electricity and, a few hundred yards away, the runway for the missionary's small plane. A struggle against sin and microbes. Prayer and technology. The upshot is a disinfected, pasteurized Amazonia over a few hundred square yards. But all around dwells the real Amazonia, which besieges the temple of the Good, and which one resists, thanks to bottled pure water and cans of food brought in by the pastor's personal airlift. There is this guarantee of life on earth: the label "made in the U.S.A." All over the pastor's home are piles of goods. The man can hold out. He has the Gospels for his soul and the miracle medicines of the modern world for his body. The jungle and the mato have become a favorite among American missionaries, who create small artificial worlds for their artificial work. Penicillin is stronger than the Catholics' hosts . . .

Money pours from the pastor's hand upon the S.P.I. station: packages, crates, sacks of flour, antibiotics and powdered milk. This is given under certain conditions; that the poor naked Indians, with their overly large eyes and their wild hair, be brought to true life through baptism; that they become Protestants—Protestants of their pastor's sect, obviously. He must be able to write to his superiors: "I've had a budget of x, and y number of conversions . . . " The return on investment. The end product—the Indian, who has become a member of a certain congregation—changes his wild pagan name for a nice, civic, Christian one, like Lincoln, or like David, Joshua or Solomon. It is most important that the convert, if asked his name, knows how to reply proudly, "I am Abraham." He should say this with a convinced air, in the manner of a man close to God, a man who listens respectfully to the pastor's sermons, whose lips he sees moving without being able to understand one word. It is essential that the savage be transformed, not just into a "civilized" but into an "americanized" man as well. One even makes the attempt to teach him a few words of English . . .

It is all a matter of appearances. The S.P.I. functionary, in exchange for the playacting he allows, quickly sees to it that he pockets all the gifts that the missionary intends for the Indians. For his own use, and, even better, to sell. It's great business. How far away one is from the wretched little trading of yesteryear, where one had to be satisfied with exploiting the naked Indian. Times now happily distant. Prosperity has come. As for the Indians, their situation is somewhat better, not much . . .

In reality, there is almost always a gentleman's agreement. What the missionary wants is to send home good statistics to his headquarters, and what the S.P.I. type wants is to benefit without a lot of bother. He gracefully agrees to lend his Indians out for a bit—provided that they aren't spoilt! Provided that he relinquishes none of his power over life and death, over his pleasures. When relations between the American and the functionary become strained, the latter screams, "I'm the chief, I'm the chief." And to prove his rights, he gets drunk on whatever he has, whatever he has stolen. He gets his hands on the flasks arranged in the American's pharmacy, and in his ether delirium, finds the courage to bawl out the pastor, particularly if the latter has the poor taste to state, "You're intoxicated on my disinfectants." A courage rarely found by the S.P.I. man because of what is represented by "Protestant power," puritan power, American power, the only one able to make a dent in this Brazil, where generally nothing undertaken against the established order succeeds. So, faced by the Bible and dollars, the Protector of the Indians manages to restrain himself most of the time. And, as always, the Indians suffer.

Of course there are missionaries who are sickened by the atrocities, who denounce the horrors, cause an outcry, write newspaper articles about them, and become a perfect nuisance. And in Brazil, there must never be nuisances, even American ones. It's regulated in the Brazilian manner, very discreetly and efficiently, without fuss. This is how a woman missionary died mysteriously. She was absolutely determined to make revelations about poisoned sugar. And, on the open mato, it was discovered that she had swallowed some herself. What a tragedy, lamented the local senhores, who informed Rio de Janeiro by radio, when it was too late to save her. A plane sent urgently brought back just an arsenic-loaded corpse. It all goes to show, once again, that in Brazil you have to play by the rules of the game. Which is well understood by most of the men of God from the U.S.A.

The latter, imported from St. Louis or Wichita, are almost caricatures of a good conscience, solid and thick with its certainty, and niggling from its rigidity. So many from the same mould: glasses over their blue eyes, crew-cuts, blond hair and freckles, a smooth, precise, coldly warm, and implacable way of speaking! They have a certain fanaticism, which sometimes gets distracted, but which always returns to this criterion: "The point is . . . " But what is this point? It is more than the glory of God—it is the glory of the American Bible.

A strange new beginning—for had not the moralizing Middle West, which furnishes the missionaries, once been a Far West where killing the savages was a necessity? In Amazonia, of course, the Far West of the selva, the fathers are not there to bless the murders. Certainly not. If only for the reason that their job is evangelization, and the Indians are their raw material. But they do not genuinely sympathize with the misfortunes or genocide of the tribes. They are guided by a sacred cynicism, which consists of doing what they believe to be right, and tolerating all the outrages of reality. It is the curse of the Americans, in Brazil as throughout the world, that in practice they always ally themselves to the worse cause . . . And, at least in the case of the pastors, in all innocence.

For their interest lies elsewhere—in the Book, the prophets and the verses. The bodies and souls of the Indians can only be saved by the Word, which engenders penicillin, the dollar and the whole of puritanical civilization. But the Word takes precedence—even over the massacres. The essential thing is that Christ's Words be brought to these Stone Age savages. The result: missionaries are translating the Bible into over 100 Brazilian Indian dialects— languages that are as unknown as the savages who speak them, or that consist of some 100 words at the most, or that serve no more than a remnant of a tribe. This enormous task is presided over by an American linguistic institute. Millions of dollars. Vast apparatus and technology. America in her splendor. For before translating the Bible into these extraordinary languages, you practically have to manufacture them. To extract them from the prehistory of the jungle. To give a meaning to all those unknown sounds, catalogue them and make dictionaries of them. The Truth is henceforth dished up in "languages" where there was nothing to express the least truth, since truth does not exist for the Indians. To them, nothing exists, except the concrete. So to place God in the Indian languages of Brazil, it is first necessary to improve them . . .

The work is easy in the stations of the S.P.I. Mr. Civil Servant provides talking Indians—bearers of the language to be recreated—for "his" pastor, in his office, in front of his tape-recorder, batteries and cameras. If the Indians are "civilized," and speak a gibberish sort of Portuguese, they lend themselves to the fantasies of the whites. Their S.P.I. protector is always hovering over them, telling them to do as they're told. For he has an agreement with the missionary that the latter should pay them a cruzeiro an hour. The American believes he is making it attractive to the Indians, who understand nothing, absolutely nothing, about money. The functionary rakes it in.

When the American is less naive, he pays his indebtedness by means of gifts—which are the delight of the Indians, at least until the gifts are handed over to their protector. Things often turn into high comedy. One day, the savages refused to speak, and the S.P.I. man beat them to make them continue. The missionary had a crisis of conscience. Waxing indignant, he told the civil servant, "Don't take my presents for the Indians with you." But the Indians did not appear again, and the pastor had no recourse but to submit to the conditions of the protector if he wanted to finish his dictionary.

Anything is possible, including the S.P.I. man's telling the American: "My Indians want electricity. You will provide them with a generator as their pay." The missionary makes some calculations: "The motor is worth such and such. So the Indians will have to dedicate so-and-so many thousand hours to me." The machine is installed; at nightfall, the thing snores and the naked bulbs light up. The functionary is wild with pride and satisfaction at the miracle of light which leaves the Indians totally indifferent. They are recompensed, however, in the sense that as their S.P.I. protector has attained his ends, he is less keen to lend them to the missionary. The latter groans with indignation: "I've only had a third of my hours; how can I finish my dictionary?"

There are complicated cases—say, when it is a matter of a few males and females who can only communicate with each other and who are separated from the rest of the world by a barrier of words. These primitives only know from whites the language of blows and insults that is at the level of their intelligence. But what terror when they are delivered up to the pastor, with his smile of earnest good nature! The American adjusts all his machines for recording, his levers and knobs, his films and tapes. He is faced with petrified eyes and silence. He has to tame these beings, who are living thousands of years behind, as he would tame timid wild creatures.

Once they are reassured, he culls their vocabulary by surprise—one or two words a day is a good result. He captures these words through drawings. Dull glances, limp bodies—suddenly, he shows a sun on a piece of paper, hoping for a click, for the moment when the creatures will recognize the star with such astonishment that they will cry out its name—then the sun is "in the box," registered on the tape. In the same way he obtains "fish," "jaguar," "manioc," "rain," the 400 or 500 noises expressing all the phenomena that constitute their world. Thereafter, imagery no longer suffices: even these people have verbs. Action is needed: to obtain "run," someone has to run in front of them. Generally you tell a "civilized" Indian to gallop; and while he does, you wait for the gurgle meaning "run" to fall from the lips of one of the primitives stupidly watching this exercise. Sometimes the pastor, and even the functionary, set to, trotting up and down, up and down, quite out of breath, for the sake of uncertain results . . . And this is not all. For there are also some grammatical rules. But when the pastor has got this far, up to the syntax, his dictionary is practically finished. Everything is easier, because these savages from the depths of time have broken the sound barrier from their side, and jabber a few words in every language from Portuguese to English. A triumph of civilization: one more unknown language is known. And soon the triumph of God, who will be able to express Himself in one language more . . .

Happy the pastors who do not admit to a fundamental contradiction. They are in Rondonia to save Indians by means of the Book. They have God with them. But they also have other Americans, who are not religious at all. Men on business, on missions, who work, directly or indirectly, for the U.S.A. How gladly the missionaries welcome their compatriots into their bungalows! Suddenly, amid the loneliness of the mato and the jungle, where there is nothing but wily senhores and barbarous Indians—both people from another planet—suddenly American fraternity is recreated. American drinks,

American meals, American jokes—at last, the American way of life. The pastor blesses the food, the pastoress bustles about her housekeeping, and the children romp sturdily like good little Americans. Time passes as if the pastor does not know that his guests are doing jobs which, in the end, inexorably condemn their flocks, the wretched Indians of Amazonia . . .

Brazilian expansion. In fact, it is much more of an American expansion. So many American coffers—official, semiofficial, and private—to pour in dollars, provided that the Brazilian government is not too "bad." So many organizations, economic, cultural, and military, so many enterprises of espionage or charity, all with innocent names like "Alliance for Progress," tirelessly functioning. Often concealed, camouflaged, and Brazilianized on the surface. But one only has to scratch to find, almost always, the poorly disguised American colossus underneath. The highway, the road that is killing the Indians, the road of Brazilian penetration, conquest and civilization, would not exist had not the daunting machinery taming the mato been provided, one way or another, by Uncle Sam. The highway is also the artery of colonization by the United States.

The serious work is done by "technicians." They are not secret agents, but how they love secretiveness! What fury when they are discovered! Their principal task is a geological one, the systematic inventory of petroleum, uranium, and rare metals, looking ahead to the day when the United States will need them and come to exploit them massively in the Brazilian selva. This exploration is made with the agreement of the Brazilian government, and even with its collaboration—but the interested parties prefer to draw a veil over such activities, to avoid giving the people of Brazil the impression that the Americans are stealing their national treasures.

A comical scene took place one day at Vilhena, which is not even a village, just a few straw huts in the mato, 200 or so miles from Pôrto Velho. Absolute poverty. Luxury at Vilhena is represented by the bar where an unsavory caboclo sells warm beer, pricing it according to the looks of his customer. Even so, in this lost spot, there is a fine landing strip, and every week a short-winded Dakota lands there, a rusty, tattered and altogether seedy machine belonging to the F.A.B., the Brazilian Air Force. This is a plane which makes a round of the most distant nooks and crannies, an aerial bus where everything is open and above board, from the engines and crew to the freight. It has been like this for twenty or thirty years. Mail sacks and crates are piled into the plane for the stations. A little bit of contraband is stashed there too, a little profit for the pilot to augment his salary. And into the bargain, whether there is room or not, people are put on top of all this—kids, women, anyone who turns up. This is how Brazil is, and how things work.

One day, in this Vilhena which barely exists, a twenty-year old Parisian got off this flying bus for a stopover. He's a youth who is part of the French "culture" of Rio de Janeiro—which is nothing compared with the American set-up. He is charming, and naively well-informed. For his own amusement, he often wanders about the vast spaces, by any means available, often with the slatternly and hospitable F.A.B. . . . . A communion with the marvelously exotic. His luggage consists of a duffel bag, a toothbrush and a camera.

At Vilhena, then, this delightful Frenchman was filming the desolate and yet captivating poverty of the place. He was in the middle of haggling over a bottle of orangeade when an enormous thing descended from the sky and encrusted itself at the other end of the terrain, which was completely deserted. As if to avoid anyone looking. It was a large four-engined plane. The boy sidled up to it. On the cockpit was a flamboyant coat of arms—the crossed flags of the United States of America and the United States of Brazil framing this social explanation in large letters: "Cartographic Mission." An apparently innocent explanation, but what was this monster of aeronautical technology doing there? Its back end yawned opened and showed a hold full of impressive equipment: jeeps, amphibious engines, pieces of a bridge, radios and machine guns. It was unloaded—but with what precautions!—by tough-looking men in dungarees and blue jeans, all of whom had been brought by the plane. By their dark skin and sharp features, you could see that they were Brazilians—a confidential working force, for some discreet business. At their side were a few other Brazilians. These gentlemen were in large hats and boots, and had all the postures of straw men, destined for a secret mission. They waited, speaking to each other in low tones. Among them was a man with somewhat more reddish skin, perhaps the Indian who would be their guide in the jungle. A rough, tall fellow was directing the operation with military precision, giving his orders in perfect Portuguese. He was an American.

The nice Frenchman started up his camera. At the noise the American whirled around. He was icily furious. White to the lips. He pounced on the indiscreet youth and proceeded to interrogate him with a dry, hurried, precise brutality, as if he had captured a spy in the middle of a war. He questioned him in Portuguese:

"Are you a journalist?"

"No."

"Why are you filming us? Are you paid for it?"

"No."

"Who are you working for? For the Communists or a second bureau?"

"For no one. For my own amusement."

"You are a foreigner. Do you have any authorization?"

"Why should I need one? What are you doing here yourself? You aren't any more Brazilian than I am . . . "

"Who are you?"

"A French student. I'm travelling with an F.A.B. plane to Pôrto Velho. Go ahead and call the police if I'm in the wrong."

One of the straw men in straw hats came to hiss a few words into the American's ear. The latter, after shaking his head, barked at the "spy":

"Leave. Leave at once. And don't let me see you prowling around here again."

The Frenchman returned to the side of the Dakota and his gallant pilots—their uniform was the only spotless thing there. (In Brazil, the crease of the pants is the symbol of nobility in the midst of squalor.) They were in the middle of finishing loading up the people and all those heterogeneous packages. A tropical fairground that was just the opposite of the unloading of the big mystery airplane.

One of the boys in the crew chuckled, and tapped the Frenchman on the shoulder:

"These Americans, the ones involved in cartography just like the ones in geology, don't like curious people. You're lucky to be French with genuine papers."

Laughter. Obviously the whole population of the selva was in the know. The mystery-making of the Americans only served to make them more obvious.

The Brazilian gave the key to the whole matter, with a volubility that was rare in this Rondonia where people speak so little. But perhaps it was because this little swarthy pilot, who lived off miniscule deals, was jealous of the formidable American schemes which were so profitable to those who knew how to work them.

"That team," he said to the Frenchman, "is that much touchier and nastier because it's involved in one hell of a business. You know that people have been talking about uranium in the district for some time—to such an extent that a lot of people, and even some Yankee pastors, have been strutting over the mato with geiger counters disguised as watches on their wrists. What a hope! But this time it's said to be for real. There really is supposed to be a radioactive deposit. Anyway, all the big wheels are in full swing. You see how some sort of C.I.A. has sent this group of storm troopers, these super-experts, to take a closer look, under strict orders not to make themselves obvious."

So Americanism is everywhere on the Pôrto Velho highway, on its edges and in the interior—Americanism in its greediest and most efficient form. American planes, with American pilots from American companies are photographing every square yard of the jungle. Right in the jungle, American teams are taking borings and making analyses wherever there is a clue. But all the results they obtain are kept in the United States itself. Not one negative or one document has been communicated to the Brazilians. But from now on, the U.S.A. knows everything about minerals in Rondonia, which could one day be as useful for American industry as for a great American war waged with atom bombs.

Who doesn't know that at Pôrto Velho the real landowners are American? At least half the territory of Rondonia belongs to Americans, either individuals living in the United States or companies whose headquarters are in the United States. None of it is really exploited, but just kept in reserve. Ownership is so well concealed that the legal proprietors—but where is the legality?—are Brazilian senhores of every stamp: politicians, policemen, grocers, seringalistas etc. No one will admit such a thing, but the whole city is in the racket, and lives off it already. The population is composed only of straw men, whose lips are sealed.

Pôrto Velho. The capital of Americanism, with the decor of a scruffy Brazilian dump. Where are the high days and holidays of the borracha of old? It is just a banal village in a Far West bolted into its secrets. Still with not more than a few thousand inhabitants. Low houses with facades, pediments and sometimes tiles. Along the streets of beaten earth file jeeps filled with cowboy-style people—ten-gallon hats, guns, and cartridge belts—sitting on piles of animal skins. For travellers, there is only one hotel, which looks like a huge fortress.

There's an appalling stench over the whole town. Mostly from excrement— and yet sanitation has been installed throughout Pôrto Velho. But no one pulls the plug, everything is stopped up and broken. A taste for discomfort through laziness. This lackadaisacal attitude does not stop people from working their brains overtime to keep abreast of all the coups being prepared. Then they are immensely energetic . . .

The peculiarity of Pôrto Velho lies in its severity, mistrust and refusal to talk. The lower rung of caboclos, killers, contraband runners and capataz scrutinize all the newcomers, Brazilians as well as foreigners, with hooded glances. (If a man is undistinguished and not dangerous—that is to say, he is not involved in any coup which would annoy such and such a senhor—he is left to his secrets. There are plenty of the most unlikely people. You'll even find a wooden-legged author of crime stories.) But the heaviest looks are sent out by senhores reading the newspaper, their newspaper, the upper Madeira paper which daily proclaims that all is honesty in Rondonia. These are the men waiting for a genuine American, the billionaire preceded by introductions; the person whose presence alone causes prices to rise. But that kind of American does not come there very often. He prefers to send his straw men into the city of straw men. Misfortune can happen to those who have too many pretensions without sufficient weight. In Brazil it doesn't do to make a mistake in one's analysis.

Such is Pôrto Velho, the headquarters of a double Americanism: of one which permits profits today and of a second which promises big business later on, when America will install herself massively. These two forms of Americanism are intertwined; the profitable present prepares for an even more profitable future.

To be truthful, America is most visible at Pôrto Velho under the guise of the Brazilian barracks—the home-grown army is very American. Thus, close to the cruddy city of the civilians, there is the finer and more modern city of the military. Its men pursue the highway farther and farther for the double expansionist delirium of Brazil and the U.S.A.

One of these roads is supposed to go to Manaus. But how will it get there? On the other side of the waves of the Amazon? It would need a bridge some one to two miles long. No one knows how it can be built and yet perhaps it will be built, thanks to the Brazilian miracle, the extraordinary dynamism in apparent laziness.

But it is the other highway which matters, the one which is to plunge into the territory of Acre, still fabulous with its Rio Purus and its Rio Branco, and where murder is the first reflex. A vast and unexplored space wedged into the cordillera of the Andes, at the foot of the ranges, where they get lost in the vegetation. Where there is the terror of the Jivaros, the head-shrinkers, and the hope of unimaginable wealth.

The highway which will triumph over this barbarism will be the highway of imperialism. The imperialism of the U.S.A. and of Brazil. For the route will scale the Andes, cross Peru, and fall into the Pacific Ocean. It will be the sacred and strategic artery, the Pan-American, which will join the civilization of Rio and Brasilia to the colossal civilization of the United States. The commanding post will be in Washington, the White House, the State Department and the Pentagon. And so, by means of this highway, running through the pampa, the mato, the selva, and the giddy peaks to the endless shores of the Pacific, Uncle Sam will completely dominate the two halves of the immense continent. After the colonialism of the cement slabs of strategic airdromes built with American money during the Second World War, this will be the colonialism of the highway.

In fact, in Pôrto Velho, Pan-Americanism sets off by train, the ancient western train of the borracha. On it are put the trucks of adventure, and sixty miles away they will be taken out and made to cross the Madeira on rafts; and they will try to move along the highway, which is not even completed in the middle of the vegetable desert. So the trucks move first thanks to the empire of the railway, an aging empire whose death they are bringing about. For the line is doomed, to the benefit of the highway.

A dying civilization of rubber and its railway line. On the railway, there are stopovers for coffee, fresh water, and refreshments. A chat with the caboclos in their huts. Tables, chairs, a small sideboard, and hammocks. A transistor radio. Always someone close by sharpening his axe against a stone. It is comfortable and yet stifling. On the threshold of a slightly less poor house, there is a basin, a pot of water and a napkin: an employee earning a few extra pennies by serving dinner. Everything belongs to the railway company. From time to time a man protected by a bodyguard appears at the doorway and distributes small handfuls of bank notes—the company's paymaster. Large thumbs are held out and pressed onto a notebook—the signature on the receipt. Thanks to the generosity of the railway, there are schools. They are in the open air, roofless, on slatted planks supported on props. In the open air are the blackboard, squatting little boys and girls, and some ragged girls with bare feet who are their teachers. Apparently, in order to make a living, they are also prostitutes, in the midst of the virgin jungle. This is the sediment slowly deposited by the civilization brought for fifty years by the railway, which will soon be taken over forever by the jungle. This prosperity will disappear in favor of the modern style prosperity which will be established along the highway.

Then the trucks are set back onto the ground, the motors revved up and their drivers, bristling with nerves and weapons, are shut up in their cabins, to penetrate into the jungle like deep-sea divers . . .

Against so many cruelties, civilization has to be cruel. The toughest of the adventurers are inadequate for the task. The army has to be there constantly, with machinery that is even more gigantic than Rondonia's chewing down an even more fantastic natural growth. And to occupy the terrain, there are curious "military colonies," camps of pioneer soldiers, with barracks in the depths of the jungle and ploughs and women in addition to weapons. Brazil is a Carthage whose mercenaries are occupying lands, instead of seas. The country has gone on expanding into wild and distant spaces at the expense of Paraguay, Bolivia and Peru. Brazil conquers somewhat in the fashion of a boa constrictor—she captures land endlessly and then begins to digest it slowly; methodically, with military colonies on all the frontiers, which she pushes out farther when they are imprecise. This is what is happening in the territory of Acre, with the blessing of the Americans, who rely more on well-behaved Brazilian greed than on the Iberian pride of neighboring countries, which can take any direction.

In these depths of the depths of Amazonia, there are still some Indians alive. They are terrifying, determined, wily, courageous, and completely unapproachable. They are aided by prodigious natural surroundings. So real wars have to be waged against these people, so far away that no one speaks of them. Almost nothing is known about them except that death reigns in the direction of the Rio Branco. Unknown massacres.

There is horror on a grand scale there, but there is also trouble for the white killers, who are often killed themselves. The Indians in this jungle are almost invulnerable. The most modern equipment for liquidation is inadequate against them, and the equipment's efficiency is lost in the immensity of the great vegetable night. It has to be a hand-to-hand struggle. The civilized have shadows against them, attacking with arrows, and even bullets—for there are always bad traffickers who sell arms to the Indians. These traffickers are, in theory, shot, if they are caught, but never in practice, because of their connections. And also because, for money, everything is permissible, even arming the Indians whom one is supposed to be killing.

Trade: rifles exchanged for gold, diamonds, resins and, best of all, shrunken heads, whose best manufacturers are the Jivaros. The Jivaros haunt the borders of Ecuador, Peru and Brazil. They are a great tribe, war-like, magical and perverse, and they kill—they kill the whites from hatred and as a precaution. They also kill other mysterious Indian tribes to have the raw material for their rite: skulls. These miniaturized heads are not only used for incantations, but for business; a thriving international trade with white purchasers.

In Rondonia, the Indians are decimated and enslaved. But in the hidden depths of Acre, genocide has hardly begun. Of course, the final solution will come one day—it has to, because of the inter-American highway. Meanwhile, there is still the high adventure of madmen who believe that the Indians could possibly become customers. They attempt to imbue the savages with the concept of self-interest, to make them understand that in exchange for these objects, like metals, skins and shrunken heads, which—except for the shrunken heads—mean nothing to them, they will get what they most desire in the world: guns and axes. In Acre, because of the highway, these negotiations will certainly end one day, for lack of Indians.

But this kind of transaction is being undertaken where there is still no highway or navigable river—in central Brazil, near the Xingu and fief of the Vilas Boas brothers. There too some supermen of adventure have been trying to induce the savages to trade, by taming, while still respecting their savagery. I learnt about them while I was with Orlando and Claudio. Indeed, don't the two brothers, for all their goodness and philosophy, have a part in it. Commerce is no stranger to them: commerce in otter skins.

V THE VILAS BOAS BROTHERS' SECRET

ONE DAY the "little" Frenchman arrived at the Vilas Boas brothers, the boy who, in Rondonia, had got himself so badly bawled out by the agents of the "cartographic mission" at the height of its quest for uranium. But he is one of those nice young people, very sweet and very well brought up, whom nothing stops, just like those field mice with bright eyes and sharp noses who keep pattering about. Curiosity is his demon. He sneaks into everything, by any means handy, the choir boy of the jungle, with a purity that is not astonished by any impurity or any atrocity. The fantastic appears normal to him. He knows everything, and he notes it all down. Even in the harsh world of Amazonia, his warmth opens up the most shuttered heart . . .

So he had continued to shuttle about with the planes of the F.A.B. And here he was on the Xingu. To tell the truth, he had already been there—Orlando and Claudio were old acquaintances of his. Everybody embraced.

Once he is here, the boy prowls around the brothers' fief, looking innocent. He noses about, going off by himself and palavering in bad Portuguese with the Indians of the villages. In every tribe there are always one or two Indians who know a little of the language of the senhores. How delighted these "savages" are to be able to speak freely! They love to complain—one never discovers whether it is because they enjoy it or whether they have some cause to.

On returning from one of his rounds, the little Frenchman told me this:

"It's a delicate situation—as the brothers would never make ends meet with the government's money, they have their Indians run a contraband in otter skins. Orlando and Claudio survey this traffic closely; they insist that everything goes through their hands. The Indians kill the animals, and the Vilas Boas negotiate the furs—and what's more, they do it very fairly for everybody.

"This fairness doesn't prevent endless quarrels. You know the inveterate suspicion of the natives; they are sure that they are being done. They used to try to sell on the sly to adventurers who slipped into the reservation. But the brothers have their own police, who drive these hustlers out. The tribes are furious. The chieftains come and say to Orlando and Claudio 'Give us more or we'll all leave your reservation. We'll go somewhere where we'll be free to deal with more generous whites.' "

The little Frenchman unveiled for me the shady side of the reservation—as always, nothing is simple with the primitives. And I at last understood the true reason for the sulkiness painted on the bushy faces of the brothers.

"There is competition in the forest," went on the Frenchman. "New ways of making money are still being invented here. Of course the majority of the big operators are the well-established senhores, who have their own neck of the jungle; the old exploiters, the enslavers, the ones who have the Indians killed. Conventional respectable people, Catholic and of good character if you don't count their practices vis-à-vis the murder and rape of the Indians. But for some years, I've been meeting men of a new type, on the big planes, in the palaces of the cities, and sometimes in the open mato, thousands of miles from any comfort. Very rich, and very tough. Tireless in the canoe, tireless in the select nightclubs. Champagne. Women. Even a generosity—a frank laugh. No sinister faces, no killers at their side—they are known to everyone, and yet they are as if they had no identity. Anonymous—a past that is lost and forgotten, in the night, in another country. But just imagine what each of them represents in the way of adventure!

"These people are nowhere and everywhere, they are always mysteriously on the move. They set such store by their incognito and total freedom that they often don't have their own home. Perpetual motion. When they descend on a town, they generally install themselves in private establishments of great luxury. I know of one of these hotels, at Manaus: the ground floor is laid out as a nightclub; there are two floors above for the rooms of the girls, who are all very beautiful; on top of that is a restaurant, and then higher still there are two floors without prostitutes, where the gentlemen may rest and hold discreet discussions. It's all very gay, without any hint of brutality or secrets.

"I had an entertaining time with some people who, rings on their fingers and beauties on their knees, invited me to sit at the bar and have a drink with them, for the pleasure of it, knowing that I was French. Most of them spoke several languages. Parties at night with guitars and nostalgic songs, an attentive maître d'hôtel and everyone's respect. And in this setting, these good companions chatted. Of course they didn't tell me everything—for example that they had flotillas of boats and planes which went everywhere and were registered nowhere. Everything that belongs to them is intangible, almost immaterial, although it certainly exists and functions all the time. They are the kings of contraband. They don't boast about that, but they do recount freely how they tried to get the Indians interested and make them work for them. Because what they transport fraudulently toward French Guiana are the products of the jungle—diamonds, gold and skins. And they have discovered that getting them from the Indians themselves, of their own free will, is what costs the least. But to achieve that, what cunning and diplomacy in making the first contact, discussions, the whole grind, all in the heart of the jungle—even if afterwards they go off to live it up in some metropolis. Intelligence counting for more than force.

"These men are quite extraordinary: aged generally around forty, of any and every origin, and most of them fairly cultivated. Adventurers who've got their instruction in Amazonia—imagine what this entails! They're usually foreigners, but they've already meddled in countries of this sort, and in their traffics, for a long time. They're somewhat international but not at all the well-known models—such as presidents of American trusts, whom you glimpse between two banks, or the dregs of European aristocracy who can be bought and sold. They are not experts nor technocrats. They are little Onassises at their debut, above sadism for sadism's sake, or pride for pride's sake. They believe in all the possibilities, even in the possibility of man. At bottom they are just as hard as the others, but they have a newer understanding of 'dough.' All the same, to pile up billions as quickly as that, to cut such a swathe in Brazil, from nothing but brain work, this smacks of prodigy, this demands genius . . .

"There are no more closed faces by their side. No more hospitality with that little backdrop of fear. When you meet one, it's he who introduces himself first, very cordially, offering you a name and a cigar—a false name and a genuine cigar. And then of his own accord, he begins to give you dribs and drabs of stories; true stories, and false ones with quite a lot of truth in them . . .

"Once when I wasn't in one of the F.A.B.'s Noah's Arks, and my ticket had been paid for, I was in a Caravelle gliding discreetly towards Manaus. A man was in the next seat. Nothing of note except for a somewhat phosphorescent tie, a cigarette case studded with diamonds and a few gold teeth. Swarthy features, strongly hewn, but sort of dulled by that detached, disinterested, bored expression of travelers on civilized airlines, bathing in that indifference which is considered good breeding in the world of airports. Anonymous until a hostess with a tray had linguistic troubles with me, when she proposed roast beef to me.

"And then this guy lavished exclamations in the language of Molière from his metallic yellow jaw in a hash of accents in which the foreigner and a sort of Burgundian dominated:

" 'You're French, so you're my friend. I am completely at your service. Mr. Ramirez, professional hunter. I was a pupil of your nuns, many of whom had originally come from Dijon, at Santiago-du-Chile. My father was a banker. Went bankrupt. So I came to try my luck in Brazil. Spent years in the jungle. On the Xingu a jaguar lacerated my face. At Manaus a surgeon from your country patched me up. I love France. I've got trackers, half-castes and Indians too, to kill the animals for me. I have 1,000 of them ... at Manaus, you shall live with me, and you'll live very well.'

"And it happened just like that. We were in the famous hotel-bordello. During the day there were serious visits to which I wasn't invited—swift and enigmatic faces which left not a trace. In the evening, we paid court. The festive band of Mr. Ramirez were all very nice, even if they were missing a few eyes and a few noses. Courtesy in all the mad gaiety, girls treated like queens, the court of love and also real comradeship. No threats of drawing knives and no heavy asides. Laughter. And one night my host began to tell me his life story, as if there were no law of silence. And he let me record his recital on the tape recorder. If you'd like to hear it ... "

And so it was that an unknown, curiously rocky and peasanty voice, recounted, in the home of the Vilas Boas who are so poor, how to make a fortune on the Xingu, which is their river. It told how to get rich when you are craftier than they are, when you know how to use the Indians better than do they, who are the great specialists in these Indians. The situation was the more paradoxical because this lesson in savoir faire was given in French, a language of which the Vilas Boas do not understand a word. It is because they have never gone to the nuns to learn how to speak Burgundian, which is such a good upbringing for a man to have. The brothers yawned as the so-called Mr. Ramirez unraveled his secrets—some of them anyway ...

"I arrived in Altamira—which is where the wild Xingu flows into the Amazon—in 1963. The only men to go there, threading up the rivers, are the hunters. Yes, I started off as one of them. What saved me was that I had, hidden on me, in a wallet attached to my body, $200 in bank notes. I wasn't obliged to sell myself. For it was the period of the market of men. In July it would be the dry weather, and the trackers would set off for months and months in their canoes along the water, penetrating further and further upon unknown rivers. But before they set off into the greatest loneliness in the world, they had to have munitions and arms; sometimes they daydreamed of possessing a radio. They didn't have a penny for these acquisitions, so they used to come to supplicate rich 'patrons.' The latter interrogated them, felt their muscles and asked them: 'Are you brave? Tell me what you've already done.'

"Thanks to my dollars, I at any rate stayed my own master. I equipped myself at my own expense. But I bought what was indispensable secretly. If the senhores had known that I had remained a free man they would have had me killed—I would have been a bad example. I was suspicious of everything. In the wretched boat that I'd procured, I loaded up my possessions at night and fled. The start of my expedition was a flight. I didn't even want to have a companion with me. I was obsessed with the fear that he would assassinate me. To go alone where I wanted to go was madness and yet the reasonable solution . . .

"I ascended rivers for two months as far as the borders of the Mato Grosso. I kept on paddling, surmounting the rapids and avoiding men. At last I spotted a favorable place. I set up my camp in a creek and buried my treasure there: sacks of flour and boxes of cartridges. There was no question of plunging into the interior. I used to hunt on the banks. I ignored the reptiles, the snakes and the alligators which teemed there, because their skins wouldn't bring in enough. In the beginning, I used to kill a suricu or an anaconda, in the belief that I was preserving a store of meat for myself. They made tons of meat. There were some of these monsters in holes in the bottom of the river. They used to come out at night. I would see their eyes with my lamp and shoot. It was easy to kill them, but it was too much work to strip the skin off the enormous coils of their bodies—it took almost a week. Then it fast decomposed into uneatable carrion which attracted all kinds of filthy little creatures. I gave it up. To feed myself, I used to dive into the water to catch large tortoises. You had to be a good swimmer. It was a matter of diving behind them as they rose to the surface and then taking them by surprise. Often the noise of the battle attracted the piranhas. The ones in the Xingu were the biggest kind. As soon as the river began to boil, I made a dash for the bank. A few seconds late, and I would have been drowned. To be honest, I've eaten a great many of these piranhas that didn't eat me. When I started to fish I caught so many that I had indigestion. Often, for fun, I would chuck a bit of flesh into the current, and these vile fish would begin to gobble each other up by the thousands. A nightmare. It was like a cannibal river.

"All of this was more spectacular than dangerous. But the real hunting—the matter in hand, tracking down the wild animals—used to exhaust me. First of all because, when I slept, it was as if I were stealing my own time, short-changing myself. I was obsessed by the eldorado-hunters' obsession, that sickness, that greed which prevents them from closing their eyes. For there were cats everywhere, crouching on the watch, howling with love, coupling, prowling, climbing, ready to pounce, searching for their prey which could be me, me who so badly wanted their skins. One skin, at Altamira, or at Belém, was worth from $50 to $100. Thinking of that was enough to dazzle you. But to collect enough of them, you really had to risk your life.

"Some of these cats, like the ocelots, I captured in traps. But the jaguar I had to confront with a gun. It was him or me. I would summon the one I wanted to slaughter by night—in his own language, if I may say so. I used to pass myself off as a lady jaguar by imitating with my lips the noises made by the female, and the male would come along. There was also a strange trick—rubbing a tree trunk with a thong cut out of the scaly skin of a certain kind of fish. The to-and-fro rasping on the bark reproduced exactly the amorous grunts of a female in heat—which unfailingly attracted the very real jaguar which I'd got my eye on. The animal, so curiously deceived, approached me as I crouched, camouflaged, and clutching my Winchester. Four or five yards off, the beast became suspicious, froze and snuffed the air. This was the moment I was waiting for. After pointing the lantern, I took aim between his eyes and pulled the trigger. If it was a good shot, 300 pounds of teeth, claws and muscle would collapse—and all I had to do was take my knife and cut it up. It was as if dollars were running into my pocket. But if the animal was only wounded, he suddenly started again to advance, to run at me and, with a blow of his jaw or his paw, would knock the gun out of my hands. That was always its tactic. The jaguar knew what it had to do and was no longer afraid. He believed he had me at his mercy. But in a fraction of a second, I whipped out my revolver and, almost body to body, shot upon his bulk. That's how I extricated myself from the business several times.

"The time I was put out of commission, I hadn't prepared anything or seen anything. It was my turn to be caught in a trap. The invisible cat balanced on the branch of a tree. He bowled me over and ripped open my face. In the end I had him, but my face was just one wound, a paste of blood, gaping flesh and crushed cartilage. It was dusk; I couldn't see any more, and I thought I was blind. It was laughable to think of any aid, either human or divine. I could do nothing but remain where I was, as I was, in my corner of the jungle. To wait in order to wait. A certain vision returned to my eyes. And my ravaged face knitted up, dried out and scarred over little by little—as tormented as an old battlefield. It wasn't until much later, when I had become rich, that I was able to have myself made over as a beauty, or at least as a normality, thanks to facial surgery . . .

"As I got better, I started hunting again, to pile up the spoils, those striped, speckled and shaded skins which were my reward. They were still in their wild state, almost raw, slightly salted. I had stashed them with infinite pains into a chest, which I had buried. One evening, on returning from my rounds, I found only a hole where I had hidden my booty. The 'skin pirates' had passed by. Experts. Their profession was to spot the lairs of the hunters as they paddled up the rivers. When they had found one, they used to wait to operate until the men had left on his trails. They would ransack his camp, and every time they'd discover the hideout of the furs however subtly the furs had been disguised. They knew all the old tricks, making short work of the devices thought up to camouflage the furs. As soon as they had got their hands on them, which took just a few minutes, they left.

"In the jungle, despair is death. You have to be stubborn to survive. So I perservered. The robbers had overlooked my ammunition—so once again I reentered the lists against the jaguars. I made a new pile of their skins. This lasted until, on the path, I saw arrows planted on the ground. Enormous, sinister arrows, with their tips swaying in the direction of my lair. I knew what this meant—it was the symbolism of the Indians of the jungle, their ultimatum which said: 'Leave if you want to live.' I was paralyzed with fear. I had gone too far, almost into the domain of the Solimis Indians, who were so feared that there were no men near them, only wild animals. Just a few years before, their warriors had massacred all the garimpeiros of a big gold camp. The gold had been abandoned in the jungle which belonged to these Indians. I myself was to find a kind of cadaver of an object, an old rusted sieve, all that remained of this particular eldorado. But it is a rule that, in the jungle, one incongruous object, one iron thing, often remains as a witness of past disasters, whereas the flesh and bones, the entire skeletons of human victims have been devoured in a few hours by nature. A little later on, however, some skin-hunters had slipped in, in the belief that they would kill the jaguars and escape the Indians. The Solimis had put arrows through most of them and ordered the others to be off. They had fled and I, in my turn, fled too.

"For a few days I descended the river I had come up by. I met up with another hunter. What precautions we both took before accosting each other! We chatted, and joined forces. This man taught me that tortoises' eggs, which were buried in sandy banks, were a great delicacy to jaguars. They used to come in force into one spot which was a veritable vegetable field of eggs. We began to lie in wait for them. But some Indians turned up who were equally keen on this manna. General surprise. General scuffle. And in the end everybody got the hell out, animals, savages, and hunters. Luckily those Indians were not too ill-disposed. They were slightly civilized Caiapos, who, after all this turmoil, returned to eat on the tortoises' laying grounds instead of pursuing us.

"At the end of six months, I returned to Altamira. I had only a few skins, and I only got a few hundred dollars for them. So little money for so much pain. This wasn't the big bankroll which I needed to launch my business. In order to get myself my initial capital, there was only one way: deadly gold. To go into a gold garimpo, one of those marvelous and cursed places where you could make three or four pounds of the yellow metal per week. But where the men were infinitely more dangerous than the jaguars—where they killed one another for fun, liquidating each other at an average rate of ten or fifteen per cent a month.

"Constant gold piling and massacring, empty wealth which you kept nothing of and every chance of dying. But I was determined to make my fortune and to stay alive. A double gamble.

"I left the Xingu and its gold deposits that were forbidden by the Indians. I embarked tamely enough on a steamship which was ascending the Amazon. At Santarém, a tributary flows into the Amazon, parallel to, but even larger than, the Xingu; more bloated with waters from far and unknown lands, yet somewhat less mysterious, for its rapids, waterfalls, and whirlpools are not quite so treacherous, and men get past them with somewhat less terror. This twin brother of the Xingu is the Tapajós, the river of gold.

"At Santarém, I obtained the sieves and equipment necessary for my new profession. And then, once again, I began to paddle against the endless waves. Two weeks to reach the last village with the vaguest pretense of civilization, and another two weeks, ascending from river to river and bypassing on foot I don't know how many terrifying cascades, to reach a curious hamlet. Some cabins, with a few ' merchants ' selling old beans and old meat at fifty or a hundred times their real price—and also the most fabulous luxury articles, such as you could only find in a few boutiques across the civilized world. Everything you bought, you paid for in grams of gold.

"It took another two, three, four days to reach the eldorado. Deep in the virgin jungle. All of a sudden there were thousands of men churning up the river. Five or six thousand alarming human beings. For the people of the gold form a class to themselves. They are the most appalling dregs, straight from the underworld of the big town. Assassins only. Criminals only. Nothing in common with the garimpeiros of diamonds and precious stones, who are just the reverse: men of the jungle, caboclos and half-castes of the great jungle. The latter respect a law—even if it's an unwritten one. They have a sort of love for adventure for its own sake, adventure which wears them out and in the end kills them. They are a true part of the world of Amazonia, whose lure consumes them. They are the members of a society, where it hardly matters to them that they are the slaves of senhores who exploit them to the last breath. For they have known the great illusion.

"With gold there is none of this romanticism. None of this community of the great jungle. No sentiment. There it's truly a republic—but what a republic! A republic of freed convicts. Nobody has any masters. They make short work of the senhores and the cops.

"All the same, there was a law—gratuitous murder. 'Virile' murder—to prove your superiority. There were killings at night. Always the same challenge: 'I am the one who's the man.' Anyone who didn't take up the insult was immediately an outcast, a coward whom you bled or buggered, at will. The real men demonstrated their capacities and sustained their physical and moral claims with the knife, the revolver or sometimes the ax. Straightforward duels or general brawls. And so you got a hierarchy of values, expressed by nicknames. Your only name was this sinister pseudonym. When I arrived, the reigning terror was known, deferentially, as 'come vivo'—the eater-alive. He was a stunted man aged twenty-six, and the king of the knife. On the horn haft of his dagger were twenty notches—one per corpse. He was an evil character, stabbing without warning until the day he would be stabbed himself. The hierarchy of the gold garimpo often changed . . .

"Sometimes a woman would turn up—several more deaths. And yet for the first days, it was like a love court. The creature had her charms admired by one and all. But at the end of a week or two, she had to choose 'her man.' That was the custom. A hardnose would always wait for this moment to say to the lover who'd just been chosen: 'I want her.' The proprietor had to make up his mind in a second. He either killed the brute or gave up his darling. If he capitulated, he would suffer the ultimate in humiliation. For the conqueror, after enjoying his conquest to the full, would come over to the man he had dispossessed: 'Now I order you to take back your own '

"This world that I was entering was dangerous for me. Not to give these men a hold, that was my problem. Useless to deny that I wasn't of their sort. I had to get myself respected as an enigmatic creature, one apart, who'd come from an even more dreadful world than their own. I behaved in such a way that the rumor went round that I was an American gangster on the run. A certain detached coolness in one or two bad brawls confirmed the story—and without my saying a thing. After that I was left in peace. For six months I was able to pile up gold.

"There was another difficulty. This collection of men was' like a privat club, with its own code. Rule number one: gold must not be money, the well-loved bank note, capital, or a way of becoming important. Gold must be thrown away. It was a matter of honor to get rid of it by the most outrageous orgies. It was permissible to leave for Rio de Janeiro and even for New York in order to dump this ballast. Whereas the diamond hunters were despoiled like poor wretches, here it was a matter of great lords voluntarily looking down their noses at riches. Glory to the craziest whims. The type who thought he'd hoard treasure and become a big shot in society was a traitor.

"A closed club, with its own domestics. Like those tradesmen who used to make incredible profits at the expense of members of the circle. Like the pilot who used to come every day to parachute 200 pounds of meat down into the garimpo, where there wasn't even a landing strip. *He* had the right to become a millionaire. How I would have liked to be in his shoes!

"My obsession: to evacuate my pile. At the end of six months I had some 100 pounds of gold. It was then I began, ostentatiously and grandiously, to have delirious daydreams. Naked women covered with minks. That had been done already. But I said: 'I shall drive through the garimpo at the wheel of a Cadillac.' Incredulity. I showed them the letter with the order and explained, 'I'm going to Rio to pick her up. I'll have her taken apart and a pilot will parachute the pieces down here. I'll come back with a mechanic who'll put my car back together and I'll run you all over with it . . . ' This was how I got out with my pile of yellow metal. No need to add that the very next day at Rio de Janeiro, it was put in a bank.

"My first capital. The most precious. But what should I do with it? What was more, it was better for my health to disappear from any town for some time, because of the gold seekers and their sensitivity, their strange conception of honor. Unlike them, I only wanted to succeed. I searched around for a good business and then I thought back to the Xingu and its brave animal hunters. Simple, honest men, those ones . . . People whom it should be easy to take in hand. And the skin business could bring in a pile, provided you were businesslike. A truly modern man of affairs, as much at ease with the primitives as with the bankers—particularly the American bankers, as all the furs ended up on the great New York market.

"Altamira. But this time I was there as a millionaire appearing among crud and misery. The arrogant, dangerous senhores themselves courted me. These big mouths were almost broke. Thanks to their enslavery, they just had phantoms for hunters, physical and moral wrecks who were no longer any good for facing jaguars. And why should the hunters have any courage, when all the skins they brought back just plunged them still deeper in debt?

"But I spoke in a language never uttered before. I said: 'I want real men. Those that show me that, I will make rich.' I was in a bar. At my side was a sack of notes and pistoleiros to guard me. I stuffed a wad of $200 into the hand of everyone I engaged. The man's eyes were incredulous as he saw the notes; he had the thunderstruck expression of a humble man before a miracle. And a kind of fear in him. I had to reassure him: 'I have chosen you. If I'm mistaken in you, I shall lose my money and you will stay a tramp. But if I'm right, not only will you bring me in a lot of money, but you'll have five, ten times the dollars you have now. And most important of all, you'll have won your liberty . . . ' Often my promises only increased their incomprehension. I had to explain again: 'These $200 are for you to equip yourself. If you return from the hunt with ten furs, we will be even. If you bring back 100, I will give you $2,000 more. Two thousand dollars for yourself. So the more you risk, the more you will be paid, for I will pay you. It's in my own interests to pay you . . . '

"I was only able to recruit 200 hunters that year at Altamira. These caboclos and half-castes that I wanted to employ had a funny kind of mentality. They were riddled with suspicion. They just didn't believe me. They couldn't even imagine a world where a rich man, to get richer, wouldn't use his intelligence to cheat and misuse the poor until they died. My fine words could only conceal a frightful trap. Moreover, the capataz, the senhores' overseers, put on nice smiles and began to offer rounds of cachaça. In the drinking binge that followed, the story went round that I was the devil.

"My difficulties were really incredible. But I tried everything. There were still some seringals in the jungle, each one employing 100 'bleeders.' The seringalista always lived at Belém. He used to sell all his borracha to the Bank of Amazonia—a state bank—at a high price. There was a political combine in favor of domestic rubber. But on the spot, in the jungle, a brute of a steward used to continue the century-old practice of selling things to the seringueiros at thirty or forty times their real price. Men normally used to die at the age of twenty-seven or twenty-eight, earlier if they were trouble-makers who showed a poor spirit or zest. A man was done for if he didn't make more than five quarts of latex a day. If, thanks to exceptional determination, he managed to produce enough of them to free himself from his debts, the boss had him 'put down.' A brawl, the police used to say. Nothing more. Oh yes, there are still things happening, even now, that are enough to make you shudder.

"So then I told myself that such unfortunates would follow me, because it just wasn't possible for them to sink any lower. And in fact, 100 of those convicts came along with me. What a storm among the seringalistas when they saw their slaves leaving! They got together a gang of killers and even put a price on my head. But I had surrounded myself with my own highly paid pistoleiros. Paying, that's what's made me succeed. There were deaths, but not among my own.

"The year after that, I managed to have 500 or 600 hunters. They all had faces that were more nearly human, better nourished, less sullen and lost in suspicion. They were scattered over a territory twice the size of France, in deep jungle. They used to work in little groups of two or four. It was always a father and his sons, or a handful of brothers. Kinship was the best precaution to avoid interkilling. But I didn't stay at Altamira. I knew how hard the men's job was. I had to encourage them and keep an eye on them. To their amazement, I would emerge from a canoe, after weeks and months of wandering in those damned rivers, with a smile and with money. I used to pay them for the skins that I took. I stacked them inside barges: this was the beginning of my fleet. These primitives began to trust me. I even gave them news of their families. They would ask me: 'Has my wife become a prostitute?' 'Oh no, she's living and eating well, she doesn't need to sell herself.' What's more, I watched over that, too, in Altamira. Now my men often used to return the cash that I'd just given them: 'You take care of that too.' Everything was going fine. I had a lot of skins, the international rates were good, and I got to know an American buyer who used to come right into Altamira I had tiny runways constructed in the jungle where I could land in a little plane. My first plane. It saved me months . . .

"I used to see a lot of bad things everywhere. The big companies were buying up land, particularly in the Mato Grosso. The people who were the biggest nuisance to me were the S.P.I. At every station, they extorted from my hunters a tax of twenty per cent on their skins. They used to send their

Indians to steal skins from my men. And they even had these Indians, the ones whom they had reduced to slavery, hunting the animals for nothing, to their own profit. They treated these Indians abominably.

"Because of this, there was a permanent war between the wild Indians and the semicivilized, the caboclos who were working for me. It was a catastrophe. It could ruin me. If my people were strong enough, they used to kill the Indians. It was in their blood. But if the tribe was too powerful, then it was my people who decamped. They abandoned the best hunting grounds. And the worst thing was that the S.P.I.—this S.P.I. composed of killers— denounced me to the authorities as a massacrer of Indians. I had to pay extra to the politicians not to have problems.

"Things were going badly. Even so, I tried to push my men forward towards the game. One of my hunters was brought back in a canoe dying, run through with two arrows. But my greatest misfortune was that one of my groups was almost entirely wiped out while they were making their rounds of the ocelot traps. Three men out of the four dead, their bodies stuffed into the traps meant for the cats. This was the work of the Solimis, the same Indians who'd chased me off two or three years before.

"Everything that I had done could crash in ruins. I decided upon a bold move: to go myself to the spot with ten of my toughest boys. I gave the order not to kill the Indians. To set the traps in the usual way. We were all very frightened. At each trap I used to leave a gift and a distinctive mark. My sign: a parrot's feather—the bird was considered lucky in the jungle. I wanted to create an association of ideas in these primitives' heads, to touch off a reflex: that where there was a gift and a parrot's feather, all they had to do was to pick it up, enjoy it and let us be. Let us hunt. This 'education' took me six months. The Solimis no longer attacked but they remained just as unapproachable and just as invisible. They clearly didn't want to go a step further along the path of collaboration.

"But I was really obsessed. I used to imagine to myself over and over what a marvelous business it would be to have hundreds of Indians as hunters. Indians who would hunt for me of their own free will because they had understood that it was in their own interest: that they could get everything they wanted—all the magical marvels of our civilization—in exchange for animal skins. For months and months I held councils in the virgin jungle with almost no results at all.

"The Indians I was trying to tempt were the Caiapos, who were not completely wild; indeed they were classified as semicivilized. I did have one first result: I brought them peace. I broke the old fatality of reciprocal fear which had been the age-old mesh of the jungles. I said to my hunters, 'I will kill anyone who kills a Caiapo.' They knew that I meant it. Then I approached the savages with an escort of my men, displaying signs of joy and fraternity. I invited the Caiapos to a fiesta. It was a tremendous fiesta deep in the jungle. My own men still thought that we were just going to start over the age-old ruse to make slaves of the Indians. I disappointed them. I wanted this new and incomprehensible thing—the friendship of the Indians. I was festive, I held endless discussions with the caciques and their warriors. But where I tripped up was that I could never manage to din into their heads what interested me the most—the notion of reciprocal self-interest, the notion of commerce.

"There was nothing you could get a hold on the Indians with. I asked them for jaguar skins. To please me, they used to bring me one from time to time. When I said to them, 'Give me some others and I'll present you with a gun,' they were dumbfounded. They didn't see the relationship between the furs and the guns. They asked themselves what I could possibly do with more skins. They were well-meaning, charming, but stubborn. They had a deplorable lack of any notion of the plural, which was enough to prevent any real commerce based on exchange and mutual profit.

"But I didn't completely fail with them; I kept to the old procedures—trade, compromise and pretense—but I didn't give in to any sadism or bad faith. It is to my own interest to be moral. So there are thousands of Caiapos who give me furs when they feel like it, and I give them little objects. It's not going too badly. Now, on the Xingu, I've almost my own fief, with my half-castes, my Caiapos, not too much war or famine, with women who oblige everyone; naturally, without being obligated in return—which avoids any problems. I haven't realized my dream of being the protector of an 'Indian kingdom,' with a modern 'king' whose friend and associate I'd have been. But it can't be helped. I am working honestly and I am rich, even very rich, which is a consolation. And making a fortune in the jungle without wrong-doing is something which has never been seen before, and despite everything it is progress, and a new technique."

That was the end. The tape recorder which was speaking of the Xingu on the edge of the Xingu where we were, stopped. There was a drowsy silence in the house of the Vilas Boas brothers. Everybody stretched.

I noticed that there were a few Indians with us, some long-haired, naked men and an old Indian woman, whose skin was so pleated that it fell over her genitals like an apron. The Indians squatted there, come from who knows where, so far from these white-man conversations and yet vaguely vigilant. The atmosphere of immobility was broken by the mischievous laughter of some children who scampered off—little Indians have still not acquired the mysterious or stupid solemnity (one doesn't know which) of their parents.

Orlando woke up at the sound of these chirpings with a jump, and said heatedly:

"I realized that that was Ramirez speaking. A robber. A dirty trafficker. He's the one who's been buying up my otter skins from my Indians behind my back. He's corrupting them. That's all he does. A dishonest man. If I were to get hold of him . . ."

Huge sighs of rage from Orlando. At the end of the room, on a rack, the barrels and triggers of his rifles gleamed. I thought to myself that in certain cases Orlando must have to take a hard grip upon himself, on the power of his temper and his muscles, not to shoot and kill. He is as large and explosive as a barrel of gunpowder. Poor Orlando.

The little Frenchman, who knew his Vilas Boas, made a sign to me and was very careful to refrain from giggling. It certainly wouldn't have been the moment. There would have been a scene, with at least some ugly shouting or fists pounded on the table. Orlando's eyes, which were glittering with fury, went out; they became scabbards without daggers, things folding for a good sleep. Orlando flung himself into a hammock and began to snore.

"I don't know how much Ramirez is worth," went on the little Frenchman with his deceptive innocence. "How could anyone know in a Brazil where business men are as shadowy and mysterious as the jungle they exploit? What's more I don't care. He's a really sympathetic adventurer and he's also somebody—at least for the moment. This month he's worth billions all the way to New York. If he becomes penniless again, he'll make out again and begin over, for he's one of today's money-breed; not honest, not dishonest, neither good nor bad; he doesn't even ask himself such questions, except for the gallery; his only concepts are money and amusement. And then what an amazing imagination he has! It's an interesting species, but a known one. He is one of the international set of those 'doers', those fantastic and prosaic doers who proliferate in the disorder of the world, like efficient microbes, radiating possibilities, yet who are not surprised at even their finest successes.

"In Manaus I lucked upon a person who was less easily classifiable, and more genuinely astonishing. It happened in a large store, a kind of bazaar, with plenty of little people shopping for little things. But at one counter there was someone who looked like a gentleman, who was saying to a

salesman: 'I want 300 large sieves.' 'For what use?' 'For gold.' There was no
surprise at these words. 'You can have my merchandise delivered,' the
purchaser went on, 'this afternoon at my hotel. A man named Francesco will
be waiting for them.' 'Certainly, senhor.' Just a shade of respect in the
assistant's voice. As if this were a normal order . . .

"In fact the purchaser was anonymous because of his ordinariness. He had
the build of a little middle-class townee, of some office employee. A finely
drawn face, but rather expressionless; medium height, gentle, modest and
youthful; he was not quite thirty. Nothing to remark upon. No scars. You
really had to look at him to see him. But he fascinated me. I finally noticed
that his skin had a special grain to it; it was very elastic, and a very warm,
almost ochre color; his hands seemed to be a reddish copper. This exotic skin
was dressed in dull, good quality cloth whose cut was that of an ultraselect
tailor, in London or New York. Suddenly I was dazzled; how could I have
failed to notice a battery of gleaming diamonds on his fingers? A waterfall of
stones on the knuckles of a very insignificant man, a man who suddenly came
towards me with a swift, noiseless step, and who was upon me with the speed
of lightning. I was afraid I would be stabbed. But all I got was a charming
smile revealing delicate teeth:

" 'I have bought those sieves for my tribe. I am a cacique. My father was a
pure Indian, my mother a caboclo. My parents were killed and I became the
chieftain. I make my people work for gold, diamonds and animal skins. Does
that displease you? Do you have any objections?'

"I certainly didn't. And then at a dizzying speed, we became friends. We
went on great binges in the nights of Manaus, in the nights of that lovely
colonial city that was rising again from the ashes of its death fifty years back.
How I love Manaus crushed by the sun during the day, with the shadows
heavy beneath her marvelous trees; the colonnades and pediments that have
escaped the stranglehold of the forest; those houses that are no longer ruins,
but which, during their sleep, have lost their tinfoil madness and hideous bad
taste to become grave, austere, and serene.

"I found myself back there again, because the Indian, much more than
Ramirez, was a part of this splendid world which lavished good humor instead
of evil until you were exhausted. And of course, suspended in the
air-conditioned atmosphere were a few words which you knew it was not nice
to say, because they represented billions.

"With the Indian, life was far more unbridled than in Ramirez' company.
For Ramirez didn't really live it up, he just went through the motions. He

didn't really consume girls and he hardly consumed champagne. But the Indian never sobered up from money, chicks and booze. And yet he was never drunk. His eyes were always lucid, with no doubt the same look as his ancestors had had as they scrutinized the mysteries of the jungle. That's how he contemplated the permanent orgy, but with an unimaginable grace and gaiety. He always had notes at his finger tips to give out, and even little diamonds in his pockets to make presents of. One day he offered me a bulky envelope. 'A surprise,' he said. Inside was a note: 'To remember me by,' and a one carat diamond.

"Was this a primitive, a crazy Indian in the process of feathering his nest? Absolutely not. Serious gentlemen came to greet him from all around. One day, he said to me, 'This is a delegation of custom officers.' He burst out laughing: 'I do just as I like. Everything is corrupt.' And—an even surer sign of his importance—Americans in bow ties came up to him with their briefcases, their handshakes and their documents to be signed . . .

"Who was he? I never knew his real name; he had 100 names. One night he told me a story, his story, a little bit of it, with omissions, silences and sudden flights of the imagination. But among its mythical unrealities there was still some fact which I could verify:

" 'I am the only person who always knows where my tribe is. It obeys me. I send my warriors off as my prospectors and workers. They go when I tell them to because they know that during that time I will keep their families safe. I camouflage the soft belly of the clan, the women and children, the old and the sick, in the heart of the jungle. I move it at the smallest suspicious sign. What's more, I have everything ready to butcher anyone who might appear unexpectedly. I can't take any risks. The men would murder me on their return if any misfortune had happened to their own while they were working for me far away.

" 'Up till now, nobody has found the village. So I don't have any trouble in recruiting strong young boys—they have the bodies of wild animals, a primitive caution, and the reflexes of the jungle along with some of the knowledge of the whites whom they almost never see. They know how to use a compass and a radio, but I leave them their deep soul. They go off to search for me. They make great treks, two or three in a canoe, naked and ostensibly primitive, paddling along the rios and igarapés over most of Amazonia. They brandish their bows, and no one suspects that, carefully concealed in the bottom of their canoes, they have the most modern rifles. Their orders are to use them only in extremity, if there is no other way of saving their lives.

Their most important task is not to make themselves obvious. They have to appear like poor devils of Indians, wandering in the wilderness for some puerile and incomprehensible savage whim. In fact they have been very well trained by me. No one can beat them, with their sharp Indian eyes, at detecting a vein, a deposit or a mine. They spot the treasure by imperceptible signs; a certain coloring, a certain granulation of the soil, water or mud. They never make mistakes. Then they return. Some of them are able to send me messages in Morse; others know how to show me the right place on a map.

" 'So I go there with my work unit of 100, 200 or 300 men from the tribe. Everything depends upon speed: a commando attack upon the treasure. I embark my troops on motor boats with powerful motors. To reach the sources of the igarapés, we use lighter outboards. Then we disembark, sentinels are placed around and we set onto the eldorado like ants on a bone. They work like madmen to get out the treasure, in two weeks at the most. We must never stay long in the same place. We have to withdraw before the eyes or ears of strangers begin to spy. Then we leave as quickly as we can. It's as if nothing had happened. We've even wiped out every trace we could. A helicopter has come to collect the diamonds or gold.

" 'My mystery, my power and my wealth—the civilized in Manaus have learned to respect these. They are astounded: they can hardly believe in an Indian who is their equal, an Indian who surpasses them. Of course they are familiar with some wild creatures who've been collected by priests or pastors, and stuffed into school, where they've shone as pupils. But round about the age of sixteen, they've all been successively attacked by a sort of paralysis, like a mental block. Not one of them was able to pass an important examination. But I am the Indian who hasn't fallen apart in civilization. On the contrary, I've been hardened and fortified by it. I know very well that the whites are waiting for the infantilism of my race to catch up with me. While I wait for that, I am making billions and doing all that I want.

" 'Why? Because I am a double personality. I'm a genuine Indian, and at the same time I've become a genuine Caraibe—a white. There are two men in me. I'm just as much at home in my Indian clans as here at Manaus or at the New York Stock Exchange.

" 'And my Indians? I give them the assurance of living, and even of living better. I am worth 100 Vilas Boases. They actually belong to the other camp, and I don't. I am the one who can give the Indians everything and ask almost nothing in return. I am the only one who can.

" 'Now I own not just one tribe, but several. All unknown, all mysterious and happy. They all produce an incredible amount, and I know how to sell what they bring me.' "

While the little Frenchman was telling the strange story of the billionaire Indian, evening had fallen upon the Xingu. Orlando was still snoring. The electric motor began to snore too. The naked lamps hanging from the bare beams had curtains of mosquitoes for lamp shades. The sun sank in the darkening sky, after a last glowing flicker which lit up the clouds for a few moments. As it did every night, all around us the black mass of the jungle seemed to close in on the bungalow, where the conservations continued.

Our circle of speakers had been enlarged by two young men, whose eyes gleamed through bushes of beards. They had got off the F.A.B. plane. Friends of Claudio's, Brazilian intellectuals, apparently anthropologists, apparently Indianizers. They had joined our group the moment they had arrived at the station. They charged its atmosphere with a certain tension. Beneath all that hair, their faces and lips were thin. They were from a different time than the Vilas Boas brothers, who, in their good works, adjust as well as they can to the world and to society. But these others are "against." In their eyes Rondon is a windbag, and positivism a lot of hot air which was used by the aristocrats of the old days to keep their consciences clean. They dare not say that Orlando and his younger brother are outmoded, or that they have, in a way, sold themselves. With them, love for the Indians is not love—it's politics, progressivism, a forceful argument against the established Brazil, against the U.S.A., and against the capitalist world. Thanks to these young men, the martyred Indians unconsciously serve as an ideological weapon.

The two youths were friendly, but they had the dry, sarcastic, biting intonations of people possessed by certainty. They said to the Frenchman:

"Your 'good' cacique doesn't exist. A billionaire is always a bastard. An even bigger bastard if he makes his money from the Indians. We know the bit about the secret tribes, which are the property of someone who's both benefactor and beneficiary. It's the latest step in horror. If a clever man discovers a tribe of Indians, he doesn't exterminate them these days, he keeps them for himself. The jungle is a concentration camp where he makes his robots work. Robotizing instead of enslaving. A new technique. And then it's enough to claim that one is partly an Indian, a big chieftain possessing thousands of men. The false Indian goes to sell his real Indians to Americans, trusts or banks.

"A so-called botanist introduced himself to a large consortium. He said that he had explored a part of the jungle and discovered there a creeper of great value, from which an essence basic to the perfumery business could be extracted. He had tamed a nearby tribe and it had agreed to collect the plant which was so imperceptible that it needed an Indian eye and hand to pick it. This was fine—except that the primitives in question were very demanding. They even wanted money.

"The project was accepted by the trust, and millions paid to the 'botanist.' A few months later he was discovered living it up at Manaus. He was asked for an explanation. 'The Indians deceived me. They took the money and refused to do anything. They almost killed me; I escaped—and I am boosting my morale with my last few notes.' Everybody knew that the man hadn't even set foot in the jungle, and had lost everything by gambling. But he must have had accomplices in high places. People preferred to believe his fables, and even launched a military expedition of reprisals against the tribe to resolve the matter honorably. The tribe did genuinely exist, and was punished by total massacre."

Stories. Stories. Changing and eternal Amazonia. What is permanent and what fluctuates? The debaters spoke of the family of Sousa Aires de Almeida—the father Leandro and the son Jordan—to depict the reality of the semi-Indian exploiters of Indians.

The Sousa Aires de Almeidas live where the upper Amazon is still called the Solimões. In the middle of the river, the islands of Armação and Araria have a population despite the isolation; several thousand leprous Indians have been deposited there. They have been thrown into these prisons of nature. With vast stretches of water as their walls. They are condemned to a slow death, without medical care and without food, living and dying without any aid—cannibalism, animals and insects make everything disappear in a few hours. Besides the lepers, the white bosses bring all their human dregs there, to get rid of them forever. It's the depository, almost the morgue, for Indians suspected of "nonproduction" because of a disease.

Some sixty miles away is a sleepy market town: Tabatinga. Nearer still, almost opposite the lepers' island which is barely visible—there is just the wilderness, the leaden river, and the sheer vegetation—is a prosperous place piously called Belem, (no relation to the large city situated far away downstream), or Bethlehem. On a hill, sheltered from the sixty-foot floods, stands the fine property of Senhores Leandro and Jordan Sousa Aires de Almeida. They have a large house, a terrace, hangars full of barks of trees, animal skins, borracha and gums. Pious pictures and an iron cage to chastise the disobedient. The Almeidas are making several thousand Indians of the Ticunas tribe work.

Yet God is there. He has had his prophet, the brother Jeronimo—a genuine monk. Some thirty or forty years before, the Ticunas used to say "No" to emissaries sent by Leandro, who promised them happiness if they would but come to his house at Belem. The Indians had fled into a lost valley in the jungle. Every ruse had failed until this monk had arrived among them and groaned that the end of the world was at hand. "But there is a haven of grace, and if you follow me there, I shall save you." This was how brother Jeronimo brought the whole tribe to the place of safety, which turned out to be the fazenda of the Aires de Almeida family. All the savages were immediately tied up and tortured by the senhor's men. They were told: "You owe a lot of money to Senhor Aires de Almeida. You will each bring twenty pounds of rubber a month. You will abandon your wives and villages, and live near your trees." An old language. Old customs. Classical, commonplace atrocities, dating several centuries back and following the well-known techniques of "making the Indians work." So it was that the men fell into complete degradation. At the smallest error, they were whipped on the senhor's veranda while he watched. Iron yokes were put on them, they were delivered to the ants, they were tied up naked under the sun for days without eating or drinking. The whole gamut of refinements. The Indian girls served the pleasures of the capataz, to satisfy them and help to break the men's will. Many of the men had the poor taste to die. Happily, Brother Jeronimo, who was a regular house guest, had the charity to confess them before they expired.

The Ticunas dared not flee, much less disobey. Finally, a certain "Verissimo" escaped and even found a Brazilian to listen to him—the captain of the Seventh Company of the Frontiers. That didn't stop Verissimo from being returned to his owners. On the famous veranda, in front of the senhor's fine house, he was flayed with a whip. He was tied to a pillar with one arm left free—he was forced to hold his little daughter, whom he tried in vain to protect with his free hand. But he survived and finally succeeded in running away for good. As soon as his escape was known, Senhor Leandro Sousa Aires de Almeida became afraid that all the other Ticunas might disappear into the jungle as well. So he reassembled them in his own home for a few weeks of reeducation. Blows. Blows. Blows. Those who complained were jammed against bars, standing, their hands and feet padlocked together, excreting on themselves, shriveling little by little into human rags which collapsed without being able to fall.

This happened recently. It would all have been hidden but for a surprising event. One day gentlemen arrived who came to ask for "explanations" in the name of the Government. They brought Verissimo with them, but not to deliver him up for a just and definitive punishment. As an accuser. Stupefaction on the part of the Almeida senhores when they were asked questions of this kind: "Have you beaten any Indians?"

"Oh not very much, just for their own good, for they are a lazy, lying set of thieves; they owe us a deal of money, but have no sense of gratitude; we would be ruined if we didn't oblige them to rid themselves of their debts by odd jobs."

The Almeidas were full of their rights. And yet people continued to pester them with other equally foolish accusations. Coarse laughter when they were asked: "Have you forced Indian girls to have sexual intercourse with you?"

"Oh there's no need to force them to that. They all do it of their own will, these girls. But we haven't deflowered a single girl . . . "

Then the inquirers had the Ticunas brought from the fazenda, all just untied, still covered with wounds. Among them were lepers who were not yet leprous enough to be sent to the isle of Armação. Even without fingers, they had been kept as prisoners and beaten so that they would work. There were also children, pitiful, pregnant little girls, their emaciated faces eaten by their great black eyes, their bellies enormous. But the Indians who were told to speak, did not speak—they were too afraid of the reprisals which they believed inevitable. The capataz had murmured to each during the night: "One word and you will die." Hardly ten men even vaguely confirmed Verissimo's allegations. A little thirteen-year-old Indian girl, Lita Jacamin, was braver: "After what Jordan did to me, I became large and had a miscarriage. This has happened to all my playmates."

In the town of Tabatinga, honest people brought the whole affair back to proper proportions. In their eyes, Leandro was the patriarch, the good adventurer of Portuguese blood, the benefactor whitened in severe trials. He had done everything for the area. It had been frighteningly desolate when he had arrived as a young man. It was he who had tamed the Ticunas, who had taken them into his care, who had made them live better, almost like civilized people. The paths, houses, churches, hangars and boats were his work. Obviously it took a certain firmness, but a fine and just one. It was unfortunate that he'd married a pure savage, an Indian from the jungle, who was Jordan's mother. It's as if there were a curse—that every man with half-Indian blood in his veins should become the scourge of the Indians. Jordan had organized the system of terror, with his gang of armed killers, his whips, his iron cage and his brutal punishments. He was amoral and violent Even the holy days had been mocked. Every year, in the fazenda, Jordan used to preside over the election of the Virgin. He had previously distributed cachaça to all the Ticunas until they collapsed onto the ground in their orgy. Jordan used to choose from their pell-mell bodies a little girl so young that no one in the tribe had touched her. Then he would proclaim her as the Virgin and use her . . .

So Jordan, the almost Indian, the scourge of the Indians, was released by the whites of Tabatinga. He was prouder and more powerful than ever, for when he was brought to court to be placed in preventative detention, the magistrate declared: "I cannot punish him. I do not know the penalty. How could I, since we are in the land of the free?"

Stories, stories. But underneath everything there is an extraordinary permanence: the rule that the unwritten law is above the Law. Here lies the strength of Amazonia, in spite of all the changes and any progress.

Stories, stories. To top off all the adventures, there is this last adventure: contraband. Some contraband is open and venerable. The most respectable is the one that takes place on the railway line of the Corumba, the line which is the glory of Brazil and is almost transcontinental, crossing Brazil from the Atlantic towards the Andes, Bolivia, and the Pacific.

On the frontier with Bolivia, whole trains are filled with merchandise which gentlemen from São Paulo intend to sell to the natives of Santa Cruz and La Paz on the other side of the frontier. In return they bring back cocaine, narcotics and maté. It's such a sacred practice that the traffickers went on strike when someone wished to harm their rights.

It was a well-established custom that they would get out to smoke a cigarette at the customs station during the visit, and get in again immediately after. To compensate for this deference, it was understood that the customs officers should never find anything in carriages which were so many walking bazaars. But it once happened that a new departmental head, in an excessive display of zeal, started to search the train and threatened to write a report. No doubt this was just a little blackmail to increase the amount of the traditional kickback, so much per train. But to breach the conventions like that, when you aren't particularly strong, is a very serious mistake in Brazil.

The contrabanders would not have marked their displeasure adequately by simply killing the man. What is one corpse? To show their fury properly, they decided to strike. A blow like this fell so hard upon the economic prosperity and well-being of the people that the authorities immediately knuckled under. Apologies. An agreement was signed which guaranteed the maintenance of the old customs. Commerce was only begun again after the promulgation of a kind of charter.

Contrabands of all and every kind, including stallion sperm for insemination, dropped by parachutes over large ranches. Coming from European or North American bulls, this sperm is very precious—and highly taxed at customs. A few ounces are poured into a flask, which is placed into a miniature refrigerator, and wrapped in layers of cotton, plastic and aluminum. A large packet is released from a plane like any other on the end of a parachute over the agreed and secret spot.

What isn't possible? Even sinking a ship—on paper. A cargo leaves from Santos, a cargo of coffee (an ordinary product purchased from a state institute). Suddenly you learn that the boat has been lost at sea with all hands. Condolences to the owner. A few weeks later, a ship with an entirely different name, documents and cargo shows up at Belém or Manaus. Nobody recognizes the former craft, least of all the customs officers. The captain, when he pays his protocol visit, tells them that he is bringing in second-hand American cars for the new highways of Amazonia. They are disembarked virtually without dues, as scrap iron, and publicly auctioned off at low prices. Each car is deformed: a door is missing, and so on. The purchaser goes to get his car delivered in some distant shed, very discreetly. His vehicle is gleaming. The missing door has been put back. All he has to do is to pay a substantial supplement to reach the real price; for, of course, the car has a new engine and is the latest model.

So, in the station of the Vilas Boas brothers, we went on recounting tales. In the bungalow, the electric generator misfired and the lamps winked. It would soon be time to turn them off. But before they went to bed, one of the Brazilian intellectuals, his hair volcanic, launched an accusation against America, an America which in his view was responsible for everything:

"It is the progress by the Yankees that has given the poor taste to the country. In the old days one used to say indulgently of a man that he 'stole Brazilian style.' Now almost all the people in high places 'steal American style.' This is our misfortune. This is how contraband is being corrupted. In Amazonia, it has become American instead of Brazilian. And it's killing many more Indians.

"Formerly the fazendeiros, garimpeiros and seringueiros used to liquidate the tribes. Evilly and yet almost paternally. They, at least, had feelings, even if they were only cruelty and hatred. With the billionaires of Manaus, model 1971, and their American patrons, it's all become impersonal, indirect and distant. These people speak like pastors and act like machines. The Indians don't count any more, their life no more than their death. In the end this is more murderous.

"America is hidden—except in one place. At Amapá. It's half way between Amazonia and Guiana. Some garimpeiros discovered eighteen hills of manganese there, in what was terra incognita a few years ago. The Americans came into this country of horror and conquered it with laughable ease.

"In the immensity of the vegetable night of the jungle there is light and space. And in it, an ultramodern city, not a futuristic one, but the quintessence of the American way of life. Just a few houses in a park, with walks, lawns, flower beds and a few marvelous trees. How nature has been tamed! The fierce orchids of the jungle have become domesticated, well-behaved flowers tended by gardeners. In this island in the midst of the green ocean, calm, dedicated, and methodical existences are passed, always in the same way, always following the same timetable, between the bungalows where people live, the supermarkets, the temple, the club, the bar, the office, the factory and the mine. Factories without chimneys and mines without galleries.

"There are very few men. What use would they be when a few gigantic machines do all the work so cleanly and efficiently? There are machines for clawing the mineral from the soil. Machines for the first refining operation. Thirty engineers and workers in one building are enough. No hand ever touches the stuff. They manipulate levers, and everything happens by itself, as if by magic.

"The metal marches to the waiting trains, which have brought provisions essential to the life of Amapá. Trains run incessantly along the 115-mile line which has been especially built to transport the manganese. Manless trains transporting manless minerals which the trains pour into manless boats—or almost manless. The boats are the carriers of Bethlehem Steel, which are moored to the quays of Macapá, specially constructed for them in the northern mouth of the Amazon. They depart with their portion of Brazil.

"It's a closed circuit. An American circuit. From Bethlehem Steel to Bethlehem Steel. Nothing but for and by Bethlehem Steel. Everything happens as if Brazil itself didn't exist. Almost the only Brazilian thing about it is the label stuck onto the actual company—the fake label of Amapá.

"Amapá is a chunk of jungle transformed into a chunk of America. It is surrounded by a boundary, a no-man's land a few yards wide where a half-cleared vegetation is sprouting. Occasionally the boy scouts of the enterprise risk going into it. Their chief, a man in glasses, constantly warns them: 'Don't go to piss in the jungle; a few steps too far and we'd lose you forever.'

"The hour of pure Americanism has not yet come. This is the hour of compromise: the old Brazilian system americanized by dollars, bibles and contraband. This has engendered in us an even more questionable greed, one where puritanism has sharpened the ancient wickednesses. I tell you this—if, these last few years, people have started killing the Indians again en masse, it's America that's the real culprit."

BUT WHERE is the real culpability? Who could define it? It is all so interwoven. In the nineteenth century the Americans systematically exterminated the red Indians of their prairies and Rockies. But in Brazil they don't dirty their hands or even their brains. Their consciences are clean. They have no imperative need for genocide. On the contrary, in their own country, in their own churches, they even contribute money for the little "Redskins" of Amazonia. They do not know what is happening. And insofar as a few missionaries, businessmen, or agents are aware of what's going on, they say: "Is it our fault if the progress we bring with us into the jungle and the matos makes the Indians perish, from a sort of allergy? We can't do anything about it." This kind of reasoning is that much more acceptable in that if, in the ground swell of the American way of life, there are almost always some murders, the murderers are not Americans but Brazilians devoted to American prosperity.

The ambiguity is that much greater because, even if proAmericanism kills the Indians, antiAmericanism liquidates just as many of them, if not more. What does antiAmericanism consist of? An obsession: that Brazil should be made the greatest country in the world, but by the Brazilians themselves. Without selling themselves to Washington, and therefore against Washington. The principle of this antiAmericanism is that there should be still more sensuality, still more cross-breeding, and that the demographic explosion should fill the country with 200,000,000 inhabitants. Brazil will colonize itself, instead of being colonized from the exterior—even though this fantastic task will take 100, 200 years, perhaps more.

In 1940, the signal for the crusade was given by the extraordinary Getulio Vargas, the creator of the modern concept of Brazil. A crusade waged in the name of all the skin colors of the Brazilian race. Alas, this civilizing rainbow resulted in the elimination of one color, the red: the color of the Indians. It was then that their great degradation befell them.

And here too, lies the remorse of the Vilas Boas brothers. An old remorse, genuine and deeply felt, for they once took part in the great military expedition into central Brazil. This was the expedition that was supposed to make the Indians enter into the national community, and which instead made them outcasts after a gigantic fraud. What has become of the Chavantes, the noblest of all the Indians? A proud race which no longer exists despite Orlando and Claudio, and even because of them—because without knowing it and without wishing it, they had been, in their early youth, the instruments of its destruction.

I was going to leave the Xingu. This was my last conversation with the two brothers—Orlando, craggily good-natured; Claudio, melancholically sweet. More than ever, they seemed to me hobos, haughty, tender, fundamentally sad. They had already told me of their bitterness, of all their regrets and their disappointments, of their wasted lives, of their work that was so small and useless amid the immense engulfing of the Indians. But this last day of my presence, they confessed to me what lay heaviest on their hearts. This was their fundamental remorse, their "secret" which spoiled every joy: the affair of the Chavantes.

Orlando used a solemn tone to warn me that he was pronouncing sentences that were the key to his life:

"Who knows if a better solution couldn't have been found for the Chavantes? In the mines of Uberlândia, recently, I saw a wretched Indian scratching in a hole. This creature, this ridiculous scarecrow, asked me for money. He told me that he was a Chavante; I thought to myself that a few years ago he would have been a proud warrior who could have killed me or offered me his friendship.

"I used to know so many of them once, the Chavantes who fought against me, but whom I made my companions, my messmates and my brothers. They believed in me, in my word and my promises. And because of me they were suppressed, and became these shadows whose land has been taken away. For these ferocious fighters were peasants before anything else. This was the whole problem. People kill the Indians of the jungle for eldorados. But they kill the Indians on the borders of the jungle, even more, to take their territory for cultivation.

"There is no way they can escape. In the heart of Amazonia, tribes can still disappear into nature, but there on the Rio das Mortes, the river which serves as a frontier against the vegetation, the conquered are without shelter or camouflage; they are doomed men. There is just a steppe, deadly because it covers a fertile soil. I never suspected that bloodthirsty madness on the part of the whites for getting hold of land which didn't belong to them. I was young then."

Orlando had a curious way of confessing his sins—he rolled his eyes. Round eyes in a long feline slit of eyelids, protruding, angry eyes which wished to express his naiveté. But this rather querulous good nature was suddenly corrected by a metallic glint when the pupils narrowed, as they do in animals, for a biting sentence. In this touching, yet disturbing way, Orlando told me his life, a life which had begun by an error:

"There were ten of us children. Our father was a lawyer at São Paulo. An upright, stern and good man who originated from Ceará, the distant Northeast of hunger and thirst. He had experienced all the sufferings of people in those parts. He had leftist ideas, hoping for a better future for men. Although it left its mark on us, we were happy and lived in a large house. Our parents were marvelously in love with each other. So much so that when my father died in 1942, my mother died almost immediately afterwards. This caused the family to scatter, and our poverty. The girls got married. As for us four boys, we found little jobs in capitalist societies, telephone companies, refrigerators, goodness knows what. Mediocrity, shabbiness, and a prospect of days and years that would be always drably alike, scratching at paper under the boot of the rich. This lasted until Getulio Vargas proclaimed the march toward the west, *la marcha para o Oeste.*

"Vargas had been our god ever since he'd tied up his gauchos' horses to the railings of the palace Tiradentes, the parliament of the old-style aristocrats and coronels, who used to quote Voltaire, Rousseau and Washington in the course of their long eloquent debates where they maintained all the old injustices. Vargas was just the opposite; he wanted the Brazil of the people liberated from the financiers of Wall Street and from the prostitutes of Paris. The god of the new—or so we believed.

"He had a great deal of national sensitivity. He had been most upset when a certain French politician—Paul Reynaud—had declared that the whole of Central Brazil was one vast unexploited wilderness, and that it behooved Europeans to occupy it. He'd said that before the Second World War. So once France was crushed in 1940—a France whose president of the council happened to be the boastful Paul Reynaud—Getulio took his revenge. In

1943, he decided that he himself, the great Brazilian, should 'occupy' his center of Brazil, unknown Indian country, the fief of the Chavantes.

"The Chavantes had enjoyed world fame ever since they had killed Percy Fawcett in 1927. He was an Englishman of the Lawrence of Arabia kind, a former colonel, an aesthetician of adventure. He had a strange capacity for achieving the impossible. He had spent his life among the jungles, a gentleman at ease among terrifying tribes. He was already a myth in his lifetime. One day the world learned that he and his son had disappeared in the forbidden heart of Brazil. For a long time, it was one of the great mysteries of South America. International journalists prowled around the Rio Araguaia and the Rio das Mortes for years to try and pierce the enigma. These rivers were then in the hands of the Chavantes who were believed to be the assassins, even though the Chavantes were renowned as much for their faith-keeping as their cruelty. Why had they violated the laws of hospitality accorded to Fawcett, who had been bound to them by sacred ceremonies?

"After this drama, the Chavantes retired into themselves more than ever. They made the Rio das Mortes into a frontier—a real military frontier, fortified Indian style. There were warriors on the watch; the tribe was mobilized against a world that wished to penetrate its secrets; as if the revelation of this secret would be a curse, which would infallibly cause their death, as the witch doctors had predicted. So the Chavantes slaughtered anyone who was foolish enough to come near them, attracted by their mystery. Some patrols of soldiers sent to reconnoiter were destroyed, as well as two missionaries, sick with faith, who approached them brandishing crucifixes. Martyrs, but fools as well! But the pressure of the civilized still increased, until Vargas proclaimed the Great Expedition of Central Brazil and Xingu-Roncador.

"For this expedition ever to take place, we had to have a gaucho in power, a genial autodidact, a bespectacled witch doctor, whose strength lay in saying things the little man could understand. How could Vargas, the father, better arouse the enthusiasm of his millions of sons than by announcing the conquest of Brazil by Brazil? No one in this country had ever spoken like that to so many ordinary people. From then on they lived through him. What did it matter if so many of his marvelous projects were just day-dreams? But in this case, in the march to the West, Getulio was superb. He was a connoisseur of primitive passions, and made use of nationalism, which had been poorly exploited until then. At that very moment, oddly enough, the new Brazil wished to make an affirmation against Europe in crisis and in defeat, and not against the United States, which was giving her aid.

"The minister João Albert organized the preparations. There was a levy of volunteers. My brothers and I enlisted as regular soldiers, to get out of the grayish tone of our existences. One problem: we had to conceal the fact that we knew how to read and write. In those days, there weren't many people among the Brazilian troops who could, so they were very precious. If anyone had discovered it, we would have been put into offices and headquarters as secretaries, bookkeepers and warehouse keepers. We, of course, wanted to campaign and forge ahead. But one day Claudio was caught red-handed in the act of 'non-illiteracy.' What a fuss! In the end we were allowed to form our own commando troop by proving that, since we could read, we could also read maps; and this was so useful that they should send us on reconnaissance.

"1944: the 'army' was assembled at Chavantina, the last outpost facing the Chavantes. Getulio came to inspect the expedition there, and then we crossed the Rio das Mortes.

"The serra do Roncador lay on the other side. Mato on top of rocks. Soft tangled hill tops, Chavante country. Eight terrible months without sleeping. There were sixteen of us, ahead of the troops. I had hand-picked my men from convicts and criminals, the toughest and also the bravest breed in the world. Brutes who just wanted death and blood—indeed this was a state of mind common to the whole of the expedition, which was coming well behind us.

"But I said to my few madmen: 'There are very few of us, and we are too far in advance for anyone to be able to come to our help. If we kill a single Indian, the Chavantes will kill us all. We have to go about things in a different way.'

"I had an idea. The Chavantes must be stunned with amazement, and perhaps with terror, as the army advanced toward them. These savages, too, had their councils of war where they pondered the best decision to take. Certainly they were preparing for a ferocious struggle. It was like a general mobilization. While we were climbing up the tall, thorny grass that tore at us, there was a permanent oppressive presence all around us, the dull sounds of gourds, terrifying shrieks and shadows. No attack, but a surveillance, or rather a waiting. As if these poor people were saying to themselves that to engage in combat would be collective suicide. I told myself that this was perhaps my chance: to manage to convince them that their only hope of safety lay in peace.

"An almost impossible task. For one sole corpse, be it white or red, would immediately mean thousands of corpses. My first task was to restrain my own outlaws, who were becoming very restless. All around us the Indians became more numerous, more intangible, and were closing in on us as if to take us by surprise and slit our throats. One of my terrors revolted, and aimed a machine gun at the vague patches that were all we could glimpse of the Chavantes. I had to act.

"My authority was reestablished, but it was hell. I couldn't even drop off to sleep for a moment. I didn't trust my people that much, who, though apparently obedient, were each capable of sticking a knife through me at the least inattention on my part. The Chavantes had begun to shoot arrows at us. We strained our eyes to peer through the darkness of the vegetation and the darkness of the night. The torture of keeping watch the whole time. We marched five, ten, miles a day. Before nightfall, we dug ourselves into six-foot trenches. Now the Indians started to attack. Five attacks, with hordes of savages rushing up to our trenches. Twice they came within a few yards. We fired, but we fired over their heads. To get to us, the savages began to dig communicating trenches; they were snaking along them, and we had to go and stop them up. It was a war of positions!

"Months without a death. A terrible but subtle game. As if the Chavantes wanted to avoid the irreparable by not pushing their charges to the very end. Why didn't they come to me for parleys? What held them back at the last fraction of a second? I was discouraged. I no longer understood. It hadn't turned out badly, but there had been no results. And so it was, in terrible physical and moral trials, that I crossed the country of the Chavantes.

"It took eight months for the first emissaries to come to me. No doubt because, behind me, the bulk of the advancing expedition alarmed the Chavantes and I appeared like their savior. I held interminable palavers with their honorable old men. They believed me, but could I guarantee all the other white invaders? I gave them my word: 'We will not enslave you. We only want to cross your territory, to go further into the interior. Once we have passed, you will be completely free again.' That's what I said, but I believed what I was saying. For the official aim of the expedition was to explore all the unknown center of Brazil, to pacify and Brazilianize it, but without domesticating the Indians in any way.

"That much was true. The army departed on a long trek; it took them two or three years to get all the way to the Amazon and Manaus. I received a special mission; to shed some light on the famous mystery of Fawcett's death, a mystery that was darkening the good name of Brazil. To do this I set off with the last of the unsubdued Chavantes, a particularly savage subtribe within the big tribe. These people were called the Calapagos. Their men looked like women, with their hair coiffed into chignons. I plunged into the terrifying jungle with them. I passed four years in their company, leading their life, miles from anything civilized. I was one of their own. They behaved with me as if I had become an Indian, and even a Calapago. Sometimes I thought that Fawcett must have been accepted in the same way, and that this had not stopped them from butchering him one day. It was generally believed that it was these Indians who had killed him. But never, never, despite our brotherhood, could I draw one word out of them on the subject.

"In a certain way I began to love these Indians; they were so marvelous with me, trusting and gay, and talked to me about everything, except that one thing. They behaved as naturally as if there had never been a secret: but I knew that the secret existed and that it could destroy me.

"My best friend and constant companion was a young warrior by the name of Naimura. Why, one evening like any other, after so many evenings together, did he suddenly begin to tell me the mystery?

" 'It was my father who found the bodies of three men on the banks of a little creek, Fawcett's, his son's and an Indian's of an unknown tribe, who always accompanied them. We knew nothing about it. We were informed about it. We learned that the Europeans had been hunting some ducks; as they shot the birds down, they went and collected them. Suddenly Fawcett made out some Indians quite near him: he took them to be poachers and fired at them. The Indians cut the throats of the civilized, believing them to be bad. We, the Calapagos, were inconsolable. We wept. Fawcett had never been hostile towards us. He was good, and he'd been our guest, and suddenly he was no more. It could bring us misfortune. So we all kept silent, from fear, and also to ward off fate. If we behaved as if nothing had happened, perhaps we would escape from the vengeance of spirits and men.'

" 'But who were the Indians who killed Fawcett?'

" 'They were not Calapagos. We were never able to find out who it was . . . '

"Was that what it was, just a misunderstanding in the jungle, the Fawcett affair that had excited the world, provoked the invasion of central Brazil and actually changed the course of my life? Was that all it was? At the end of it all this mixture of truth and falsehood. Naimura had not told me everything. And yet the truth must have been something like that. I sensed it. Except that his father was the poacher and the killer. It all made sense. Fawcett had had the reflexes of a British gentleman against poachers, and the savages had had the reflexes of maddened savages. A stupid death.

"Later, a buffoon of a billionaire, a newspaper magnate in the Brazilian style, who'd taken the name Assis de Chateaubriant, 'discovered' Fawcett's remains and sent them to England with pomp and circumstance. But whose bones were they really? The drama of the jungle ended in an advertising stunt.

"I turned back to the Rio das Mortes, where the expedition had set out from, long years before. What a state I found my Chavantes in, the ones who'd stayed in their territory trusting in my word. Poor people. Instead of the liberty they'd been promised, there was 'pacification'—in other words, every kind of oppression. In the first influx of people, the scum from the big towns had pounced on the Indians; they didn't even know they were Indians. They tortured them to make them confess where they'd hidden their gold and treasures, as if the Indians had ever cared to have any. The Chavantes fled and hid themselves in small groups. But they didn't go far away, because they were also peasants. They loved their land and wanted to defend it. They stayed on the watch, very agitated, menacing absurdly, for they knew how powerless they were now, and how badly they had been cheated. They couldn't resign themselves completely, and sometimes they let off a few arrows. The authorities became concerned and told me to calm them. And I began again to look for the Chavantes and tame them again, handful by handful.

"What a lot of patience it took. It took months to recuperate a terrorized people who no longer believed in me. Yet I was sincere. I told them that we would chase away all the bad whites forever. Oh yes, I believed it. But I wasn't strong enough to hold the adventurers in check, so I asked for help from the regular Brazilian army. It arrived in great pomp and was really splendid. One general helped me considerably. He came into the Indians' territory in full uniform, on horseback, like a sovereign. At the head of the column, a brass band of 100 decorated bandsmen played national hymns and sambas. It was really marvelous. The 'bad guys' fled and the Chavantes came out of their hiding places to form ecstatic circles around the soldiers.

"I had completed my task and was happy to have succeeded. I set off for the distant jungle for other pacifications. I still believed that I could save many Indians all across Amazonia. Had I not saved the Chavantes? What a blow it was for me when, a few years later, I returned once again to the Rio das Mortes. The river deserved its name more than ever, for there were no more Chavantes left alive worth speaking of And those who were left no longer had the desire to live

"It's an inexorable process. First, there had been direct and indirect slaughter. The garimpeiros had reappeared; they had assassinated and then spread the germs of deadly diseases. Half the Chavantes had perished. This time there was no one to inconvenience the murderers—just the reverse. They no longer worked for themselves in the hope of illusory eldorados, but got a good pay, provided by the fazendeiros.

"The fazendeiros. The gentlemen in the big cities; the first really distinguished gentlemen to emerge in the savagery. In Rio de Janeiro and São Paulo, they had heard this story: 'On the Rio das Mortes, there are lands for the taking. They are good quality and not too far away. All you have to do is to get rid of the Indians.' For this they employed killers. There'd been a good blood-letting of Chavantes, but it hadn't been enough. For there were still some fanatics clinging to the soil who, over some thousands of miles, had created a new frontier between their own fields and the whites.' And these Indians no longer shot off arrows to defend themselves, but exhibited documents signed by me, by officers, by generals and by all the other pacifiers who only recently had guaranteed them their lives and properties forever. But this proved an illusory defense, too. For other papers were to be opposed to theirs.

"In Brazil, what kills more than anything else—more than the killers—is the law. The hypocrisy of the law. In this country, there are twenty-two states with twenty-two senates, not counting state and federal organizations. Imagine what this represents in the way of politicians! And what it produces in the way of decrees, ordinances and stipulations! You can be sure that there's some dirty business corresponding to every text.

"But the best people at making a law to measure are in the chambers of the Mato Grosso. It's all done very quietly, with deliberations, a vote, and a paper in an official journal. And now and again, a revolver shot or two in the middle of the debates. The upshot is an official decree, in suitably forbidding and pedantic jargon. The conspirators—for there's a coup every time—hold the keys to a fortune in lands. And the others, the ordinary people, are faced with ruin or death. It's all done in the Brazilian way, very decently on the surface, ferociously underneath, and terribly well-calculated.

"Poor Indians! This is how they lost everything in two sleights of hand. In a generous decree, number 903, dated the 28th of March 1950, the Governor of the Mato Grosso recognized the Chavantes' rights of possession of 12,352 square miles. And a few years later, on the 15th of December 1956, a small text consecrated and ratified the decree with this qualification, added as if routinely: 'All the territory which hasn't been demarcated and registered within two years will be returned to the State.' The Indians knew nothing about it, but the S.P.I. was admirably well informed. The very day the time ran out, the S.P.I. confiscated the Chavantes' territory on the grounds of 'illegality!' And then the little senhores of the S.P.I. divided it into lots which they sold to the big fazendeiros senhores. Obviously, everything had been worked out in advance between the interested parties. The purchasers didn't even need to kill the Chavantes, for with nothing left they were dying out slowly from starvation, poverty and despair.

"You could also sell these last Chavantes, if you happened to have any. This was the fruitful operation which the most powerful of the fazendeiros, one Orlando Ormeto, devoted himself to. He had got hold of so much territory that he found himself saddled with more than 1,000 Indians. What should he do with them? Kill them? That would be expensive, possibly mean a row. Reduce them to slavery? That was to give oneself a lot of trouble, probably for nothing. But 625 miles away there were some men who felt they had a vocation for getting the Indians to work—the Salesians of São Marcos, an Italian brotherhood. They had turned up plumb in the middle of virgin territory, "acquired" it thanks to the piety of the authorities, and had started off by founding a fine monastery, amid rich, fertile prairie soil which was waiting around to produce a blessed crop. They had an idea: What would be more edifying than to have nature's harvests grow thanks to a harvest of men? The double advantage of enriching the monks while they saved souls. They should procure the Chavantes remaining on the market, convert them and introduce them to the redemptive power of the law of labor. Wasn't this how the dedicated Jesuits of Paraguay had gone about it, two centuries ago? That had been a remarkable period, which the São Marcos brothers proposed to start over, on a more modern and businesslike scale.

"The deal was made, and Orlando Ormeto handed over his Chavantes to the brethren. They were stuffed into planes and brought to São Marcos by a miniature airlift. As luck would have it, over half of them caught a strange disease, a sort of scarlet fever, in the course of the flight. Many of them died, but the survivors learned good habits, litanies and the catechism. The Indian ladies were guided along the right path by the good sisters, the kids served as choir boys and the men were promoted to the dignity of agricultural workers. An eight-hour day, rounded off by mass at dawn and vespers at dusk. Their daily recompense was a ticket, which gave them the right to a plate of rice or manoic. Supplementary hours were paid for by a system of 'good points,' which enabled them to obtain clothes. Now you can see sturdy Chavantes in dungarees on tractors. But where is their soul, where is their life? I'll tell you—they're ecclesiastical serfs.

"What is left of the Chavantes? First, there are the 700 robots of São Marcos. But they're better off than the two other surviving groups, pitiful collections of living dead gathered around the S.P.I. stations, close to the Rio das Mortes. There are 200 of them at Arevese, and 300 at Pimentel. I can't begin to describe their fate. There is one particular brute among the S.P.I. people. As I speak, the 300 at Pimentel are in the process of being destroyed. They are not being given anything to eat, and they are forbidden to get anything themselves. When one of them was caught chewing, a civilized in the station hit him as he yelled, 'You've been stealing.' If no help is brought them from the outside, there will be no more Chavantes left alive at Pimentel in a few weeks. But where could this aid come from?

"The Chavantes have been reduced to nothing. In a sort of way, it's as if I had been reduced to nothing. When I was young I set out, at Vargas' summons, to make the Brazil of the people, with the Indian nations as the jewels of the people. But what happened to Getulio? Did he deceive or was he deceived? Men hid behind him who were even crueler and greedier than the traditional senhores they replaced. Formerly there weren't any 'professional politicians.' The power belonged quite naturally to the rich and the strong. But around Vargas this species of men new to Brazil was created—the bosses, the specialists in the public realm, the masters of the apparatuses. They said they loved Getulio, and they said they loved the people. But the people who mattered most to them were the nouveaux riches of big business, the big, ill-bred billionaires, who'd started from zero, too, from São Paulo. An extra skyscraper a day sprouted in that metropolis! Forty thousand more factories in the Brazil of those days, southern Brazil, a fantasy of modernism and prosperity, a Golden Calf in rut.

"It was the supermen, the powerful and the wily of São Paulo's Brazil who profited from Vargas' crusade to 'conquer' the rest of the country. As you know, I started from São Paulo, too. And so, when my work with the Chavantes was done, it was the people from the town where I was born who benefited from it. By perverting it. It was this alliance of senators and bankers who had my Chavantes killed, to get hold of thousands of square miles of soil for free. This war is not over; for now that the Indians are eliminated, the victors are tearing each other apart for their spoils.

"So go and see what's happening on the Rio das Mortes, my old

In the Vilas Boas reservation. The Indians rediscover some of their joy of life, their mores, customs, and ceremonials when they are freed from their fear of the Whites. But how long will this last? The advance of civilization is inevitable. The Indians stand in the way of civilization. Let them all die. No one says it, everyone thinks it.

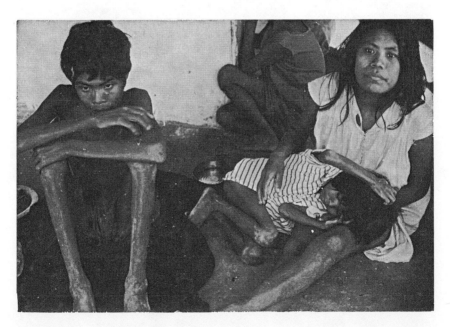

The Indian's abysmal poverty. These Indians were chased from their lands by the whites, hunted down. The Vilas Boas brothers, Claudio and Orlando, found them starving and terrorized. It will take long to calm them, give them some trust and a new longing for life. And then what can the future offer them?

'battlefront,' which has become the battlefront of thieves. Go to Chavantina, the town where I set off from, in my youth, to 'pacify' the Chavantes. There's not one Chavante there. But it's still a battlefield—a battlefield of greed."

I had lived with the Vilas Boas for some days, and they had told me the story of their lives with a noble and profound simplicity. They had been willing to express their thoughts. As noblemen. A masterly virility. Perhaps a little bit of ham in the performance, but still excellently well played. And a genuine virility, at that. I was among men. Sentiment, but no emotion—until the last few moments of my departure. And even then, no friendly slaps on the back, in the Brazilian manner. Just a pressure from their cheeks rough with beards, and a hug from their ragged sweaters. When I climbed into my little plane, I left them as they wished to be, in their legend.

Adieu Orlando. Adieu Claudio. Adieu, the hobos with pride, the tough with generosity. Adieu, the realists with the dream, and the obstinate with the noble ambition. Adieu, the brothers, disappointed in a formidable project.

I flew towards civilization, toward Brasilia, with a half-way stop at Chavantina. But Chavantina doesn't exist—in a completely modern way. There is no mato, there are no huts, no Indians, not even any half-castes. Just dozens and dozens of artistically placed gasoline drums, adorning rosebeds and walks. They composed a military aerodrome, where the F.A.B. machines took on supplies before soaring off towards the Far West. Conquest had passed by, and left in its wake a stopover in solitude and beauty for these stage coaches of the twentieth century.

Voices echoed in an open colonnade, where plants were twined and where the boss of the place, some commander or colonel, was bustling about. He was a stout, upright worm, yellowish from his own fat, in a khaki outfit which seemed like one more fatty layer. He did his best to embrace "my" pilot with his sausage-like arms—the fellow who'd transported me for the whole of my trek, who'd been so good at "giving" old clothes to the Vilas Boas brothers' Indians that he looked like an empurpled Nero in the feather finery he'd received in exchange. His pretty booty was now neatly stowed away in the little plane which had landed us at Chavantina.

Hugs between the base's punching clown and my young brave. They were old cronies. Jokes and gossip. How good life was! They paid no attention to anything else but their pleasure and their friendship—until Fatty unfolded one eye to look in the direction of the fruit hanging over our heads. The gourds clung there obscenely, plump pouches enclosing some empty, juicy interior. He tore himself away from his caresses, and started to walk portentously toward the most sumptuous fruit. As one hypnotized, he fingered them at length with expert hands. Suddenly he made his choice, cut the cord which held one of them up, swollen as if from some elephantiasis, and deposited the thing in the cupped hands of my pilot. It was a very important gift—whether from the intrinsic value of the object, or symbolically, I don't know. Anyway it ought to be the symbol of fraternity between two fine Brazilians, happy, adept, and prosperous, who knew how to fend for themselves, who understood each other . . .

Other good Brazilians had agglutinated around us: a fat lady and her kids, and a slender, tapering little man. Fraternity. I was asked to take these people in my plane. They were family, they were cousins, they were colleagues, I wouldn't know how to refuse . . .

Weasel-face was prepared to pay for his passage, with words. He'd been told that I was a senhor journaliste. So he agreed to the "game," allowed me to question him and even replied copiously. Honestly, too, it seems to me.

"The lands. They've caused a lot of quarrels. The best land belongs to the good Salesians of São Marcos . . . "

This was the religious order that Orlando had just talked about so caustically. But it was true that the Vilas Boas are unbelievers. Here I was going to get another version.

"Good monks. I know them well—I went on a retreat in their monastery. It's very large, square, two stories high, with rooms, refectories, cells and workshops, all painted in bright colors. There are a lot of people there. These monks do good, but they're very rich.

"It's caused a tremendous amount of jealousy. A few years ago a fazendeiro, Senhor Machado, went there in person, with some ten armed men. Surrounded by his guard, he shouted that the lands were his; he had the genuine property titles, and the monks' titles were fake. 'I'm going to give you a good lesson, as advised by my friend the prefect of the region. Pack up and go, or I'll kill you.' It's obvious that the senhor fazendeiro had a lot of political support, enough for him to dare to plunder men of God. When the prior said no, Machado had him seized by his men, and started to horsewhip him himself, on the face. The superior, covered with blood, accepted the blows as he prayed.

"It was the Chavantes who worked the monks' fields who saved them. The monks had the idea of ordering their Indians to paint themselves up in their war colors, and take up their bows and arrows. Strange are the ways of the Lord! For the defense of God's possessions, they'd been told to turn back into a savage horde. They snaked along, naked, and suddenly burst out around Machado and his killers, once again the terrifying, shrieking, dancing Chavantes. The senhor and his little troop fled, and the monks held a thanksgiving service in the pealing chapel, filled with scrubbed and decently reclothed Indians murmuring their prayers.

"Why did the Chavantes fight for the monks? Because Machado would have exterminated them. At least with the monks they are alive, and have rediscovered a certain taste to life, even if it's not their own. But how do they feel toward their masters? How can one know? They never show any feelings. They are docile—perhaps too much so. Everything belongs to the monks, nothing to them. After the scarlet fever crisis, there was a food crisis. Some of them fell sick from hunger. Then their regular allowance was improved, and now they look good, but they're kept out of the way, in a native village, and are closely supervised in everything they do. Sometimes the monks get discouraged, and talk of ingratitude. Yet their Indians work well and the monastery's fortunes continue to increase. But won't the monks be massacred one day out of the blue? With the Indians, I can tell you, you can never anticipate things, ever . . . "

Laughter. In the bungalow at Chavantina, this evaluation of the Chavantes occasioned general hilarity. It takes a monk, and even one hell of a monk, to believe that one can manufacture "good Indians." Is it the love of God which blinds the brethren, or their cupidity? The question was left respectfully unanswered.

The wind made the fat fruit sway above us. No one seemed afraid that they'd fall on our heads. Weasel-face said:

"You'll learn the most at Brasilia; that's where the biggest land coups are cooked up."

Brasilia. I knew that there weren't any Indians there. But the federal capital had been provided with an Indian outpost, 300 miles to the west, on the river Araguaia. It's where Indians are exhibited to visitors: the island of Bananal, the largest inland island in the world, hugged by two arms of the Araguaia. A palace of a hotel has been built there. There is a custom-built Indian village, with Indians on display. It's all very expensive, but the 'savages' are within arm's reach. There is, of course, a price list, but it's disregarded. Prostitution of every kind: "Do you want to go fishing? Hunting? Do you want a magic ceremony? A marriage? A war?" But everything is shoddy, from the feathers to the tattoos, which are no longer made with red-hot irons, but with paint. "Do you want to take photos? With us dressed or naked?" The Indians are dressed with the sole aim of undressing and revealing a charged-for nudity. So the migrants of the world, elderly American women, pay large numbers of dollars for a look at genitalia, while anywhere else the Indians' genitalia are free, and in superb abundance.

The Indians of Bananal! They are the Indians who were refused admittance to the hospital of Santa Isabel, close to the palace, at the time of an epidemic. The ones who had to scatter in the jungle, carrying their dead and dying in canoes. The remnants of remnants. I decided not to go to Bananal.

So en route for Brasilia, to find out whether it is the Americans or the Brazilians who are consuming the most Indians.

VI CIVILIZATION THAT KILLS

I'VE SEEN so many hard faces in the jungle—hard, flabby faces or hard, weather-beaten ones. White men bloat or dry out mysteriously, in the steam bath of bitter-sweet pestilence, the suffocating and marvelous night of Amazonia. Only the Indians—those who have not been condemned to a swift or slow death—are beautiful, with a natural splendor as of Eden. But all the civilized fall sick in body and in soul. Whether they are too fat or too thin, they are all stamped by an expression of impassivity, which you can sense is dangerous: the mask worn by wild creatures lying in wait. Even the Vilas Boas brothers, in spite of their "goodness," are of this kind. So what a marvel it was for me to find myself suddenly face to face with an archangel. It was as if I had leapt across centuries and worlds. And yet it had only taken an hour to fly from Chavantina to Brasilia, where I saw this apparition.

You entered the building as you would enter a mill, by the tenth, by the hundredth door on the ground floor—this time, in the rear of a futuristic palace. This one hadn't been finished. It had the flavor of a backstage as well as of a construction site. But there was nobody there, not even a vigilant type to play the part of the muscled doorman. From the upper stories and the endless corridors came voices of young people. Clear voices, absorbed in a gay task. I walked on and discovered boys leaning over some plans.

Then I entered a large room which wasn't an office, which wasn't a workshop, where there was nothing and which was nothing. Just a large table of bare boards, over which a man was stooped, also poring over plans. Then he straightened up. It was the master; you knew it, and yet there was nothing, no solemnity, no portentousness, to tell you so. He was tall. Slender, almost fleshless, his face sort of floating, slightly unreal, and yet very much there, as in certain pictures of sanctity. A broad forehead jutted out over slightly sunken eyes. He had one of those finely wrought heads, inscrutable and modest, such as are fashioned by thought. Such as are fashioned by faith. Passionate and disinterested thought and faith. As I approached him, he smiled at me. He had absolutely no idea who I was, but because I came to him, I was a "friend." A friend from universal friendship. And yet I might well be an informer—he was well aware that the police were watching him. As if that mattered to him! He had been a Stalin prize winner, and even now he was surrounded by Picasso's doves saying "Peace" in five or six languages. The doves were the only decoration; an extraordinary provocation in present-day Brazil, which is the Brazil of marshals and military dictatorship, where one is well advised to toe the line. But he has refused to renege on any part of his dream—the ideology for which he had fashioned the perfect material, and which he had clothed in flesh and blood.

Who would dare to raise a hand against the creator of the most astonishing and beautiful city in the world, the city made for love, Brasilia, which had risen from the desert thanks to strokes from his pen? Whether I was from the police or not, before I'd even spoken, before I'd told him that I was French and a journalist, he greeted me with this remark: "At Rio de Janeiro, the students are doing fine. They kept their ground against the charges of mounted riflemen, as they shouted 'Vive Che Guevara!' Some of them were trampled under the hooves . . . " And then, his eyes shining, he went on: "At Goiânia, the archbishop gave asylum in his cathedral to all the protesters. The troops stormed right into the chancel to shoot." His way of speaking reminded me of what the first Christians must have been like, declaiming their credo at every opportunity. Is he a Christian? I don't know. But he is a mystic. He is Oscar Niemeyer, the greatest architect, the greatest builder in the world, the man who wanted to unite in one eternal alliance, socialism, surrealism and beauty. Their reconciliation is to be found in Brasilia . . . a reconciliation in marble, but not in men. And there lies his tragedy.

Brasilia. A flight towards beauty, for the city is like a gigantic plane on the point of taking off towards the marvelous future, towards paradise, towards socialism. High on the ruddy barren plateau where there is nothing but gravel and swamps, you see a fantastic fuselage one-and-a-half-miles long, with immense fins. It is Brasilia, ready to depart for the Golden Age; Brasilia that is already skimming along toward the year 2,000. Everything is futuristic. Everything is ideas, each form, each building is an idea soaring endlessly upward. What in other towns used to be a function, has here been transfigured into magnanimity.

As its cabin, there's a sort of "royal way," a great highway surrounded by everything that goes to make up the beliefs, the knowledge, the hopes and the laws of man, in the guise of airy alloys and costly materials. First,

intentionally, there's a wasteland, the desert of the spirit, which is studded
with monuments, the spirit's jewels. There is culture here, with a theater and
a university. There is even religion. This is represented by a subterranean
cathedral enclosed beneath a cover of glass, a porthole toward the sky—it was
difficult to find a plexiglass which didn't overheat the interior. Above this
incubation of prayer is the belfry, a painful and glorious loftiness, a
consummate sacrifice. It is a wreath that is bound ever tighter, like a crown of
thorns lacerating as they tighten. The absolute symbol. There was no need for
these steel talons to torture the face of the God-made-man—no need for a
Christ. Just His most essential incarnation, a little cross on the very summit:
to show that what is the hardest in Christianity, its very essence, keeps vigil
over a Brasilia which wishes to consecrate itself to brotherhood on earth, to
an atheist happiness. No enormous idol like the one beetling over the
sugarloaf mountain at Rio de Janeiro, that pot-pourri of all human pleasures.

The purity of Brasilia: the most utilitarian thing is sublimated. What is viler
in itself than the administration, the ministries and the government? Here in
Brasilia principles are materialized. The Great Way terminates in the grandeur
of the public realm. First of all, on each side of the fabulous highway, like
connecting rods, are five rigorously parallel units. These are the perfect
machines fashioned to administer a vast Brazil. It's the factory of bureaucracy, the cluster of all the ministries. Their wheels turn far from the base
blows of chance, without noise, without crowds, without squalor, and
without refuse. They're almost abstractions—long glass boxes. Inside them are
thousands of transparent cells, as if there were nothing to hide, as if all were
light. They are the offices of the highest civil servants, where a man should no
longer think of himself but of the people. The old Brazilian egotism has been
replaced by the technocracy of the good, and with the good as its driving
force. Well, that's the theory anyway . . .

Apotheosis. The unexpected dead end. For quite close to these buildings,
The Great Way ends with the law. A crescendo. This highway, which has been
bordered by the monuments of ideas, which has passed through the buildings
of bureaucracy, leads to the supreme sovereignty. You complete the ascent
towards ideology and socialism by reaching a very curious ensemble which
bars your way. A kind of mobile, set on the ground. It can also look like an
ultrahuge, ultramodern toilet. In the middle, two translucent slivers are
planted side by side, together assaulting the heavens—but they could just as
well be towel rails. Below there are kinds of basins. The one on the right,
which is put in a normal position, might contain water. The one on the left is

inverted, as if you'd chucked out the water after using it. All this is
Parliament. The Secretariat is installed in the two dizzying slabs; beneath the
upright cup is the Senate, and beneath the upside-down cup is the Chamber.

Although everything is transparent in Brasilia, the two Assemblies are
enclosed beneath these superstructures. Inside there is a labyrinth of immense
corridors, involuted staircases, things that resemble dead ends and bottle-
necks, with sudden openings onto quantities of rooms. All the cubicles that
you need to prepare yourself to legislate—toilets, libraries, bank counters,
post offices, bars, restaurants, places to talk in and places to spit in. Crowds
of people converse in this sumptuous troglodyte universe, the electricity
throwing into harsh relief the mustaches and skins, with the effect of
bootblacking the complexion. Bursts of voices, strumming of fingers, cabals,
nonchalance, solemnity, the whole political scene with its triumphs, its
profiteers and its servants. Every material and intellectual comfort has been
installed—the latter comfort being the least used, despite the stocks of books
and newspapers, the whole of literature, science and the world's press in
incredibly well-ordered rooms, the only rooms to be somewhat empty.
Elsewhere it's like the inner city and the subway put together. All of this
culminates in the two semicycles where the official law is wrought—not many
people there, either. But what a crowd in the corridors and lobbies making
the real law, or so they say, in what I have called the bottom of the "cup."

Light and shade of the Brazilian realization. The savage chiaroscuro of
jungle and men is continued in the purity of Brasilia. But there is light and
shade in the superhuman architecture of Niemeyer as well, the architecture
conceived for the perfect creatures of a radiant socialism. This artistic
opposition he has fully intended. It can best be seen quite close to the square
of the Three Powers—where the Judiciary and Executive buildings flank the
Parliament like annexes—in an extraordinarily beautiful edifice. It is called
the Palace Itamaraty. It's a ministry which is not integrated into the complex
of ministries; it's the ministry of Foreign Affairs. That is to say, it's the
supreme incarnation of Brazil as she would like to be, the face that she shows
the world. The intelligence is, of course, Niemeyer's, the only one capable of
the technical ability and the innovative discoveries for such a design.

At first it's a cavern. It's all marvelous, but in a way you don't know where
you are or where you are going. You emerge from trap doors, ramps and
passages, and come across water or grass, a courtyard, a closet like a
sanctuary, or some huge lonely object, or reflections and mirages. You are
there as if shut up in a dream. You bump against the dream. It's all

deceptive—there is no space. It's stifling. There is no real day, but the electricity and the air-conditioning have been worked over enough to make another day, impalpable, strange, fabulous, precise and false. High and low ceilings collide, walls separate or draw near. The dream can procure the nightmare. The machinery of the marvelous; the fantasia of the trompe-l'oeil—and yet there is nothing which is not genuine. A tangle of marble, steel, mirrors, and woods where the distant jostles against the near, where stress is mingled with solace and light with dark. All this darkness, these heavy wrappings, are made of jacandando, the tree that is the heavy soul of the jungle.

In this palace I feel as if I were in prison. There are too many symbols. An interior world where you are interned. Is this the liberation? It is madness purged by all the heavy abstractions; it is the sublimated translations of the darkest complexes of man and nature. It is the zenith of art at its most refined, a delirium of the delicacy which is perhaps the zenith of primitivism. The jungle is here, and yet there is almost no greenery, just a few tufts of thick plants. Walls of glass separate you from the sky and the grass. Inside, mysterious paths lead from marvel to marvel, from secret to secret, to arrive at a miniscule notch. Beyond this is a rectangle of water or grass, which is not the vast space of the country, but just limits, just frontiers. And never, never are there any flowers. It is cerebralism gone mad, the unknown factor in instincts and hopes governed under art.

But is art, particularly this art so imbued with the contradictions and dramas of man, the solution? Is it the solution for the wretched masses, to whom Brasilia is a name that triggers the national pride, like the victory of a football team? But Brasilia is pride by proxy. For Brasilia is not the people; it is an aristocracy which thinks, which believes it thinks, for the people, and which in the name of the people, has created something that is more than Versailles, Angkor-wat, or the Pyramids. Or which is, at the least, all of them in terms of the twentieth century. The matchless expression of modern times whose style has not yet been discovered. An astonishing success—but an astonishing waste as well. For it is the act of a despot.

An abnormal city—even a monstrous city. The opposite of a Paris or a London, which has been formed by centuries of civilization. The opposite of a New York or even a São Paulo, which has shot up under a fantastic pressure of forces. Until Brasilia, in the history of the world, cities had been made for their inhabitants. Brasilia is the first city to be born not for beings as they are but for the idea of what they ought to be.

Where are the people? Together. All the people who have the same occupation are together in their cuadras and their supercuadras. These are "habitational units" which are completely self-sufficient and where the occupants are completely self-sufficient. They are like convents; there is the convent of culture, where all the "cultured" live culturally in a community; there is the banking convent where even a fortune is not supposed to count—so the millionaire director is lodged with his employees, from his doorman up. Of course, the word convent isn't used—instead one uses the word sector. Forty-eight sectors altogether, with a common work, common leisure, common occupations and preoccupations.

You would think you were in the capital of a socialism that had reached the peak of its evolution. With humans like insects between glass slides. Insects submissive to the Party and all-powerful thanks to the Party. It is conceived as a city of "cadres," being perfect in their humility and their power who, from the cuadras, telecommand the whole people. The sacred city of the bureaucrats consecrated to the people who aren't there. Of course, it was necessary to have thousands of workers come to build it in the open desert; and when it was completed, the working class was chased out. The ordinary people are crowded into teeming satellite cities, with some 20,000 to 40,000 inhabitants in each, all compulsorily more than twenty miles from Brasilia. There lives the normal Brazil, with its squalor, misery and joy, its women and fripperies, its stench and drama—life in its fullness, whereas Brasilia in its beauty is as if dead, as if soulless. A terrible piercing boredom oozes from everywhere.

A fantastic misunderstanding. That Niemeyer has given to his masterpiece the face of socialism in its purest state, the face of political commissaries in a totally futuristic Kremlin, is obvious. But the truth is that there is no socialism in Brazil and no socialism in Brasilia. It is only a dream . . .

The art of governing by dream, long before Brasilia, had been invented by Vargas, Getulio the hairless, with the crooked nose, alone in his palace. To understand Brasilia one must go back to Getulio who sincerely loved the humble and the poor, but who had no program for them. Nothing but his charm and the jobber's art of blowing hot or cold with the contemporary wind. He passed through a certain fascist period at the time of Hitler and Mussolini, whom he liked to be compared to. But it was a watered-down fascism. A kind of democracy. At the time of the Allied victory, he even sent an expeditionary force to Italy. In reality there was nothing but paternalism.

He was a debonair autocrat, and that was enough. As a system, he had himself and people like him, politicians who had risen from lowly beginnings. He had replaced the "coronels"—so called because they had commanded battalions of the national guard at the time of the Brazilian empire—who used to govern with the ferocity of their forebears. Vargas and his men were spellbinders. They dabbled in socialism after a fashion, which allowed them to get into everything. When Vargas created syndicates, the funds were in the hands of the states and the syndicalists were his good friends. Nothing had been changed in depth. Vargas' strength lay in the fact that he was sincere in his lack of scruples. And that he knew how to make it, à la brazilienne. No blood was shed; if he had any captains who revolted, he made them majors. And he lasted.

This was easy enough, for thanks to the Second World War, it was the golden age. The Americans and the English needed all the eldorados of Brazil and they were buying up everything. Unlooked for prosperity. And then peace brought back misery. There were immense problems to resolve—a partially modernized country had to provide for the masses who were beginning to have a vague consciousness of themselves. Vargas knew nothing of economy and his prestige was exhausted. He left after fifteen years of "rule." But after him things got worse, and in 1950, at sixty-seven years of age, he returned to power.

The country was paralyzed. As a recourse, Vargas had himself acclaimed as president. But he had to find new recipes for applause—to achieve this, he propounded Brazilian expansion. Words replaced money. To Vargas, it had always been very easy. What was simpler than for him to proclaim "I'm doubling all the salaries the day after tomorrow." That had been a catastrophe. Getulio was obliged to look for magisterial words: "I'm going to make Brazilian steel." It caused immense popular excitement. The Americans weren't too unhappy with this sort of socialism, because they financed it. "I'm going to make Brazilian petroleum," he said, but this time the Americans were excluded from the business. It escalated. Vargas was waging war, in spite of himself, against the rich and against the gringos, the Americans.

There was a certain Carlos Lacerda, a young and already thickset man, with regular features, a leaden mask of a face, and a massive body, who was a violent enemy of the regime. He was connected with the billionaires, but he was even more the hero of all the people who were afraid for their pennies. Lacerda shouted "Vargas is mad ... " It was an odd situation, the aging

Vargas in the middle of his crusade with this hue and cry against him. Just then a huge Negro named Gregorio, a professional assassin, shot at Lacerda. Clearly under orders. The bullets, instead of riddling the populist, killed a very respectable officer. A fantastic scandal. Vargas, in his palace, without understanding it, suddenly saw ignominy surrounding him. Vargas himself was innocent. The true criminal was no doubt his son, who was said to head a band of killers called the "Black Guard."

Vargas began to realize that in his entourage there was only complicity, corruption and trafficking, which had been covered by his name. Many politicians, his own disciples, were no better than bandits. But instead of admitting himself defeated, Vargas put his last efforts into resistance, trying to sublimate himself and his works. He was called upon to resign. He refused to abandon the presidency except by death. One day, at dawn, in 1955, he put a bullet through his heart, a proud and tragic end after months of filth. He had perished because he had given the people too many illusions. All the same he had set Brazil on a certain path—the belief that everything was possible for Brazilians. And it was this technique of the "dream" which would one day lead to Brasilia.

However, after Vargas, the daydreams nearly collapsed, for the politicians of Getulio's school were almost eliminated when the new president was elected. It was a gesture from a genuine hero who saved them, the famous Luis Carlos Prestes. Prestes the ferocious, Prestes the revolutionary, Prestes the innocent. More than a man, a legend.

Prestes had been a philosopher-officer, just like Rondon, who had consecrated his life to saving the Indians. Prestes had wanted much more—to save Brazil, the whole of Brazil destroyed by injustice and oppression. And he had become an outlaw.

Rondon and Prestes were two products of that strange Brazilian army which once believed so strongly in Auguste Comte, in positivism and in virtue, an army imbued with the goodness of man and the triumph of the good. A studious, serious army, distinguished and well-informed, composed of braided intellectuals, the best sons of the middle class—an army reluctant to impose virtue by the force of its bayonets. It was cast in the role of moderating power; the generals emerged from the shadows to guide the nation through her great crises. They used to make fundamental choices following their consciences, generally without bloodshed, without even using their soldiers. When they had set up the civilian who seemed to them to be the best choice, they effaced themselves behind him, at least until they were obliged to intervene again for the good of the country. And so the military was always there, obedient, but with a kind of right to disobey when necessary. One word from them was usually enough. It was they who had seen to it that Vargas had been elected, dismissed, taken back and finally humiliated, to the point of suicide. But by and large they accepted society as it was, confining themselves to serve as its pilots when there were reefs to avoid.

Prestes, like his father, had been a professional soldier. But he had scarcely reached the rank of captain when he led a revolt. The revolt was a failure. Far from abandoning his purpose he had then begun his "long march" across Brazil, with 2,000 men. He had but one goal: to overthrow what existed, to destroy the evil, to make the revolution—but of what kind? Prestes did not know. He and his phantom column spent years wandering through the jungles, the catingas, the matos and the prairies without being caught. He was adored by everyone. He spent years wandering like this, without ideology and without program, with only his generosity of spirit.

This lasted until he found the Red Gospel. And suddenly he was inspired: "It is Communism which is the truth for Brazil." In 1930 he went humbly to Moscow, where he was "educated" for four years. On his return in 1935, he acted. His solution was to instigate an insurrection of the army, which he organized methodically. Several regiments were involved. Putsch, defeat, capture. Vargas—the Vargas of the fascist period—had him condemned to fifty years in prison.

Prestes spent ten years in jail and was reprieved after Vargas' first "retirement" in 1945. He was ordered by Moscow to obtain power by legal means. He almost triumphed. Prestes the secretary of the Brazilian Communist party, Prestes the senator, Prestes obtaining almost 600,000 votes for the Party in the election, Prestes with fifteen deputies on his side, Prestes the great revolutionary figure of the whole South American continent. Was Brazil going to fall into his hands? He led a crusade against Washington, and suddenly there was nothing left. On a sign from Washington . . . his party was dissolved, his deputies dismissed and Prestes himself accused. It all happened with laughable ease; he was allowed to flee and once again he was a hunted man—although not genuinely so, for he had many fewer men around him than before and much greater sympathy from the authorities. He was not persecuted and he was even left his aureola of the noble outlaw, which lasted through Vargas' return and after Vargas' death.

When Getulio Vargas killed himself, there was no talk of Prestes. In spite of his sincerity, and his efforts, he had not changed his own nature. He believed he was a Communist, but he had remained a cavalier, a tropical Robin Hood. And all the wretched of Brazil who had protected him, who had hidden him in the course of his endless underground activities, all the unfortunates who had voted for him in the brief but dazzling moment when he had emerged from illegality, had not become Communists any more than he had. These poor people were nothing but fanatical supporters of the superman redresser of their wrongs. But Prestes had organized nothing among the masses which had any resemblance to a party constructed for revolution. Indeed his strength was approximately the same emotional base as that exploited by Vargas, and which the man who claimed his succession also wished to exploit—Vargas' disciple, Juscelino Kubitschek.

It was as if Prestes had vanished into his legend. But before entirely vanishing he gave one decisive thrust to the destiny of Brazil. After the suicide of his implacable enemy Vargas, in order that conservatism, the great feudalism of trusts, of the coronels and Washington's straw men might not triumph, he ordered his remaining supporters to give their votes to the man who took over from "our father Getulio." It had turned the scales; Kubitschek carried the day. So in this way Prestes made his contribution.

Who was Juscelino Kubitschek, the unknown with the prosaic name? He was solid, tough and self-taught. Like Vargas the gaucho and like all the men in Vargas' band, he too was a man from the interior of Brazil, with all the opportunism that this implies. He was born in the backwoods of the state of Minas Gerais, among the Indians and the garimpeiros. His birthplace left its mark. He was also very intelligent and incredibly ambitious. He quickly set about making himself one of the middle class, studying, taking exams, and earning a doctor's diploma. And at the moment that he had intended, he became a politician—a technician-politician in the style of Vargas. His father was named Oliveira. But there were millions of Oliveiras in Brazil, so to distinguish himself, he took from his Czech mother, as his last name, Kubitschek, to show that he was different.

But Kubitschek had that very Brazilian flair for modern marvels. It has been the characteristic of Brazil at all periods. One has only to recall the crude billionaires of Manaus in 1910, the rubber barons who made the most dazzling city of the Belle Epoque rise out of the heart of Amazonia. This strange sense of the avant-garde had remained in the country. Alongside its primitivism, and mingled with it, there was always this taste for novelty pushed to its furthest point. After the Brazil of the jungle and the sacred rococo, after the Brazil of the jungle and the nouveau riche Parisianism, there was the Brazil of the jungle and futurism—with Kubitschek to officiate over it.

Vargas' Brazil had been divided into great fiefs and distributed among his lieutenants; Kubitschek was the governor of his birth state of Minas Gerais. Vargas had intended Kubitschek to be a classic governor, with his gang and his organization and without any imagination. But Vargas was outshone by Kubitschek, who knew so well which way the wind of his epoch was blowing. If he stole, he also created; he had a mystique for creation. And so it was that he made his first great leap into the future. He brutally jettisoned the capital of Minas Gerais, the city of Ouro Prêto, because it was antiquated, even though it was a prestigious antiquity with all the splendors of the civilization of gold. He had a new capital made for himself, somewhat more in the interior of the continent, at Belo Horizonte. In place of the ancient outmoded treasures, this was a city consecrated to the metals of the twentieth century, from iron onward. It took ten years, from 1920 to 1930, to build. Kubitschek used Niemeyer for his Belo Horizonte. Niemeyer made him a church in the form of round blisters, hangars for the faithful overlooked by a pyramid that tapered at the base.

In 1955 Kubitschek became the president of the Republic. First and foremost he had to make himself "Juscelino" to all the proliferating, teeming, swarming Brazilians of the masses. This fantastic tidal wave of human beings had swelled from 4,000,000 to almost 80,000,000 in a century and a half. If the Indians died, those of mixed blood seemed to have the same luxuriance as the jungle, where everything intermingled and reproduced.

Vargas had realized that for the Brazilians—passionate about football and carnivals—politics had to be a spectacle, and since Vargas' time, the same rules had applied to senators, governors, and the president of the Republic. Each of these people introduced himself in a relevant role, like an actor, with his series of gags, grimaces, and side effects that he could count upon to cajole or menace; he had his accessories, from cloaks to Tommy guns, and a retinue of grave secretaries as well as gentlemen with killer faces. Idolatry had to be unleashed, and every trick was acceptable. One genre that was much appreciated was "emphatic clowning." Nothing was too vulgar. And then in their staff headquarters, the politicians turned back into the bosses, and devoted themselves seriously to their own affairs.

Like everyone else, President Juscelino Kubitschek promised marvelous happiness for all. They wanted the dream. So he gave them the most sublime dream of all: Brasilia. The moment he was in power, he took a plane and had himself set down facing the jungle. The magic city, the capital, would rise where he'd landed. It was a capital that started off from nothing, because beyond Belo Horizonte there was nothing. The dream he was offering was the dream of Brazil the giant, Brazil the resplendent, Brazil of all the eldorados taking shape without the help of Americans, foreigners or exploiters by the invincible might of Brazil herself. It was this dream of national pride which naively, almost childishly, inflamed 80,000,000 Brazilians, even the darkest of the half-castes—for they, too, obscurely would feel themselves taller and stronger. So what did it matter how much it would cost?

How Vargas was outdistanced! For he, though the precursor of modernism, used to copy the rest of the world. Kubitschek paid no heed to it. Everything was possible. To the staid who predicted ruin, bankruptcy and catastrophe, he eulogized folly. Folly alone could tame the Brazilian gigantism and transform into a blessing what had been believed to be a curse. What was needed was the extraordinary; to deny the laws of finance and all the other prosaic laws, and at one blow, to create Brasilia and give Brazil a new heart. Beneath the accursed flowers of the Green Hell, was there not all the wealth imaginable? Brazilians had only to make themselves masters of it for their Brazil to be the greatest country in the world.

The wily Kubitschek had a piece of bravura ready for his astounded European visitors. He laughed in front of their stupefaction:

"In Europe all the nations are old and have depleted their resources. So you must count your pennies. But why should we bother ourselves with that in Brazil, with all our fantastic eldorados? Our only problem is to have them all issue en masse. And for that, one magisterial phrase is enough, the magic words, ' I want it. ' Surrealism is the real realism."

Surrealism? Juscelino's right hand was Neimeyer, who was oblivious to money, and who came from an aristocracy so disinterested and sure of itself that it found its most natural expression in "progressivism." Niemeyer genuinely believed in it. But to Brazilians with less genius and generosity of spirit, it was a fashionable snobbery. It was "good taste" to love the people. So you adored the masses by the conception of Brasilia, whose procreation was an extraordinary circus of technology, intellectualism, and avant-garde worldliness. This select group had its own spectacle: its international juries and conferences, which out of twenty-six plans designed by world leaders in urban planning, chose Niemeyer's. Niemeyer was the first man in history to have limitless means to build his unique city. As the construction progressed, Kubitschek put his initials "J.K." everywhere, and gave each group of new buildings the first name of one of his sons.

A miracle of ferocious and absolute will. The mammoth work was completed in five years, from 1955 to 1960, and Brasilia sprang into life with her facade of socialism. But the truth about Brasilia was that Brazil's finances were on the rocks, all her people despoiled by a ruinous inflation, and that the big operators had gone on a money-making spree. Profit had become the soul of Brasilia.

Yet the financial collapse had served to pay for a certain economic progress. A curious arithmetic—the more inflation, the more progress. Pounds of papers for one little purchase, the cruzeiro so bloated with figures that it was bursting from indigestion, the budget of the State at zero and its credit pretty well dead. But Niemeyer's buildings, those made for virtue, doubled their prices every month, for they were coveted by the nouveaux riches, the rich who were born of Brasilia, who lived off Brasilia, and who made Brasilia live. The artificial city's prosperity was incredible, thanks to dishonest civil servants, corrupt politicians, and rabid speculators. Brasilia survives like a nest of egotism. Another irony: Brasilia, which was built against the Americans, is now in the clutches of the Americans, who are more powerful and numerous than ever before. The curious "success" of Brasilia has brought with it the result that all the land in the interior of Brazil is being auctioned off—to the benefit of the Americans, who have gone on a wild spree of buying up jungles, rios, serras, matos and prairies. They have bought up millions of acres, at least a quarter of Brazil—with the consequence, the eternal consequence, of the death of ever more Indians.

Brasilia was supposed to bring happiness to all the Brazilians, including the Indians. But it happened at its completion that the managerial offices of the Service for the Protection of the Indians were burnt to the ground, in a fire which destroyed all their dossiers and archives—as if some one had an interest in annihilating them forever. As if it were necessary that no one should notice that instead of the felicity specifically promised by Kubitschek to the Indians, there had been nothing for them but still greater horrors.

"BRASILIA IS Brasilia. She's accepted now. She's nuts but she exists. She's won the battle and she'll last. But she only just made it. The construction was completed three or four years ago—the city was superb, but incomprehensible. She frightened everyone. All you thought about was getting the hell out. She was considered a whim of a megalomaniac, the biggest whim ever, and the one that had had the most money shelled out for nothing. All of us believed that this brand-new city would soon be just a dead city, overrun by the mato. We could already see the vegetation beginning to crack the marble. What changed everything was the arrival of the dollar and the Americans, after power had been taken over by the military who disliked Brasilia as the work of the politicians whom they'd overthrown and whom they loathed. It's a paradoxical survival, isn't it? The army so hostile to Brasilia and saving her despite itself, because of the appetite of their American allies!"

A husky voice. I didn't know the man who was speaking to me—it was just a traveler's chance encounter in a bar. I was at the National Hotel, the palace of progressive hoteliers which had become a sort of super-Hilton. There was nothing there which wasn't rich, pretentious, and stuffy; there were so many diamonds on the women and rolls of flesh on the nape of the men's necks, so many batteries of lobsters displayed on the tables, that it was suffocating. Everywhere the smell of money. Everywhere flunkies, whose infinite nuances of suspicion vanished miraculously in the face of certain gentlemen: the big operators—the true masters of Brasilia and Brazil—a few senhores, and some Americans. In a brochure, advertisements for a Pepsi-Cola factory. The reign of "Brazilo-Americanism."

The only place there was a crush was in the cleverly somber bar, which was sort of two-tiered, with its seats too low and its stools too high. Virtually no one there but men. The unknown peered from all those faces as honed as the blade of a knife or as rounded as juicy pumpkins. Very respectable faces, if a little feverish from the alcohol and the calculations whirlpooling in their brains. The bar of the modern eldorado.

I was suddenly assailed by calls in French which came from someone unrolled upon the edge of the bar. Everything on his head and face ran to length; features like gutters, a predominence of cartilage, large ears growing downwards, colorless eyes, colorless hair and a long thin slit for a mouth. The most solid thing about him was his sharp teeth which cut the flow of his words, words which were somehow both piercing, grating and insipid. Cordiality and impudence, and the rather sleazy tranquility of someone who has seen everything, who is surprised by nothing, and who knows how to make out. What nationality? A mystery. But as he had spent a long time in Paris, he still had an excellent French vocabulary with a strong, thick, yet indefinable accent which he had kept throughout all his peregrinations. A man who could speak thirty-six languages in the same way. All his perambulations had made him one of the most respectable senhores in Brazil, one of those who had really arrived, to judge by the servile smile of the bartender serving him dry martinis.

"When there's a Frenchman," he shouted to me, "I spot him immediately. They're rare in these parts and it gives me a change of scene. All my past returns to me. Paris. I was young . . . I needed a country like Brazil. I've been here over twenty years. It's the kind of backwoods where a bright boy, if it doesn't kill him, can make his bread and butter. But what a lot of fleecing has to be gone through first. You're rooked once, twice, ten times. There's no pity around these parts, I can tell you that. Everything's crooked. I was had the day I got off the boat. It took me years and years to become my own despachante, to manage for myself and even to render service to my friends.

"I had to learn everything, the language and the customs. My hardest lesson was to understand that even in the heart of the Green Hell, everything is always calculated with unimaginable precision. It's always a battle where there has to be a winner and a loser. Things are never as they seem. You think that such and such a senhor is the "boss." It's not he; it's just his double. Two senhores spread the word that they're enemies; they turn out to be accomplices. It all has a complexity and a subtlety that you wouldn't believe, a spider's web. Force and fortune are in command, but you can never see the way clear. And yet you know that for every affair, there is a "right way" to manage it. To understand Brazil is to manage to find the right way, at least now and again; and then instead of being squeezed, you put the squeeze on others. That is success . . . "

Why did this man speak to me like this? He certainly wasn't a small-time crook showing me some shabby swindle. In the first place, there were only well-off people in the National Hotel. Nor was the man fishing for a fool. Still, he had a sort of need to talk about himself, to tell the truth about himself, his life and Brazil, at long last. What he kept quiet about was the period before, what he had been and what he had done in France. I had the feeling that he must have gotten himself tarred in those days as a collaborator, or rather that he must have been one of those marginal men, without origins, more or less without a country, whom the Germans used to use for so many of their jobs. (Could he have been one of those White

Russians who used to serve the Germans as jack-of-all-trades, interpreters, spies, giving leads to the inside story, the touts and the V.I.P.s of the black market? The slang which he bandied about was certainly from that period and that milieu.) Obviously I couldn't question him. I shall never know anything more, I shall just be left with an impression, perhaps a false one. But what does it matter? The man had launched into Brazil.

"I am in real estate. I sell jungle and Brasilia—in other words, I'm a grileiro, but just a small one compared with senhores who make deals of 1,000,000 acres at a time. My operations don't exceed a few thousand acres at a go. But it's already making a profit.

"I do to people what was done to me. I arrived here with the idea of starting my life over in agriculture, of becoming a fazendeiro. With the little money that I had, I bought what was guaranteed as first-quality land. What made up my mind for me was that someone had me meet a well-known politician—who swore, the bastard, that the government was going to build a highway in the region of my territory. He told me: 'Nobody knows about it, but it's forecast for the next plan. It will multiply the value of your ground tenfold; you're making a golden deal.' I was given papers; I didn't suspect that they were valueless. Anyway, it really wasn't important, because the place wasn't worth anything. I found myself at the end of the world, on the edge of a river in the marshes. I tried hard, all the same. I set out to destroy the snakes and mosquitoes, but there were too many of them. And the Indians were disgusting. The place was full of them. They used to arrive some days very friendly, offering me their wives or anything else. But they used to change from one day to the next. They would set out to provoke you, in such a way that you would get into a blazing temper. Then they would have a good reason for butchering you. And they didn't even have anything to be afraid of if they mucked about a few 'fools of immigrants' who had already been duly despoiled by the bright boys who'd sent them off to rot in a patch of jungle. We were the people whom the Indians could kill without being in any danger of being killed themselves. It was a good riddance.

"Those rotten Indians! They pulled their tricks on the country people, the half-castes and the real fazendeiros. Not too far from my hole there was an honest-to-goodness fazenda, with a senhor and his caboclos. The savages waited for months until almost all the men left for the town, where they would sell their cattle and buy salt. The expedition took several weeks, with rivers full of piranhas to get the animals across. During this time, the Indians appeared one day at dawn on the defenseless estate, and wiped out everything they found there, old men, women, and kids, only sparing a few girls, whom they took off with them. When the caboclos returned, they found nothing but ruins and bones, and the Indians vanished, no one knew where.

"As for me, I got out fast. Poisoned arrows, Indians who suddenly turned into raging maniacs, I didn't care for that at all. Not to mention the rest—the seed I'd sown, which never came up, my few pigs which attracted the boa constrictors, etc. I found myself back at Cuiabá. I had learned. In Brazil it takes years to acquire a good technique and good connections, as well as a mastery of usage and customs. What a place! I was really put through it. You can't imagine how I groveled and crawled with hunger first while I didn't know Portuguese. But once I could write it, I was saved.

"Most people in the interior were illiterate, so I did the secretarial bit for lots of little local politicians, for the Far West civil servants and for senhores who were trafficking. Then I became a canvasser, a straw man, a man in people's confidence. I had a few tough breaks, and started from zero each time. It was a dangerous profession, but I was trustworthy, I didn't blab and I even started to propose ideas which made money. There's nowhere else in the world where that's appreciated so much. But I'm not going to tell you my transactions of the old days—I'd be skinned for it, even these days when I'm worth quite a lot of money. Let's just say that in the end, thanks to my deserts, I insinuated myself into close friendships with a few big operators and was accepted by them.

"In a certain way, Brazil is a club. I served as a tout for a grileiro and then I established myself on my own account. I, who had begun by being done, by buying a miserable chunk of jungle, was now retailing it in bulk. But times had damned well changed since then. You couldn't pull off the phantom-road trick of the old days, sending off some poor devil into a Green Hell where there'd be nothing at all. You see the country was beginning to be generally developed. Like a shot I turned my hand to honesty, because it was honesty that would pay the most. I used to choose a region that was pretty well virgin, calculating that it was there that the next slice of modernization would fall. My thing was to foresee progress a few years in advance. I used to buy when it was worth nothing, a dollar for two and one-half acres. Then I used to wait. I have a flair for smelling it out just right. As soon as the first path that was vaguely suitable for vehicles had been laid out, as soon as the jeep replaced the canoe, my land rose to five or ten dollars for two and a-half acres. To at least twenty if it was a real highway. To more if it was a dam project—to even more if anyone discovered asbestos, nickel, magnesium, not to mention uranium.

"I walked into three miles of pure pencil, graphite. And near it, close by Nickelandia, was the biggest pile of nickel in the world, next to Canada's. Of course the colossal deals were not for me, they were for the big grileiros, the ones who dealt directly with Washington and the large trusts. I've no idea if everything that's told about these vast treasures is true. Even the geologists don't agree. What's more, I don't give a damn. Whichever way it is, it raises the prices. What I need is a trace, just the smallest trace of asbestos or of anything else, on my land. It really doesn't matter very much whether it's exploitable or not—I would even rather it weren't—it would be too much, I would be emptied out. I just need a semblance. For then it begins to take off, at $50, $100 for each two and one-half acres, and more. That's how I fobbed off all my property onto Americans, nice ordinary Americans, the kind who dream of Texas as it was fifty years ago. Nice clients. It was my first big business deal . . .

"To be quite honest, it's wrong of me to boast. I should be a billionaire. I would be one if I hadn't bungled Brasilia. I ought to have known that in Brazil, when there's an enormous waste of money, particularly official money, there are stupendous fortunes to be made by the crafty. All I've done is get a few pickings. I didn't get more because of my prudence, because I didn't manage to believe it. As if one ought to be prudent under the circumstances, in this country!

"For Brasilia, the cruzeiro had had it—and so had almost the whole budget of the State. It wasn't enough. The State put the printing presses to work, in a big way. It was a very Brazilian phenomenon that the good people throughout the country who'd been bled for Brasilia didn't balk too much. Notice that for the big debtors and big customers, it was a good thing. As for the merchants, their prices went up faster than the inflation. Every week they stuck a new tag onto their merchandise with figures swollen by thirty or forty per cent. The rich managed to make do one way or another. But the masses were really hard hit—the poor who had no debts to wipe out nor property which automatically increased in value, the poor who lived from day to day, managing to nibble at something, to have a beer, a piece of ass, or a turn of samba thanks to a crappy bank note that had been earned with so much trouble.

"But the printing presses didn't do the trick. Brasilia still needed more real dough. The construction sites thirsted for billions so as not to stop. So Juscelino ordered all the social organizations, all the Prudential institutes, the institutes for assistance, insurance, health and instruction, all the syndicates and all the mutuals to pour in their funds and their reserves to finance Brasilia.

"But it was still not enough. It was at this point that the government went sniveling to the capitalists, the business men, the speculators, the bankers and the grileiros. To sell them the city in small pieces, portion by portion, even before it was built. But at that time almost nobody bought it. Brasilia was being touted like any other piece of real estate, like a mammoth resort. But what kind of resort? What was to be done with Brasilia? A simple luxury Washington? An improved Chicago for the opening up of the vast spaces of the West? A super Las Vegas of pleasure? Nobody knew. Nothing was adapted to anything. Things just went on.

"The gentlemen from Congress who were destined to the Parliament, and the bureaucrats promised to the glass sliver buildings refused to go into that 'tomb.' They all had nice tidy little lives at Rio de Janeiro or on the coast. A cushy existence. Even foreign diplomats didn't want to abandon the delights of Rio de Janeiro. In Brazil, it is not proper to give orders to gentlemen of this importance, you have to entice them. 'You will get dobradima—double salary—in Brasilia.' 'You will be housed in masterpieces of modern art.' 'These marvelous apartments will be yours. You will pay for them in twenty years by a monthly payment of twenty dollars.' These last words proved magical. Wave after wave of civil servants broke over Brasilia. They all signed deeds of sale with the authorities and immediately demanded a change of post. But before they retired to Rio or to São Paulo they all resold what had cost them practically nothing, for 40,000,000, 50,000,000 or a 100,000,000 cruzeiros. Sometimes, instead of selling, they would let the apartment at a steep price. One woman, who was head of a bureau in a ministry, told me: 'I had myself appointed to Brasilia. I got myself granted a superb, five-room apartment. I had myself put on permanent leave by my service and installed a tenant in my flat—he pays me 700,000 cruzeiros while I only hand over a few thousand to the State. Like that I can go off to my husband and my children who've remained in Rio. I shan't need to work nor shall they and we shall be comfortably well-off.'

"That started it! Dishonesty was the saviour! I came to Brasilia too, and like the others I was convinced it would end in catastrophe, but that there was some money to be made first. We speculated like madmen, on short term at top speed, dreading a crash. There was a frenzy of buying and an even greater frenzy of selling. Everyone was afraid of burning his fingers. I was satisfied if I doubled my investments. When I had got a deal on an apartment for 10,000,000 cruzeiros, I couldn't sleep until I'd palmed it off again for 20,000,000. Everybody was doing just what I did. Except for Parliament, the ministries and the statues, I believe that Brasilia has been sold and resold, in separate pieces, at least five times, with a hike of 100 per cent each time. If I'd only hung on to what I bought, I'd be a billionaire! But how could anyone foresee that?

"In the long run the senators got into the habit of living there, as did the civil servants. For a breath of fresh air, a certain boulevard W 3 was constructed which skirted the futuristic city. It was certainly not Niemeyer who did it. It was the opposite of Niemeyer's Brasilia. It was engendered by money and for money. It was the ultimate in refreshingly bad taste, super-luxurious with restaurants, bars, snack bars, pizzerias, and night clubs for the rich who wished to escape the boredom of Brasilia.

"Brasilia had become the capital of an immense internationale of grileiros, compradores and speculators from all over the world, men with billions, in dollars: Chinese and Japanese, Syrians and Orientals, not to mention people who've originated from central Europe; many Americans, some of them sharks or promoters, but also a goodly quantity of gulls. And, of course, Brazilians, who traffic in land and act as their protectors. As usual, you can do nothing without at least a governor or senator up your sleeve; these days you need a general as well.

"The most powerful of these land-sellers is Juan Ignatio. He's also known as 'White Martin,' among other names. No one knows his real one. He was a civil servant in the Title Office, which has enabled him to become the biggest forger of false registers, dossiers and property-titles ever. But in Brazil, the false is worth more than the true, and even becomes the truth if it's applied by force. And Ignatio was colossally powerful, and rich. Ministers and governors used to dog his heels. He had intimate liaisons with some extraordinarily shady characters, international adventurers with billions of their own behind them, respectable only thanks to their dollars, vultures who dug their claws into Hong Kong as readily as into Pretoria or Brasilia. Ignatio is on a first-name basis with many men of this kind, and provides them with everything they want; he's even sold the highest mountain of Brazil, Peak Neblina! He's said to have procured 5,018 square miles for an American, a certain Stanley Seelig; a huge chunk of jungle which the American's turned into his own kingdom.

"All these transfers are illegal, but, once again, what difference does it make? Ignatio is retailing Brazil like a whirlwind, operating in almost all the states of the Confederation—in Amazonia, Goiás, the Pará, the Mato Grosso, the Maranhão, the Minas Gerais and in the territory of the M.A.P.A. You can imagine what a web of intrigue that involves! It's a web with endless ramifications, proliferating into all the little local senates and chambers; not to mention the army of civil servants, policemen, judges, and military under his orders. In addition to Ignatio's gang, there are eight other huge organizations of grileiros, who trade over vast zones of Brazil and Latin America, sometimes pulling off deals as far as Asia.

"There are also private individuals with genius who succeed in outbidding the others. A terrific victory. Do you want the figures for the largest properties? Three thousand seven hundred seventy five square miles for Lancashire Incorporated; 1,648 for a certain Daniel Jeres; 915 for one James Bryan; 537 for the Japanese Takishuma Miamoto. Compared with these people, Rainier of Monaco is a pygmy: his domains in the Mato Grosso are only twelve times as large as his principality. Leopold, ex-king of the Belgians, hardly has a better share.

"The real victims of this unbridled international speculation in Brazil's virgin spaces are the Indians. They have lost their lives by it. You will tell me that they have always been killed. In the old days it was clear, simple and obvious. One used to liquidate them to be rid of them. But now it's quite different. They are useful. Whites use them, their legal existence and their recognized rights, to eliminate their equally white rivals in the battle for territory. It's only after the Indians have—in spite of themselves—fulfilled their function that they are made to disappear.

"The extermination of the Indians was begun again because, since Rondon, they'd been the only men to have official rights to the land. It's what happened at the time of the push toward the west. When people wanted to obtain Indian lands, they saw to it that they would no longer contain any Indians at all. From that point on, the lands were something that belonged to nobody, and which one could take in peace and quiet. But there were more and more amateurs in land and the game became more complicated. It was then that the state of Mato Grosso promulgated ordinances about the cession of soil. The authorities used to 'sell' several hundred or several thousand acres to desbravadores—'brave men.' Some excellent conditions were imposed upon them. At first the 'purchaser' could only get his terrain registered after having improved it. He was supposed to build a little church, a little hospital or a little airport. He had to employ an increasingly large number of laborers and regularly augment the extent of cultivated land. At the end of eight years it was all his, provided he had respected all the clauses. In other words, it never happened.

"My job was to see that it never happened. At that time I was still young. The moment a fazenda started to increase its value, my boss would want it for himself for almost nothing. I was responsible for going to find the poor devil who'd broken his back over the land, and telling him: 'Sell it.' I used to speak in such a way that I was understood. I almost always was. If not, I would return with policemen and a Mato Grosso civil servant. This was an inspector who used to inspect the land. He always discovered an omission— not enough statues of saints in the church or something like that. Confiscation. Resale to my senhor. This time without any regulations or conditions, and registration was immediate and easy.

"Sometimes it was necessary to pull off the 'Indian trick.' When the fazendeiro to be fleeced was already quite a somebody, with friends and supporters, we used to set the business up by putting into it people more powerful than our opponents. When everything was ready, I would arrive with the cops and gentlemen from the Mato Grosso's State Office for the Repartition of Land. The latter used to say: 'On the 193 square miles that we've given you, there's a tribe of twenty families. We are obliged to annul the concession.'

"The discussions would often take a nasty turn. I have been wounded by a burst of gunshot in my time. But we were particularly careful to keep a good guard around the Indians, to avoid their being eliminated in the meantime which would have spoiled everything. It was only once the deal had been made that they would disappear. The Office of the Repartition of Land showed no surprise. Nobody wanted to know.

"I did even better: I managed to put a tribe on the territory which we wanted to take. I used to say to a cacique: 'Go and install yourself with your people on the edge of such-and-such river . . . ' This was done on the quiet and then we 'discovered' these Indians, informed the authorities and denounced the fazendeiro whom we wanted to rob as a 'stealer of Indian territory.' After that everything followed the outline I've just given you.

"There are always technical improvements in the land war. The minute the big senhores are confronted just by Indians, the legitimate landowners, they settle the boundaries and register the land, and everything is immediately, so to speak, regulated. The state of the Mato Grosso set the example, or to be more precise its chamber and senate did.

"The politicians of Cuiabá proposed a plan whose intent was to restore to the Kadirrem Indians the land from which they had been dispossessed. To do this, the politicians harked back to a treaty of peace and perpetual friendship signed in 1791 between this tribe and the Portuguese crown—the only treaty of its kind in Brazil. They set about rendering justice to the tribe with dogged zeal—restitutions, boundary drawings, and a series of accords reconstituting the Kadirrem's territory. But the governor of Aruda vetoed it. No doubt he could foresee what was due to happen in 1958. In that year, the parliamentarians of the Mato Grosso, in a burst of enthusiasm, voted in a great law which definitively conceded a vast region to the Kadirrems.

"Oddly enough, however, they arranged that the governmental press office should only publish two copies of its text. One was destined for the archives and the other was brought by the deputies in dead secret to Campo Grande, the seat of the Office for the Repartition of Land in the Mato Grosso. There was a rush of deputies claiming, in their own names and that of their relations, portions of the territory that they had just attributed to the Indians. The moment the Kadirrems had been recognized as the masters of these hundreds of thousands of acres, it was as if the Indians had passed from life to death. All that was left to do was to divide the spoils. Eventually, the affair leaked out. Which is to say every kind of person demanded his part of the spoils. But the deputies were the only ones to receive satisfaction. They alone possessed the territory of the Kadirrems, each one getting the number of acres corresponding to his importance. Which was only fair after all, since it was they who had hatched the whole plot, with such pains and effort.

"But what are the parliamentarians of the Mato Grosso compared with the great grileiros of today, compared with Juan Ignatio, or the other gangs? These don't even need to put themselves to such difficulties. When they swallow Indian territory, the tribes are conjured away even faster, without any fussing, any complications, or even leaving any trace. You can't even speak any longer of genocide. Their disappearance is a phenomenon on its own.

"Barely fifteen years ago, Brasilia was Indian territory. Take a look and see if you can see any Indians in the city consecrated to human brotherhood. Where are they? Who bothers to ask?

"And then look around about Brasilia. There were once vast spaces with savages, garimpeiros and adventurers. No longer. There was one village of the far west, the Pillar of Goiás, facing the jungle, and it's become the highly prosperous state of Goiás, which is being fully developed. Now there are 2,000,000 inhabitants, including many Japanese and Syrians. A provincial capital has shot up from nothing at Goiânia: 200,000 inhabitants, a skyscraper and banks. In what used to be desert there are huge estates, ranches and mechanized agriculture. The principal products are rice, cattle and minerals. But where are the Indians in all of this? Who knows?

"Yes, there is someone. Ludovico. Governor Ludovico, the former governor who was sacked by the military. They had to station several regiments around his 'Palace of Emeralds,' his palace at Goiânia, to get him to resign. It was like overthrowing a king. And to tell the truth, he *had* ruled the region for years; he'd always been there. He was one of Vargas' men, one of the better ones. An empire builder. It really was he who made the state of Goiás in thirty or forty years out of nothing. He's spending his retirement in Brasilia. Once the only words he spoke were orders. Now he's diminished, a kind of pensioner with a few fine remains—and a well-hidden but fantastic hatred. You could talk to him about his great era. And if you were to ask him what he did with the Indians when he was creating his Goiás, he wouldn't tell you very much, I'm sure. But that would be even more revealing."

YOU'D THINK it was a fat insect, with a gleaming, gray metallic carapace and wing sheaths folded over a hard belly. The thing was installed in an armchair, filling it up. In fact this was a piece of human vermin: a man who looked like a cockroach. I found this little creature in the home of Governor Ludovico; the governor himself, as I'd been told, looked like a great deplumed chieftain, engrossed in holding up his pants in which his shrunken posterior was swimming. He was in his shirt sleeves; an almost orthopedic harnessing was keeping up his trousers: the system included huge braces, brand-new and multicolored, stretched over his fleshless ribs and collarbones, and also a belt, whose buckle replaced a navel that had disappeared into the folds of his belly. Ludovico was a ruin, who spoke to me with the now rather laughable majesty of the past. But it wasn't he who riveted my attention. It was the other character. The one who sat stiffly apart in his arm chair, a bald forty year old, whose round pudgy face was hidden by black sunglasses. The knobs of his revolvers and the projection of his stomach didn't prevent him from comfortably crossing his arms and legs as if he were looking for the best position to take a nap. The whole effect was one of a mound of firm grease with brown skin and khaki clothes. That's all I could see of this person who was faking sleep, betraying himself by a kind of smile which was the epitome of insolence and vigilance, the tropical suspicion displayed by the sinister, trusty thug.

A very odd scene. It was set almost at the top of a cuadra. All very ordinary to begin with. A huge and almost empty apartment, with a newness that was already dusty, but not dirty, with heavily conventional modern furniture dotted about, of the kind you get in big stores. No decoration, except for a little crucifix. This wasn't poverty, it was more of a carelessness, an indifference to contingencies. Such was the lair of the solitary old governor . . .

When I rang the bell, he opened the door himself. His moth-eaten look took me by surprise. He looked like an Indian grandfather. Everything about him was dry and pendulous—his skin, his nose, and his features sagged, but nobly. Like an ancient mask worn down by time. The mask grimaced with a painful cordiality. A handshake, and then silence. And discomfort. And sentences which fell slowly, one after the other, from the lips of this old man who was forcing himself to speak, to tell me something, anything polite: "I am familiar with French culture. Previously I used to go to France every year . . . "

The night before, I had informed the governor, by telephone, that I wanted to meet him to talk about the Indians. He hadn't dared refuse to receive me, but he had taken his precautions. The cockroach was one of them. He was not introduced to me. I was not told who he was or why he was there. He himself didn't utter a word or make a gesture. There he was, well in evidence, pretending to pretend to snooze. He was a menace—how and why? He was an S.P.I. man, I was to learn later, who knew all the ins and outs.

A funny sort of welcome. No question of my playing the curious. We sweated. We found a subject without too many dangers: how Ludovico had created the state of Goiás. For one hour, emphatic words fell jerkily from the old man's mouth. The S.P.I. killer—no question of killing me; just a polite warning—ground some rings which he had on his fingers and gave me a meaningful look. Ludovico was full of golden teeth; in his informal clothes, he wore a somber tie, adorned with a fat pearl which, on the end of its pin, seemed to perspire no less than he. Time passed slowly. He was going to have to come round to the Indians, to say a few words about them. To do this, the governor took on an air of extraordinary detachment, of profound forgetfulness. Suddenly, as if his memory were returning for an unimportant question, which he only remembered as a matter of duty and from an exaggeration of probity and honesty, he let fall the following with a carelessness that weighed a ton:

"The Indians? I believe that you're interested in them. The problem was solved in the Goiás. It had never been very serious. Now, from time to time, there are still outbreaks between the Indians and the fazendeiros. But it's quite natural, quite natural. The Indians steal, and this produces some clashes. When I was still governor, I used to give an order, and it was all straightened out immediately.

"Mark you, I've done a great deal for the Indians. When I created the Goiás, I granted them a zone of 38 square miles; I mean 76. A great many of the civilized reproached me in those days for giving so much land to savages who would spoil it, but I held firm, and I gave the fazendeiros to understand that they must be charitable, and that this was the best way of not hearing any more from these Indians, by putting them all alive in a little corner of their own . . . Since then, there's been no kind of trouble at all."

I drank in these words. The effort of saying them made sinuous violet veins stand out on Governor Ludovico's broad forehead. In his voice, a sort of asthma. His eyes were glassy and his old teeth were huge and yellowed with tobacco, as yellow as the skin of his kippered, smoked face. Even his wrinkles tried to play the part of his fellow-feeling, of his love for the Indians. A somewhat pathetic attempt. The sunglasses of his acolyte were trained on me like weapons. You'd think he was blind, but behind those portholes you felt the intense gaze of a killer. It was definitely he who had been the executor of Governor Ludovico's Indian policy, and who was there so that I shouldn't discover the truth.

But I knew the truth already. Ludovico had buried the Indians alive; he had handled them in such a way that they died on their own, like sick animals, without assassins. This was the so-called policy of "mildness," in other words the policy of hidden violence. In 1941, he had started, with the experts of the S.P.I., his generous policy which wiped out the problem of the Indians at the same time as it did the Indians. No more than a few remnants were left. Success.

What Ludovico now feared was that I should learn and spread around what his mildness had really been towards the Indians. I was touched by this shattered politician, the humiliated good fellow in his retirement, the titan who had become almost senile, who had only one obsession: to be, in the eyes of posterity, the irreproachable, unblemished founder of the state of Goiás, a sort of William Penn à la brésilienne. He was terrified that those dirty painted Indians that he had had to destroy would return to sully his legend.

His fear was unnecessary. I quickly realized that, in Brasilia, Ludovico was already considered old hat. For his system let some Indian remnants remain; not many, but some, an excess. Here lies the novelty: they don't want any Indians at all.

As it has advanced, progress had left behind it, in the midst of modern, civilized and populated states, fragments of tribes. There used to be some of them beside the great cities. They were ignored, it was as if they had been forgotten, for the Indian shanty towns were hardly a nuisance. But a few years back, it became impossible to put up with them any longer, and those who had survived the ancient exterminations have been exterminated. In the Brazil which gave rise to Brasilia, there now are massacres not only in the Far West, not only on the frontiers, but also in the hinterlands, in the old historic provinces of rococo, Negroes, the holy Virgin and buildings in the style of Le Corbusier.

A tribe like the Maxicalis, beside Kubitschek's Belo Horizonte, on the old metallic lands of the Minas Gerais, is abandoned. The Maxicalis are forbidden everything, even hunting and fishing. Many have died and others are wandering around. Their children have the enormous bellies that come from poverty and vermin. The adults have holes without teeth for mouths. The women prostitute themselves for a mouthful of anything. When they are too famished, the Maxicalis, bristling with bows and arrows, encircle a fazenda at night, to fall upon anything edible. But they are expected and slaughtered with Tommy-gun fire. The Indians are systematically pushed towards hysteria. The fazendeiros sign contracts with pistoleiros to kill the Maxicalis or distribute that tropical bludgeon, alcohol. The Indians are increasingly aggressive against the whites; they even rage against each other. There are sacrilegious wars within the same tribe, villages destroying each other, ten or twelve Maxicalis killing one another a week, their bodies lying at the foot of totems, their heads split by knives or axes. A haze of alcohol hangs over everything; the power of the cachaça—such a desire to drink that an Indian sells his last sack of beans to get a bottle of it. He drops dead at the height of his alcoholic ecstasy. It has all been calculated by the fazendeiros who say, "Let's finish up with these Indians."

Of the Indian "stains" in the process of being "cleaned up," there are some as far as the sugar coast, as far as the sertao of thirst, in the oldest part of Brazil. In Brasilia, a Brazilian recounted for me his voyage to the end of the night of the Indians of the Northeast.

"There is a whole little marginal way of life down there which is a mockery to God and to the world. At Aguas Bellas, the city of the civilized and the village of the Indians have been side by side for centuries. These two inimical worlds, opposed to each other in everything, are yet almost alike in their misery. It is this frightful resemblance that so struck me. The real difference is that the whites have an insane pride, whereas the others are overwhelmed by their failure.

"I arrived at Aguas Bellas at dusk. The town is made of cracked cubes, from colorless dried mud. It is surrounded by a countryside gray from dust, pierced by thorny bushes. It seems not to have any existence. A quiet, dull little world of its own, sunk in the torpor of poverty. Everything was constrained and sullen. There was a total silence, as if the noises had been absorbed by the over-heated air. The sun was sinking behind a ridge. Between two buildings, a man was toiling with some oxen to plow a furrow in a field. Otherwise there was virtually nobody, just a few shadowy men and women who moved sullenly and slowly towards home. The church bells began to chime. This was the city of the whites; that is to say, of half-castes and mulattoes.

"I was looking for the Fulni-O Indians, the powerful tribe which in past centuries had possessed the whole countryside. But I didn't see any of them. I began to look for people to give me some information about them. They threw me dirty looks and didn't reply. At last, in a bar, a black hole between leprous walls, a tall raw-boned boy told me: 'They're in their village, a half mile from here. They can come to town, but they prefer to stay away.'

"A thickset man of about forty, with blue eyes, and covered in leather, a kind of human closet, planted his bulk opposite me. I was afraid he'd take out a knife, but he only took out what he had on his mind:

" 'I have nothing against the Indians; but they are an infected, dirty, disorganized, rowdy race, who fight each other, get drunk, steal and rape and would go as far as killing if they were allowed to.'

"Have any of them been caught in action?"

" 'Not recently. But in the old days they were great assassins.'

"And the chieftain killed by the police last year? Was he causing trouble?"

" 'He was a man who behaved himself, even when he drank. He was a friend of the police. So it wasn't they who got rid of him, but another Indian.'

"At this point the tough left me in peace. The boy offered to show me the way to the Fulni-O's village. The path was appalling, a river of thick dust; on its banks emerged cubes of filthy-colored mud, the color of weather and drought, very small—hovels in geometric shapes. It had some resemblance to the town, but it had a misery that was much more striking. As I walked forward, I found only emptiness. Screens closed the holes that served as windows and doors. Through a chink I noticed that there was no furniture inside. All these rabbit hutches looked alike, stuck one by the other, without space in between, each one a little over two yards long by two yards wide and two yards high. My white companion told me that there were swarms of Indians inside, eight or ten in each cabin. I continued not to meet a living soul.

"In the center of the village some Indians materialized. They thought that we had lost our way, because white men never came there. So they called the new chief. He came running, hurrying like a man coming to ward off some misfortune. He was a tall strong man, with a huge knife in his belt. He could have been taken for a sertanejo. A few steps away from us this colossus stopped short, seized by sudden apprehension. He muttered to us: 'No stranger can stay here.' He called the 'paje' to his aid, the witch doctor, who came along, an old, withered, mothy man. After repeating that the place was reserved for Indians, he asked us for cigarettes. As he began to smoke he agreed that we might remain a while. We all entered a cabin to talk, where men were sleeping in hammocks. Those who woke up got out of them and joined in the conversation.

"Once the Indians had been reassured about us, they began to complain. This surprised me, because it's rare for Indians to grumble. Sometimes a few of them do it, but as an act, as a way of extracting gifts from the whites. I had never met any who believed what they were saying. But these Indians, the Fulni-O, believed in their own lamentations. They depicted themselves as men who wanted to make progress through their own efforts, but who were prevented from doing so by hatred, jealousy and greed, and who were compelled to remain in penury and hunger. It was extraordinary for me to meet Indians who, at least in words, had acquired the awareness of what civilization could be, and who were perhaps at its threshhold.

" 'The truth,' they all cried in chorus 'is that the white city is virtually at war with us. The people want our last pieces of land; they say that we're not working them. But it's a lie. If we don't grow good crops, it's for lack of money, ploughs, tractors and seed. Often we're unable to buy even the seed. We have to scratch the soil with our hands and with primitive instruments to plant beans and a little cotton. We collect honey. And we are always hungry and always lamentably clothed.'

"Is there a solution?"

" 'Yes, founding a cooperative. This is impossible because we're prevented from doing it. The government has given funds for it, but they disappeared before they reached us. In the town there is an agricultural bank which lends huge sums to any important senhor, even if he's nothing but a land thief; and we, the real landowners, are refused the smallest loan because they tell us that we don't present any guarantees. The rich are against us and the poor are against us. We are dying of hunger and we have no jobs. Even the priest is against us.'

"A crowd had gathered around; old men and women, children with enormous bellies, invalids covered with lice, sick people. The paje was scratching the lower part of his belly, because of a hernia. The handsome cacique breathed like a pair of bellows when he spoke because of a tumor. When I asked if there were a doctor, there was a great outcry.

" 'No, there isn't. Who would come to look after an Indian? And anyway they want us to die.'

"A witch of an old woman clutched me. She wanted to sell me a colorful sack so that her son might eat. Her husband confirmed the story. There had been no work in town for months.

" 'The senhores, when it suits them, offer us little jobs. They pay us very little. But the point is that as soon as they don't need us any longer, they dismiss us. After a little bit of hope, comes despair. With my salary I had begun to get myself a house built. But my boss said that I stole. I was beaten and I wasn't paid, and my house will never be finished. Now our baby is dying, for lack of a few cruzeiros.'

"Other hands clutched me—two hands in particular, of a kind which you'd believe were 100 years old. They belonged to an Indian woman who was majestic in her ignominy of being an old deteriorated creature. I followed her into her hut.

" 'Look. Look in the name of the Light of God. We used to have a huge bed; we have broken it into pieces to make coffins with its planks for our dead. Last year sixty-five children died. Last year every mother lost at least one son or one daughter from measles or some other disease.'

"Before me was a blind man; his eyes were still there, swollen globes in a withered face: 'I had learned how to make "Indian stuffs." It was a senhor who taught me. He was supposed to buy them from me. But often he buys nothing. This darkness is nothing compared with hunger. I cannot even beg, for at Aguas Bellas, nobody takes pity on the infirm.'

"Only the cacique asked for nothing. Apparently he sometimes goes off into his tribe's sacred place, two or three days walk away. There he puts his flute to his lips and plays the old dances of the jungle. All the Indian youth follow him there and dance wildly to escape their grief, as they ask God—which God?—for a better life. It's all that's left of tradition. For these magnificent orgies, the boys and girls dress in their Sunday best.

"Poor Indians, betraying the garb of Eden at their sacred galas. But the Indian girls are still lovely despite their dresses. They are so pretty that the young senhores go there to caress them. The girls let them do it but with shame. Shame, a new and modern sentiment previously unknown to the Indian girls, who used to do just what they wanted.

"Shame, frustration, and a longing to be as other men. This was the first time I'd noticed this mentality within a tribe. For that to happen, centuries of 'proximity' had to pass. And now that the Fulni-O had been caught up by the extraordinary desire to be like the whites it was impossible for them.

"I had heard about an Indian fazendeiro, an Indian tradesman, and an Indian shoemaker. But I hadn't found them. It was as if they'd been eliminated forever. All I met was an Indian 'professor.' Back in Aguas Bellas, in a school, I discovered an ordinary little village teacher, with a class of forty white children. You could hardly notice that she was 'Indian.' This was the 'professor.'

"The girl listened to me with an air of guilt. She was embarrassed. At last she said: 'I'll speak to you in a moment. Now I have to pay attention to my class, which is just ending.' When I returned later, I found her in a deserted room, sitting on a stool in front of a blackboard. She laughed as she saw me, bitterly:

" 'So you've come to take a look at an Indian who has succeeded, who is integrated into society. But my daily bread is humiliation. If someone wants to be kind to me, he says: "It's great, you don't look like an Indian." I never had the right to make a mistake. At the smallest error, somebody remarks: "Who do you think you are?" The truth is that, in the eyes of the whites, an Indian is always an Indian, just as a Negro is always a Negro. Sometimes the civilized make a show of encouraging us to learn and to work. It's just hypocrisy. They loathe our successes. They quickly see to it that we are humbled and put down. In Aguas Bellas, a peace reigns that is an undeclared war. The whites don't realize how hostile they are when they discover that Indians might be men like themselves. There is no solution.'

"I left Aguas Bellas, and its emptiness full of a heavy, crawling hatred. I used to say to myself that this hatred would still be there even after the Fulni-Os were all gone. It was the curse of the country, of this Brazilian

Northeast pickled in violence for so long. Such was the heaviness of the surroundings, of the countryside, the town and the whole region, that I had an impression of approaching catastrophe. Won't the executioners of the Indians, those harsh, bitter sertanejos, cruel because of the Indian blood that they have in their veins without knowing it, the sertanejos with troubled consciences, won't they, once the Indians are liquidated, feel a solidarity with all the other subhuman creatures of the sertao, the half-castes, caboclos and mulattos? Sometimes I wonder if, after so much cruel instability, the sertao is going to be caught up at last in a genuine social revolution."

The man who talked to me about Aguas Bellas had the pert face of a squirrel. He never stopped twitching, bubbling and jumping about. He was very slender and short. His thin features, slightly twisted and used in a kindly manner by time, were those of a malicious gnome. He was like a sneering, giddy will-of-a-wisp, who mocked everything, even tragedy itself. He was an aristocrat: he didn't give a damn for anything. He gossiped and joked. It was because he was a thoroughbred, the end-of-the-line kind, with centuries of ruins piled up behind him. He was completely broke, something of a vagabond, an unbiased . eccentric, the descendant of generation upon generation of coronels in the Northeast.

He spoke of that Northeast and the changes occuring within it:

"To understand my Northeast, take a trip to the Medical Museum in Bahia. For more than half a century Lampion's head has been kept there, in a glass jar—Lampion, the bandit of legendary fame, the Cangaceiro adored by the people and just as useful to a great many senhores. Now all that is left of him are some dead bits impregnated with formalin. The smell is frightful. It's all flattened, distended, with thick whitish gelatin. Previously his family wanted to buy his head back, but the authorities asked too steep a price. So there it stayed, in this museum. I sometimes go to contemplate it. You'll find it in a room consecrated to monsters of pathology. You can see, in their jars of formalin, bodies of Indians, bodies of blacks, corpses of kids with two heads, anything you like. The employees are very obliging for a small tip, and will show you a curious medley of colors which at first sight you might take to be erotic. But it's not love; it's a meticulous representation of 101 ways of committing suicide in the shanty towns. An extraordinary number of little people kill themselves, amid the happy indifference of everyone else. A certain sado-masochism used to assure social equilibrium under the fine patriarchal custody of the coronels.

"Lampion used to be the symbol of the strange desperate happiness of yesteryear. No one knew the catinga better than he; he could be felt behind every rock, every thorny bush. He had attached the catch of his revolver to its hammer, with a sort of handkerchief, which made him gain a few miraculous hundredths of a second in butchering the man he confronted. He was a terror; he plundered and gutted, he commanded 100 bandits, he had accomplices and spies everywhere. Children who spied for him, and mistresses, gave him information. But he was a brigand who defended the humble, the sertanejos against the so-called coronels. They no longer had any rank, but they had remained absolute landowners, and all of them, from father to son, were tyrants of the Middle Ages and pitiless toward their serfs.

"Lampion was a righter of wrongs. But not only in the name of the people. If he lasted, it was because he was integrated into the system. If he assassinated coronels, it was often at the request of other coronels. He rendered a great many services and had powerful protectors. In this way he contributed to keeping the Northeast, that country of madmen, a country of order. Thanks to the code of honor of which he was the supreme expert.

"The gentlemanly coronels lived in a fully primitive way. Honor, its subtlest and bloodiest aspect, presided over perpetual warfare between the big families and clans. They were always puzzling over whether there had been an insult or not, to determine whether they should apply the law of hospitality or of vengeance, two ever-opposed imperatives.

"In theory, hospitality was sacred. If you were riding your horse through the open catinga, in the desolate serras bordering the Rio Francisco, where there is now a hydroelectric complex, you were all right if you found a herd preparing to settle down for the night. It was the rule that someone should offer you a hammock, show you the pot where the beans, maize and rice were boiling and say, 'It doesn't cost you anything; help yourself.' But you could equally well be gashed with a knife and bled to death. Something had escaped you, the reason whereby these people acknowledged their rights to kill you without in the least transgressing the law of loyalty.

"My grandfather, the governor of Pernambuco, tracked down Lampion, in a manhunt which lasted for years. When Lampion was cornered, he would cross into another state. When my grandfather had Lampion's associates thrown into jail, there were always powerful people to intervene in their favor. Lampion remained free.

"My grandfather gave his son, my father, the responsibility of proposing an 'honorable surrender' to Lampion. My father set out to look for him in the state of Bahia. How should he find him? A coronel who lived in a fine house with a lot of servants suggested that my father stay with him for a week. 'What kind of footing are you on with Lampion?' 'I am rather dependent upon him. If some tax collectors turn up, I call Lampion, who gets rid of them for me. If my cows are stolen, Lampion finds them for me, or their equivalent. If I have an enemy . . . I pay for Lampion's services by a very reasonable monthly sum. I am his subscriber. But I don't lose by it, for I never pay a penny to the State.'

"The coronel was obliging enough to offer to make contact with Lampion on my father's behalf. So one evening one of Lampion's men arrived in the fazenda—a gallows face, a huge hat and a leather vest. He was supposed to bring my father to Lampion. Before leaving, my father entrusted his portfolio to his ferocious companion. At the São Francisco falls, the man returned it to him without a penny the less: 'Here we are, Lampion is waiting for you.' He was a very gay man, with a head well tanned by the sun—the head that you can see in gelatine in the Museum of Bahia. Agreement was not possible and my father departed. In the end, my grandfather succeeded in capturing Lampion and having his head cut off, that famous head.

"Shortly afterwards my grandfather died at a ripe old age. My father, who had a peaceful temperament, inherited his enemies. One day he learned that in order to exact a crueler revenge, they had decided to kill, not him, but the son he had just had. That is to say, me. In his anger he cried: 'If they touch one hair of my child's head, I shall exterminate them all.' He had a black as his confidential servant, a Negro carved from ebony, the son of a slave, who looked at my father with commiseration: 'But, senhor, the simplest thing would be to exterminate them all first.'

"The sertao, after centuries, is shifting. Even the hatred isn't of the same kind. It used to be a pure passion, and it's become a utilitarian one. For the people at the top, it's no longer really hatred. And it's certainly no longer honor. It's politics, which is the same as saying it's business or gangsterism, something cold and low, which preserves from the past only the sense of destiny and inexorable frenzy. In addition to the classic coronels there are judges, police, and prefects, who are even greedier for wealth and power, and who involve each other in a carnival that is funereal but lacks romanticism. It's given rise to modern 'coronelism.' People make deals with each other and terrorize each other in a cruel materialism. The paternalism of old has been replaced by trafficking of all kinds with syndicates of death. The trusty cangaceiros of former times have been replaced as executioners by pistoleiros.

"It is very involved. A Senhor Mendes was a very prosperous man and a deputy of his state. He had a large fortune, numerous fazendas and seven sons. He was feared, because everyone knew that he had ordered numerous assassinations. One day, two Indians appeared before his wife. They had found her husband's corpse, riddled with bullets, in the catinga. A year later a large bundle covered with straw was discovered on a serra. It was the body of Ze Crispin, a young man of twenty-two years, married, with three children to whom he didn't leave a penny. His profession: pistoleiro. He had already twenty men killed for money to his credit. An inquiry concluded that it was an act of vengeance on the part of the widow, Mrs. Mendes. It was the slain killer's brother who accused her, who was himself a killer in the service of a Senhor Robes, a big landowner and an enemy of Mendes. In the Crispin family, all the males were professional assassins. The order was given to arrest them all. They were all captured alive, and it was discovered that the executed pistoleiro and his imprisoned brothers had been in the pay of Mendes not Robes. They used to constitute his band of death.

"The Crispin brothers were asked if they killed Mendes.

" 'We killed him so as not to die ourselves.'

" 'But you were already in his employ.'

" 'He had hired us all at the rate of twenty escudos each a week, on condition that we were ready to kill and to die for him.'

" 'Why did you decide to execute your boss Mendes?'

" 'Senhor Robes had offered us 1,000 escudos to assassinate Mendes. But we were only paid half this sum after we had rendered this service.'

" 'What happened after Mendes' murder?'

" 'We continued to work for Robes. Two executions in one fazenda, three executions in another. Then Ze Crispin was shot down on the orders of Mendes' widow.'

" 'But why had you betrayed Mendes for Robes?'

" 'For money. And also because Robes was even more powerful than Mendes. Once his proposal had been made, we were dead men if we didn't accept it.'

"The conclusion of the matter was a light prison sentence for the surviving Crispins, and shortly afterwards, their providential escape. The proof that they had judged well, the proof that Robes really was stronger than Mendes.

"The privileged are massacring each other in a chain reaction, but let not a crumb drop for the people. For the people, it is more than ever obedience or death. It is still poverty, children who die, droughts where the "deserters" flee to find water, and where the self-flagellators stay and punish themselves to ask water of God. Old habits. And yet, little by little, a new and incredible phenomenon is coming to light. The sertanejos are discovering that life would be better without the tyranny of the powerful, and that the solution is a hatred, a hatred which will wrest from the privileged some part of the goods of this world. A social hatred—something unknown until now in the sertao which has known so many other hatreds.

"In one village we stopped at something that could almost be taken for a restaurant. Flies. A group of Negroes in a corner. A man with an evil scowl waited for us to order. He was the restauranteur. Before anybody could say anything, he said: 'There's some rice.'

"Our chauffeur went towards him: 'Do you have any chicken?'

" 'No.'

"A shudder ran through the group of blacks. The largest of them, with skin that was dark and worn, got to his feet. 'Quite a gourmet. You want all the nice things.'

"As he was speaking, the man approached our chauffeur, a machete in his hand.

" 'People who eat are pigs. I am going to bust your belly.'

"But the chauffeur drew a revolver from his pocket and pointed it. 'If you come any closer, I'll shoot.'

"The antagonists separated, both backing away prudently, step by step. The black returned to his nook and the chauffeur was by the door. With him, we made a dash outside.

"The Northeast is the fruit of our sins: the murder of the Indians and the slave trade of the blacks. From these crimes have come all the half-castes, the sertanejos of the catinga and the mulattos of the coast. Is this to be the hour of expiation for us others, the manufacturers of half-castes?

"The vast Northeast is a land of people with dark skin. The sertanejos are coppery and the mulattoes blackish. This used to make two different worlds of misery and revolt. But now civilization has imposed a uniformity upon poverty. Increasingly, there are whole regions where men no longer know from what blood they come, except that it's a blood of the oppressed. There is being slowly born the consciousness of the proletariat. A slow birth, but it has already caused alarm. If these masses of brutes were to become aware of themselves, there could be torrents of blood; even more blood than was spilt when almost all the Indians were killed.

"And the Indians? Brasilia is a monument to their corpses. But nothing has been solved, for the Indians have perpetuated themselves anonymously. Or, if you like, they've been perpetuated. It's in the Northeast that all the breeding of reds and blacks has given rise to a people who no longer have a name, whom despair can drive mad and progress make savage. And here is the true vengeance of the Indians: to insure that nothing in Brazil can be extricated from its excesses."

IN RIO DE JANEIRO, I was hunting for Senhor Jader Figueredo, the high-ranking civil servant who had unmasked the massacre of the Indians. It was he who had directed the painstaking and dangerous inquiry into the genocides and atrocities, and into the daily practice of murders. It was he who had worded the famous and shocking report; he was the one responsible for the scandal. But I never managed to find this person. At last, one day, I got a glimpse of him in a ministry—which was a marvelous mansion of painted and sculptured wood, from the old times, a show case of old Brazil. An easy-going atmosphere, debonair gentlemen in the gardens and corridors, pats on the back, laughter, empty offices, and doormen as friendly as their superiors. One big family. Figueredo, except for the once, was never there. I wanted to ask him for the key to the mystery; why had he dared to do what he'd done? For this is what no one had explained. He had, very likely, acted upon orders from the then government, the military government which wished to demolish persons placed very high up, enemies of the regime, no doubt politicians. And then the revelations had taken on so broad a scope that the army had found that it was getting involved itself. In official circles, nobody talked about it any more. When I finally discovered Senhor Figueredo, he stammered a few words and slipped away. I shall never catch him again.

I wandered in Rio in search of the truth. But I felt like a fly caught in a jungle flower, one of those enormous flamboyant things that are more like animals than vegetables. That's what Rio de Janeiro is like to me: a flower which is a labyrinth. An abyss of sado-masochistic joy, but joy first and foremost.

Not a city. Pieces like the colors in the rainbow, all separate and yet extraordinarily connected and intimate. Each fragment clinging to a piece of land between the tropical mountain, the tropical ocean and the tropical sky. The jungle and waters are united all around in endless combinations, but they are ignored. No one sees them, no one wants them. No exoticism, except for the fantastic exoticism of men packed into all the tangled corollae of Rio, the orchid city.

You would think that someone had churned together all the races of Brazil to obtain a range of homogenized products, of similar skins and of identical men. It's a geography of colors. A marriage of the ultrawhite and the ultrablack to achieve a complex mentality: the soul of Rio. Every elegance and license is permitted. Intelligence is used to create greater enjoyment. Satins emerging from hovels for the carnivals. And elsewhere, in the other sprawling quarters, there are all the shades between creamy white and boot black. There are business quarters, dormitory quarters, old quarters, and suburbs of crime where it seems as if the only industry is that of reveling.

In Rio one man was unhappy, really downcast. Colonel Vinhas, who had been the chief of the S.P.I. He was in hiding, and afraid. Afraid of what he knew.

However, a few weeks earlier, a Brazilian journalist had discovered him, and gone to see him. So many horrors devolving into mediocrity. The redoubtable Vinhas is a Brazilian of medium height, with large glasses and black eyes in an undistinguished face. His home is an apartment typical of middle-class suburbs. He was seated, half lying, on a green velvet couch. Three children; standing behind him was his wife, Doña Teresina, holding in her arms her last born, nine months old. If Vinhas was a wreck, ready to throw in his hand, she was fierce and vigilant.

A strange scene as described to me: the presumed gangster-chief of the S.P.I. was groaning. He wept:

"I've been forbidden to talk to justify myself. I have to be silent. 'They' don't want me to tell who committed the crimes."

He laughed bitterly: "I've been depicted as a billionaire. I don't have ten apartments, just this one. I've never had the use of official cars. I used to direct my services from my office, drinking cups of coffee. I'm poor. Perhaps you won't believe me, but my wife works ten hours a day in a plastic factory so that we can make ends meet."

The telephone never stopped ringing. Doña Teresina explained: "It's a friend who wants to have news. Please don't do anything that could be detrimental to my husband. He's a regular officer and he'll be put in jail at the slightest imprudent word. They are powerful. Please."

"And who are these 'they'?"

No reply. The photographer who was with the journalist prepared to take a photo. Cries from Doña Teresina: "Don't do that, for the love of God! That would be imprisonment tomorrow morning."

The question was asked again: "Who are these 'they'?"

Vinhas was on the point of saying something. He stammered and relapsed in silence. The baby was crying in his mother's arms and Doña Teresina left the living room. Vinhas opened his mouth: "I have received orders to say nothing. They were given me by the brigadier-general, the director of aeronautics. I am an airman, in fact."

"It's said that Governor Jurais Magalhaes is particularly compromised. What do you know about it?"

"He has nothing to do with all of this. He's never seen an Indian in his life."

"Then who is it?"

"I let you enter as a friend. I can't say anything. They are so powerful. There are two political men who are particularly formidable. The power that they have in this country is quite out of the ordinary."

The telephone rang. What somebody was saying to him on the phone reassured him. He returned: "A lawyer has proposed to defend me for nothing. I can't pay anything. He's supposed to come here."

The colonel was sufficiently reinflated to undertake his own eulogy.

"The army had appointed me to put a stop to the massacres. During my whole administration there weren't any. I and my soldiers used to restrain everyone. The estate owners used to cringe with fear when they came before us. I even gave guns to the Canelas tribe on the island of Maranhon, when I learned from an informer that some fazendeiros had hired some 'hunters' to liquidate them. Those Indians were able to defend themselves."

But Doña Teresina remained fearful. She interrupted her husband in the middle of his speech. "Don't talk. If you are imprisoned, who will suffer? I and my children."

The colonel went on anyway, triumphantly: "Nobody knows the S.P.I. like I do. I know all its secrets, I've traveled everywhere."

The telephone again. The lawyer wouldn't come. Nobody would come. Vinhas said no more.

Mediocrity and mystery. I was achieving nothing. Figueredo was a shadow and Vinhas had been spirited away. I went on wandering about Rio de Janeiro. I frequented the company of the "opposition."

What I found was a conscience. I was brought to the house of a man who was the incarnation of conscience. An admirer of Mao Tse-tung, of Fidel Castro, and of all the progressivists. A self-styled revolutionary. This was a doctor who looked after the poor without asking them for money. The apostle thundered before me:

"Vinhas is a brute. All the military think about is keeping everybody standing at attention. As the Indians have no notion whatever of obedience, they make them obey by the punishment of massacre. It is the regiments of the regular army which are exterminating them."

This person received me in his own home. It was a strange dwelling for the pure in heart. A little palace set in a marvelous garden. A maître d'hôtel and whiskey. Persian carpets, Chinese screens and Negro masks. Someone had me admire the Picasso of the private collection. Padded and fabulous luxury. While he spoke, the man listened to himself. A grave voice. Slightly over forty, a pasty male beauty, an aging, chubby-cheeked, silver-plated Apollo. His wife appeared. Two hundred and twenty pounds in diamonds. The lady withdrew. Heavy boredom. The master of the house was speaking like an oracle. He made much of his own worth. Famous names fell from his lips; he knew all the advanced upper crust in the world. He seemed to have nothing else to do but make speeches. I dared not ask him where the fortune that he spread about came from.

From this point on, my inquiry about the Indians became a journey to the home of avant-garde billionaires. In Rio in these circles you can't pronounce a certain name without the company emitting a gurgle of pleasure: the name of Madame B. But her friends, all her friends, only use her first name. She is a Brazilian of the purest kind. Her husband died leaving her a lot of cash. She is the soothsayer of the left.

She was holding a large reception in her house. The intellectual, worldly and political Tout-Rio was in her living room (a huge glass and metal cage). She was larger than life. A provocation to every way of living. Already ripe, but as knotted as a vine branch. Her face was a sort of embossed leather. A mixture of monkey and parrot, of old cacique and great lady, of charmer and exterminating angel. Her skin was very exotically tanned. Against a general background of chatter, hugs and embraces, gesticulations and little cries, her neck held her head forward in a position of offense-defense. Her gay way of joking could end in an attack with her claws. But usually she was a good girl, with an incredible amount of cheek, shocked by nothing and considering everything natural, offering no restrictions on her own liberty.

"It's Brazil." She loves Brazil passionately. All the same, she does have her own code of proprieties: to detest the army, to love art, and to go regularly to Paris. There is a fit of hysteria when anyone talks in front of her of the military.

She asked me: "Have you visited my Museum of Modern Art?"

This was her lifework; it was her way of consecrating herself to the people, dating from the time of good governments, from whom she had obtained the necessary funds. The museum was a temple of humanism. When I admitted to the lady that I hadn't been there, I realized that I had committed a crime. But she clenched her good will and kept her good temper. I spoke to her about the Indians. She replied:

"It is really such a pity that you haven't been to my museum. For you would have seen the extent to which painting all over the world has been inspired by our Amazonian tribes."

I was pushed towards the sea of guests. A former minister first of all, a minister of Social Affairs, obviously from the period before the army came to power. An "ex." But all the people there were "exes." In physical appearance, this gentleman was a drop of oil.

"Our country is three countries. There is the South in the forefront of progress. There's the coastal region of the center which is being fully developed, and then there are the vast spaces of Amazonia. That's another world. We shall need at least a century to civilize it. But we have the time."

"Will the Indians have disappeared before the era of civilization?"

"What Indians? Who do you mean?"

The man's mouth fell open and his amazement was apparently sincere. Then he corrected himself:

"Oh yes, I see. But that's just a small problem, a question which is economically completely negligible."

The Indians were swept aside. This is how I definitively lost them in the living room of the grande dame of Rio. After Mr. Oil Drop, Mr. Tuberose. A long and lean gracefulness that never seemed to end. All the tender attentions paid to a delicate skin, all the little pains taken over elegance. Perfume, creams, jewels. It fell just short of caricature. This was a young man who shuddered constantly. His arms and legs were like vibrating antennae. His oval head had large, outraged or rolling eyes.

What cries of distress, what an emotional breakdown when this pearl learned from my lips that I was a working journalist. You would think he was at death's door. Death's door in French, because Miss Tuberose manipulated this language with exquisite refinement. This perfection in our language has become rare in Brazil, where the well educated who detest America are more and more prone to an American accent.

"I sensed it, an instinct warned me. You're going to write frightful things. You're going to see my country with square eyes. But my vast Brazil is poetry and innocence. You're going to trample upon it all with your large feet and your large intelligence, because you'll trust to appearances, you'll believe what you're told. Be it known that a great many things, which are more or less authentic, are not truly true in Brazil."

"Are the Brazilians really in the process of liquidating their Indians?"

"Go to Ouro Prêto, the city of marvels. My cousin lives there in an eighteenth-century house. She is as lovely as an Inca princess. In the flower of her youth she has all the pride and tenderness that are the soul of our race. I will give you a note for her. She will talk to you about the Indians, and you will know the truth, for she has the blood of bandeirantes and caciques in her veins. She is descended from a great and noble tribe through her maternal line."

I requested the word of introduction, but Miss Tuberose had already started to moan again and left me flat. I learned that he was an ornament of the young gilded homosexuals of Rio de Janeiro. They formed a select and recognized club, which was admitted into good society.

At Carnival time, I am told, a procession of proud American cars drives around a large square. On each hood stands a creature in a dress from a great Paris couturier, waving veils. It is a procession of homosexuals. Apparently also, on a sidewalk, amid wild sambas, a fat man and a fat woman shake themselves, facing each other for hours, in a grotesque dance until one of them collapses and admits himself defeated. This is a combat between the king of the pansies and the queen of the queens. That's what I'm told. And anyway, what does it matter, for there you have the famous Brazilian innocence.

I was plunging deeper into Rio de Janeiro. I took myself off to Cachias, at the end of the suburbs, about fifteen miles away. There was none of the favela, of the human sewer. This is a dormitory quarter. From it, thousands of decent male and female employees leave every day at dawn to go to work in Rio. These hard-working crowds return in the evening and, as the night falls, do their shopping in the thriving, well-lit stores close by.

And yet Cachias is a capital of crime. Everyone knows it. The great professional killers of Rio live there: it's also *their* dormitory. As Cachias is on the boundary of two states of Brazil, it's difficult to control. That's the official explanation. The truth is Tenorio, the senator who was always reelected. A curious figure. He likes the gangsters because, he says, they are humble, exploited men of the people. He collaborates with them. The army has chased Tenorio out of his senatorial seat but he is still in the area, and still powerful.

Set off from the main streets, and close by an empty lot, is the steeple of a small new church, the kind built by worker-priests in Paris suburbs. It looks more like a social center than a church. Inside is a round face, the ruddy solid face of a good Breton—a priest's face. He's a former chaplain from parishes in Indochina, and he remembers the Asian war as a good time. Besides which, he's one of the saintliest people around.

"There used to be nothing for God in this part of the world. The clergy didn't dare risk themselves here. I've built this hall with my own hands and found the money for it. There's nothing to be done with the old people. Now that night is falling, can you hear those tom-toms and gourds? Soon it will be the time for matrons with snakes around their necks and for saints who dance as they smoke fat cigars and drink glasses of cachaça; sacrificers in white robes who slit animals' throats; hysterical women foaming prophecies and spirits speaking from beyond the grave. I am constantly besieged by this alienation.

"The young listen to me better, particularly the girls—the ones who don't want to be prostitutes. I have made them workshops with typewriters and sewing machines. It's empty now, they've all just left. Later on they're too afraid."

"Of what?"

"Of being raped in the streets, of course."

We had one glass of red wine and then another one. A farewell round. Clearly, the good man was afraid to talk to me about the realities of Cachias.

Cachias made you afraid. I searched in vain for someone who would speak openly with me, until I found an addict in a bar—he got his supplies there. He knew a great many people. I swore not to reveal anyone's identity.

We drove for a long time and left Cachias behind. Houses became rarer. A landscape of an inhabited no-man's-land. We stopped near a sort of public garden. A lawn climbed a kind of knoll. Trampled grass, bare earth. Shadows of men and whispers. Higher up, a few trees blackened the sky. Up there were the two chief selling points. My mentor told me to stay below, and went off. Prowlings all around me. Nothing. The man returned, smoking a cigarette with a thick odor. He told me that it was some "good grass," but he didn't know its name. Everything had gone off all right.

"Often there's gunshot, brawls and a death or two. It's a place where corpses are a dime a dozen; it's the gangsters killing each other. It's worth it, it's big business. They're selling the stuff over there as if it were a supermarket. Sometimes the police are killed. This makes Tenorio unhappy, because it's a proof that his cops have tried to make deals by bypassing him. No one dares attack him. He lives in a house completely built of armor plating, like a battleship. It's huge. I'll show it to you in a little while. Occasionally Tenorio has his own cops assassinated—he has his own killers. Sometimes they kill for fun or for some fantasy. A lot of corpses, I can tell you that."

A "friend" of my companion got into the car. He guided us to Tenorio's house. We drove into Cachias. Once again macadam and sidewalks. We stopped. A few mulattos loitered near by, avoiding looking at us so as not to get mixed up in anything. At the angle of two streets was a parallelepiped. A smooth, cold thing without any opening, with high vertical walls stretching for fifty yards and a completey flat top like a lid. It had the look of a can of food, a leaden coffin, and a strong-box. It was Tenorio's fortress. I touched the wall. It was made of metal; a carapace of pure steel, pierced with tiny holes for observation and aeration. Not one window. Just formidable walls where sliding panels could be pressed to reveal weapons. I heard a click. Something had been put into position. But nothing. They must have been satisfied with observing us and listening to us.

"I've been inside it once," said the addict's pal. "In the interior there are Tenorio's apartments, harem and offices. Sheltered from everything. He lives there with his women, his kids and his killers. On the terrace there's a swimming pool and a garden. In every joint and angle there are well-screened machine guns. But there are also antennae registering everything that happens outside. Tenorio, himself, in his lair, smokes cigars in his pajamas."

The addicts took it into their heads to have me meet Tenorio. I'm sure they knew him better than they claimed. As for me, I was not going to say who I was ... They began to thump with their fists against the formidable armor plating. It remained just as closed, just as dead, but it gave the impression that anything could happen, particularly a hail of bullets. I walked along the armored walls until they finished. There was a garage, stores and an entrance there. These were the outbuildings, not fortified but under the protection of Fort Tenorio. A magnificent Negro in overalls was scrubbing the interior of a Cadillac. He was amiability itself.

"Senhor Tenorio's car?"

"Yes."

"And Senhor Tenorio?"

"He's out." A gargantuan smile from the black. I went off again and started up the engine of my car. I asked the addicts if Tenorio really had many bodies on his conscience. They laughed:

"Him! At least 10,000 men. That's an overall figure. There's no way of keeping count. He used to have all his adversaries assassinated. It used to happen in their own homes, or right in the street. Sometimes he used to have them kidnaped and brought into his fortress. Then he would interrogate them himself. There were no rules to his methods of roughing them up. It all depended upon the occasion and upon his temper. He used to take it out on the rich mostly. He made them spit blood or money or both. The little people liked him. He was also a great friend of Kubitschek. He almost became governor of Rio de Janeiro."

"How?"

"He knew how to get people to vote for him. What a presence he had! He used to hypnotize the crowds. His speech! His eyes! And his black cloak, lined with blood-red, that he strutted about in. And the machine gun that he waved in front of the people as he shouted that it would be used to exterminate all their oppressors. He used to do whatever he liked with the blacks, the half-castes and the mulattos. But he wore a mail coat on his chest as a precaution. He was so popular that the government had to send a battalion to Cachias to break his dictatorship. Now he is old and sick, but still rich and still able to get anyone killed who displeases him."

"But it's a reign of terror!"

"Oh no, it's part of a way of life. The chief of a lottery gang had a score of big winners killed. The boss of a samba school liquidated all his rivals in the quarter. It didn't shock anybody . . . I know a hotel where all the pipes are broken. It drips everywhere, making a noise like a heavy tropical rain storm. But from beyond this deluge come strange voices and moans. 'For pity's sake, bring us some water.' These noises come from one side where there is a commissariat of police. It's been going on for years. It's like that every day and every night. Everybody's used to it. It even creates a distraction."

Murders and tortures at Cachias: a spectacle, a spice to life. So how can one be surprised that, in wild Amazonia, the genocide of the Indians is a peccadillo? There's not much pity for life and death in this sensual Brazil. And everything is pullulating too much for anyone to be concerned over the extinction of some savage tribes in the jungles and matos. It's not indifference, but a sense of fatality

286 MASSACRE OF THE BRAZILIAN INDIANS

But there are some young, handsome, and new—if one can say so—Indians left, from the Indians who you would think had all been liquidated. Quantities of unknown red men are in the process of emerging from the jungle. This was the great news that I learned from an adventurer in a deliciously disreputable spot.

Down there was the Brazil where vice is like a virtue. It's a few hours from Rio. A soft humidity, tropical plants, tender pastel colors, a sylvan landscape. A stream flows nearby. A little further on the sea splashes softly on the beach. A few thatch roofs, supported by columns which are still virtually tree trunks. Little orchestras playing sambas; it is fairy-like.

There was a somewhat larger house which you'd think was full of idylls. At rustic tables there sat young girls without makeup, in charmingly low-cut dresses, with expensive jewels, and gleaming amber skin. They sat nicely at the tables like students. Some men were courting them, in a polite way. These girls were the prostitutes. They laughed, they didn't discuss their price and they waited until they were spoken to. They were all very well brought up. Their clients were almost their lovers. Now and then a couple would rise and go towards the bank of the little river, where there were log cabins, each of a different color. Every hour an old servant went by to change the sheets. Rustic love. One of these kids told me that her mother knew what she was doing, but her father, a cab driver, did not—or at least officially did not. There was no sense of sin or degradation.

"I am making my dowry. I want to get married. In the daytime, I am a salesgirl in a boutique; I make a supplement in the evening."

Another foreigner was there . . . He was a French-Canadian with wrists that looked as if they were oxidized. And metallized skin. We offered each other whiskey.

"It's very nice, this country brothel," he said. "But there are much better ones near Manaus. Meadows grow there on the huge swamps and become floating islands, turning round as they drift slowly. With trees, vegetation and men. Some flimsy little reed houses are stuck side by side, and there are light canoes nearby. It's a watercolor world."

I was curious, and I inquired about this unusual man's profession. "You can see from my skin that I'm a diamond fisher. You only acquire this carapace among clouds of Amazonian mosquitoes. I've reached the point where I don't even feel them any more. Seven months of work, five of rest. We've just gone on leave. I have a Frenchman and an Englishman as my fellow workers. What do we do? We scrape the bottoms of rivers. We were working in Guiana. It went very well, more than $200,000 to share between us at the end of the year. But we got the news down the pipe line that the Rio Zenio was even better. It's at the end of Rondonia at the end of Brazil. We never really knew if we'd got the right spot; it was all so uniformly alike.

"We started off by making boats with axes, and then we dragged a pipe along the bottom of the river. We had two black divers to hold it. They got ten per cent of the profit and were happy enough. The mud which was brought back by the tube was poured into a sieve installed in one of our boats. It was arranged in a slope—first the dirt stopped, then the pebbles, and at the end there were just gold and diamonds left. It's not a romantic profession at all. We are the sewer men of the rios. We don't seek the company of the garimpeiros; we put up with each other. But our millions have their merits. I'm off to buy myself some property in France."

"And the Indians?"

"They were believed to be all liquidated. This was once the region of the Cintas Largas, who had been dynamited, machine-gunned and cut into pieces to the last man by the senhores' killers. Everybody considered that the 150,000 miles all around had been "cleaned up." But one day we heard melodies, singing and cries rising from the jungle. It seemed to us that we glimpsed bodies of naked men slipping over the river banks. Smoke was rising from clearings as if there were villages. It was as if the massacred savages had been resurrected. We were sure we'd get hit with some arrows. The authorities refused to believe it. And today it's admitted that once again there are several thousand Indians. Not those of the old days, obviously—they had been very well liquidated. But others, completely unknown, coming from no one knows where, who are probably unaware of the executions—they don't appear hostile at all. They're very pacific, very well disposed. There's a question of sending them an expedition of pacification."

I returned to Copacabana, in the Rio of the rich. Cement hotels. A macadam road in front of the sea. A parapet. All rather ramshackle. Not a blade of grass, not a plant, not a palm tree, not a terrace, not a café. It's a lifeless speck in a Brazil full of life. Yet it's a place renowned world wide for its charms and pleasures. In reality it's a fortress against the infamous tropics. Only the sun and the sand are admitted, and the bodies of the well-bred in the process of cooking themselves. Snobbery has reached an abstraction; bronzing considered as the supreme Brazilian value.

There were apparently no Indians here, nor blacks. A few ebony-colored gentlemen who behaved like senhores were catalogued as "whites." For money has the gift of whitening the skin. But there weren't many of them. Copacabana is chiefly the domain of snowy white boys and girls who are just artistically browned. Sunburn serves to camouflage any residual pigmentation.

And yet kindness still emerges just as some flowers manage to make their way between chinks of concrete. A cynical kindness, the kindness of half-castes.

This is what the Philosopher recounted to me. That's what I called the magnificent fellow who had come from Europe to be the condottiere of pleasure in life, a little professor in a university—teaching Brazilian style, which meant only a few hours a week. But his chief role was as the Immoralist who understood and enjoyed Rio.

"Your killed Indians," he told me, "are part of Rio. The wretched Negroes are a part of Rio. Rio is the result of massacre and love. It's a demonstration that life is stronger than death. So Rio is the true heart of all the Brazils.

"There is a modern Brazil which looks to deny its mixtures. I know a blond boy who no longer wants to make love to Negro girls. This attitude shocks his mother, an old-time dowager, who scolds him: 'But it's against all the customs. Your father, your grandfather and all your ancestors always courted black girls. It was considered a social duty.'

"There is also a Brazil where everyone is seeking to improve the quality of his blood. It is true that a man from a people of reddish or blackish complexion dreams of pale carnations. But I can also introduce you to girls from the fashionable white world. If they are slightly dark they claim they have an Indian ancestor, so that they won't have to admit to black forefathers. All the Indians can be killed at the present time, but they are in a worldly way considered superior to the Negroes.

"Even the white who is purifying himself by an unbridled international snobbery has a side to him which comes from the jungles of Amazonia and the sugar mills of the coast. So the alchemy of blood is not the terrifying and tragic thing that it is in the United States. Here, as all the bodies and all the souls are mixed up, the result is this marvelous ambiguity; an oddly dosed and complex naturalness which permits everything, which is in everything and which is completely dominated by the rules of the game: sadism and felicity at the same time. We are in a hypocritical world which understands, enjoys and savors. The foreigner can't pick his way between all the charms and the cruelties, but the people from here are perfectly at ease in this crazy world, whose madness is always governed by a secret logic. Everything is sensual and everything is cerebral.

"Every evening, when night is about to fall on Rio, the city waits for its pleasures. This atmosphere of luxuriant anguish doesn't exist anywhere else in the world. Everyone knows that something will happen to him; he doesn't know why or how. Brazilians wrack their brains in the preparation of carnal pleasures, tortures or the confection of corpses. They have the gift of playing with each other like children playing with a ball. It all has a happy ending.

"The best place to see Brazil as an enchanted land is at the Carnival of Rio. It's not an orgy, for love is the daily bread which people never go without. At the Carnival, on the other hand, it's a matter of making a journey to escape the world of misery and reach the true eldorado. There are no more poor people, no more favelas, no more half-castes, just millions of archangels, kings, princesses and empresses in their finery.

"Hardly is the carnival dead when it starts to be reborn. They are already preparing the next one. In this way, they live constantly in brocades and treasures, while they forget the prostitution, the murders and the stench of the huts. The carnival is the great redemption."

A few months later, I came upon the Philosopher again in Paris. He was like the mournful cavalier:

"I don't know if I shall go back to Rio. It's become very sad. The little tramway of Orfeu Negro is dead, the bus loaded with black humanity that used to climb up to the hills of the favelas. This was the good Brazil, with the kids clinging to the planks of the old bone-rattler. No one ever dreamed of paying. A cave-in carried off the rails and the authorities refused to repair them. They were ashamed of this symbol of the old Rio.

"And so many other painful events! Our friend the soothsayer, Madame B., was thrown into a prison for prostitutes. They tortured her by taking her fingerprints thirty-five times. She was released after a few days and showed her wounded and bandaged fingers to Tout-Rio. But what would once have been a crime of lèse majesté only shocked the festive left a little bit more. The army no longer respects people from high society. They go to jail just like the students and the intellectuals.

"I no longer recognize Brazil. The officers, who were the only honest Brazilians, have gone mad. The old generals who were sold to America were relatively decent. Now there are 'integrists' who are organizing commando hunts against the communists, that is to say the leftists. And worst of all, the young lieutenants are dreaming of a 'pure and harsh'—if one can say so—revolution against both Marxism and dollars. There's even a new Prestes, a captain who's deserted called Carlos Lamarca, who is preaching a gospel of city guerilla warfare. He has attacked and pillaged some banks in the name of the people. It's a dirty menacing confusion instead of the good old confusion of the old days, where the rich used to profit and the people have a good time. Will there still be a Brazil where everything has a happy ending?"

Suddenly the Philosopher burst out laughing: "You can never anticipate anything in Brazil. Look, the Indians that your river-scourer talked to you about—the adventurer from the country brothel—are in fine shape. There are at least 2,500 of them now being recuperated. And they're even Cintas Largas.

"I was present at their pacification. I arrived in a tent village in the heart of the jungle. It belonged to Mirales, a fanatic supporter of the Indians, but very different from the Vilas Boas brothers. He's a nobleman; a soldier monk, a solitary autocrat, a military cavalier. He's devoted himself to the Indians because of a wound which left him with a limp.

"You could see nothing but jungle, but you knew that Indians were quite close. Mirales gave this order: 'When the Indians appear, you will let them do to you what they like and as they like.' A long week of waiting. At last twenty-five naked, handsome, young and slightly effeminate men emerged from the vegetation. They all wore on their waists a large belt to which a thong was attached which was wound around their genitals. These were the Cintas Largas, alive indeed, well nourished, not too scared, and full of curiosity and greed. These ones clearly didn't know about the extermination of the other tribes of their nation. We will never know from what back end of the jungle they come.

"Before they arrived, Mirales had had hidden all the things that we possessed; he had made us close our tents and our cabins with chains, padlocks and bars. But all these precautions were useless. During the night, the Indians battered everything down. Where an obstacle withstood them, they dug subterranean galleries to get into the middle of our tents anyway. They took everything, underpants and tubes of toothpaste, even old cans of preserves. Only food didn't interest them. They were wild with delight. Mirales was equally satisfied. He didn't mind being plundered; his affair was working out very well. He had just saved his dog in time by ordering it to be taken into the jungle.

"It was a great joke. The Indians began to feel us. They opened the men's flies to see their hair, as they don't have any in the pubic area. There was a nurse there. Her white skin fascinated them and they began to undress her. 'Let them do it,' shouted Mirales. She only struggled when the Indians wanted to take her away. The noble savages didn't insist and departed toward the rest of their tribe, happy as sandboys, loaded like pack horses and obviously absolutely intoxicated.

"The pacification season is off to a good start. Mirales is counting on taking six months to rally together all the Cintas Largas. His rivals, the Vilas Boas brothers, are in the middle of setting up an expedition to finally tame the blond Indians of the Xingu."

"Has a method been found this time to make the pacified Indians survive?"

"No, of course not. These ones as well, the ones that they're recuperating right now, will only survive a few months. There is no solution. There never will be. It is civilization that kills them."